The Civil War in Tennessee,
1862–1863

ALSO BY JACK H. LEPA
AND FROM MCFARLAND

*Breaking the Confederacy: The Georgia and
Tennessee Campaigns of 1864* (2005; paperback 2011)

*The Shenandoah Valley Campaign
of 1864* (2003; paperback 2010)

The Civil War in Tennesee, 1862–1863

JACK H. LEPA

McFarland & Company, Inc., Publishers
Jefferson, North Carolina, and London

The present work is a reprint of the illustrated case bound edition of The Civil War in Tennessee, 1862–1863, *first published in 2007 by McFarland.*

LIBRARY OF CONGRESS CATALOGUING-IN-PUBLICATION DATA

Lepa, Jack H., 1949–
The Civil War in Tennessee, 1862–1863 / Jack H. Lepa.
p. cm.
Includes bibliographical references and index.

ISBN 978-0-7864-6431-9
softcover : 50# alkaline paper ∞

1. Tennessee — History — Civil War, 1861–1865 — Campaigns.
2. United States — History — Civil War, 1861–1865 — Campaigns.
I. Title
E470.4.L47   2011   976.8'04 — dc22   2007006738

BRITISH LIBRARY CATALOGUING DATA ARE AVAILABLE

© 2007 Jack H. Lepa. All rights reserved

No part of this book may be reproduced or transmitted in any form or by any means, electronic or mechanical, including photocopying or recording, or by any information storage and retrieval system, without permission in writing from the publisher.

On the cover: *Battle of Lookout Mountain,* Kurz & Allison color lithograph, 1889 (Library of Congress)

Manufactured in the United States of America

*McFarland & Company, Inc., Publishers
Box 611, Jefferson, North Carolina 28640
www.mcfarlandpub.com*

Table of Contents

Preface   1

1. Preparing to Fight   3
2. The River Campaign Begins   14
3. Fort Donelson   21
4. Turning Point in the West   32
5. Johnston Risks All   45
6. First Day at Shiloh   53
7. Shiloh — Day Two   69
8. Shiloh's Aftermath and Subsequent Campaigns   78
9. Rosecrans Takes Command   88
10. Slaughter at Stone's River   95
11. A Victory of Sorts   104
12. Spring 1863   110
13. A Campaign of Maneuver   116
14. A Fight Is Coming   125
15. Chickamauga — First Day   136
16. Chickamauga — Second Day   142
17. Chattanooga Under Siege   152
18. Grant Goes to Work   162
19. Nothing to Do but Wait   171

20. Lookout Mountain	180
21. Missionary Ridge	188
22. An Impossible Victory	195
23. After Chattanooga	204
Chapter Notes	209
Bibliography	221
Index	227

Preface

During the American Civil War Tennessee was probably the most important single state to both sides in terms of strategic and practical value. For the Union the state was the route to the Deep South and Atlanta. The rivers provided avenues of transportation in all directions and control of Tennessee and the Mississippi River would cripple the Confederacy's ability to move troops and supplies from the western states to the east. The Confederacy needed to maintain control of Tennessee to protect its southern states, and also because large amounts of agricultural products and mineral wealth came from Tennessee.

Many of the worst battles of the war took place for control of Tennessee: Shiloh, Stone's River, Chickamauga, and Chattanooga. Many of the men who rose to the top of the Union high command by the end of the war learned to command armies in Tennessee, including Henry Halleck, Ulysses Grant, William Sherman, George Thomas, and Philip Sheridan. This book describes the two years during which the fate of Tennessee, and possibly the nation, was decided.

I would like to thank the staff of the University of Nevada, Las Vegas, for their help with research and locating material used in this book. The staff of the Interlibrary Loan Department of the Las Vegas-Clark County Library District provided significant assistance in finding older and rare books that I would not have had access to otherwise. In addition, the Honnold-Mudd Library at the Claremont Colleges in Claremont, California, has an excellent selection of books from the nineteenth century that I was allowed to use.

1

PREPARING TO FIGHT

The American Civil War was less than a year old at the beginning of 1862. Men on both sides were still enlisting to go on what they believed was going to be a great adventure with bands playing, flags waving, and pretty girls waving at the brave men in their dashing uniforms as they marched off to fight for a righteous cause. The nation had not yet become familiar with the term "rivers of blood." After four terrible years this war would end as most wars did; one side was victorious, one side was defeated, and families on both sides mourned the loss of all those brave men who had given "the last full measure of devotion."[1]

While most of the attention was focused on Virginia, it was really in the western states where the Confederacy's doom was sealed. Foremost among those states was Tennessee, especially in 1862 and 1863, where the Union forces won their first major victories and opened the way to invade the Deep South. Clearly, it was Tennessee's position on the map that gave the state its strategic importance. And, like the nation, Tennessee was a house divided.

The meandering Tennessee River forms in the eastern mountains near Knoxville, and flows southwest to Chattanooga then across northern Alabama to near the Mississippi border. The looping river then heads almost straight north, through Tennessee again, and into Kentucky where it finally empties into the Ohio River at Paducah. The course of the river cuts Tennessee into three sections; the three regions had vastly different outlooks on the war. The eastern portion of the state around Knoxville is a mountainous area that was mostly occupied by small farmers who were loyal to the Union. In Western Tennessee, along the Mississippi River, cotton was a major component of the economy and the area was heavily Confederate. As might be expected the central portion was a mixture of both.[2]

Because of their support for the Union, President Abraham Lincoln had a special place in his heart for the mountain folk of East Tennessee. From early in the war he was constantly pushing the acting Union commander in that area to liberate the people from Confederate control. The political reasons for Lincoln's concern were clear enough, but he also could see that there would be military advantages to early movement in Tennessee, since it was clear that the state would bear the burden of defending the Deep South.[3]

In addition to its strategic location, Tennessee's natural and man-made resources made it a prime target. In the east the Unaka Mountains contained the majority of the

Confederacy's copper mines and large supplies of saltpeter, necessary for the manufacture of gunpowder. In and around Nashville were located some of the largest powder mills in the Confederacy. Both Nashville and Memphis contained a large number of machine shops and foundries that produced weapons and other military equipment. Railroad lines that were vital to the Confederacy for troop and supply movement traversed Tennessee in all directions. The rivers that flowed through Tennessee were also of great importance to the South. The Tennessee River brought trade from the Ohio River all the way to northern Alabama, while the Cumberland River could be used by large steamships to Nashville, and by smaller ships much farther east. The Mississippi River on the west was of course important for trade and military movements for both sides.[4]

The richness of Tennessee was also the cause of many of the problems in defending the state. The Confederacy could not afford to lose any portion of the state: not the mineral wealth of the east, nor the farming and industrial areas of the center, and not the Mississippi on the west. By attempting to defend everywhere the limited number of available troops had to be spread out across a vast territory.

In November of 1861, Major General George B. McClellan was appointed general in chief of all the Federal armies. A native of Philadelphia, he was a gifted engineer who graduated from West Point in 1846, second in his class. McClellan served in the Mexican War and returned to West Point as an instructor. In 1857 he left the army to go into the railroad business where he quickly rose from chief engineer of one railroad to president of another. McClellan returned to the army when the war broke out and after the embarrassment of Bull Run was appointed commander of the Army of the Potomac and then general in chief. It didn't take him long to realize the command structure in the western states needed to be changed to bring order out of the chaos that had been created by John C. Frémont in the Department of the Missouri.[5]

As Frémont's successor McClellan chose Major General Henry W. Halleck, who was second on the list of major generals and had been considered for the post of general in chief that went to McClellan. Halleck was an engineer who graduated near the top of his West Point class. He was a well-known writer on the art of warfare authoring *Elements of Military*

Henry W. Halleck (courtesy Library of Congress).

Art and Science and a translation of Jomini's *Life of Napoleon*. Resigning from the army in 1854, Halleck became a successful lawyer in San Francisco, and was offered a seat on the California Supreme Court, which he declined.[6]

Henry Halleck was balding and overweight with a bad temper and considered by many to be an overbearing intellectual, behind his back he was less than affectionately called "Old Brains." None could deny, however, his obvious talents and his success in all walks of life inspired confidence in his ability to administer his new command. The Department of the Missouri included Missouri, Iowa, Minnesota, Wisconsin, Illinois, Arkansas, and Kentucky west of the Cumberland River. Within a few months of taking command Halleck brought much needed order to his department and improved the living conditions and efficiency of about 90,000 soldiers and the naval units under his command.[7]

Another appointment made by McClellan that would have an important impact on the war in the west was that of his close personal friend, Brigadier General Don Carlos Buell, to command the newly created Department of the Ohio, composed of Ohio, Michigan, Indiana, Kentucky east of the Cumberland, and Tennessee, with headquarters in Louisville, Kentucky. Buell's regular army colleagues considered him to be one of the best commanders in the service. Buell was a tough disciplinarian with a gift for turning new recruits into capable soldiers, but he lacked any sort of charisma and found himself unpopular with his men. He was a methodical soldier who seemed to sometimes regard the enemy as an inconvenience that threatened to disturb his perfect plans. He once wrote that if caution and following the rules of warfare limited the number of actual battles fought causing the army to "sometimes miss the accidental success which folly or recklessness might have gained," this was acceptable because, eventually, observing the rules would bring victory.[8]

Although Buell was certainly committed to the cause of the Union he was a conservative Democrat with no interest in supporting abolition; in fact he had owned slaves. He was fighting for the preservation of the Union and to maintain the Constitution as it was; he did not approve of an escalation of the war. Unfortunately for Buell the pace of the war and its political goals had already changed sufficiently to put him one step behind by the time he took over his new command. In many ways Halleck and Buell were too much alike, turning them into competitors, which made cooperation between the two difficult.[9]

To oppose Halleck and Buell the Confederacy was counting on one of the most highly regarded soldiers on either side, Albert Sidney Johnston. A graduate of West Point from Kentucky, Johnston served with Confederate President Jefferson Davis in the Black Hawk War. Resigning from the army in 1834 he joined the fight for Texas independence and also fought for the United States in the Mexican War. In 1857 he commanded the expedition against the Mormons in Utah. When war broke out Johnston commanded the Department of the Pacific and was offered a high command in the Union army. When his adopted state of Texas left the Union, however, Johnston followed his heart and made his way across the southwest to offer his services to the south.[10]

Johnston was fifty-nine years old, tall and handsome, possessing undoubted courage and military ability. He looked like a general. Jefferson Davis thought Johnston was the ablest soldier on either side, and gave him command of the Western Military Department. Johnston's huge command encompassed all Confederate held territory from the Appalachian Mountains west to the Ozarks. Johnston had about 70,000 men under his command, totally inadequate to defend a line from Kentucky to southwest Missouri.[11]

For both Federal departments in the west the Confederate military forces were only a part of the problems that had to be overcome. Both Halleck and Buell lacked any aggressive spirit and could not agree on what moves to make or where to strike first. Buell was frequently being informed by Washington how important it was to liberate East Tennessee and its pro–Union citizens. Halleck, who looked at the situation from farther west, believed that the formidable Confederate position at Columbus, Kentucky, was the key to taking control of the Mississippi Valley. It was clear, as Halleck soon realized, however, that the Tennessee and Cumberland rivers provided the most feasible all-weather routes to split the Confederate forces in Tennessee and destroy them or drive them from the area.[12]

Albert Sidney Johnston (courtesy Library of Congress).

Right from the beginning of the conflict the Confederacy built up its defenses against Federal incursions on its rivers, especially the all-important Mississippi. At Columbus, Kentucky, less than twenty miles from Cairo, Illinois, Confederate general Leonidas Polk fortified the two hundred foot high bluffs overlooking the river with 140 guns. Considered by both sides to be a Gibraltar-like position, Columbus was unassailable from the river. With the addition of several forts stretching down river, including Island No. 10 and the impregnable position at Vicksburg, the Mississippi River was effectively closed to Federal ships.[13]

With so much of the Confederacy's limited resources devoted to protecting the Mississippi they were left with somewhat limited means to protect other important waterways. Among these were the Tennessee and Cumberland rivers that led into the heart of Tennessee and farther south. Two modest forts protected these waterways near the border with Kentucky. Fort Henry, on the eastern bank of the Tennessee, was fitted with seventeen guns and a garrison of a few thousand men. About twelve miles to the east, Fort Donelson was positioned on the western bank of the Cumberland. Guarding the water route to Nashville, Fort Donelson was an imposing obstacle mounting about forty guns with outer works that could hold over fifteen thousand troops.[14]

In addition to defending the rivers General Johnston had to somehow build and hold a defensive line that stretched from the Mississippi River across Southern Kentucky and Northern Tennessee. One of the places that the Confederates did choose to defend was Bowling Green, Kentucky, a small town strategically placed on the Big Barren River and the line of the Louisville and Nashville Railroad. Johnston established fortified works and was able to build up a garrison of about 20,000 men commanded by Major General William Hardee. As a stepchild to the war in Virginia, Johnston's department was never given resources adequate to counter the much larger numbers of Federal forces he faced, and Johnston had little hope that it would ever get any better although he made every effort to increase his available forces.[15]

General Johnston was constantly receiving demands from state and local political leaders that their territory must be defended. In an effort to increase the size of his forces Johnston suggested to President Davis that departments not directly threatened could spare units to reinforce areas that faced imminent invasion, such as his own. In January an aide sent to Richmond to ask Davis in person for more troops was quickly informed that there were none to spare. On January 22, after learning of the Confederate defeat at Mill Springs, a frustrated Johnston wrote to Confederate adjutant and inspector general Samuel Cooper saying that if forces from other parts of the Confederacy could not be spared to reinforce Tennessee a greater effort to raise troops had to be made. "No matter what the sacrifice may be, it must be made, and without loss of time. Our people do not comprehend the magnitude of the danger that threatens. Let it be impressed upon them."[16]

Adding more fuel to his argument Johnston prophesied that Federal operations elsewhere might be suspended till spring but "to suppose with the facilities of movement by water which the well-filled rivers of the Ohio, Cumberland, and Tennessee give for active operations, that they will suspend them in Tennessee and Kentucky during the winter months is a delusion." The Confederacy would have to marshal all its resources for the defense of Tennessee.[17]

On the last day of 1861 and the first day of 1862, President Lincoln issued another call for action and cooperation between the commanders in the West. In a wire to Halleck the president asked: "Are General Buell and yourself in concert? When he moves on Bowling Green, what hinders it being re-enforced from Columbus? A simultaneous movement by you on Columbus might prevent it." The next day he wired Buell: "I think you better get in concert with General Halleck at once," sending essentially the same message to Halleck about Buell. While it was clear that the western commanders would accomplish more by working together their rivalry for the top command in the west was preventing any meaningful cooperation.[18]

The president was fully aware of this rivalry, and added to the lack of action by McClellan and pressure from Congress to get the war moving, the answers he received from Buell and Halleck only increased his frustration. From Buell came the admission that "There is no arrangement between General Halleck and myself. I have been informed by General McClellan that he would make suitable disposition for concerted action." So Buell would wait until he received instructions from McClellan. From Halleck came a strangely similar reply: "I have never received a word from General Buell. I am not ready to co-operate with him. Hope to do so in few weeks. Have written fully on this subject to Major General McClellan. Too much haste will ruin everything." Halleck, too, would sit and wait.[19]

On January 2, Halleck wrote to Buell from St. Louis warning him not to expect any assistance in the immediate future because "I have had no instruction respecting co-operation." Halleck went on to say that he could not make any meaningful campaign against Columbus since "all my available troops are in the field except those at Cairo and Paducah, which are barely sufficient to threaten Columbus." Halleck then suggested that perhaps in a few weeks he might be able to render assistance to Buell but for now to withdraw troops from Missouri would be "almost impossible."[20]

General McClellan wrote to Halleck on the 3rd, apparently in agreement with the president's wishes, to promote cooperation between the western commanders. "It is of the greatest importance," he emphatically wrote, "that the rebel troops in Western Kentucky be prevented from moving to the support of the force in front of General Buell." To achieve this goal McClellan suggested "an expedition should be sent up the Cumberland River, to act in concert with General Buell's command." He proposed that this expedition be composed of at least two divisions accompanied by gunboats and that a demonstration against Columbus be made at the same time. He closed by asking Halleck to submit his own views on the situation. George McClellan may have had a difficult time moving his own army but he could see clearly enough the best course of action in the West.[21]

Also on the 3rd of January, Buell wrote to Halleck with his own suggestions for a combined movement. Buell stated that it was "not extravagant to say that the great power of the rebellion in the West" was between Columbus and Bowling Green. The center of this strategic area was "about where the railroad between those points crosses the Tennessee and Cumberland Rivers, including Nashville." Because of the railroad the Confederates could quickly concentrate troops at any point along their front. To prevent this Buell proposed a "combined attack on its center and flanks, or at least demonstrations which may be converted into real attacks, and fully occupy the enemy on the whole front." Included in this plan were expeditions on both rivers. It was a struggle but the strategy for the Federal armies in the West was slowly taking shape.[22]

On January 7, an increasing impatient President Lincoln wrote to Buell, "Please name as early a day as you safely can on or before which you can be ready to move southward in concert with Major General Halleck. Delay is ruining us, and it is indispensable for me to have something definite." The president, desperately trying to stir up some action by one or both of his western commanders, sent a similar wire to Halleck.[23]

That same day, in a lengthy reply to the president's wire of the 1st, Halleck tried to explain the situation in his department estimating that the enemy has "about 22,000 men at Columbus, and the place is strongly fortified." After allowing for the minimum number of troops to guard Cairo and Paducah, Halleck could put only about 15,000 men in the field to cooperate with Buell. "It would be madness to attempt anything serious with such a force," he continued, "and I cannot at the present time withdraw any from Missouri without risking the loss of this State."[24]

General Halleck went on to say that he believed the "authorities at Washington do not appreciate the difficulties with which we have to contend here." Confederate raiders and sympathizers had "so enraged the people of Missouri, that it is estimated that there is a majority of 80,000 against the Government." Halleck was convinced that he was "virtually in an enemy's country." In addition to the enemy Halleck had to deal with unruly and untrained troops and a lack of trained officers to train and discipline those troops. The frustrated general colorfully compared his situation to that of "a carpenter who is required to build a bridge with a dull ax, a broken saw, and rotten timber."[25]

As far as cooperating with Buell, Halleck admitted that he knew "nothing of General Buell's intended operations, never having received any information in regard to the general plan of campaign." Guessing that Buell wanted to move on Bowling Green while he advanced against Columbus, Halleck emphatically wrote that this would simply repeat the errors that caused the Federal disaster at Bull Run. "To operate on exterior lines against an enemy occupying a central position will fail, as it always has failed, in ninety-nine cases out of a hundred. It is condemned by every military authority I have ever read." On the copy of this dispatch a disheartened President Lincoln wrote, "It is exceedingly discouraging. As everywhere else, nothing can be done."[26]

While Halleck might agree with Buell's assessment that control of the Tennessee and Cumberland rivers was central to any meaningful Union victory the problem was that both men wanted to be the one to claim that victory. Halleck was not enthusiastic about attacking Columbus and sending expeditions up the two rivers so that Buell would have an easier time of capturing Bowling Green and Nashville, and almost assuredly the overall command in the West. Buell, on the other hand, believed that Nashville was the great prize in the region and since the city was in Buell's department he was not interested in sharing that prize with Halleck. Another factor in the equation was that once Buell had Nashville he could turn his attention to Eastern Tennessee and Knoxville, which would greatly please President Lincoln.[27]

Both Halleck and Buell wanted to fight a war with minimum risk to their forces and their reputations. They decided that by thorough preparation along with slow and cautious movement, avoiding actually fighting as much as possible, the administration's goals could be achieved. Both commanders were more interested in campaigning by the map and occupying strategic points than in going after the Confederate army. Halleck saw the advantage of using the rivers to advance but since Nashville was out of his jurisdiction he was not all that enthused about helping Buell capture the city. Buell could not see beyond his land advance on Nashville or how important control of the rivers would be in the future. Back in Washington, McClellan was so involved in fending off pressure from Lincoln and Congress to take some action in Virginia that he was unable to offer any tangible suggestions on the problem. Someone or some event was needed to convince the Union commanders to take action whether it was in their personal interest or not.[28]

That someone surprisingly turned out to be a short, scruffy looking brigadier general named Ulysses Grant. An 1843 graduate of the U. S. Military Academy, he had served with distinction in the Mexican War. In 1854 Grant resigned his commission after spending several dreary years on the West Coast without his family and earning an enduring reputation as someone who loved the bottle a little too much. In the years before the war Grant tried several civilian trades, including working for his father, none of which he was very good at, and his future looked grim. The war saved him, as it did many former officers, from a life of nondescript boredom.[29]

Grant's first command was as colonel of the 21st Illinois Volunteers. In his first action Grant led his regiment to attack an enemy camp near his own. On finding that the Confederates had retreated as the Federal troops approached Grant realized that the enemy commander "had been as much afraid of me as I had been of him," a valuable lesson that Grant never forgot. Promotions came quickly to experienced officers early in the war and the former captain who had resigned from the army under a cloud was soon promoted to brigadier general. Serving in Halleck's command and stationed at Cairo, Illinois, Grant's first real fight was at Belmont, Missouri, where he led five regiments in an attack on a Confederate camp. Confederate reinforcements arrived and Grant had to quickly pull his men out of harm's way, displaying his soon to be legendary coolness under pressure.[30]

On January 6, in the middle of the blizzard of telegrams between St. Louis, Louisville, and Washington, Halleck had ordered Grant to make a demonstration toward Mayfield, Kentucky, about thirty miles south of Paducah. The objective of the advance was to prevent the enemy from reinforcing Bowling Green and Grant was to "make a great fuss about moving all your forces towards Nashville, and let it be so reported by the newspapers," while keeping the true reason for the move secret. The ever-cautious Halleck also ordered that Grant should not "advance far enough to expose your flank and rear to an attack from Columbus, and by all means avoid a serious engagement."[31]

Grant was happy to get some action and organized a multi-pronged advance. The department's naval commander, Flag Officer Andrew Foote, would send gunboats up both the Tennessee and Cumberland rivers while Brigadier General Charles F. Smith, a tough old soldier who had been one of Grant's instructors at West Point, led a force from Paducah toward Fort Henry on the Tennessee. Grant would lead another force of about 6,000 troops from Cairo, to the west of Smith's column, toward Columbus. Despite Grant's enthusiasm for the movement it was not a pleasant experience as he remembered. "The weather was very bad; snow and rain fell, the roads, never good in that section, were intolerable. We were out more than a week splashing through the mud, snow and rain, the men suffering very much."[32]

The expedition turned out to be mostly a long walk in terrible weather that brought few immediate results. However, General Smith learned that Fort Henry, and the still under construction Fort Heiman located across the river, were vulnerable. Smith went back up the river in a gunboat and exchanged a few shots with Fort Henry, reporting on the 22nd, "I think two iron-clad gunboats would make short work of Fort Henry." Here was information that Grant could use to make a move that might actually produce some important results and he spent much of the next week trying to get Halleck to approve an expedition up the Tennessee.[33]

Any movement along the rivers would require naval support and it was for this purpose that a new weapon was created that would substantially ease the Federal efforts. During the fall and winter the shipyards at Cairo, St. Louis and other river towns were busy building warships for the Union cause. The most formidable of these were seven shallow-draft ironclads created by James B. Eads of St. Louis. These ships were wide, flat-bottomed paddle wheelers encased in iron armor up to 2½ inches thick across the front and thinner plating on the sides. The armor formed a sloping casemate that earned the ships the nickname "turtles." They were also slow and underpowered but with thirteen heavy guns they were more powerful than any ships the Confederates could send against them and could shell fortifications from out of range of most enemy artillery.[34]

Early in the war the warships that operated on the inland rivers, while commanded by naval officers, fell under the jurisdiction of the army. The crews to man these vessels were a mixture of riverboat sailors, civilian volunteers, and a few seafaring naval veterans. Still woefully short of crewmen Grant issued a call for experienced sailors from the ranks of the infantry who were willing to transfer to the gunboats. Soon the ships had their full complement of crew and were ready to sail in mid–January.[35]

Henry Halleck may have been slow and cautious to a fault but he was certainly intelligent enough to see that the rivers offered the best opportunity to advance Federal armies into Tennessee. On January 20 he sent a lengthy message to McClellan outlining his ideas. He began by criticizing the Federal war effort so far, calling it a "pepper-box strategy — scattering our troops so as to render them inferior in numbers in any place where they can meet the enemy." He was careful, however, to point out that this was not McClellan's fault but rather that of scheming politicians trying to serve their own interests.[36]

Halleck then went on to say that a move down the Mississippi was not practical at this time but "a much more feasible plan is to move up the Cumberland and Tennessee, making Nashville the first objective point." This would probably force the abandonment of Bowling Green. In addition, "Columbus cannot be taken without an immense siege train and a terrible loss of life.... But it can be turned, paralyzed, and forced to surrender." Surprisingly, Halleck agreed with Buell in that "this line of the Cumberland or Tennessee is the great central line of the western theater of war," but, careful as ever, he could not recommend taking any action with less than 60,000 men.[37]

Aside from the obvious military benefits that could be derived from a campaign up the rivers into Tennessee there were also outside forces at work that helped convince Halleck to finally make a move. On January 18, General George H. Thomas won a small but important battle at Mill Springs in eastern Kentucky, a victory that reflected favorably on General Buell. Another factor that Halleck had to consider was a telegram he received from Washington informing him that Confederate general G. P. T. Beauregard was heading west to join Johnston with fifteen regiments. If Halleck were going to act it would be best to do it before these reinforcements arrived.[38]

Since early January Grant had been requesting a meeting with Halleck to discuss plans for a campaign along the rivers. After General Smith's report concerning Fort Henry, Grant again requested an audience with his department commander, and this time it was approved. Arriving in St. Louis on January 23 Grant later wrote that he "was received with so little cordiality that I perhaps stated the object of my visit with less clearness than I might have done, and I had not uttered many sentences before I was cut short as if my plan was preposterous." Grant returned to Cairo disappointed and embarrassed. In addition to his naturally cautious nature, one of the factors that caused Halleck's hesitation in approving Grant's campaign was the fact that Halleck had little faith in Grant himself.[39]

Ulysses Grant was nothing if not persistent and he quickly recovered from his rebuff in St. Louis. He was also able to enlist Flag Officer Foote in the effort to convince Halleck to approve the expedition. On January 28 both men put forth their arguments. Grant wrote, "With permission, I will take Fort Henry, on the Tennessee, and establish and hold a large camp there." In a separate telegram Foote added: "Commanding General Grant and myself are of opinion that Fort Henry, on the Tennessee River, can be carried with four iron-clad gunboats and troops to permanently occupy. Have we your authority to move for that purpose when ready?"[40]

The next day Grant sent a more detailed message: "In view of the large force now concentrating in this district and the present feasibility of the plan I would respectfully suggest the propriety of subduing Fort Henry, near the Kentucky and Tennessee line." Suggesting that the Confederate river defenses might soon be materially strengthened and that a forward movement would have a positive effect on the morale of the troops Grant diplomatically closed with, "the advantages of this move are as perceptible to the general commanding as to myself, therefore further statements are unnecessary."[41]

It would be reasonable to assume that the increase in troops under Grant's command shows that Halleck was already contemplating some sort of movement but it is also probable that Grant's urging combined with that of Foote and the news of Beauregard's approach finally convinced Halleck to allow the river campaign to proceed. On January 30 Halleck told Grant, "Make your preparations to take and hold Fort Henry. I will send you written instructions by mail."[42]

That same day Halleck wired McClellan acknowledging the information about Beauregard and stating: "General Grant and Commodore Foote will be ordered to immediately advance, and to reduce and hold Fort Henry, on the Tennessee river." Halleck also said that the railroad between Columbus and Bowling Green would be disabled although in the dispatch he made a mistake on its location.[43]

Grant began organizing the expedition immediately. He wired Halleck that preparations for the campaign were being made quietly without drawing undue attention and he was "Awaiting your instructions, which we expect in the morning, I have not made definite plans as to my movements, but expect to start Sunday evening, taking 15,000 men." The expedition would travel by steamer as far as possible and either Brig. General John A. McClernand or General Smith would be left behind to command Fort Henry after its capture. At this point the expedition was still being thought of in limited terms: take Fort Henry and return.[44]

On January 31, Grant received Halleck's full message of instructions for the campaign. Grant was to gather all the troops he could from the various garrisons under his command, leaving sufficient force behind to guard them against enemy raids. The roads were almost impassable so the troops and supplies would travel by steamers, escorted by Foote's gunboats, and the objective being, "Fort Henry should be taken and held at all hazards." Halleck wanted the road to Dover cut so that reinforcements could not reach Fort Henry and then cavalry was to be sent to destroy the railroad. Halleck also informed Grant of the approach of Beauregard stating that "It is therefore of the greatest importance that we cut that line before he arrives. You will move with the least delay possible."[45]

On February 1 Grant sent orders to McClernand to be ready to move the following evening with a three-day supply of rations for the troops and forage for the animals. Grant also wrote to Smith to bring all the troops he could spare from Paducah and Smithland and that the move was scheduled to begin Monday, February 3, and the only objective mentioned was Fort Henry. Little was known about the Confederate defenses along the rivers, especially Fort Donelson, and at this time Fort Henry was considered the biggest prize.[46]

Halleck informed Buell of the expedition on January 31, to which Buell responded with an offer of assistance, in several days. In dispatches on February 1 and 2, Halleck informed Buell that he did not require any assistance since "at present it is only proposed to take and occupy Fort Henry and Dover [including nearby Fort Donelson], and, if possible, cut the railroad from Columbus to Bowling Green." A successful assault on Fort Henry would open the Tennessee River to the Federal fleet but Halleck admitted, "how far we may venture to send the gunboats up the river will be left for after consideration." And, finally, a clear picture of what Halleck hoped to accomplish by concentrating a large force at a captured Fort Henry: "Troops must be withdrawn either from Bowling Green or Columbus to protect the railroads. If the former, you can advance; if the latter, we can take New Madrid and cut off the river communication with Columbus." Thus, Halleck was looking for much broader results than the capture of a small riverfront fort. In addition to the military and political advantages of expelling the enemy from large portions of Kentucky and Tennessee this scenario, if it were played out properly, would likely gain for Henry Halleck one of his prime objectives, the overall command in the West.[47]

It had been much too long in coming, but movement was finally here. After months of President Lincoln trying to get his generals to do something, months of bickering between those generals as they tried to gain some advantage over each other, and months of debating strategies, the Federal army in the West was finally advancing. It doesn't happen all that often in war but the Army of the United States had the right man in the right place at the right time. And the day after he sailed from Cairo to begin the campaign, Ulysses Grant, who in the past had never really been a success at much of anything except mediocrity, sent a simple little message to General Halleck that would soon bring about dramatic results in Tennessee and begin the long and bloody journey to reuniting the nation: "Will be off up the Tennessee at 6 o'clock. Command, twenty-three regiments in all."[48]

2

THE RIVER CAMPAIGN BEGINS

The next morning, February 2, the fleet set off from Cairo. As the ships slowly moved out into the river Grant's chief of staff, John Rawlins, thought that Grant seemed nervous and until they were well away he frequently looked back as if fearing Halleck would have a change of heart and cancel the expedition at the last moment. The warships in Flag Officer Foote's fleet consisted of the ironclads *Carondelet*, Commander Henry Walke; the *Essex*, Captain William Porter; the *Cincinnati*, Commander Roger Stemble; and the *St. Louis*, Lt. Commander Leonard Paulding, along with the less formidable wooden gunboats *Conestoga*, *Lexington*, and *Taylor*.[1]

Steaming up the Ohio River the fleet reached the Tennessee that evening and arrived near Fort Henry by the morning of February 4. As they reached the vicinity of the Confederate works several mines, or torpedoes, were discovered in the water but they were improperly prepared and easily disposed of with little danger to the ships. By afternoon the steamers arrived a few miles below Fort Henry and the transports began unloading McClernand's men along the eastern shore. Grant accompanied Foote and the four ironclads up the river to inspect the fortifications and exchange a few cannon shots to test the range before the main action began.[2]

Fort Henry had been built on low ground in a bend of the river. The location allowed the guns along the waterfront to fire directly down the river but it was also poorly engineered and prone to flooding when the river was high. The fort itself contained seventeen heavy guns. Around the fort were entrenchments and rifle pits to defend the land approaches. Large tracts of the surrounding fields and woods were not much more than swamps, making a land-based assault against the camp and fort even more difficult. The total number of Confederate defenders was about 2,800 men commanded by Brigadier General Lloyd Tilghman. He was from a Maryland family that had served the nation since the Revolution, a graduate of West Point, and had served with distinction in the Mexican War. Tilghman would lose his life in May of 1863 during Grant's Vicksburg campaign.[3]

Although Fort Henry's garrison was not all that large for so important a position, reinforcements from Fort Donelson, only about eleven miles away by two good roads, were easily obtainable. Grant felt that the two positions were so important to the defense of the rivers "that it was natural to suppose that reinforcements would come from every quarter from which they could be got. Prompt action on our part was imperative."[4]

On the hills above the west bank of the river, across from Fort Henry, the Confederates had begun work on another set of fortifications called Fort Heiman that were in a much better position to control the river and resist attack. Together the two forts would have presented a formidable obstacle to movement on the Tennessee but Fort Heiman was unfinished and the position indefensible.[5]

Grant wrote to Halleck on the 4th explaining that McClernand's troops had been set ashore about three miles below Fort Henry but because sufficient shipping was not available to transport the entire army at one time a large number of steamers were returning to Paducah for General Smith's troops.[6]

Grant also wrote to his wife, Julia, on the 4th: "All the troops will be up by noon to-morrow, and Friday morning, if we are not attacked before, the fight will commence. The enemy are well fortified and have a strong force. I do not want to boast but I have a confidant feeling of success."[7]

With the arrival of General Smith's troops Grant had about fifteen thousand men under his command and on the 5th he published Field Orders, No. 1, detailing his plan for the coming assault. On the east side of the river the First Division, commanded by McClernand, was to advance until reaching the roads linking Fort Henry with Fort Donelson and Dover. "It will be the special duty of this command to prevent all re-enforcements to Fort Henry or escape from it, also to be held in readiness to charge and take Fort Henry by storm promptly on the receipt of orders."[8]

Two brigades of General Smith's division were to secure the incomplete Fort Heiman on the western shore and establish a battery of artillery there so as to fire into Fort Henry. Smith's third brigade and any troops not needed to secure Fort Heiman were to be transferred to the eastern bank and either prepare to assault the fort or support the First Division, as was deemed necessary. In addition to the land forces Foote's gunboats were to steam straight up the river and bombard the Confederate works.[9]

While Grant's troops were moving into position around Fort Henry, inside the works General Tilghman was facing a grim reality. As the Confederate general knew, both the fort and the surrounding works were well within range of Federal artillery from numerous points on both sides of the river. Add the firepower of the large guns on the Federal ships and it was obvious that Fort Henry could not be held for very long. In commenting on the poor choice of location and layout of the fort the Confederate commander felt that "the history of military engineering records no parallel to this case." He decided to remain in the fort with just enough men to work the guns while the remainder of the garrison escaped to Fort Donelson to fight another day. It was clear to Tilghman that "Fort Donelson might possibly be held, if properly re-enforced, even though Fort Henry should fall; but the reverse of this proposition was not true."[10]

The attack was scheduled to begin on the morning of February 6. As often happens, however, the weather had a major effect on the plans of mortals. Although the morning was fair with a light breeze, it had rained most of the night and it wasn't until almost 11 o'clock that McClernand's force was able to begin their march. The roads were ribbons of mud and the going was so slow that it took the Federal infantry hours longer to reach their assigned position than was expected. On board the flagship Foote and Grant were aware of the poor conditions on land and Foote even commented that he would force the surrender of the fort before the land forces could come up. General Smith moved his men forward on the opposite side of the river and before noon the gunboats moved to the attack.[11]

The ironclads approached the fort four abreast with the *Essex* on the right, then the *Cincinnati*, *Carondelet*, and *St. Louis*. The wooden gunboats were stationed behind the ironclads for their protection but were close enough to be able to assist in the bombardment if needed. As Commander Walke reported:

> The Cincinnati fired the first shot as the signal for the other to begin. At once the fort responded from her eleven heavy guns, and was ablaze with the flame of cannon. The firing from the armored vessels was rapid and well sustained from the beginning of the attack, and seemingly accurate, as we could occasionally see the earth thrown in great heaps over the enemy's guns.[12]

The Federal ships opened fire about 1,700 yards from the fort and continued closing the range until they were within 600 yards. As the ships came closer to the fort the accuracy of the fire from both sides naturally improved. The ships were hit more than fifty times but the *Essex* suffered the only major damage. A heavy shot pierced the armor, killed a sailor, and smashed through the ship, blowing up a boiler and scalding twenty-nine men with the pilot being killed at the wheel. This disabled the ship forcing it to fall out of line and drift off downstream.[13]

The three remaining ironclads continued to pound the fort as they moved closer and closer. After about an hour and a half of bombardment the interior of Fort Henry had become a shambles. There were wrecked guns and pieces of gun carriages along with mangled bodies and wounded lying everywhere. One of the defenders' most powerful weapons, a twenty-four-pound rifled gun, burst early in the fight. Another large gun was disabled by an accident. Captain Jesse Taylor later wrote that the fire from the Federal ships "penetrated the earth-works as readily as a ball from a navy Colt would pierce a pine board, and soon so disabled other guns as to leave us but four capable of being served." Although the garrison that stayed to fight was small casualties were mounting, the men were exhausted and there were no replacements available. The Confederates had fought bravely but it was obvious to Tilghman that the fort was lost. He had held out long enough for the infantry to make good its escape toward Fort Donelson and further sacrifice was pointless so the Confederate flag was lowered in surrender.[14]

General Tilghman made a formal surrender on board Foote's flagship. The surviving garrison numbered about eighty officers and men. Tilghman was allowed to send a report of the action through the lines in which he wrote: "I take occasion to bear testimony to the gallantry of the officers and men under my command. They sustained their position with consummate bravery as long as there was any hope of success.[15]

The relative ease with which the gunboats had forced the surrender of Fort Henry helped to create the idea that earthworks could not stand up to a determined naval bombardment. Apparently the fact that the fort was poorly located and designed, was inadequately armed, and was partially flooded by the rising river made little impression on Federal commanders. In fact, Captain Taylor commented that "If the attack had been delayed forty-eight hours, there would hardly have been a hostile shot fired; the Tennessee would have accomplished the work by drowning the magazine."[16]

After the surrender Grant quickly put garrisons in both Fort Henry and Fort Heiman and sent a short wire to Halleck: "Fort Henry is ours. The gunboats silenced the batteries before the investment was completed. I think the garrison must have commenced the retreat last night. I shall take and destroy Fort Donelson on the 8th and return to Fort Henry." Whatever rivalry might have existed between the services did not affect the commanders and Grant made sure Foote's ships received credit for the victory.[17]

In a more detailed report that same day Grant wrote:

> The garrison, I think, must have commenced their retreat last night or at an early hour this morning. Had I not felt it an imperative necessity to attack Fort Henry to-day I should have made the investment complete and delayed until to-morrow, so as to have secured the garrison. I do not now believe, however, that the result would have been any more satisfactory. I shall take and destroy Fort Donelson on the 8th and return to Fort Henry with the forces employed, unless it looks feasible to occupy that place with a small force that could retreat easily to the main body.[18]

Almost as soon as Grant told Halleck he was going to take Fort Donelson it was apparent that there would be delays. On the 7th Grant decided to take a look at Fort Donelson and with a small escort approached to within a mile of the works. Grant's opinion of the two senior Confederate generals in Fort Donelson appear in his *Memoirs*:

> I had known General Pillow in Mexico, and judged that with any force, no matter how small, I could march up to within gunshot of any intrenchments he was given to hold. I said this to the officers of my staff at the time. I knew that Floyd was in command, but he was no soldier, and I judged that he would yield to Pillow's pretensions. I met, as I expected, no opposition in making the reconnaissance and, besides learning the topography of the country on the way and around Fort Donelson, found that there were two roads available for marching; one leading to the village of Dover, the other to Donelson.[19]

Back at Fort Henry there was much to do to secure the fort and prepare for further action. A great deal of enemy property had been captured and needed to be accounted for. The weather turned bad and supplies needed for the advance were delayed. Foote had to return to Cairo to repair his battered ships, leaving only the *Carondelet* to guard the river. There were also problems with the green and mostly undisciplined troops that had to be addressed. On February 9 Grant issued General Field Orders No. 5: "The pilfering and marauding disposition shown by some of the men of this command has determined the general commanding to make an example of some one, to fully show his disapprobation of such conduct." In essence Grant was going to hold the commanders liable for the conduct of their men. If the brigade, regiment, and company commanders did not punish known offenders promptly the commander of the unit would be punished in their place. Grant wanted the guilty parties found and punished, no excuses. In addition, Grant's order encompassed a much larger, and ultimately more important, view than just punishing some guilty soldiers. They were in the enemy's country and Grant felt "so much more could be done by a manly and humane policy to advance the cause which we all have so deeply at heart, it is astonishing that men can be found so wanton as to destroy, pillage, and burn indiscriminately, without inquiry."[20]

While Grant and his troops were preparing for the march to Fort Donelson the naval war was moving forward. The Tennessee River was now open to Federal ships as far south as Florence, Alabama, which was as far as ships could navigate. Immediately after the fall of Fort Henry, Foote sent the three wooden gunboats, under the command of Lieutenant Commander S. L. Phelps, on a raid that would yield spectacular results. About twenty-five miles from Fort Henry, Phelps landed a party that damaged a railroad bridge and tore up a portion of the track. Sailing up the river just the presence of his flotilla forced the rebels to burn three steamboats, one loaded with ammunition. Farther south Phelps captured the *Eastport*, a half-finished Confederate gunboat loaded with lumber. As the small fleet continued up the river two more steamboats were seized near the border with Alabama. On arriving at Florence three ships loaded with military stores were burned by the locals. The Federal ships had an uneventful return trip except for bombarding a Confederate camp near Savannah, Tennessee. In addition to the material damage done by the raid Phelps noted in his report:

Ulysses S. Grant (courtesy Library of Congress).

We have met with the most gratifying proofs of loyalty everywhere across Tennessee, and in the portions of Mississippi and Alabama we visited most affecting instances greeted us almost hourly. Men, women, and children several times gathered in crowds of hundreds, shouted their welcome, and hailed their national flag with an enthusiasm there was no mistaking.[21]

While Phelps' gunboats were rampaging on the river the move to Fort Donelson was becoming much more important and complicated than anyone originally expected. Grant's comment that he would "take and destroy Fort Donelson on the 8th and return to Fort Henry" would seem to indicate that, at least at first, Fort Donelson was considered to be of secondary importance.[22]

Back in St. Louis, however, General Halleck was realizing that the capture of Fort Henry had to be followed up by an attack on Fort Donelson. Not only would the capture of Fort Donelson clear the Cumberland River to Nashville but about thirty miles up the river was the town of Clarksville where the railroad crossed the river and went northeast to Bowling

Green, connecting the two parts of the Confederate army. If the bridge over the Cumberland could be destroyed Albert Sidney Johnston's army would be split in two, and with Federal gunboats patrolling the river the Confederate forces at Bowling Green would be trapped above the Cumberland, and easily crushed by the vastly superior Federal forces. Halleck seldom tried to force any action but his anxiety is clear when on February 8 he telegraphed to Grant: "If possible, destroy the bridge at Clarksville. It is of vital importance, and should be attempted at all hazards." Grant could see the importance of the bridge at Clarksville as well as Halleck but he was hampered by the weather and lack of naval support. From his vantage point Grant could also see that Fort Donelson would have to be captured before any move could be made on Clarksville.[23]

General Johnston also saw the strategic situation as clearly as anyone. The day after Fort Henry was lost he met with General Beauregard and other commanders at Bowling Green to determine a course of action. Because of the easy naval victory at Fort Henry he believed that "the best open earthworks are not reliable to meet successfully a vigorous attack of iron-clad gunboats." Johnston and the other Confederate commanders expected Fort Donelson to fall in the same way. If this should occur "it will open the route to the enemy to Nashville."[24]

It was just as critical to hold the important industrial center of Nashville as it was to save the army north of the Cumberland so Johnston ordered the commander of the garrison at Bowling Green, General William Hardee, to abandon his fortifications, move down to Nashville and prepare defensive positions around the city. The hope was that if Fort Donelson could hold out long enough the defenses of Nashville could be made strong enough to repel the Federal gunboats. This seemed to be a sensible plan considering the circumstances but for some reason Johnston decided to make a serious stand at Fort Donelson and diverted about 12,000 of the Bowling Green troops to reinforce the fort. This was probably a bad idea but if the situation called for it the troops could always abandon the fort as they had done at Fort Henry. The real problem for the Confederates at Fort Donelson was the quality of the officers who commanded the garrison.[25]

While the generals in the field were making plans and gathering their forces General Halleck was continuing to plead with General McClellan to get reinforcements and promote himself at General Buell's expense. On February 8 Halleck wrote that he was "decidedly of opinion that if General Buell cannot move on Bowling Green, all his available forces not required to guard Green River should be transferred to the Cumberland, to move by water on Nashville." Halleck's forces could not advance on Nashville because he was afraid of being cut off by Confederate troops at Bowling Green.[26]

On the 10th of February, Halleck, fearing a non-existent attack, pleaded his case to McClellan:

> Do send me more troops. It is the crisis of the war in the West. Have you fully considered the advantage which the Cumberland affords to the enemy at Nashville? The whole Bowling Green force can come down in a day, attack Grant in the rear, and return to Nashville before Buell can get half way there. We are certainly in peril.

In another telegram a few hours later Halleck again requested reinforcements saying, "Give us the means and we are certain to give the enemy a telling blow." Halleck didn't seem to realize that he already had the means, a non-descript-looking fellow named Grant who was preparing to strike a blow that would change the course of the war.[27]

From his headquarters in St. Louis, General Halleck continued to send troops to bolster the expedition to Fort Donelson. On February 11, several regiments arrived and were formed into a new brigade for General Smith's division. Halleck also transferred two men who would have an enormous impact on Grant's career and the war in general. Brigadier General William T. Sherman, who was wasting away in a training camp in St. Louis, was sent to take command of Paducah, beginning the partnership with Grant that would eventually produce victory for the Union. Another officer, Lieutenant Colonel James B. McPherson, was assigned to Grant's column as an engineer. He would quickly rise to become one of Grant's most trusted subordinates and eventually command the Army of the Tennessee. In July 1864, the 35-year-old McPherson was killed in action in front of Atlanta. Sherman considered him the most promising officer in the army and a close personal friend. The tough old soldier wept when he received the news.[28]

Anxious to get moving but knowing that he had to have the support of the gunboats Grant wrote to Foote on the 10th asking him if he could at least send two ships from Cairo and offering to supply artillerymen to man the guns if the crews were deficient. On February 11, Halleck wrote a dispatch to both Brig. General G. W. Cullum, his chief of staff, and Flag Officer Foote urging them to "push forward the Cumberland expedition with all possible dispatch. I will give you plenty of support in a few days. Time now is everything for us. Don't delay one instant." That same day Halleck sent another message to Foote: "You have gained great distinction by your capture of Fort Henry. Everybody recognizes your services." Suggesting that taking Fort Donelson would make Foote famous Halleck continued, "The taking of these places is a military necessity. Delays add strength to them more than to us. Act quickly, even though only half ready. Troops will soon be ready to support you."[29]

On February 11 the expedition finally began to take shape. Foote wired Halleck that he was "ready with three gunboats to proceed up the Cumberland River, and shall leave here for that purpose in two hours — 8:30 P.M." Foote left Cairo with the ironclads *St. Louis, Louisville* and *Pittsburgh*. The *Carondelet* and the wooden gunboats, just returned from their raid up the Tennessee, would rendezvous in the Cumberland, below Fort Donelson. While steaming up the Ohio River the warships were joined at Smithland by transports carrying six new regiments to join Grant's army.[30]

Also on the 11th Grant wired Halleck that "every effort will be put forth to have Clarksville within a few days." Grant admitted later that he was "very impatient to get to Fort Donelson because I knew the importance of the place to the enemy and supposed he would reinforce it rapidly. I felt that 15,000 men on the 8th would be more effective than 50,000 a month later."[31]

Grant's General Field Orders No. 11, issued on the 11th, directed that one brigade of McClernand's First Division would move by the Telegraph road to within two miles of Fort Donelson. The other two brigades were to move by the Dover or Ridge road and spread out so as to join with the first brigade the same distance from the fort. Two brigades of Smith's Second Division at Fort Henry were to follow on the Dover road to be followed by the troops stationed at Fort Heiman. One of Smith's brigades was to be sent to Dover to cut off a Confederate retreat, if practical. General Lew Wallace was left in command of Fort Henry with some of Smith's troops and several new regiments but could be quickly transported by river if needed at Fort Donelson.[32]

3

Fort Donelson

Grant's army moved out for Fort Donelson on the morning of February 12. Once past the flooded low country around Fort Henry they made good time. The weather had become unseasonably warm and as soldiers often do many of the men thought it was too much trouble to carry their overcoats and blankets and discarded them along the way. McClernand's troops arrived at their destination early that afternoon.[1]

During the afternoon and evening the Federal lines were formed around Fort Donelson. General Smith's troops were on the left covering the northwest portion of the fort extending to Hickman Creek. McClernand was on the right, controlling the escape routes to the south with his right flank extended to the flooded area south of Dover. Grant felt that his position was a good one as he explained, "The troops were not intrenched, but the nature of the ground was such that they were just as well protected from the fire of the enemy as if rifle-pits had been thrown up. Our line was generally along the crest of ridges." Grant ordered Lew Wallace to bring up his troops and as soon as the gunboats arrived the attack would begin.[2]

Grant's plan of attack was relatively simple, basically the same formula that he wanted to use at Fort Henry. The infantry would cover the Confederate outer works, prevent troops from going in or out, and set up artillery to bombard the land fortifications. Foote's gunboats would pound the fort into submission, as they had done at Fort Henry. Cut off by land and river the fort would quickly surrender. This sounded easy enough but Fort Donelson was not Fort Henry. Thousands of Confederate troops had already reinforced the garrison and the fort itself was much stronger and better situated than Fort Henry. Grant and his army were in for some unpleasant surprises.

Fort Donelson was built to protect Nashville from enemy ships sailing up the Cumberland River. The Cumberland flows to Dover from the east and just south of the town makes a right turn heading north toward the Ohio River. Fort Donelson was located on a high hill on the left bank of this bend, looking north, about two miles above Dover. The majority of the Confederate artillery was stationed high on the hill overlooking the river. They were lighter pieces with limited range but because of their height were able to send shot plunging down upon the decks of any ships that got too close. The most intimidating armament of the fort was facing toward the river on the hillside with two well-protected batteries that had been cut into the bluff at least thirty feet above the waterline. There were only a dozen guns here but they were the most powerful in the fortifications and ships approaching the fort would have to sail straight into their fire.[3]

The land approach to the fort was also well protected. On the far northern side of the fort lay a swampy, flooded area that was impassable and prevented any land attack from that direction. The fort itself was not all that large but around it was an entrenched camp of about one hundred acres with fortifications laid out along the hills and ridges that curved south from the northern swamp around to the east until the works met another flooded area just south of Dover. The fortifications consisted of rifle-pits protected by logs running along the high ground. The areas in front of the works had been cleared to provide a good field of fire and abatis from felled trees with branches facing outward gave additional protection. The ground around the works was very broken up with woods and ravines making it even more difficult for an attacking force to approach. All in all Fort Donelson would be a much tougher nut to crack than was Fort Henry.[4]

Fortunately for the Federals the strength of Fort Donelson's works was at least partially offset by the weakness of its commanders. To command the twenty thousand men at Fort Donelson General Johnston picked Brigadier General John B. Floyd and it would have been difficult to find a worse officer in either army. Floyd was a Virginian and had been secretary of war in the Buchanan administration. Many in the North believed he had secretly transferred military equipment to southern states in anticipation of the conflict and he was one of the few Confederates about whom the word "traitor" was freely used. He was a political general with little knowledge of military affairs and less about his new command, which he assumed as the Federals were getting their positions set on the 13th. Second in command, and in charge of the left wing, was Brigadier General Gideon J. Pillow. He did have some experience in the Mexican War but was almost as useless as Floyd. Among the senior commanders the only one who could be called a real soldier was Brigadier General Simon Bolivar Buckner, who commanded the fort and its immediate vicinity. Buckner was a West Point graduate, and a courageous and intelligent officer, as he was to prove. Buckner was also a personal friend of Grant's from his previous army service.[5]

On the morning of the 13th Grant was still waiting for Lew Wallace's troops and Foote's gunboats to arrive so that the assault could be launched and properly supported. The only gunboat available was the *Carondelet*, under Commander Henry Walke, that had steamed up from Fort Henry. Anxious to get something going Grant advised Walke, "Most of our batteries are established, and the remainder soon will be. If you will advance with your gun-boat at ten o'clock in the morning, we will be ready to take advantage of any diversion in our favor." Walke was willing to help and a little after nine o'clock he opened fire from long range under cover of a point of land. The ship and fort exchanged fire for several hours with the fort suffering no noticeable damage. The *Carondelet* was not so fortunate as one of the fort's large guns sent a massive solid shot through the ship's armor, wounding twelve men. Mostly this was an exercise in wasting powder and shot for both sides.[6]

During most of the morning of the 13th the land forces were quiet except for some light artillery fire and occasional skirmishing as troops moved around. In the early afternoon, however, the fighting started in earnest on McClernand's front. He sent three regiments to attack a battery that had been firing on his troops intermittently during the morning. McClernand launched his attack without approval from Grant, who was not too happy about it. "The battery was in the main line of the enemy, which was defended by his whole army present. Of course the assault was a failure, and of course the loss on our side was great for the number of men engaged." This was probably the beginning of Grant's dissatisfaction with McClernand that would ultimately lead to Grant's relieving him of command of an army corps in front of Vicksburg and sending him home.[7]

General McClernand had "deemed the opportunity favorable for storming redan No. 2, which lay in front of the Second brigade." Colonel William Morrison was ordered to form his brigade, consisting of the Seventeenth and Forty-ninth Illinois along with Colonel Isham Haynie's Forty-eighth Illinois, to make the assault that would be led by Haynie. The attacking regiments were formed in line of battle about a quarter of a mile from the target with the Forty-ninth on the right then the Seventeenth and Forty-eighth on the left. There was a question of seniority between the two colonels prompting Haynie to say to Morrison, "Colonel, let us take it together."[8]

The Federal troops moved forward crashing through some thick underbrush down one hill and up the side of another toward the Confederate works. They were met with increasingly heavy artillery fire and as they approached within fifty yards of the enemy works "encountered an almost impassable abatis, made by felling trees crosswise of each other." Working through this obstruction the attackers came into an open area when the Confederates in the rifle pits let loose with a heavy fire that looked like a wall of flame. Haynie reported, "As near as I can judge, we maintained our position under this most galling fire of rifle, shot, and shell for an hour." While leading his brigade Colonel Morrison was wounded in the hip, solving the question of who was in command. McClernand sent the Forty-fifth Illinois to reinforce the attackers but that only increased the Federal casualties. Haynie finally decided it was pointless to keep his men under this murderous fire and retired back down the hill eventually returning to the main line. Flavel Barber, of the Third Tennessee, thought that the retreating Federals looked like "a flock of sheep, leaving their track in mangled corpses."[9]

After the fighting on McClernand's part of the line ended, the Federal troops settled in for what would be one of the worst nights of their lives. The mild weather they had been enjoying suddenly turned into a harsh winter storm with cold rain changing to sleet then snow. By nightfall the cold became intense with thermometer readings of well below zero, highly unusual for this region. The men who had thrown away their coats and blankets on the march from Fort Henry suffered severely. No fires were allowed on the front lines and no warm food or hot coffee was available. In some commands the men stood to arms and kept moving all night because they couldn't bear to lie on the wet, frozen ground. Colonel Richard Oglesby wrote, "On the morning of the 14th the sun rose upon our forces, who were nearly torpid from the intense cold of the night." It wasn't until it started getting light that fires were allowed and the men huddled around small campfires trying to get a little warmer as they boiled their coffee.[10]

It was just as cold in the Confederate lines that morning and despite the repulse of McClernand's assault at least some of them were beginning to understand how dire their situation was. In the camp of the Third Tennessee Flavel Barber acknowledged that "For the first time we began to realize that we were surrounded and actually besieged by the enemy." With their overwhelming numbers it appeared as if the Federals would simply be able to wait until famine and exhaustion forced the Confederates to surrender. "Hereafter our contest was to be not an effort for victory but a desperate struggle to escape."[11]

In addition to the terrible weather the early morning hours of February 14 brought Foote with his gunboats and steamers loaded with reinforcements. General Wallace arrived with the troops from Fort Henry and the newly arrived regiments were formed into the Third Division, commanded by Wallace, and posted in the center of the line. This allowed McClernand to move his command farther to the right toward the river covering the road that led from Dover to Nashville and further isolating Fort Donelson from the outside.[12]

The arrival of the gunboats and reinforcements gave Grant the confidence to write to Halleck: "Our troops now invest the works at Fort Donelson. The enemy have been driven into their works at every point. A heavy abatis all around prevents carrying the works by storm at present. I feel every confidence of success...."[13]

To his wife, Julia, Grant wrote: "The taking of Fort Donelson bids fair to be a long job. The rebels are strongly fortified and are in very heavy force. When this is to end is hard to surmise but I feel confident of ultimate success."[14]

To General Cullum back in Cairo, Grant wrote:

> Appearances indicate now that we will have a protracted siege here. The ground is very broken, and the fallen timber extending far out from the breastworks, I fear the result of an attempt to carry the place by storm with raw troops. I feel great confidence, however, of ultimately reducing the place.[15]

With the arrival of the reinforcements and the gunboats Grant felt ready to begin the assault, but first he wanted to try to reduce the fort by bombardment as had been done at Fort Henry. Foote was asked to join the land artillery in a combined bombardment on the afternoon of the 14th. Based on the experience at Fort Henry and the poor results from the *Carondelet's* long-range fire Foote decided to close in and blast the fort apart. Most of the morning was spent preparing the ships for battle, including piling lumber and bags of coal on the upper decks to help protect against the plunging fire of the higher Confederate guns.[16]

About three o'clock the gunboats came within long range of the fort. The *Louisville* was on the right, then the flagship *St. Louis* and the *Pittsburgh*, with the *Carondelet* on the left. The wooden gunboats *Tyler* and *Conestoga* were about a thousand yards behind the ironclads. About a mile from the fort the *St. Louis* opened fire and the other ships immediately joined in. As Foote continued to close the range, eventually to less than 500 yards, the guns from the fort pounded the ships. The problem for the Federal fleet was that as they got closer to the fort more of the short-range Confederate guns in the upper works could reach the ships with a plunging fire that went through the lightly protected upper decks. In addition, the shorter range made it more difficult for the Federal gunners to hit the batteries high above the river. The lower Confederate earthworks were shot to pieces but it usually took a direct hit to disable a gun, so the Confederates were able to continue firing amid the debris.[17]

It didn't take long for the Federal ships to show the effects of the pounding they were taking. Decks were slippery with blood from dead and wounded sailors, holes appeared along the waterlines, and fires sprang up on the wooden decks. The *St. Louis* alone was hit 59 times, one of which killed the pilot and wounded Foote. Both the *St. Louis* and the *Louisville* had their steering ropes shot away and began to drift helplessly in the current. The *Pittsburgh* and the *Carondelet* were also severely damaged but closed in on the two drifting ships and covered them until the current carried them out of range. The battle lasted about an hour and a half with the ships losing 54 men killed and wounded. Together all four ships had been hit over 140 times and would need extensive repairs before they would be fit for further service, thus removing any threat to Fort Donelson from the river.[18]

After the repulse of the gunboats General Grant knew that the best course of action was to wait for more reinforcements and "make the investment of Fort Donelson as perfect as possible, and partially fortify and await repairs to the gunboats." Accordingly, when Wallace's troops filled out the center of the line and McClernand moved farther to the right in an effort to cover the half-flooded area south of Dover his lines were stretched thin, especially on the far right near the Clarksville road. It might have been anticipated that this weakness on the right would have invited a Confederate attack but Grant would later write that he "had no idea that there would be any engagement on land unless I brought it on myself."[19]

On the other side of the lines the Confederates were not just sitting around waiting to be starved into submission. They knew as well as Grant that Fort Donelson had become a trap, and the only way to save the army was to break the Federal lines and retreat as soon as possible. As General Floyd put it, "I had already seen the impossibility of holding out for any length of time with our inadequate numbers and indefensible position." During the evening of the 14th the Confederate commanders met and formulated a plan to save the army, even though it meant giving up the fort.[20]

The most logical place to break through the enemy lines was on the Federal right, where their lines were thin, and then get away to the south toward Nashville. It was decided that General Pillow, with about ten thousand men, would sweep down on McClernand's right flank and push it back toward the center. Buckner was to attack Wallace's green troops in the center while leaving enough men to man the trenches. If these attacks succeeded the right and center of the Federal army would be pushed back like a door swinging open. Buckner would then use his forces to guard the flank while the Confederates made good their escape down the Clarksville road. The Confederate commanders finalized the plans and the attack was set for early on the morning of the 15th.[21]

The weather that night was just as bad and the men in the Federal lines suffered just as much as the night before. Thomas Durham, of the 11th Indiana Volunteers, wrote: "We had no tents and were not allowed any fire; we lay on the snow and frozen ground with our wet and frozen clothes that night. With our suffering from the cold and the bombardment which was kept up all night, there was no sleep for us."[22]

Before dawn on the 15th Grant received a message from Foote asking him to come to the flagship for a meeting because Foote's injury kept him aboard ship. As soon as it was light enough Grant rode out to the boat landing leaving instructions for the division commanders not to start any fighting until he returned. Foote informed Grant that he needed to return to Cairo to repair his battered fleet. A disappointed Grant tried to convince Foote to remain a least a little longer and in the end Foote agreed to leave the two least damaged ships to support the land operations while he took the other two back for repairs. The meeting ended about noon and Grant was on his way back to headquarters when he received shocking news: the distant firing that had been heard was not just the normal everyday skirmishing but a heavy attack against McClernand's lines and the army was headed toward disaster.[23]

The Confederate attack to force their way out of Fort Donelson had begun right on schedule. W. S. Morris of the 31st Illinois Volunteers remembered that the Federal troops did not even have a chance to make their morning coffee before the Confederates came charging out of their works, and "burst upon McClernand's division with loud and defiant yells." The assaulting troops were supported by field artillery advancing with the infantry and "shrapnel, grape and canister, supplemented the musketry with fearful precision and deadly effect."[24]

Dick Oglesby's brigade held the right flank of McClernand's division with three regiments under John McArthur in support. Pillow's men struck them hard but Oglesby's men formed quickly and fought them off, at least for the moment. The Confederates came on again in greater strength this time and soon most of McClernand's line was heavily engaged. Dismounted cavalry from Nathan Bedford Forrest's command joined in the attack from the flank and rear and soon the Federals were in trouble.[25]

McArthur's regiments quickly found themselves in the thick of the fighting. To the left of Oglesby the brigade of W. H. L. Wallace was soon engaged. The fighting on his front went back and forth, but continued hour after hour. Heavy smoke began to obscure the fields; the snow was stained red from the dead and wounded; and the Union troops, ill prepared for a battle, were running low on ammunition. Lieutenant Colonel Frank L. Rhoads, of the 8th Illinois, reported: "The fire was murderous, as the long list of the dead and wounded sadly shows." The Federal troops put up a good fight, among them the Thirty-first Illinois under Colonel John A. Logan, who was later wounded; they offered fierce resistance but were simply overpowered. By ten o'clock the pressure of the Confederate attack was pushing Oglesby's men back to the west, taking McArthur's men with them. The Confederate plan was working just as they had hoped it would.[26]

McClernand was in desperate straits; he sent a message to Lew Wallace for help. Wallace referred the request to Grant's headquarters for approval before transferring any of his troops. With Grant absent, however, no one there had the authority or the initiative to act on his own and Wallace's request received no answer. Soon McClernand repeated his plea for assistance and Wallace sent Colonel Charles Cruft's brigade to the right. Unfortunately they were misdirected, arriving too late to be of much assistance, and eventually joined McClernand's troops as they fell back.[27]

By now most of the First Division's original position was in Confederate hands and Wallace sent Colonel John A. Thayer's brigade to stem the tide before his position was also overrun. Thayer took up a position that was protected by heavy woods on each side and waited for the enemy. Many of the retreating regiments formed up around Thayer's line, receiving ammunition and a short breathing spell to regain their composure. Soon enough though the Confederates hit this new line, but this time they could make no more headway. The fighting was desperate but the Federals stood firm, the Confederates pulled back, and there was finally a lull in the battle.[28]

It was during this mid-afternoon break in the fighting, while McClernand and Wallace were conferring in a small clearing, that Grant rode up carrying a handful of papers. Grant was all business as he listened to the reports of his subordinates. What they told him would have disheartened most men. McClernand's division had lost nearly 1,500 men and had been driven back into Wallace's position. The road to Clarksville was wide open for the Confederates to make their escape. General Smith, on the left, was too far away to provide any help. General Wallace described Grant's reaction to what could not be called anything but a disaster:

> In every great man's career there is a crisis exactly similar to that which now overtook General Grant, and it cannot be better described than as a crucial test of his nature. It cannot be doubted that he saw with painful distinctness the effect of the disaster to his right wing. His face flushed slightly. With a sudden grip he crushed the papers in his hand. But in an instant these signs of disappointment or hesitation cleared away. In his ordinary quiet voice he said, addressing himself to both officers, "Gentlemen, the position on the right must be retaken."[29]

Why the Confederates had pulled back was not known, perhaps they were regrouping for another attack, but it gave the Federal troops time to regroup. Many Union soldiers were bewildered, looking for their units, searching for food or ammunition, and going through the haversacks of the dead Confederates. In his memoirs Grant wrote:

> I heard some of the men say that the enemy had come out with knapsacks, and haversacks filled with rations. They seemed to think this indicated a determination on his part to stay out and fight just as long as the provisions held out. I turned to Colonel J. D. Webster, of my staff, who was with me, and said: "Some of our men are pretty badly demoralized, but the enemy must be more so, for he has attempted to force his way out, but has fallen back: the one who attacks first now will be victorious and the enemy will have to be in a hurry if he gets ahead of me." I determined to make the assault at once on our left. It was clear to my mind that the enemy had started to march out with his entire force, except a few pickets, and if our attack could be made on the left before the enemy could redistribute his forces along the line, we would find but little opposition except from the intervening abatis.[30]

Grant was going to turn the tables on the Confederates by having General Smith attack their weakened right flank. Wallace was to attack the enemy lines in his front and every effort was made to rally the men in McClernand's command to join Wallace's assault. Grant wanted to attack on all fronts so, crippled or not, the gunboats must join in. Although Grant appeared calm on the outside he was fully aware of the danger his army still faced and expressed his concern in a message to Foote:

> If all the gunboats that can will immediately make their appearance to the enemy it may secure us a victory. Otherwise all may be defeated. A terrible conflict ensued in my absence, which has demoralized a portion of my command, and I think the enemy is much more so. If the gunboats do not show themselves, it will reassure the enemy and still further demoralize our troops. I must order a charge to save appearances. I do not expect the gunboats to go into action, but to make appearance and throw a few shells at long range.[31]

Here is the first show of Grant's military philosophy that would eventually take him higher than anyone who knew him would have ever dreamed he could go. He had done all the right things in the field: order an attack where the enemy was weakest, regroup the beaten troops, counterattack to regain the lost ground and try to get the gunboats to contribute what they could. Besides all this, which most competent commanders would have done, Grant knew that sometimes the morale of the troops was what made the difference between victory and defeat. Grant was well aware that many of his troops were demoralized and felt the battle was lost, but he also knew that the Confederates had just failed in their bid to escape and were now right back in the same trap as before the battle, so they were no better off than the Federal troops. It might look like the Federal forces had been beaten but Grant would not let his army admit that it was beaten. Grant realized that during almost every battle there comes a time when both sides are exhausted and he believed that when that time came the side that could muster one final effort would gain the victory. He felt that now was that moment, and the final effort that brought victory would be made by his troops.

So, the broken Federal army was brought together. The men were urged to fill their cartridge pouches and rejoin their regiments. They had not been beaten and now they were going to attack and snatch victory from the enemy's hands. As the men reformed their battle lines Grant rode over to the left to give his orders to General Smith.[32]

On the right of the Federal line the brigades of Colonel M. L. Smith and Colonel Cruft were preparing to attack. While they were waiting the order to advance Thomas Durham of the 11th Indiana Volunteers noticed that Colonel Smith was casually smoking a cigar while sitting on his horse waiting to begin the assault when suddenly, "A bullet cut the cigar off close to his mouth." The colonel just "spit the stub out, took another cigar from his pocket and called to one of the boys to give him a match. He lit it with such coolness that it had a very quieting effect on the high-strung nerves of the boys."[33]

Colonel Smith led the Eighth Missouri and the Eleventh Indiana forward, followed closely by Colonel Cruft's brigade and two Ohio regiments. They moved quickly, firing as they advanced over the rolling and wooded terrain, driving the enemy steadily back in the direction from which they had come that morning. The Federals reached a hill where they re-formed their lines then continued to push the Confederates back until they were back into their original entrenchments. The Federal troops stopped about 150 yards from the enemy works and the positions of the two forces were about the same as they had been before the early morning Confederate attack. More importantly the escape route to the south was effectively closed.[34]

The Federal counterattack had gone almost too smoothly considering the vicious fighting that had taken place earlier in the day. As it turned out Pillow had changed his mind about breaking out and marching south. Just before Colonel Smith moved forward Buckner was moving his troops out of their trenches to begin moving south when Pillow ordered him back into the works on the right. Floyd, technically the overall commander of the Confederate forces, discussed the situation with Pillow and approved his orders. Pillow also began pulling his men back to their own lines on the left. When Colonel Smith led his men forward the Confederates were already in the act of falling back and they put up much less resistance than they might have.[35]

It is difficult to understand what made the Confederates give up all they had gained from the morning assault. Pillow reported that he had decided to end the attempted breakout "after seven and a half hours of continuous and bloody conflict. After the troops were called off from pursuit orders were immediately given to the different commands to form and retire to their original position in the intrenchments." It is understandable that after several days in the cold, open trenches and a full day of fighting that the Confederates were simply exhausted and Pillow wanted to give them a brief rest before setting out on a long night march. What is difficult to comprehend is why they basically gave back the ground they fought so hard to capture. It is even more difficult to understand why the Confederate commanders thought Grant would just sit there and leave the route south open for the Confederates to use when it was convenient.[36]

Over on the left Grant had given General C. F. Smith orders to attack and carry the works directly in his front, and Smith wasted little time in doing just that. Smith posted John Cook's brigade to make a feint on the left and, with close artillery support, Jacob Lauman's brigade, led by Smith in person, would attack and overwhelm the thinly manned works. The Federal troops who made that charge would remember it all their lives. It was tough going at first, the abatis stalled the advance and the Confederates did not give up without a courageous fight, but the most memorable thing about that battlefield was General Smith.[37]

The old general was out in front, erect in the saddle, saber held high, urging the men to follow him. At one point the troops wavered and Smith yelled to them: "Damn you gentlemen, I see skulkers, I'll have none here. Come on, you volunteers, come on. This is your chance. You volunteered to be killed for love of country, and now you can be." With the combination of oaths and example Smith led his men up the slope to the Confederate works and over. The fighting was deadly but with the general in the thick of it the Federal troops quickly took control of part of the outer line and brought in artillery to consolidate and expand their foothold. Smith lost about four hundred men in this charge but it was the deciding factor in the siege. With Federal troops controlling a portion of their lines further resistance by the Confederates was pointless.[38]

Pillow admitted in his report that Smith had captured a commanding position in the line "being immediately in rear of our river batteries and field work for its protection." From this position Smith could easily attack Buckner's troops from behind "or he could advance, under cover of an intervening ridge, directly upon our battery and field work. While the enemy held the position it was manifest we could not hold the main work or battery."[39]

The only hope the Confederates in Fort Donelson had of escaping was now gone. Their lines were breached and it was clear that they could not hold out much longer. In a council of commanders that evening Pillow made the suggestion that they try to fight their way out again. General Buckner stated that his command was so tired and demoralized that they could not be counted on to put up another good fight: "It would cost the command three-fourths its present numbers to cut its way out; that it was wrong to sacrifice three-fourths of a command to save one-fourth, and that no officer had a right to cause such a sacrifice." Pillow then suggested that they hold out one more day and try to escape on the river, to which Bucker replied that he expected an attack at dawn and that his men could not hold their position for half an hour. All the senior officers at the meeting agreed that there was only one thing left to do.[40]

Now occurred one of the most bizarre scenes recorded during the entire Civil War. Both Floyd and Pillow were concerned that they might be treated as traitors rather than prisoners of war. Floyd refused to let himself be captured. Pillow's nerve also failed him. So Floyd turned the command over to Pillow, who immediately turned the command over to Buckner, who, being a real soldier, decided to share the fate of his troops. Floyd and several of his Virginia regiments boarded a steamer and made their way down to Nashville, followed by Pillow. General Forrest, disgusted by the entire situation, mounted his cavalry and simply rode off through the flooded area south of the fort.[41]

While the generals were debating how to save themselves the troops in the field were suffering through yet another terrible night. Between the two armies there were several thousand casualties, many of the wounded dying during the night while lying on the freezing ground. Ira Blanchard, of the 20th Illinois, remembered how miserable he was: "Famished and chilled we huddled around our fires to doze, to freeze on one side, to burn on the other; while the wind sent puffs of smoke and ashes into our powder burnt faces. Thus we writhed and twisted on that damp cold ground, all that gloomy night."[42]

Thomas Durham later wrote that the night of February 15 was the worst he could remember: "Lying in the snow, the night fearfully cold, suffering from hunger, my clothes still wet and frozen from my half night spent in the mush ice and water of the bayou, the suffering from the cold was almost beyond endurance. I thought I would certainly freeze to death."[43]

About three in the morning a Confederate officer with a flag of truce came into General Smith's camp with a letter for the commanding officer. Smith took him to Grant's headquarters and Grant read the communication from Buckner who proposed the "appointment of commissioners to agree upon terms of capitulation of the forces and post under my command, and in that view suggest an armistice until 12 o'clock to-day."[44]

Grant read the note then asked General Smith what he thought about it. "No terms to the damned rebels," Smith barked. Grant chuckled then sent one of the most famous messages in American history to Buckner: "Yours of this date, proposing armistice and appointment of commissioners to settle terms of capitulation, is just received. No terms except unconditional and immediate surrender can be accepted. I propose to move immediately upon your works."

Smith remarked, "It's the same thing in smoother words," then took the dispatch to be delivered to Buckner.[45]

Grant was not making empty threats when he told Buckner that he would move on his works. Orders had already been sent to all three division commanders to renew the attack on the Confederate works as soon as it was light. The attacks were about to begin when Buckner's answer was received:

> The distribution of the forces under my command incident to an unexpected change of commanders and the overwhelming force under your command compel me, notwithstanding the brilliant success of the Confederate arms yesterday, to accept the ungenerous and unchivalrous terms which you propose.

Years ago, when Grant left the army under difficult circumstances, it was Buckner who lent Grant the money to return home. Perhaps Buckner expected Grant to remember that and give him more lenient terms. Clearly he was mistaken.[46]

When the sun came up on February 16, the battlefields and fortifications around Fort Donelson were unusually quiet. At first the Federal soldiers just stood around wondering what was going on, then they heard cheering from Smith's division and word of the surrender began to spread. Wallace occupied the enemy works in his front and rode into Dover, where he found Buckner and his staff having breakfast in a tavern. Grant joined them shortly and had a pleasant conversation with Buckner during which Grant offered the new prisoner any assistance he could to help Buckner get through his captivity. Grant would not allow an old friendship to affect his actions during the fighting but once the guns were laid aside he was ready to do all he could to help a friend in need.[47]

Grant quickly got off a telegram to Halleck announcing the capture of Fort Donelson and "from 12,000 to 15,000 prisoners, including Generals Buckner and Bushrod [R.] Johnson; also about 20,000 stand of arms, 48 pieces of artillery, 17 heavy guns, from 2,000 to 4,000 horses, and large quantities of commissary stores."[48]

In a later telegram Grant, who was always willing to give credit when it was due, wrote that he "ordered a charge upon the left (enemy's right) with the division under General C. F. Smith, which was most brilliantly executed, and gave to our arms full assurance of victory."[49]

Ira Blanchard, of the 20th Illinois, remembered the surrender for the rest of his life: "Soldiers threw up their hats, pulled off their coats and fell to whipping one another until their wind gave out, or their coats went to pieces. This was the first great victory of the war, and the greatest day of rejoicing I ever saw."[50]

4

TURNING POINT IN THE WEST

The capture of Forts Henry and Donelson and the subsequent opening of the Tennessee and Cumberland rivers immediately changed the entire military situation in the West. Suddenly most of Tennessee was opened to Federal invasion. Johnston could do little more than pull his badly outnumbered troops south and try to find a place to make a stand near the border with Mississippi.

The twin victories also brought rejoicing throughout the North. These were the Union's first substantial triumphs and the discouragement that existed since the calamity at Bull Run was replaced by jubilation. Another result was that a once obscure brigadier general named Grant was now famous. He was the man who knew how to beat the rebels and his demand for "immediate and unconditional surrender" at Fort Donelson was repeated across the nation. Grant, however, was not the type to sit back and enjoy his newfound fame. He didn't have the time because with victory came more work.[1]

The conditions in and around Fort Donelson were chaotic. About 14,000 Confederate prisoners had to be accounted for, cared for, and shipped to prisoner-of-war camps. Bodies of dead soldiers and animals were lying all over the area and the men needed to be identified, when possible, but in any case all had to be quickly buried to avoid the spread of disease. Military equipment and supplies of all kinds were also scattered everywhere and what could be used had to be gathered up. There were huge piles of rotting pork on the waterfront that had to be quickly destroyed. In addition to the military and supply problems hundreds of civilians soon descended on Fort Donelson. Some came to look for loved ones or assist in caring for the wounded, but many were there to pick up souvenirs or see if they could find a way to profit from the confusion.[2]

Almost immediately after Buckner surrendered Grant acted to correct the problems he had just inherited, at least the problems that could be seen at the time. General Wallace was ordered back to Fort Henry with two brigades of infantry, including artillery and cavalry detachments, to hold that position against any possible enemy attacks. Generals McClernand and Smith were ordered to create a special detail of about two hundred men to guard the ammunition and stores in Fort Donelson. The prisoners were rounded up and disarmed and the wounded of both sides were put up in makeshift hospitals. The weather soon turned bad and a heavy rain began but it looked as if the Federals were getting things under control.[3]

The day after the surrender Grant issued a formal order of congratulations to the men of his army:

> For four successive nights, without shelter, during the most inclement weather known in this latitude, they faced an enemy in large force in a position chosen by himself. Though strongly fortified by nature, all the safeguards suggested by science were added. Without murmur this was borne, prepared at all times to receive an attack, and with continuous skirmishing by day, resulting ultimately in forcing the enemy to surrender without conditions.
>
> The victory achieved is not only great in breaking down rebellion, but has secured the greatest number of prisoners of war ever taken in one battle on this continent.[4]

As a reward for bringing victory to his department General Halleck gave Grant command of the new district of West Tennessee that included the territory from Cairo to the Mississippi state border between the Mississippi and Cumberland Rivers. Since the Cumberland flowed mostly east this left the actual limits of the new district in that direction open to interpretation. Meanwhile, Grant just wanted to get on with the war. With the enemy retreating south it was obvious that now was the time for pursuit, don't give them a chance to rest and re-group. In Halleck's original orders Grant had been told to destroy the railroad bridge at Clarksville, about thirty miles up the Cumberland, and on February 18 he began to move.[5]

Flag Officer Foote, still nursing his wound, sailed up the Cumberland with the gunboats *Conestoga* and *Cairo*. On the 20th the Federal expedition found the fortifications at Clarksville deserted and much of the civilian population, who were afraid of Federal reprisals, also missing. Foote reported this to Grant and suggested that he could bring up more gunboats and easily head upriver to Nashville.[6]

On February 21, Grant sent a message to General Cullum in Cairo saying, "It is my impression that by following up our success Nashville would be an easy conquest; but I only throw this out as a suggestion.... White flags are flying from here to Clarksville, and rumor says the same thing extends to Nashville." Grant added, however, that he would not make any move without orders. That same day Foote, who also felt that the city could be easily taken, sent a dispatch saying that he and Grant were ready to advance on Nashville but, "We were about moving for this purpose when General Grant, to my astonishment, received a telegram from General Halleck not to let the gunboats go higher than Clarksville."[7]

Canceling what appeared to be the relatively easy capture of such an important enemy city would seem to make no sense, but there were things going on behind the scenes that Grant had no knowledge of. Ever since Grant began the campaign McClellan, Halleck and Buell had been burning up the telegraph wires with messages back and forth. All three of these men were considered brilliant generals before the war, but apparently it takes time to be brilliant. They needed time to consult each other, time to arrange for all the details of supply and transportation, and especially time to promote their own views and maneuver for personal advantage. In the midst of all this planning and organizing Grant had won two significant victories by simply taking the initiative and acting. Now the pressure for more action was building and Grant was beginning to look like a man who had created more trouble than opportunities.

Halleck, who never had much confidence in Grant, tried several times to demote, or at least rein in his enthusiastic subordinate. On February 8, the day Grant told Halleck he would take Fort Donelson, Halleck was asking Secretary of War Edwin Stanton to promote Brig. Gen. Ethan Allen Hitchcock to major general and assign him to Halleck's command, which would result in his replacing Grant in command of the Tennessee River expedition. Hitchcock was an aging but capable soldier and the request was quickly approved, but Hitchcock ended up declining the offer due to poor health.[8]

Halleck also tried to expand his command by suggesting to the War Department that a Western Division be established containing the departments of the Missouri, the Mississippi, and the Ohio, commanded respectively by Gen. David Hunter, Hitchcock or Sherman, and Buell. Of course Halleck would be the overall commander of the new division. Grant, apparently, had no place in this new command structure.[9]

In another attempt to promote himself Halleck wired McClellan on February 17: "Make Buell, Grant, and Pope major-generals of volunteers, and give me command in the West. I ask this in return for Forts Henry and Donelson." Just two days later Halleck tried to get General Smith promoted: "Brig. Gen. Charles F. Smith, by his coolness and bravery at Fort Donelson when the battle was against us, turned the tide and carried the enemy's outworks. Make him a major-general. You can't get a better one." While Smith certainly did deserve recognition for his role at Fort Donelson, Halleck seems to have forgotten who was in command.[10]

Continuing to advocate his plans Halleck wrote to Buell on the 18th to say that he had recommended to the president that Buell be promoted to major general, after which he should move to the Cumberland: "The battle of the west is to be fought in that vicinity. You should be in it as the ranking general in immediate command.... Help me, and I will help you.... You will not regret it." What Halleck failed to mention, and Buell undoubtedly understood, was that Halleck would then be in overall command.[11]

Becoming even more blatant Halleck wired McClellan on the 20th, "I must have command of the armies in the West. Hesitation and delay are losing us the golden opportunity. Lay this before the President and Secretary of War. May I assume the command? Answer quickly." The next day Halleck informed McClellan that because of the threat of an attack on his rear from Columbus he had been unable to act as promptly as he might have on the Tennessee and Cumberland, but insisted that "I cannot possibly be mistaken in the strategy of the campaign."[12]

McClellan did not hesitate in replying to Halleck's presumptuous messages. "Buell at Bowling Green knows more of the state of affairs than you at Saint Louis. Until I hear from him I cannot see necessity of giving you entire command. I shall not lay your request before the Secretary until I hear definitely from Buell." McClellan also quickly advised his old friend Buell to report conditions in his department every day and suggesting that the advance on Nashville "is of the greatest importance," and that if it would be quicker for Buell to move along the Cumberland he would order Halleck to concentrate on Memphis and Columbus.[13]

Trying to enlist additional help in his personal campaign Halleck wired Assistant Secretary of War Thomas A. Scott, in Louisville, on the 21st, advising him that the Confederates were falling back and based on reports from Grant and Foote it appeared they would not stop to defend Nashville. Halleck asked Scott to "divide the responsibility with me? If so, I will immediately prepare to go ahead. I am tired of waiting for action in Washington. They will not understand the case. It is as plain as daylight to me."[14]

Secretary Stanton replied to Halleck's requests saying that he liked the ideas Halleck had submitted but the president's son was ill and "on account of the domestic affliction of the President I have not yet been able to submit it to him." The positive nature of Stanton's wire led Halleck to make one last appeal, directly to the secretary. Commenting on how much time had already been lost Halleck noted that he needed control of Buell's army to strike a fatal blow, "I am perfectly willing to act as General McClellan dictates or to take any amount of responsibility. To succeed we must be prompt. There is not a moment to be lost. Give me authority, and I will be responsible for results."[15]

On the 22nd Stanton finally gave Halleck an answer that left no room for further discussion. President Lincoln had gone over Halleck's telegrams and Assistant Secretary Scott's reports and decided to leave the command structure as it was. Stanton also wrote that the president "desires and expects you and General Buell to co-operate fully and zealously with each other, and would be glad to know whether there has been any failure of co-operation in any particular." In addition, of the several names Halleck had submitted for promotion to major general President Lincoln only sent one name to the Senate, Ulysses S. Grant. The promotion was quickly approved and Grant now outranked everyone in the West except Halleck himself.[16]

While the telegrams were flying between St. Louis and Washington, General Grant was just trying to keep things moving in his little corner of the war. There were two clear enemy targets in sight and Grant meant to go after them: Nashville, which by February 21 Grant believed to be virtually undefended, and Johnston's army, which was in full retreat. Although Halleck had refused permission for Grant to advance to Nashville he soon found another way to achieve the desired result.

During the siege at Fort Donelson, General Buell had obligingly sent a division of infantry under Brigadier General William Nelson to reinforce Grant. These troops arrived at Fort Donelson on the 24th, too late to help there but just in time to head to a different destination. The last anyone knew, Buell was slowly making his way from Bowling Green toward Nashville and since Nelson's division was part of Buell's army it seemed only reasonable to send Nelson to rendezvous with his commander. Not giving Nelson time to unload his transports Grant ordered him to immediately move up the river to Nashville and report to Buell. If Buell was more than two days away Nelson was to stay on the ships until Buell did arrive. Grant also took pains to report this to headquarters in a message to General Cullum: "As requested, the gunboats have gone up to Nashville. Johnston, with his army, has fallen back to Murfreesboro.... General Nelson reported to-day with his division. I forwarded them immediately to Nashville."[17]

Nelson quickly moved up river to Nashville and entered the city with no opposition. Buell's army had arrived on the opposite side of the river from the city and he was a little indignant that one of his divisions had taken the city without him. Buell was also fearful of a Confederate attack on Nelson's division and quickly wired Clarksville for reinforcements. Stretching things a bit Grant took this as a sign that he should intervene and go to Nashville himself and advised General Cullum, "I shall go to Nashville immediately after the arrival of the next mail, should there be no orders to prevent it."[18]

Grant received no orders prohibiting his going to Nashville so on the 27th he took a steamer up to Clarksville where he met briefly with General Smith. The ships that had taken Nelson's division to Nashville were loading troops as Grant arrived and Smith showed him an order from Buell: "The landing of a portion of our troops, contrary to my intentions, on the south side of the river has compelled me to hold this side at every hazard. If the enemy should assume the offensive ... my force is altogether inadequate." Smith told Grant the order was "nonsense" but of course he would obey. Grant continued on to Nashville expecting to meet Buell there.[19]

Buell was not in Nashville, however; his headquarters were still on the north side of the river and on the evening of the 27th Grant sent him a message that he had hoped to see Buell in the city but it was getting too late to wait any longer. Grant offered to send more troops in addition to Smith's men but he saw no need as the enemy "are not far north of the Tennessee line." Grant's note was a little brusque and he signed it as U. S. Grant, Major General, just so Buell knew who was senior.[20]

It turned out that Buell was on his way into the city and Grant met him on the way to his ship. The meeting was civil, and that was all. Grant reiterated some of the points he made in the note and mentioned that all the information he had convinced him that the Confederates were retreating as quickly as they could. Buell replied that he had information there was fighting just ten or twelve miles away and that he believed the city was in danger of being attacked. Grant believed that any nearby fighting was only the enemy rear guard protecting their wagon trains. Buell insisted that his troops were in danger and Grant decided to let it go, commenting later, "Smith's troops were returned the same day. The enemy were trying to get away from Nashville and not to return to it." The first Confederate state capital was now firmly in Union hands.[21]

Not too many days before Grant and Buell met, Albert Sidney Johnston's army had been streaming into the city on their way from Bowling Green. It was immediately clear that the city could not be defended against the Federal gunboats since there were few fortifications in place. In addition, the bridge over the Cumberland was the only feasible escape route for the Confederate army, and with Foote's gunboats able to sail up and destroy it at their leisure, Johnston had no choice but to evacuate the city on February 23. The citizens were in a panic and no one knew what to expect, but the worst was assumed. The people imagined they would be subjected to all the horrors of medieval sacking and pillaging. Many could think of nothing but escape and soon the roads were filled with carriages, wagons and open carts, filled mostly with women and children slowly heading south in the cold rain.[22]

Johnston's army fell back to Murfreesboro, but that was just the start of a long grueling march that ended in Corinth, Mississippi. In the Mississippi River fortress of Columbus, Leonidas Polk could clearly see that if he remained he would be inviting the same fate of siege and eventual surrender that had befallen Fort Donelson. So a few days after Nashville was evacuated he abandoned his fortifications and also headed toward Corinth. The Confederate forts along the Mississippi were now isolated from the rest of the Confederate army in Tennessee.[23]

Now, all that stood between the Union forces and the heart of the South was the remnants of Johnston's army. These men were tired, hungry, poorly armed and lacking in almost everything needed to make war, and their morale had sunk to a new low. Of course, a storm of criticism was heaped upon General Johnston. Newspapers that had recently praised him called for his removal. Elected officials and private citizens complained to Jefferson Davis who responded by saying, "Gentlemen, I know Sidney Johnston well. If he is not a general we had better give up the war, for we have no general."[24]

As General Beauregard later wrote the loss of the river forts caused "a feeling of consternation, anxiety and distrust that spread over the entire section of country comprised within the bounds of General Johnston's department." The citizens were panic-stricken and much of the army was demoralized. Criticism of General Johnston came from everywhere. But, "he withstood the storm with firmness and manliness, and was uncomplaining."[25]

General Johnston commented on the flood of personal attacks on his character in a March 18 letter to President Davis:

> I observed silence, as it seemed to me to be the best way to serve the cause and the country. The facts were not fully known, discontent prevailed, and criticism or condemnation was more likely to augment than to cure the evil. I refrained, well knowing that heavy censures would fall upon me, but convinced that it was better to endure them for the present, and defer for a more propitious time an investigation of the conduct of the generals.... The test of merit in my profession with the people is success. It is a hard rule, but I think it is right.

Johnston didn't waste much time in worrying about his reputation but went right to work preparing to reverse the recent Confederate losses.[26]

Around the end of February and well into March, while Halleck angled for promotion, Nashville was being occupied, and the war was moving up the rivers, a situation developed that could have produced dire problems for the Union war effort and did slow things down. The communication system between Halleck and Grant had failed, and neither man was aware of it. Messages between Halleck in St. Louis and Grant's forward positions were relayed through Fort Henry. It was not learned until much later that one of the telegraph operators at Fort Henry was a Confederate sympathizer and some of the messages that came to him were not forwarded in either direction. The result of this was that Halleck had little idea what Grant was doing and Grant had little idea what Halleck wanted him to do.[27]

When Halleck realized that his efforts to get Buell's forces put under his command were not going to succeed he decided to concentrate on an advance along the Tennessee River. Halleck ordered Grant to pull Smith's troops out of Clarksville and concentrate the field army near Danville, some thirty-five miles upriver from Fort Henry, and prepare for an advance away from Nashville. Grant knew nothing about these new orders and it was at this time that Halleck learned troop movements had been taking place that he knew nothing about, including sending Smith to Nashville.[28]

On March 1, an unhappy Halleck wrote to General Cullum in Cairo inquiring who had sent Smith's division to Nashville: "I ordered them across to the Tennessee, where they are wanted immediately. Order them back. What is the reason that no one down there can obey my orders? Send all spare transports to General Grant up the Tennessee." The transports were needed because also on the 1st Halleck sent a message to Fort Henry for Grant, who was not there, to start a movement up the Tennessee. "The main object of this expedition will be to destroy the railroad bridge over Bear Creek, near Eastport, Miss., and also the connections at Corinth, Jackson, and Humboldt." After destroying the bridges Grant was to return to Danville and then advance to the town of Paris, on the west side of the river.[29]

At the same time that Halleck was ordering Grant to move up the Tennessee, Grant was sending his own report to Halleck. Grant remarked that he had been sending messages to Halleck, through the chief of staff almost daily. Grant also stated that many of his men were suffering from dysentery and "If I am compelled to move suddenly, it will be with a very weak force compared with what the major-general commanding probably expects. The loss in battle and the number who have sickened since reduces my force considerably."[30]

Henry Halleck had a great deal to be concerned about in early March 1862. Brigadier General Samuel Curtis was pursuing Confederate troops in Missouri and General John Pope was in the middle of a campaign to capture the enemy strongholds along the Mississippi at New Madrid, Island No. 10, and Fort Pillow, in addition to Grant's move which was supposed to assist Pope by cutting the railroad connections that supplied the enemy along the Mississippi. The strictly military problems were compounded by Buell's constant messages asking for cooperation and requesting a face-to-face meeting, and Washington's rejection of Halleck's frequent requests to be given overall command in the West. Halleck also received reports that the troops at Fort Donelson had engaged in looting and that discipline was extremely lax. Finally, Halleck now became aware that none of his plans for movements up the Tennessee had been executed. A normally irritable man, this pushed his temper over the edge.[31]

On March 2 Halleck sent an angry message to McClellan complaining that he had not heard from Grant for more than a week and that he had left his command to make an unauthorized trip to Nashville. Halleck didn't like to condemn a general right after he won a victory, "but I think he richly deserves it. Satisfied with his victory, he sits down and enjoys it without any regard to the future. I am worn-out and tired with this neglect and inefficiency."[32]

This dispatch was grossly unfair and untrue. More likely than not, in the time honored tradition of middle management, Halleck was simply attempting to show his superiors that whatever problems had arisen in his department the fault lay with some one else, in this case Grant. Of all the officers under Halleck's command no one had tried to take the fight to the enemy or was more anxious to push after the beaten Confederates than Grant. Grant's visit to Nashville was, at most, a minor stretch of his authority since the limits of Grant's command were not specifically established.

Back in Washington, General McClellan responded to Halleck's wire as might be expected; he supported whatever action Halleck needed to take to bring his subordinate in line. On March 3, McClellan replied: "The future success of our cause demands that proceedings such as Grant's should at once be checked. Generals must observe discipline as well as private soldiers." Halleck was authorized to arrest Grant if necessary and replace him with C. F. Smith. McClellan continued, "I appreciate the difficulties you have to encounter, and will be glad to relieve you from trouble as far as possible."

To illustrate how serious the matter was being taken Secretary of War Stanton also signed this message.[33]

Not content with his first message Halleck decided to pour more fuel on the fire in another wire to McClellan on the 4th: "A rumor had just reached me that since the taking of Fort Donelson General Grant has resumed his former bad habits. If so, it will account for his neglect of my often-repeated orders." Halleck decided not to arrest Grant but did place General Smith in command of the expedition up the Tennessee. The former bad habits were, of course, Grant's previous problems with alcohol. Along with instructions to relinquish command to Smith, Halleck wanted to know, "Why do you not obey my orders to report strength and positions of your command?" This was Grant's first inkling that he was in trouble with his commanding general.[34]

The next day Grant wired Smith with the news that he would be in command of the expedition up the Tennessee. Informing Smith of the strength of the enemy forces that the expedition might encounter Grant passed along words of caution that the bridges should be destroyed, if possible, but "a general engagement is to be avoided. The idea probably is there must be no defeat, and rather than risk one it would be better to retreat." That same day Halleck sent amplified orders on the raid up the Tennessee saying that if the raid successfully destroyed the bridges at Corinth and Bear Creek the troops should "encamp at Savannah, unless threatened by superior numbers."[35]

Still not aware of how potentially serious the situation was Grant wrote to Halleck on the 5th to inform him that General Smith had been put in charge of the expedition and inquiring if Clarksville should be abandoned. Grant then went on to state that he was unaware that he had ever disobeyed any order and that, "I have reported almost daily the condition of my command and reported every position occupied." Grant had not received troop returns from Smith but believed that was because of Smith being ordered to Nashville by Buell, which fact was reported. Grant further noted that his reports had been made to "General Cullum, chief of staff, and it may be that many of them were not thought of sufficient importance to forward more than a telegraphic synopsis of." Mentioning that the terrible conditions brought on by almost continuous rains would make moving troops difficult Grant went on to say that his command contained "forty-six infantry regiments, three cavalry regiments, and eight independent companies, and ten batteries of light artillery," with an average strength of 500 men per regiment. In ending this dispatch Grant told Halleck, "You may rely on my carrying out your instructions in every particular to the very best of my ability."[36]

This should have ended the matter. Grant sort of apologized if he had done anything wrong, reported the information Halleck had been waiting for, and promised to follow future orders to the last detail. Both Grant and Halleck had better things to do, like get on with the war. Unfortunately Halleck just could not let the situation end without having the last word so on March 6 he sent Grant another reprimand complaining that he had ignored repeated orders to report the strength of his command. In addition, "Your going to Nashville without authority, and when your presence with your troops was of the utmost importance, was a matter of very serious complaint at Washington, so much so that I was advised to arrest you on your return."[37]

Ulysses Grant always gave the appearance of a calm and mild sort of man. In reality there was nothing meek about him. When aroused Grant had a temper like anyone else, he just had better self-control than most. In his reply to Halleck's latest complaint Grant invited Halleck to prove his allegations:

> I did all I could to get you returns of the strength of my command. Every move I made was reported daily to your chief of staff, who must have failed to keep you properly posted. I have done my very best to obey orders and to carry out the interests of the service. If my course is not satisfactory, remove me at once. I do not wish to impede in any way the success of our arms. I have averaged writing more than once a day since leaving Cairo to keep you informed of my position, and it is no fault of mine if you have not received my letters. My going to Nashville was strictly intended for the good of the service, and not to gratify any desire of my own.
>
> Believing sincerely that I must have enemies between you and myself, who are trying to impair my usefulness. I respectfully ask to be relieved from further duty in the department.[38]

Now neither man was willing to back down. On the 8th Halleck told Grant: "You are mistaken. There is no enemy between you and me." Halleck once again stated that he had received no information on the number and position of Grant's command since the capture of Fort Donelson and informed his subordinate that "General McClellan has asked for it repeatedly with reference to ulterior movements, but I could not give him the information. He is out of all patience waiting for it." Grant replied the next day stating that he had 35,147 infantry; 3,169 cavalry; and 12 batteries of artillery in his command with just over 25,000 men assigned to Smith's expedition. There were about 5,700 men at Fort Henry waiting for transportation and the rest were spread around in garrisons at Fort Henry, Fort Donelson and Clarksville. Grant also sent a separate dispatch continuing the argument:

> I will do all in my power to advance the expedition now started. You had a better chance of knowing my strength whilst surrounding Fort Donelson than I had. Troops were reporting daily, by your order, and immediately assigned to brigades. There were no orders received from you until the 28th February to make out returns, and I made every effort to get them in as early as possible. I have always been ready to move anywhere, regardless of consequences to myself, but with a disposition to take the best care of the troops under my command. I renew my application to be relieved from further duty.[39]

Halleck had to send one more dispatch on the 9th informing Grant that his letter of the 5th was the first information received at headquarters. Again mentioning that "General McClellan had repeatedly ordered me to report to him daily the numbers and positions of your forces." Halleck continued that he was embarrassed that he could not provide this information to the general in chief because he could not get Grant to respond to repeated orders and warned Grant, "Don't let such neglect occur again, for it is equally discreditable to you and to me."[40]

At this point it seemed that Halleck wanted to put the matter aside for he continued the dispatch: "But to business," ordering that Forts Henry and Donelson could be manned by regimental size garrisons and that any available troops should be sent up the Tennessee as soon as possible. "As soon as these things are arranged you will hold yourself in readiness to take the command. There will probably be some desperate fighting in that vicinity, and we must be prepared."[41]

The matter should have ended now but Grant received a dispatch sent on the 6th in which Halleck enclosed a letter sent to Judge Davis, president of the Western Investigating Commission. In this wire Halleck went on to complain about "the want of order and discipline and the numerous irregularities in your command since the capture of Fort Donelson," which had attracted the attention of Washington. "Unless these things are immediately corrected," he added, "I am directed to relieve you of the command." The letter from an unnamed source alleged that looting and the sale of government supplies to private businesses were taking place in Grant's command and little or nothing was being done to stop it.[42]

On March 11 Grant sent an angry reply that took the situation to the next level. Having received Halleck's message of the 6th with the letter to Judge Davis concerning fraud Grant wrote that his orders to suppress marauding were "the only reply necessary. There is such a disposition to find fault with me that I again ask to be relieved from further duty until I can be placed right in the estimation of those higher in authority."[43]

In other words Grant had had enough. He wanted an official court of inquiry to review the whole situation. This was something that Halleck did not want and he quickly tried to calm his angry subordinate. "You cannot be relieved from your command. There is no good reason for it." All that was being asked was for Grant to use his power to enforce discipline. Halleck then came to the real reason he didn't want to lose Grant: "Instead of relieving you, I wish you as soon as your new army is in the field to assume the immediate command and lead it on to new victories." Apparently this new tack worked. In his reply on the 14th, Grant revealed that he had felt that it would be impossible to continue in command without a court of inquiry. Halleck's telegram, however, "places such a different phase upon my position that I will again assume command, and give every effort to the success of our cause. Under the worst circumstances I would do the same."[44]

The situation between Halleck and Grant had almost gotten out of hand but now it appeared as if things were back on track. What Grant was unaware of, however, was that much more had happened than a disagreement about reports. McClellan's slowness to act had finally cost him his job as general in chief and he now commanded only the Army of the Potomac. Halleck, on the other hand, had been given that which he had campaigned for so hard, overall control in the West, which brought Buell under his command and relieved much of his anxiety.

Another factor that helped Grant's case was that the president had gotten involved. Lincoln was not willing to see the man who had given the Union its only major victory persecuted and perhaps driven out of the army without at least a fair hearing. On March 10, Brigadier General Lorenzo Thomas, adjutant general of the Army, wrote to Halleck:

> It has been reported that soon after the battle of Fort Donelson Brigadier-General Grant left his command without leave. By direction of the President the Secretary of War desires you to ascertain and report whether General Grant left his command at any time without proper authority, and, if so, for how long; whether he has made to you proper reports and returns of his force; whether he has committed any acts which were unauthorized or not in accordance with military subordination or propriety, and, if so, what.

This dispatch in effect forced Halleck to decide if he wanted to file formal charges against Grant, and prove them, or let the matter drop.[45]

Halleck was more than ready to drop the issue. He had covered himself with his superiors by reprimanding Grant, he no longer had to answer to McClellan, and he must have known that charges against Grant would be difficult if not impossible to prove. On March 15, Halleck responded to Thomas that although Grant and some of his staff did indeed travel to Nashville without authorization it was clear that "General Grant did this from good intentions and from a desire to subserve the public interests." Whatever lapses in discipline may have happened at Fort Donelson were in violation of published orders. Halleck went on to state that Grant had explained the situation and had been directed to resume his command in the field. Halleck requested that "As he acted from a praiseworthy although mistaken zeal for the public service in going to Nashville and leaving his command, I respectfully recommend that no further notice be taken of it." Any problems with Grant's reports were partly from the failure of his subordinates to supply him with information to pass on to Halleck and "partly from an interruption of telegraphic communication. All these irregularities have now been remedied."[46]

In his final word on the subject Grant wrote to Halleck on March 24 stating that "In regard to the plundering at Fort Donelson, it is very much overestimated by disappointed persons, who failed in getting off the trophies they had gathered." Orders issued at that time confirm that Grant tried to curb such problems. Grant also believed that under the circumstances it was proper for him to order Nelson's troops to Nashville and then follow up in person to confirm that the enemy had fled and to confer with General Buell. Grant wrote that he did not believe he had neglected any of his duties and had communicated with headquarters on an average of once a day since leaving Cairo. In closing Grant said, "I most fully appreciate your justness, general, in the part you have taken, and you may rely upon me to the utmost of my capacity for carrying out all your orders."[47]

The gratitude Grant felt at the time was surely authentic and it was not until years later that he learned Halleck had been the cause of the problem. In his *Memoirs*, Grant's anger was still apparent when he wrote that less than two weeks after the victory at Fort Donelson "I was virtually in arrest and without a command." This was an exaggeration since Grant was never under arrest, but his bitterness against Halleck only increased when Grant learned that "it was his own reports that had created all the trouble."[48]

Although in the long run this situation did Grant no real harm it must have been an emotional roller coaster for someone who had only recently tasted success after years of mediocrity. Dr. John Brinton, a military surgeon and friend of Grant, later wrote, "The treatment received by General Grant from his superior officers at this time cut him bitterly. He obeyed his orders to the letter.... His fault was in being too strong and active." The situation was finally resolved, Grant was off the hook, Halleck had his new command, and the war could now proceed.[49]

While Grant and Halleck were exchanging letters the Tennessee River expedition, now commanded by General Smith, got under way on March 10. Despite all the bickering between the commanders a substantial Federal army was finally advancing up the Tennessee. The three divisions that had seen action at Fort Donelson commanded by McClernand, Lew Wallace, and Smith (now commanded by W. H. L. Wallace since Smith was in overall command of the expedition) were joined by two new divisions commanded by Brigadier Generals Sherman and Steven A. Hurlbut. The expedition landed at Savannah on the 14th where Smith split his force, sending Sherman's division on steamers, with an escort of gunboats, up the river toward Eastport to begin the destruction of the railroad bridges as originally ordered by Halleck. The next day Sherman's little fleet landed thirty-some miles from Savannah to destroy the railroad at Iuka when the weather took matters in hand. Heavy rains flooded the countryside and turned creeks into raging rivers; the Tennessee rose so high that most of the boat landings were under water. Sherman re-boarded the steamers and turned around back toward Savannah, but stopped instead about nine miles upriver on the west bank at Pittsburg Landing, where he found General Hurlbut's division.[50]

Sherman later related how Pittsburg Landing was chosen to be the army's campsite: "During the night of the 14th, we dropped down to Pittsburg Landing, where I found Hurlbut's division in boats." Sherman left his troops there and reported to General Smith who instructed him to return to Pittsburg Landing, disembark his and Hurlbut's troops and "to take positions well back, and to leave room for his whole army; telling me that he would soon come up in person, and move out in force to make the lodgment on the railroad, contemplated by General Halleck's orders."[51]

General Grant resumed command of the army in mid–March and found "about half being on the east bank of the Tennessee at Savannah, while one division was at Crump's Landing on the west bank about four miles higher up, and the remainder at Pittsburg Landing, five miles above Crump's." Grant could see as well as anyone else that the rail center at Corinth was the most important position in the area. He at once decided to concentrate his army at Pittsburg Landing, "knowing that the enemy was fortifying at Corinth and collecting an army there under Johnston." As soon as Buell's Army of the Ohio arrived Grant planned to advance against Corinth "and the west bank of the river was the place to start from." It was also clear that, while Federal gunboats controlled the river itself, eventually some sort of foothold on the west side was needed to be able to make the planned advance on Corinth and Pittsburg Landing was the obvious choice.[52]

In a report to Grant, Sherman wrote from Pittsburg Landing that he strongly believed that this was the place to be both for strategic purposes and the terrain itself. "The ground itself admits of easy defense by a small command, and yet affords admirable camping-ground for a hundred thousand men."[53]

Even though he was spoiling for a fight Grant still had to deal with the ever cautious Halleck, who sent orders on the 16th for Smith to avoid any large fight: "As the enemy is evidently in strong force, my instructions not to advance so as to bring on an engagement must be strictly obeyed." Halleck did not want Smith to leave his position or do anything that might tempt Johnston to attack him. With General Buell moving toward Savannah and at least 10,000 more men coming from Missouri, Halleck wanted no fighting to take place "until we are strong enough to admit no doubt of the result."[54]

Two days later Grant received orders that gave him an opportunity to provoke some action. Halleck wired that it had been reported that Confederate troops had "moved from Corinth to cut off our transports below Savannah. If so, General Smith should immediately destroy railroad connection at Corinth." Even though Grant knew this was not the case he moved quickly, ordering Smith and Lew Wallace to prepare their commands for an immediate advance. Grant's enthusiasm got the better of him, however, when he notified Halleck, "Immediate preparation will be made to execute your perfectly feasible order. I will go in person, leaving General McClernand in command here."[55]

This was faster action than Halleck was interested in and he quickly wired back to Grant, "Don't let the enemy draw you into an engagement now. Wait until you are properly fortified and receive orders." This put the brakes to any advance Grant was planning. He didn't mind stretching orders a bit to provoke action but Grant would not flatly disobey Halleck, especially in light of his recent troubles. On the 20th Grant wired back to headquarters: "I will take no risk at Corinth under the instructions I now have." Grant also promised to avoid anything like an evenly matched fight.[56]

On March 21, Grant informed Halleck that he believed the Confederates had gathered a large force at Corinth, with more on the way: "I have certain information that thirteen trains of cars arrived at Corinth on the 19th, with twenty cars to each train, all loaded with troops." This information, Grant admitted, "would indicate that Corinth cannot be taken without a general engagement, which, from your instructions, is to be avoided." He also believed that the enemy was still discouraged from their recent defeats and that "the great mass of the rank and file are heartily tired." This opinion would soon be proven to be totally wrong.[57]

Once again Grant's efforts to go on the offensive had been halted by his superior. He was growing restless and complained to General Smith on the 23rd: "I do not hear one word from Saint Louis. I am clearly of the opinion that the enemy are gathering strength at Corinth quite as rapidly as we are here, and the sooner we attack the easier will be the task of taking the place." Both Grant and Smith were anxious to attack Corinth. It appeared to them that the only problem they were facing was that of getting permission to strike. None of the Federal commanders at Pittsburg Landing seemed to be concerned that the enemy might be preparing plans of his own.[58]

5

JOHNSTON RISKS ALL

After the fall of Fort Donelson and the humiliating retreat of Johnston's army from Nashville the Confederacy faced a desperate situation in the region. The South's forces were fragmented and badly outnumbered. What Johnston needed most in late February and March was time: time to bring his shattered army together; time to restore his troops' morale; and time to draw reinforcements from other parts of the Confederacy to create a new army that could strike back and regain what had been lost. Obligingly enough the Federal commanders gave Johnston that time. The constant bickering and maneuvering for personal gain between the western commanders combined with Grant's problems with Halleck and the lack of aggressiveness by everyone except Grant brought the Union war effort in the area to a grinding halt. In short, the Federal authorities allowed the Confederates to live to fight another day.

It is difficult to say when Albert Sidney Johnston formulated his plan of campaign but the choice of Corinth, Mississippi, as the place to concentrate the Confederate forces in the region was certainly understandable. The town occupied a key position as the most important railroad center in the Mississippi Valley with the Memphis and Charleston line running east and west and the Mobile and Ohio connecting farther south. Once Johnston was able to concentrate his scattered troops he could wait for an opportunity to strike the enemy and reverse the Confederacy's fortunes in the West. The only way for this to succeed, however, was to strike either Grant or Buell before they joined forces and became too powerful to attack with any hope of success.[1]

The first order of business for Johnston was to reach Corinth with troops accompanying him and unite them with the other forces under his command. Winter rains that turned the roads into rivers of freezing mud made the march from Murfreesboro to Corinth a nightmare for the exhausted men. While Johnston was leading his troops south General Beauregard, who went to Columbus after Bowling Green was abandoned, set about bringing as many men to Corinth as possible. With the loss of Columbus General Polk left about half his command to defend the forts along the Mississippi and marched the rest of his force toward Corinth. Even with the addition of Polk's troops, however, the Confederate forces would number less than thirty thousand, fewer men than either Grant or Buell had. Reinforcements would have to come from outside Tennessee.[2]

The authorities in Richmond knew how important it was to hold on to Middle

Tennessee and the rail center at Corinth. Taking prompt action, President Davis transferred troops from around the Confederacy to stave off potential disaster in Tennessee. About 5,000 men were sent to Corinth from New Orleans and another 10,000 were transferred from Florida and Gulf Coast garrisons, under the command of Major General Braxton Bragg. As important as the coastal installations were Corinth was even more valuable.[3]

Throwing together different groups of men like this produced massive problems in building a cohesive fighting force. Fortunately one of the most accomplished officers in the Confederate army in the area of organizing and training new recruits was Braxton Bragg, who would have a long and varied history with the Army of Tennessee. Born in North Carolina, Bragg was a graduate of West Point. During the Mexican War he commanded a battery of artillery and fought bravely at Monterrey and Buena Vista, where his guns helped prevent the destruction of the Mississippi Rifles, commanded by Jefferson Davis. Bragg received his general's commission at the start of the war and in early 1862 his command was spread out along the Alabama and West Florida coastline when he was ordered to join Johnston's army.[4]

Braxton Bragg had a complicated personality. An educated and refined man, he believed in discipline and hard work. His men were among the best-trained troops in the Confederate army. To achieve this, however, he often drove himself and his subordinates too hard, resulting in frequent bouts of illness. He had a rather unpleasant disposition and was almost totally lacking in tact and the ability to get along with others. Over time these negative personality traits would overshadow whatever positive contributions he might have made.[5]

Braxton Bragg (courtesy Library of Congress).

After a difficult march Johnston and his troops arrived in Corinth by March 24, increasing the size of the army to about 44,000, the majority of which were "mostly raw troops, unhabituated to camp life, undisciplined, and hardly drilled." Once the army was gathered Beauregard was given responsibility for "all orders relative to preparations for the intended movement against the enemy, as well as for all details of organization."[6]

The newly formed Confederate army was at this time little

more than a large group of men thrown together by an emergency. The troops and many of their officers lacked any real experience. Bragg's troops had been well trained in camps but they had seen no fighting and the troops from New Orleans were virtually untrained. Few of Polk's troops had been in combat and Hardee's men had spent most of their time in the army quietly camped at Bowling Green. The situation was no better with the senior officers. Johnston and Beauregard had never worked together before, and Bragg was entirely new to the army as were the brigade and regimental commanders that came with him. Before any offensive movement could begin these troops had to be transformed into an army. Once again, the Federals accommodated Johnston by allowing him several weeks to organize his troops.[7]

Leonidas Polk (courtesy Library of Congress).

The Confederate commanders were a varied group but Major General Leonidas Polk was one of the most unusual officers in either army. He had graduated from West Point in 1827 but resigned almost immediately to enter the Episcopal priesthood, in which he rose to the position of bishop. Even though Polk's only exposure to the military was years ago at West Point and he had no field experience during wartime, Jefferson Davis, a classmate at the military academy and an old friend, appointed him a major general. Polk was ambitious, headstrong, and not really competent to lead a large body of men, but he wholeheartedly believed in the Southern cause, and right now that was what counted. Polk would be killed in the summer of 1864 during Sherman's campaign to take Atlanta.[8]

Beauregard had been disappointed with what he found when he arrived in Tennessee. The Confederate army was significantly weaker in both men and material than he had been led to believe. The vain and temperamental Beauregard had come west to win fame and in the middle of March the army in Corinth certainly didn't look like it could win much of anything. He later wrote that he knew "with the forces under me, gathered as they had been, and under such difficulties, no chance of success existed, were I to attempt an aggressive movement upon the combined forces under Generals Grant and Buell."⁹

When General Johnston arrived at Corinth he already knew what he wanted to do. With the concentration of the troops completed the new Confederate army would advance to the Tennessee River and crush Grant's smaller force, only about 25 miles away, before Buell arrived. As Beauregard wrote, "By a rapid and vigorous attack on General Grant it was expected he would be beaten back into his transports and the river, or captured." Time was an important factor for the Confederates and they had to act immediately but both Beauregard and Bragg were insistent that the army needed to be reorganized before any major action was attempted.¹⁰

Beauregard, who was in charge of the day-to-day activities and training of the new army, had his work cut out for him. "Our deficiencies were such, however, and so great was the inexperience of some of our subordinate commanders," that quick movement of the army was impossible. There was a shortage of trained officers in all areas, but most significantly field officers, and as Beauregard later wrote, "to my extreme disappointment, our forces were not ready and did not make the projected advance as early as I had wished and striven to have it done."¹¹

On April 2 word was received that Buell's army was closer to joining Grant than was expected and "It was then, at a late hour, determined that the attack should be attempted at once, incomplete and imperfect as were our preparations for such a grave and momentous adventure." General Johnston decided the time had come to move, whether the army was ready or not, and it was not. As the men prepared to move out, all the roads around Corinth were packed with troops and wagons and artillery; there was no room for mistakes. Johnston's army consisted of three corps commanded by Hardee, Bragg, and Polk with John C. Breckinridge, former vice president of the United States, commanding the reserve. Beauregard had given them their instructions for the march verbally so that they could move before receiving written orders. Unfortunately, Polk had decided to wait for those written orders before he moved and this, along with the normal difficulties of moving an army and the lack of experienced officers, especially in the higher ranks, produced such confusion when the army attempted to advance that the movement was postponed until the next night.¹²

At 1 A.M. on April 3, orders were issued to the commanders to begin the advance. The army that finally marched out of Corinth that morning was totally unprepared for what they were about to face. The problem wasn't really anyone's fault; there simply had not been enough time to do all that needed to be done. Bragg was one of the Confederacy's best officers when it came to training and enforcing discipline of green troops and Hardee had actually written the official infantry tactics manual of the United States Army. The weather deteriorated and rain made bad roads worse. This, combined with poor staff work by inexperienced officers, turned a one-day march into a three-day disaster. This delay would cost the Confederates dearly.¹³

For the men who made this march, especially the new soldiers, it was a most unpleasant experience. James M. Williams of the 21st Alabama wrote to his wife that he "marched from Corinth last Thursday afternoon towards the enemys lines. Friday we moved two or three miles further through the mud and water.... The rain fell in torrents nearly all night, and we suffered greatly." John S. Jackman of Kentucky's Orphan

Brigade wrote in his diary on the 4th: "At the outset our road led through a swamp, where, in some places, the mud and water was knee deep every step. The rain continued to pour down all the four noon [forenoon]. I soon regretted that I had started."[14]

In his official report General Beauregard gave some idea of the difficulties the army faced as it marched toward Pittsburg Landing. The army had been expected to be in position to launch the assault early on April 5. "The men, however, for the most part, were unused to marching, and the roads, narrow and traversing a densely wooded country, became almost impassable after a severe rainstorm on the night of the 4th." All the problems with the weather and other delays combined to prevent the weary Confederates from reaching the vicinity of the enemy until late Saturday afternoon, the 5th of April.[15]

General Johnston halted his army less than two miles from the Federal camps and began preparations to launch the attack the next morning. That night the Confederate commanders held their last conference before the battle and General Beauregard surprisingly suggested that the attack should be called off and the army marched back to Corinth. As strange as it must have seemed to the other generals in the room Beauregard did have some legitimate reasons for concern. The success of the attack depended on surprise and the length of time taken to bring the army to its present position had probably made that surprise impossible to achieve. Because of the delay many of the men had already gone through the rations they carried and the wagons with food and ammunition were still far to the rear. Worst of all, many of the untrained soldiers, wondering if their rifles would fire in the wet weather, had been test firing them during the day and the noise certainly should have alerted the enemy's pickets. All things considered the Federal army would have to be deaf, dumb, and blind not to know of the approach of the Confederates. Beauregard feared, and it seems a reasonable fear, that in the morning Grant's troops would be safely entrenched and waiting to slaughter the Confederates when they attacked.[16]

The corps commanders briefly discussed Beauregard's suggestion but General Johnston would have nothing of it and soon ended the debate with, "Gentlemen, we shall attack at daylight tomorrow." Johnston must have known that this would be his only chance for a successful fight. Any more delay and Buell would surely be up and the combined Federal armies would be too large to even contemplate attacking. A withdrawal back to Corinth would only ruin his soldiers' morale and probably completely destroy what little organization had been achieved. And once back at Corinth then what? If the Federal armies followed, which they would almost surely do, Johnston would only be setting himself up for a siege against a much larger army that he would eventually lose. No, he decided, "I would fight them if they were a million. They can present no greater front between these two creeks than we can, and the more men they crowd in there, the worse we can make it for them."[17]

The Confederate army would advance to the attack in long parallel lines of battle. General Hardee's corps was in front, spread out nearly three miles between Owl Creek on the left and Lick Creek on the right. To augment this line Brig. General A. H. Gladden's brigade from Bragg's corps was attached to the far right of Hardee's line, bringing the total number of men to a little over nine thousand. General Bragg commanded the second line, which was about 500 yards behind the first. His line was also spread out across the entire field and contained about 10,700 men. About eight hundred yards behind Bragg came General Polk's corps of a little over nine thousand men. Polk's troops were mostly behind Bragg's left wing; in addition, Breckinridge brought up about seven thousand men, mostly behind Bragg's right. Both Polk and Breckinridge were considered reserve forces to be sent forward wherever required to support the first two lines. Cavalry protected the flanks of the army and each corps brought along their own artillery. Altogether Johnston was sending about forty thousand men against the Federal camps.[18]

General Johnston originally had wanted to hit the Federal left with a massive blow and cut them off from Pittsburg Landing, forcing surrender or destruction. Sending long lines spread across the field would give no extra weight to any particular area and if successful would push the Federal army back toward the landing, where they could escape or bring up reinforcements more easily. Also, once the troops became engaged it would be impossible for the corps commanders to have any control over their men in such a spread out formation. This unusual plan of attack was drawn up by Beauregard, who insists that Johnston approved it. The real problem, once again, was time, or rather the lack of time. To re-arrange forty thousand men into a vastly different formation would probably have wasted another day. Johnston wanted to attack, and attack now.[19]

When General Beauregard made his arguments on why the attack should be canceled he was absolutely correct. If Grant's army had made even modest defensive preparations Johnston's men probably would have been slaughtered when attacked. As it turned out, however, the Federal commanders, both at headquarters and in the field, had already decided that the Confederates were not capable of launching a serious attack at this time. Apparently Grant was so focused on his own plans for the upcoming offensive that he didn't spend much time preparing for what Johnston might be planning to do.

There was no question that the Federal position at Pittsburg Landing was a strong one defensively. The terrain was varied with dense woods, thick underbrush and the occasional clear field, laced with small streams and ravines. With Snake Creek and Owl Creek on the right and the Tennessee River and Lick Creek on the left the Federals were protected against flanking movements. The only way the Federal position could be attacked was from directly in front. Sherman believed "the position was naturally strong." Some basic earthworks probably would have made the position impregnable.[20]

About two miles or more from the landing, on the ridge that divides Lick and Snake Creeks, stood a small log meetinghouse known as Shiloh. This ridge was the key to the position and this was where Sherman's division, less one brigade, was stationed. Although Sherman's division had never heard a shot fired in anger and was barely half trained Grant felt "This deficiency was more than made up by the superiority of the commander." Behind Sherman, and to the left, was McClernand's division which had fought at Fort Donelson, giving them as much experience as any men in the army. The front unit on the left was the division of Brigadier General Benjamin M. Prentiss, a forty-one-year-old lawyer from Illinois; his division was also green. On the far left, near Lick Creek, was a brigade from Sherman's division under Col. David Stuart.[21]

There were two more divisions stationed near Pittsburg Landing and considered the reserves. General Hurlbut's troops were positioned behind Prentiss and C. F. Smith's division, now commanded by Brigadier General W. H. L. Wallace, was to the right. The sixth division of the army, under General Lew Wallace, was guarding the army's supply depots at Crump's Landing, about five miles to the north. In order to make the anticipated advance the camps of the various divisions were located on or near the roads leading toward Corinth. The five divisions at Pittsburg Landing contained about thirty-seven thousand men, with Lew Wallace's having a little over seven thousand men at Crump's Landing.[22]

Apparently none of the commanders gave much thought to defense as there were large gaps between the divisions and no provisions had been made to set up any sort of line in case of an enemy attack. Warren Olney, of the Third Iowa, remembered that the troops "were camped wherever there was an opening in the woods or underbrush sufficiently large for a regiment." There seemed to have been little planning done in laying out the camps "but each regiment occupied such suitable ground as presented itself in the neighborhood of the rest of the brigade." The pickets and patrols did not venture too far from camp, which meant that there would be little warning in case of an enemy attack. The question has always been asked why the Federal army did not put up even basic earthworks to protect their position. Sherman wrote later that he "acted on the supposition that we were an invading army. We did not fortify our camps against an attack, because we had no orders to do so, and because such a course would have made our raw men timid."[23]

Grant did not want his troops to spend time digging trenches for what he obviously must have considered good reasons. The first being that he did not want the men to develop a defensive frame of mind. The army was there to advance into enemy territory; they had merely stopped at Pittsburg Landing to await reinforcements. Grant did look into the matter of fortifications and had his engineer, Colonel McPherson, study where to best set up a line of works but it would have been well to the rear of the current encampment and would have given up the protection of the creeks on the flanks. Besides, as Grant says, "I regarded the campaign we were engaged in as an offensive one and had no idea that the enemy would leave strong intrenchments to take the initiative when he knew he would be attacked where he was if he remained." Another reason for not putting up defensive works was that since the majority of the troops were new, untrained recruits Grant felt that "drill and discipline were worth more to our men than fortifications." All in all the positioning and preparedness of the Federal army was well below what would normally be considered prudent for an army in what was essentially enemy territory.[24]

The only real concern that Grant seemed to have was of a surprise enemy attack on Lew Wallace's division off by itself: "I feared it was possible that he might make a rapid dash upon Crump's and destroy our transports and stores, most of which were kept at that point, and then retreat before Wallace could be reinforced." In the last few days there had been several contacts with Confederate patrols and there was a growing suspicion that Wallace's isolation could make him a likely target. Grant had arranged for W.H.L. Wallace to send reinforcements to Crump's Landing if it were attacked but when he informed Sherman of this Grant added, "although I look for nothing of the kind, but it is best to be prepared."[25]

Grant's confidence was in some part due to Sherman. Earlier in the war Sherman had come close to having a nervous breakdown. With his confidence recovered this was his first field command since that time and Sherman was now probably the last man in the army to display any concern over the minor skirmishing that had been occurring in front of his division. On the 5th, with the entire Confederate army but two miles away, Sherman reported to Grant that he doubted there would be any serious fighting, at most the occasional picket firing. "The enemy is saucy, but got the worst of it yesterday, and will not press our pickets far. I will not be drawn out far unless with certainty of advantage, and I do not apprehend anything like an attack on our position."[26]

Grant's lack of concern was illustrated on the 5th. He wrote to Halleck saying that he had gone to the front to investigate reports of outposts being attacked but found that all was quiet. Grant then told Halleck that "I have scarcely the faintest idea of an attack (general one) being made upon us, but will be prepared should such a thing take place." Around noon that same day General Nelson's division of Buell's army began arriving at Savannah with Buell himself arriving later in the evening, although Grant was unaware of this. Colonel Jacob Ammen commanded one of Nelson's brigades and that afternoon he was visited by Grant and Nelson. When Ammen remarked to Grant that his men were not tired and could continue on to Pittsburg Landing, Grant replied that the colonel should make his troops comfortable and that boats would be sent for the men Monday or Tuesday. Then Grant confidently stated there would be no battle at Pittsburg Landing: "We will have to go to Corinth, where the rebels are fortified. If they come to attack us, we can whip them, as I have more than twice as many troops as I had at Fort Donelson."[27]

The men in the Union ranks seemed no more concerned about an enemy attack than were their commanders. Lucius Barber, of the 15th Illinois, wrote that he and his comrades had become fairly comfortable in their camp:

> The weather was delightful. Spring had just begun to open and the grand old forest was putting on its leafy covering. Our mail came regularly and we were happy as mortals could be under the circumstances. We all knew that a battle was imminent, but never dreamed that the enemy would open the strife. Our great victory at Ft. Donelson had given us great confidence in ourselves and we supposed that we rested in security for the present.[28]

William Cluett, a drummer boy in the 57th Illinois, wrote that on the evening of the 5th he was pretty bored with camp life: "Vague rumors are afloat this evening to the effect that Gen. Albert Sidney Johnston is moving toward the Tennessee River with his entire command. Not much credit is attached to it, however..."[29]

While Cluett was getting ready for an inspection the next morning, some of Albert Sidney Johnston's pickets were so close that they could listen to the music of the Federal regimental bands as they stood at their posts.

6

First Day at Shiloh

Before light on Sunday, April 6, General Johnston's Confederates were awake and preparing for battle. They ate what little they had, put aside their bedrolls and any extra clothing they carried on their backs, checked their weapons, and many probably tried to make peace with their God. A short distance away in the Federal camps most of the men were still asleep, luckily unaware of what was about to happen.

Many of the men who survived the next two days would remember that Sunday morning as one of the loveliest spring days they ever experienced. Wilber F. Crummer, of the 45th Illinois, later wrote that he never saw "the sun beam forth, shedding its golden rays on a devoted, unsuspecting army, with more loveliness." Ira Blanchard, of the 20th Illinois, remembered that the morning "opened beautiful. We were astir early, as Sunday was always inspection day and we had to have our arms, clothing and quarters in the best of order."[1]

Not far from the Federal campsites thousands of Confederate soldiers were watching the same springtime sunrise. Lot D. Young, of Kentucky's Orphan Brigade, thought that Easter morning was "so beautiful and lovely that all nature seemed proud and happy. Trees budding, flowers blooming, birds singing, everything seemingly joyful and happy in the bright sunshine of early spring." One of Hardee's men, Lt. John W. Carroll, of the 27th Tennessee Infantry, remembered that "the sun rose brightly; everything was full of animation, life, and hope."[2]

According to his son, even General Johnston was inspired by the beautiful spring morning and he was expecting to win a great victory this day. Mounting his horse the Confederate commander confidently said to his staff, "Tonight we will water our horses in the Tennessee River." Nothing less than complete victory and the capture or destruction of the Federal army would be acceptable. In a more sober moment Johnston told one of his staff who had served in Utah, Colonel John S. Marmaduke, "My son, we must this day conquer or perish."[3]

In a strange twist the first fighting of the day was an attack by Federal troops on the advancing Confederates. Well before dawn, the commander of General Prentiss' 1st Brigade, Colonel Everett Peabody, sent out a detachment from the 21st Missouri, commanded by Colonel David Moore, to reconnoiter the woods in his front. Not far from the camps Moore met some retreating Federal pickets, prompting him to call for the remainder of his regiment. The Missouri troops continued to move forward and soon

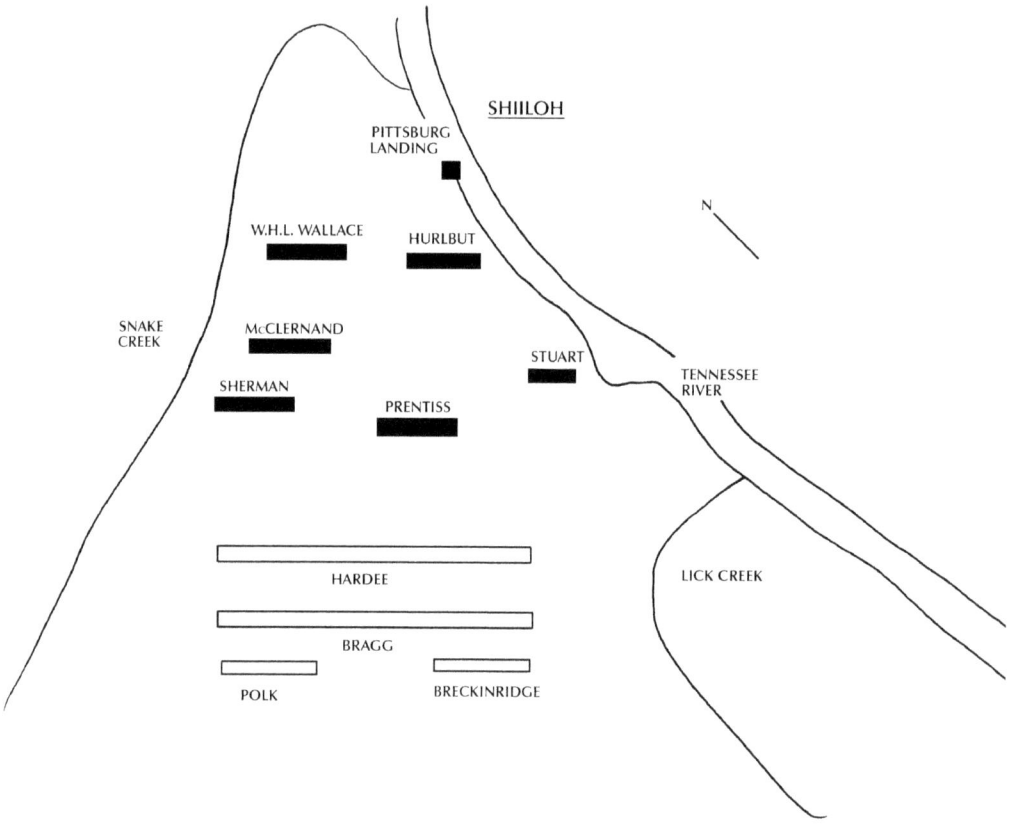

ran into a large body of Confederates coming right toward the unsuspecting Federal army. Moore's small command tried to put up a fight but as he reported, "A terrific fire was opened upon us from the whole front of the four or five regiments forming the advance of the enemy." Moore soon fell back and the battle was on.[4]

The Confederates came at the divisions of Prentiss and Sherman like a tidal wave. Although the Federals had been given some warning of an enemy attack by the firing from the reconnaissance patrols nothing could have prepared the untrained troops for the thousands of Confederates who came charging down on them. Despite all the delays in moving from Corinth, Johnston had achieved the surprise that was an integral part of his battle plan. It was not the total surprise that was later reported; Federal soldiers were not killed in their beds, nor were the camps overrun while they were sleeping, but to the mostly green troops in the two forward Federal divisions the surprise was real enough. While Federal commanders were aware that a Confederate attack was possible they were totally unprepared for the size and ferocity of what now hit them.

On the Federal left, along the road from Corinth, the division of General Prentiss was hit hard. Although Prentiss had his troops in line and ready to receive the enemy his men were just too inexperienced to stand up against the massive attack. The gap between Prentiss and Sherman gave Hardee's Confederates easy access to the flanks of both divisions and prevented any coordinated defense. Prentiss reported that "shortly after 6 o'clock the entire line was under fire, receiving the assault made by the entire force of the enemy, advancing in three columns simultaneously upon our left, center, and right." As happened all over the field some of his men would stand and fight and others would run away at the first shots. The 61st Illinois was camped on the left of the division when the fighting began. They briefly held their ground but soon most of them were on their way back to Hurlbut's camp.[5]

The fighting was fierce and one-sided. Colonel Francis Quinn, commander of the 12th Michigan, reported, "volley after volley was given and returned and many fell on both sides, but their numbers were too heavy for our forces." Soon the Federals were falling back to their camp where they resisted the Confederate horde for about half an hour. There was no time to form a regular line but the men fought in small units and individually firing from behind trees and any other little bit of protection they could find. By now Bragg's line was adding its weight to the attack and around 9 o'clock Prentiss ordered the remainder of his division to fall back again. They rallied about a half-mile back along a sunken road where, along with troops from Hurlbut and W. H. L. Wallace, they set up a strong defensive position.[6]

General Sherman's division occupying the front camp on the right was also hit with the full force of the Confederate attack. The early firing in the distance caused Sherman to ride out and take a look for himself. He hadn't gone very far when an aide was killed by Confederate fire and "about the same time," Sherman later wrote, "I saw the rebel lines of battle in front coming down on us as far as the eye could reach." Sherman always insisted that his division was not taken by surprise that morning and that "all my troops were in line of battle, ready, and the ground was favorable to us."[7]

Surprised or not, when the massive Confederate line hit Sherman's green troops the result was about the same as what happened to Prentiss' division. Some of the troops stood firm for a while then the weight of the Confederate force began to be felt. Patrick Cleburne led the Confederates on this part of their line and no one hit an enemy harder. The 53rd Ohio was one of the new regiments and its men had never heard a shot fired in anger until that Sunday morning. They were in line on the left of the camp, near the center of the battlefield. As the enemy line approached they fired a couple of volleys when their colonel suddenly shouted, "Fall back and save yourselves." Within minutes most of them were on their way to the rear.[8]

Other regiments put up a stout fight. A soldier in the 48th Ohio remembered that just as his regiment formed their line "the rebels, who were not more than a hundred yards distant, opened on our ranks, killing and wounding a number of the regiment at their first fire." Almost simultaneously the Ohioans returned fire. The Federals "made use of what little shelter the trees and logs afforded, and continued to pour volley after volley into the rebel ranks," but the Confederates kept increasing the pressure on Sherman's men as more and more came forward.[9]

As Cleburne's men continued to press the attack their casualties were terrible. Moving through the Union camp their lines were broken up by the tents and "under the terrible fire much confusion followed, and a quick and bloody repulse was the consequence." But Cleburne's men would never stop because of one repulse and the 6th Mississippi, for instance, charged again and again. The Federal fire took its toll and "only when the regiment had lost 300 officers and men killed and wounded, out of an aggregate of 425, that it yielded and retreated in disorder over its own dead and dying." Almost immediately fresh Confederates took their place and the fighting continued unabated.[10]

It was impossible for the Federal officers to put together a coordinated defense as regiments who were putting up a good fight were constantly being flanked when neighboring units fell back. Colonel David Stuart, commanding Sherman's 2nd Brigade, reported that after he formed his regiments he found a vantage point where he could view a large portion of the field. Colonel Stuart could see "fugitives, making their way to the rear," and large numbers of Confederates advancing toward his brigade. "I saw that the position of my brigade was inevitably flanked by an overwhelming and unopposed force." One of Stuart's regiments, the 71st Ohio, fell back before he returned and he had to quickly pull the rest of the brigade back to avoid destruction. That's how it was for most of the Federal units in front that morning, a brief stand and then retreat, make another brief stand and then retreat again, each movement made with fewer men than before.[11]

After the initial shock of battle Sherman more than made up for his lack of preparedness. Like most of his men this was Sherman's first major battle and he performed like an old veteran. He was everywhere that day, rallying his troops when they fell back, pushing forward reinforcements as they came up, and encouraging the men who stood and fought. Sherman was twice slightly wounded and had three horses killed under him. But, his coolness and courage could only postpone the inevitable, and the relentless Confederate pressure steadily forced his troops back.[12]

John McClernand's 1st Division was positioned behind and a little to the left of Sherman. McClernand's troops were veterans of Fort Donelson and among the best-trained and most dependable soldiers in the army. As Sherman's division was being driven back, McClernand's troops were moving up to fill the gaps on the left and try to form a solid line to halt the advancing Confederates. Colonel C. Carroll Marsh, commanding the 2nd Brigade, reported that just as his men moved rapidly to a position on the left "the enemy were seen approaching in large force and fine style, column after column moving on us."[13]

The Confederates hit McClernand's men just as hard as they had Sherman and Prentiss. Ira Blanchard recalled that his 20th Illinois deployed between two batteries of artillery. The Confederates came up over a hill and "poured into us a murderous fire.... We gave them the best we had for half an hour, but their fire was telling fearful on our ranks." Colonel Marsh reported that the enemy opened a "most terrible and deadly fire," and that "during the first five minutes I lost more in killed and wounded than in all the other actions" of the battle. One of the batteries fled and soon the enemy rushed forward and the Federal troops had to flee to a safer position. Blanchard and his comrades passed a line of troops in their rear that briefly held the Confederates in check and their officers "tried to rally the scattered companies again for another stand, but of no avail, as the boys could not be formed under so severe a fire."[14]

Colonel Marsh's 2nd Brigade quickly found itself in even more desperate straits as the Confederates flowed around his flanks. Both the 18th Illinois and the 45th Illinois were out-flanked and had to flee to avoid capture or destruction. McClernand reported that he had no support on the left "and still outflanked on the right by increasing numbers, to save my command from being surrounded I ordered it to fall back about 200 yards and reform at a right angle with the center of my camp."¹⁵

At one point in the morning McClernand was able to make a local counterattack that was a brief success, "but, re-enforced by fresh troops his wavering line was strengthened, and again he commenced turning my right and left, forcing me back." McClernand fell back to an open woods with a field in front and was joined by a portion of Sherman's division and "the contest was again renewed with increased fury on both sides." In addition to the terror there were some amazing sights on the battlefield that morning. Sergeant Alexander Downing, of the 11th Iowa, wrote in his diary that he "witnessed a wonderful sight — thickly-flying musket balls, I have never seen hail falling thicker than the minie balls were flying in the air above us."¹⁶

Over on the Union left it was more of the same for Hurlbut's division stationed well behind Prentiss with the Tennessee near his left. Warren Olney of the 3rd Iowa remembered that as he stood with his regiment waiting for the approaching enemy, "teams with shouting drivers came tearing along the road toward the landing. Crowds of fugitives and men slightly wounded went hurrying past in the same direction. Uproar and turmoil was all around."¹⁷

John A. McClernand (courtesy Library of Congress)

When the battle began Prentiss had requested reinforcements and Hurlbut sent forward the brigade of Colonel James C. Veatch. As Prentiss was forced back Hurlbut formed his two remaining brigades in line and waited. It didn't take long for the survivors of Prentiss' division to reach Hurlbut's line with the Confederates of Brig. General Jones M. Withers close behind. Many of Prentiss' men rallied behind Hurlbut's formation and soon the lines were trading vicious fire.¹⁸

Sometimes waiting for the battle can be worse than the fight itself. George W. Squier, of the 44th Indiana, wrote home that while he was nervously laying on the ground waiting for the order to fire "I simply breathed faith; 'Ever kind father preserve me.' When I arose and the firing [began I] was as cool and composed as if sitting down for a chat or shooting squirrels. The bullets whistled over our heads, shells bursting all around us, balls whiz[zi]ng past."[19]

By mid-morning what was left of Grant's army was fighting desperately in a loose and uneven front. The center of the new line consisted of W. H. L. Wallace, who had moved his reserve division forward with Prentiss' survivors, and Hurlbut's division on the left. Colonel Stuart's brigade on the far left near the river had also been forced back during the morning and was desperately trying to stop the Confederates from breaking through and getting into the rear. Sherman and McClernand were still putting up a stubborn fight but were gradually losing ground and also in danger of being flanked. The next few hours would decide the fate of Grant's army.[20]

When the battle began the army's commander was at his headquarters in Savannah. Grant had remained there because General Buell's army would come through Savannah and he wanted to meet with Buell before the armies came together. Today, however, Grant had already decided to move his headquarters to Pittsburg Landing due to some unsettling news received the day before. Both John McClernand and Lew Wallace had been promoted to major general, which meant that these two men who had little military experience but excellent political connections now outranked everyone except Grant himself. With Grant in Savannah one of them would be in command of the army in the field, and Grant was not at all comfortable with that.[21]

Grant and his staff had just sat down to breakfast when the lovely spring morning was disturbed by the dull boom of cannon fire coming from the direction of Pittsburg Landing. Grant, his staff, and other headquarters personnel quickly boarded the *Tigress* and headed upriver. Just before leaving Grant sent out two hastily written notes. To General Nelson he wrote: "An attack having been made on our forces, you will move your entire command to the river opposite Pittsburg."[22]

The second message went to Buell, who was expected to arrive at Savannah later that day but was already in the area.

> Heavy firing is heard up the river, indicating plainly that an attack has been made upon our most advanced positions. I have been looking for this, but did not believe the attack could be made before Monday or Tuesday. This necessitates me joining the forces up the river instead of meeting you to-day, as I had contemplated. I have directed General Nelson to move to the river with his division. He can march to opposite Pittsburg.[23]

This note to Buell brings into question the message Grant had written to Halleck just the day before when he wrote that he was not anticipating a major attack. There had certainly been enough warnings that the Confederate army was approaching Pittsburg Landing. Colonel McPherson stated, "It was well known the enemy was approaching our lines, and there had been more or less skirmishing for three days preceding the battle." The attack Grant had been looking for was probably against Lew Wallace's isolated division at Crump's Landing, not the main army.[24]

As the *Tigress* moved up the river the firing became louder and around 7:30 A.M.

the ship pulled up to Crump's Landing. General Wallace was on the deck of his headquarters boat and Grant simply leaned over the railing and yelled for Wallace to "get his troops in line ready to execute any orders he might receive." Wallace replied that his troops were already formed and ready to move. Seeing that all was quiet at Crump's Landing, the *Tigress* continued upstream and at about 8:00 A.M. Grant arrived at Pittsburg Landing and went ashore to see for himself what was happening to his army.[25]

Grant went to work as soon as he arrived at the scene. It was obvious from the severity of the firing that ammunition would be needed and staff officers were dispatched to get ammunition trains organized. This was more difficult than it sounds because there was no standardization of weapons in the Federal army and multiple types and sizes of bullets were required. Two newly arrived Iowa regiments were put to work in a relatively futile effort to stop, or at least control, the flow of refugees that were already flooding back toward the river. Even though it was still early in the day the area near the river was beginning to be crowded with panicked and disorganized men. Most were new recruits who had been thrown into their first battle, one of the worst of the entire war at that, with little or no training. Perhaps the real surprise is not that so many fled but that so many stayed and fought.[26]

Grant had already seen and heard enough to know that the army was in trouble. Not yet knowing that General Buell had arrived at Savannah, Grant sent another message requesting reinforcements addressed to the commanding officer advance forces (Buell's Army):

> The attack on my forces has been very spirited from early this morning. The appearance of fresh troops in the field now would have a powerful effect, both by inspiring our men and disheartening the enemy. If you will get upon the field, leaving all your baggage on the east bank of the river, it will be more to our advantage, and possibly save the day to us. The rebel forces are estimated at over 100,000 men.

The usually calm and cool Grant must have been greatly surprised by the violence of the Confederate attack since he never overestimated the strength of his opponent as much as on this morning.[27]

Going forward to meet with his division commanders Grant soon learned that he was facing not one large battle but many small, vicious little fights between brigades and regiments scattered along a fluctuating line. He also learned that the Confederate army, as untrained and inexperienced as his own, was putting up a furious fight. William Preston Johnston wrote: "The fighting was a grapple and a death-struggle all day long, and, as one brigade after another wilted before the deadly fire of the stubborn Federals, still another was pushed into the combat and kept up the fierce assault." Until now Grant had believed that the common Confederate soldier did not really have his heart and soul committed to the rebellion, but Shiloh changed that forever.[28]

Grant visited all his division commanders and saw for himself the violence of the fighting. There was little he could do that had not been done as far as the fighting was concerned other than urging them to hold fast and arranging for the distribution of ammunition and reinforcements. He briefly met with Sherman about 10 o'clock, approving what had been done so far and informing him that ammunition was on the way. The friendship and mutual confidence in the ability of the other between Grant and

Sherman began on this terrible field. In his travels around the field that day Grant says that he was "continuously engaged in passing from one part of the field to another, giving directions to division commanders." During this time, however, he "never deemed it important to stay long with Sherman."[29]

It was critically important that McClernand and Sherman hold the right side of the field because that is where Lew Wallace's division would be arriving. Grant didn't really care for McClernand, an ambitious and politically connected general, but he was a good fighter and when he requested reinforcements Grant quickly sent him the two Iowa regiments that were still back at the river, the last of the reserves.[30]

By the late morning most of W. H. L. Wallace's division had come up to reinforce Prentiss' hard-pressed survivors in the center of the Union line. As the Confederates continued their attacks both McClernand's troops on the right and Stuart's brigade on the left were forced back and Wallace, Prentiss, and Hurlbut were gradually outflanked. Hurlbut managed to extricate his men from the closing trap but Prentiss' division and most of Wallace's troops had taken refuge in front of a patch of woods in a sunken road. Grant had told Prentiss that it was imperative to "maintain that position at all hazards," and that is what he did. This was the famous Hornet's Nest where for hours the Federal troops beat back attack after attack. The name came from the fact that the firing was so heavy that many of the men thought the sound made by the bullets whizzing overhead was the same as that of angry hornets.[31]

The Hornet's Nest was the scene of some of the most brutal fighting of the day. W.J. Worsham, a soldier in the 19th Tennessee, wrote, "The roar of musketry and artillery, the bursting of shells, and the zip and the whiz of the minnie balls rendered the scene one that beggars description. We could not drive them by our fire and to charge them seemed like going into the very jaws of death." Another Confederate who fought at the sunken road, William E. Bevens of the 1st Arkansas, wrote in his diary that he and his comrades "went forward into the hottest of the battle where the roar of musketry was incessant, and the cannonading fairly shook the ground. Men fell around us as leaves from the trees."[32]

General Bragg reported that after General Polk came forward and took over command of the Confederate troops to the left of center he moved to the right to join General Thomas C. Hindman of Hardee's corps. Hindman's troops had been forced back by heavy fire from Prentiss and Wallace. Bragg tried moving more to his right and brought up the 1st Brigade of Daniel Ruggles' division and "threw them forward to attack this same point. A very heavy fire soon opened, and after a short conflict this command fell back in considerable disorder." Twice more they attacked and twice more they were thrown back with heavy casualties.[34]

General Benjamin F. Cheatham, commanding Polk's 2nd Division, reported that he had moved toward his right and joined with General Breckinridge who had come forward near the center of the battlefield. In the early afternoon he attempted to attack the center of the Federal line near the Hornet's Nest, but was forced back by a "murderous cross-fire." Falling back and moving still farther to the right Cheatham and Breckinridge continued the assaults and their troops were "actively and continuously engaged for three hours," preventing them from joining the rest of the army in pressing the attack for the remainder of the day.[34]

For most of the late morning and afternoon the story was the same all along the Union lines: unabated fighting and death. Occasionally there was a brief lull here and there, but they seldom lasted for very long. Despite the repeated attacks the Hornet's Nest remained in Union hands, but the rest of Grant's army was steadily pushed back. Ira Blanchard's regiment occupied several positions as McClernand's troops had to fall back and to the left before the continuous Confederate attacks. He later remembered, "our guns became hot from constant firing. Ammunition had to be brought up from the rear. The ground was covered with the dead and dying. Twas a horrid sight."[35]

The situation wasn't any better for the Confederates as they hurled themselves against the Federal lines. John Jackman wrote in his diary that the

Benjamin F. Cheatham (courtesy Library of Congress).

fighting raged all day long: "Occasionally there would be a lull for a short time; but the cannon were never entirely hushed. They would break out in increased thunder, and the roar of musketry would roll up and down the lines, vibrating almost regularly from one extreme to the other."[36]

Because of the confusion brought about by the constantly changing lines both Grant and Johnston spent much of their time on the field rather than in the rear directing their armies. But where Grant mostly met with his division commanders and did what he could to keep his army fighting, Johnston took a more active role. According to General Beauregard, Johnston was "uselessly exposing his person. From where he was, he could not — nor in fact did he ever attempt to — direct the general movements of our forces." While this courageous behavior might be admirable it brought about serious consequences for the Confederate army.[37]

To the left of the Hornet's Nest, the Federal line curved back to a peach orchard where Hurlbut's division was in desperate straits. On the far left Colonel Stuart's brigade had been desperately trying to hold on to the ground between this peach orchard and the Tennessee River. If he was pushed back far enough the Confederates could swarm in behind the Federal army toward the landing, bringing disaster with them. Around noon two Confederate brigades led by James Chalmers and William H. Jackson launched a savage attack on Stuart. By two o'clock Stuart had lost one of his regiments and the 55th Illinois and 54th Ohio were being heavily pressed. Stuart called for help and the 50th Illinois, commanded by Colonel Moses Bane, came to his assistance. Bane's men had barely gotten into line when they were hit hard and in about fifteen minutes they lost 79 men and pulled back.[38]

Another of Wallace's regiments that tried to fill in the line was the 9th Illinois. They walked into a storm of bullets. When the regiment began the day there were 570 present for duty. At the end of the day the 9th Illinois could put only 70 men in line. Fighting until their ammunition gave out Stuart's two regiments finally had to fall back to the bluffs above Pittsburg Landing, the last defensive line.[39]

Stuart's withdrawal put Hurlbut in a most desperate situation. Hurlbut sent his 1st Brigade to the edge of the peach orchard with orders to wait for the anticipated Confederate attack. About 2:30 that attack began and it was as savage as any that day. Warren Olney's regiment, the 3rd Iowa, loaded and fired as quickly as they could at the advancing Confederates. When the smoke cleared "they seemed to be piled up on each other in a long row across the field.... The slaughter had been fearful." But the losses were not one sided; another of the 1st Brigade's regiments, the 32nd Illinois, began the fight with over five hundred effectives and lost at least two hundred men in minutes. The Federal troops did not know it at the time but Albert Sidney Johnston was in the front lines encouraging his troops when he was struck in the leg. His staff officers saw Johnston reeling in his saddle and rushed to his aid. Johnston's horse was guided into a nearby wood where they helped him to the ground and searched for the wound.[40]

Johnston was bleeding from a cut artery in his right leg. His aides could not find the wound, which was just below the knee, possibly covered by Johnston's boots. Staff officers tried to revive the unconscious general with brandy but there was no response. Colonel William Preston, the general's brother-in-law, also tried to revive him but to no avail. In only a matter of minutes General Johnston bled to death. The stunned staff wrapped the general's body in a blanket and took him back to Beauregard's headquarters. In such a close, desperate fight the death of the commanding general could have a devastating effect on the army so Beauregard's first order as the new commander of the army was to conceal Johnston's death from the troops.[41]

For years afterward critics would complain that General Johnston had no business being in the front lines. The job of a commanding general was to stay in the rear and make sure things were moving smoothly according to the plan of battle. At Shiloh, however, because of the unusual formation, the different units of inexperienced Confederate troops quickly became mixed together as the three lines closed up during the fighting. Johnston was concerned about how his newly formed army would perform in its first big fight and felt it was important for the morale and confidence of his troops that they see him on the field.

The day was fading away and afternoon came with little change in the fighting. The Federals in the Hornet's Nest remained in place as the rest of the Union lines were forced back toward the landing. They continued to form up at one position after another, fight for a while then fall back to another position where they made a stand for awhile. On the right and center McClernand reported that his division occupied eight distinctly different battle lines that day. Supported by fragments of Sherman's division on his right McClernand was able to beat back the frontal assaults but then had to fall back when his flanks were threatened. Hurlbut finally had to pull his men back before they were trapped. As the Confederates closed in on the flank an Iowa soldier saw "men running for their lives, men every instant tumbling forward limp on their faces, men falling wounded and rolling on the ground, the falling bullets raising little puffs of dust on apparently every foot of ground." Hurlbut was able to get most of his men away and they made their way back toward the landing, to form up again.[42]

In the afternoon Grant paid his last visit to the Hornet's Nest, now just a salient sticking far out in advance of the rest of the Union line. Grant told Prentiss to continue to hold his ground. Basically Prentiss was being sacrificed to give the rest of the army time to regroup and set up a final defensive position on the high ground in front of the landing.[43]

On the right of Prentiss' troops, W. H. L. Wallace's men still stubbornly defended their portion of the field. The Confederates had been throwing men against them for hours with nothing to show for it other than massive casualties. Finally, late in the afternoon, General Ruggles brought together all the artillery he could lay his hands on and began to pound the Federal position. By this time the rest of the army had fallen back so far that Prentiss and Wallace were practically surrounded.[44]

The Confederate artillery barrage accomplished its mission. It was obvious to Wallace that he could not hold out much longer. When he received word that the Confederates were nearing the last road to the rear he decided to try to save as many of his men as possible. Two of Wallace's regiments, the 2nd and 7th Iowa, were able to escape pretty much intact, but two other Iowa regiments, the 12th and 14th, were cut off and forced to surrender. General Wallace waited until the last to leave his position, was seriously wounded and died several days later. His wife, who had come for a visit, was at his side.[45]

With all his support now gone it was only a matter of time before Prentiss would have to surrender or see his remaining troops destroyed. With Confederates now almost encircling his command Prentiss decided around 5 P.M. that "further resistance must result in the slaughter of every man in the command." He surrendered himself and about 2,200 of his division's survivors. After the surrender there was a brief halt to the fighting.[46]

This lull was just what the Federal army needed. General Grant had ordered Colonel Webster to form all the artillery he could find in a line overlooking a ravine about a quarter of a mile from the landing. Webster was able to arrange over fifty guns in a shallow crescent formation protecting the landing. Grant also ordered Hurlbut to form a defensive line, the final Federal line, from the landing around to the right and connect with the remnants of McClernand and Sherman's troops. Out in the river the gunboats *Tyler* and *Lexington* moved closer to shore and added their heavy guns to the fire from Webster's massed artillery. The Federals were preparing for what would almost certainly be the last fight of the day.[47]

While the Federals were forming on the bluffs Nelson's division of Buell's army was coming across the river. Nelson reported that "at 5 the head of my column marched up the bank at Pittsburg Landing." The fresh troops were quickly directed to join the new line on the bluffs to the right of Webster's guns. Although the Federal commanders did not realize it at the time the day's fighting was nearly over. Another thing they did not know was how disorganized their enemy was. The triple lines of Confederates that began the attack had dissolved into a huge, uncontrollable mass of men. In addition to suffering terrible casualties many Confederates had simply left their units. As Beauregard wrote, "Straggling among the men, which had begun before noon, had now assumed fearful proportions." After the fall of the Hornet's Nest, many of Beauregard's men had believed the battle was over and went looking for food and valuables in the captured Union camps. By 6 P.M. it is probable that only about half of each army was able to continue the battle.[48]

As Nelson's men marched off the steamers at Pittsburg Landing they were greeted with an appalling scene. Thousands of men were lying under the cover of the river bluff. A soldier in the 41st Ohio remembered, "The bank down to the water's edge was covered with fugitives from the battlefield." As the Ohioans moved up the bank "the men picked their way among the crowds of runaways. All of them belonged to regiments which had been 'cut to pieces' in the battle — so they said." As he led his troops off the ships General Nelson "found cowering under the river bank when I crossed from 7,000 to 10,000 men, frantic with fright and utterly demoralized, who received my gallant division with cries, 'We are whipped; cut to pieces.'" Colonel Jacob Ammen reported that he saw "such looks of terror, such confusion, I never saw before, and do not wish to see again."[49]

When General Grant went back to the landing to meet with Buell to arrange for the transport and movement of Buell's troops to the battlefield he witnessed firsthand the panic and fear of the fugitives. He thought there were as many as five thousand stragglers hiding under the bluff who were simply "panic-stricken, most of whom would have been shot where they lay, without resistance, before they would have taken muskets and marched to the front to protect themselves."[50]

General Buell also described the scene as he came ashore at Pittsburg Landing: "The face of the bluff was crowded with stragglers from the battle.... At the top of the bluff all was confusion. Men mounted and on foot, and wagons with their teams and excited drivers, all struggling to force their way closer to the river." Buell's men would have to force their way through this mob to reach their assigned position and "with few exceptions all efforts to form the troops and move them forward to the fight utterly failed." Grant saw Buell "berating them and trying to shame them into joining their regiments. He even threatened them with shells from the gunboats near by. But it was all to no effect."[51]

Buell and his supporters always felt that they had come to the rescue of a beaten army. Grant and his supporters always denied that they were beaten and felt that Buell simply brought reinforcements to continue the fight. Based on what they witnessed at the landing it is difficult to find fault with Buell's interpretation but Grant later wrote that the scene at the landing must have "impressed General Buell with the idea that a line of retreat would be a good thing just then. If he had come in by the front instead of through the stragglers in the rear, he would have thought and felt differently." Believing that the rear of the Confederate army probably looked just as bad as the rear of the Federal army Grant suggested, "The distant rear of an army engaged in battle is not the best place from which to judge correctly what is going on in front."[52]

The crisis for the Federal army was over a little before nightfall. General Nelson's fresh troops were positioned to support Colonel Webster's guns on the bluff and most of Grant's remaining troops were moved over to the right. The Confederates were just about fought out and only a relatively small force consisting of the brigades of Chalmers and Jackson tried to continue the assault. They rushed down the ravine and up the slope on the north side right into the fire of Webster's artillery and Nelson's infantry. Again and again they came on and each time they were driven back with fearful losses. Chalmers reported that his men "struggled vainly to ascend the hill, which was very steep, making charge after charge without success."[53]

Beauregard could see for himself that his army was too exhausted and disorganized to continue the battle any longer: "It was 6 o'clock, just before sunset, when I ordered the cessation of hostilities, so that our forces could be withdrawn for rest." He also had to acknowledge that before the order reached the corps commanders "the contest had already virtually ceased on the greater portion of the field." When General Bragg received the order to end operations for the day because, as the courier said, the victory was sufficiently complete and it was pointless to expose the men to the fire of the gun-boats, one of his staff, Captain S. H. Lockett, reported that the general exploded, "My God, was a victory ever sufficiently complete?" However, Bragg also later admitted that the troops were "greatly exhausted by twelve hours' incessant fighting, without food." After the battle many would say that this decision cost the Confederates an overwhelming victory but Beauregard insisted that it was "absolutely erroneous to state that some of the subordinate commanders were preparing another concerted movement, and that it was prevented by my order to stop the fight."[54]

Just before dark two other events occurred that provided a glimpse of the new direction the battle was heading. The 24th Ohio was sent out from Colonel Ammen's brigade to reconnoiter in their front. They went out about a half-mile and could find no enemy soldiers in the area. About the same time, Grant rode over to talk to Sherman where he described the failed attack at the ravine, telling Sherman that he felt that the fighting was over for the day. In addition he told Sherman "to be ready to assume the offensive in the morning, saying that, as he had observed at Fort Donelson at the crisis of the battle, both sides seemed defeated, and whoever assumed the offensive was sure to win." For Grant this day had been only the first part of the battle and he was not about to give up.[55]

By any reasonable measure Grant's army had been beaten. More than half his army had been killed, wounded, captured, or had simply run away; they had lost their camps; they had been forced back several miles and were just hanging on to a narrow strip of land along the river. But what counted even more than all these irrefutable facts was that Grant simply refused to accept defeat. Call it an inability to see reality, call it stubbornness, or call it confidence in himself and his army, whatever the reason, Grant's will became the dominant factor in the battle.

Grant would later write:

> So confident was I before firing had ceased on the 6th that the next day would bring victory to our arms if we could only take the initiative, that I visited each division commander in

person before any reinforcements had reached the field. I directed them to throw out heavy lines of skirmishers in the morning as soon as they could see, and push them forward until they found the enemy, following with their entire divisions in supporting distance, and to engage the enemy as soon as found.[56]

At the end of that terrible day the depleted Union forces had been put back together and formed a compact line near the river. Just south of the landing, overlooking the ravine, Webster's artillery commanded the front. Hurlbut formed the remainder of his division on the right of the guns, with McClernand next and Sherman extending the line to Snake Creek. All three of these divisions had suffered heavy casualties but their commanders were present and the basic organizations were complete and they were ready to continue the battle. Neither the division of W. H. L. Wallace, which had fallen apart after losing its commander and most of its senior officers, or Prentiss' division, most of whom were captured in the Hornet's Nest, were able to form in organized units and the survivors were assigned to other divisions.[57]

The only missing piece of Grant's army was Lew Wallace's 3rd Division. What happened to Wallace that day would have been almost comical if under less dire circumstances. As he told Grant that morning his division was ready to move when ordered. Wallace stated that about 11:30 an order arrived "directing me to come up and take position on the right of the army and form my line of battle at a right angle with the river." He immediately started his troops on the Purdy Road that would take them "directly to the right of the lines as they were established around Pittsburg Landing on Sunday morning," about five miles away. Unfortunately, Wallace didn't know that the army had been beaten back and he was going in the wrong direction. Around one o'clock, Grant sent Captain W. R. Rowley to find out what had happened to Wallace's division. Rowley finally tracked Wallace down and informed him that the army had fallen back and that his division was headed to the enemy's rear where it could be cut off from the rest of the army. Wallace had to turn his division around, march back the way they had come, and take the road that ran along the river to Pittsburg Landing.[58]

Of course, all this marching back and forth took time. About 2:30, the increasingly impatient Grant sent two more officers, Colonel McPherson and Captain Rawlins, to find out what was delaying his reinforcements. They met Wallace as he was moving on the correct road and escorted him back to the landing. When Wallace finally did show up it was already dark and too late to do anything but take his place on the far right of the army. Had Wallace been able to bring his division in on the Confederate flank during the afternoon he probably would have been the hero of a great victory. Instead, for the rest of his life Wallace would be blamed for his division's absence when they were so desperately needed during the battle. While he had little good fortune as a soldier Lew Wallace later in life was the author of the novel *Ben-Hur*.[59]

With the arrival of Wallace's division the final positions of the Federal army were set for the night. Grant's troops were posted on the right of the massed artillery and as more of Nelson's division was ferried across the river they joined Ammen's brigade on the left. Two more of Buell's divisions, Thomas Crittenden's and Alexander McCook's, would arrive during the night and be on the west bank of the river by early morning. The confident Grant later wrote, "Victory was assured when Wallace arrived with his division of five thousand effective veterans, even if there had been no other support."[60]

6. First Day at Shiloh

For years after the battle there would be disagreement between Grant and Buell, and their supporters, over how much Buell's troops contributed to the eventual Federal victory. As Grant stated he felt he didn't really need Buell's troops and he just barely acknowledged them when he later wrote, "I was glad, however, to see the reinforcements of Buell and credit them with doing all there was for them to do." The fact is, however, without Nelson's fresh troops in the line and the other two divisions coming up, the chances for the Federal attack the next day to succeed would have been marginal. Of Grant's original force only about half were ready to continue the fight and even with Wallace's men they would be up against over 20,000 men that Beauregard still had available. Buell's fresh divisions would be the deciding factor in the morning.[61]

All night the gunboats *Lexington* and *Tyler* sent 8-inch shells over the heads of the Federal troops. But, since Beauregard had ordered his men to fall back, the shelling actually did little harm except to keep everyone awake. It began to rain and soon thunder and lightning joined the booming of the gunboats. It was a miserable night for the men of both armies, especially the thousands of wounded who lay out on the cold, wet ground, waiting for help. Lt. Colonel Charles Jones, of the 17th Louisiana, reported that the wounded "suffered greatly, having nothing to protect them from the rain, which fell in torrents a greater portion of the night. Many of then lay that night in pools of water two or three inches deep."[62]

William Cluett, of the 57th Illinois, later wrote that he and his comrades were soaked by the cold rain and "the brain was benumbed from cold and hunger: weak men gave way to despair, and strong men cursed the misfortunes that placed our cause in such a position." The weather also caused problems for Buell's men as they made their way to Pittsburg Landing. Colonel Daniel McCook, brother of the commander of Buell's 2nd Division, wrote that "before we reached the river the storm burst, the April rain coming down in torrents. In the gloom, blinded by lightning flashes, the troops stumbled and groped their way down the slippery banks."[63]

Even generals could not escape the misery of that night. Grant made his headquarters a few hundred yards from the river. Between his painful ankle and the lightning and thunder he was unable to rest so,

> Some time after midnight, growing restive under the storm and the continuous pain, I moved back to the log-house under the bank. This had been taken as a hospital, and all night wounded men were being brought in, their wounds dressed, a leg or an arm amputated as the case might require, and everything being done to save life or alleviate suffering. The sight was more unendurable than encountering the enemy's fire, and I returned to my tree in the rain.[64]

About four miles away Beauregard was having a much more pleasant night in one of Sherman's captured tents. Bragg and several other commanders came by headquarters that night and according to Beauregard all were satisfied with the apparent victory. "No one intimated, directly or indirectly, within my hearing or that of my staff, that the order to cease firing and fall back to the captured camps of the enemy had been given too soon, or that it should not have been given at all."[65]

In fact, the Confederate army was not in much better condition than their enemy. The army was exhausted and totally disorganized. Many men just stopped where they were, making no attempt to rejoin their units. Others spent most of the night wandering around in the rain trying to find their commands. Many men returned to the Federal camps for protection from the weather and to plunder whatever food or clothing they could find. Staff officers rode through the night desperately trying to organize the scattered army. The high command of the Confederate army was also revised. Hardee was put in command of the right, Bragg moved from the right to the left, and Breckinridge from the right to the far left flank.[66]

That night Beauregard sent a message to Confederate adjutant general Samuel Cooper:

> We this morning attacked the enemy in strong position in front of Pittsburg, and after a severe battle of ten hours, thanks be to the Almighty, gained a complete victory, driving the enemy from every position. Loss on both sides heavy, including our commander-in-chief, General A. S. Johnston, who fell gallantly leading his troops into the thickest of the fight.[67]

If Beauregard could be criticized for anything it would be overconfidence. He had been misinformed that Buell had been delayed "and that his main force, therefore, could not reach the field of battle in time to save General Grant's shattered fugitive forces from capture or destruction on the following day." For some reason the news of the arrival of Buell's troops did not reach Confederate headquarters.[68]

Later that night Sherman found Grant standing under his tree with the rain pouring down. The commanding general was quietly smoking a cigar and probably contemplating what would happen in the morning. Sherman, who had been in the thick of the fighting all day, knew as well as anyone how close the army had come to disaster. Sherman commented on the day's tough fighting and Grant agreed it had been a close thing, but was confident that they would beat the enemy tomorrow.[69]

7

SHILOH—DAY TWO

The early morning hours of Monday, April 7, were cold and wet, as were the thousands of men lying or standing in the mud wondering if they would live or die that day. For all practical purposes there was no real need for the fighting to continue. Although they had come close General Johnston, and after him General Beauregard, had failed to destroy Grant's army, and now it was too late. When General Nelson's troops marched down the gangways of the steamers that brought them to Pittsburg Landing and Lew Wallace's wayward division finally took its place in the Union line the opportunity for a smashing Confederate victory had passed. The course of the war in Tennessee would not be reversed in April of 1862.

Charles C. Briant of the 6th Indiana, who arrived at the landing during the night, wrote, "I think I give the experience of every member of the old Sixth when I say that the night of the 6th of April, 1862, was the worst night of our entire three years' service." But the weather wasn't the worst part of it. With so many thousands of wounded men needing care there were makeshift hospitals set up in various locations near the river. Briant's unit had the misfortune to be stationed next to one of these hospitals and all night long "the groans and shrieks of the wounded and dying drowned every other noise except the pelting rain."[1]

Despite the death, destruction, and misery the commanders on both sides were determined to renew the battle as soon as it was light enough to see the enemy. General Grant had combined his and Buell's troops into one line. The Army of Tennessee was formed up on the right with General Wallace's fresh division on the far right and Sherman on his left, then McClernand and Hurlbut continuing toward the left. Buell's Army of the Ohio formed the left wing with McCook on Hurlbut's left, then Crittenden with Nelson on the far left close to the river. Unlike the confused fighting of the day before, the Federal army kept these relative positions throughout the day.[2]

The Confederate forces were arranged with General Hardee's corps on the far right with Chalmers' and Jackson's brigades of Bragg's corps. Breckinridge was on Hardee's left with Brig. General Charles Clark's division of Polk's corps and Bragg's troops stationed on the far left. Between Breckinridge and Bragg was an unmanned area that was filled by General Polk and the remainder of his corps later in the morning. Many of the Confederate troops were now under a different commander than they had been on Sunday and, as one might expect, confusion reigned. Altogether Beauregard could barely put twenty thousand men in the field on Monday morning.[3]

Although both sides had suffered horrible casualties on Sunday one of the most decimated units was Patrick Cleburne's hard fighting brigade. He reported: "My brigade was sadly reduced. From near 2,700 I now numbered about 800. Hundreds of my best men were dead or in the hospitals, and, I blush to add, hundreds of others had run off early in the fight of the day before." Between battlefield losses and men gone missing, many units of both armies were at half strength or less.[4]

The terrain was the same that had been fought over the day before. On the left there was open ground in front of Nelson with some woods and brush from his right to the front of Crittenden's troops. On the right of Crittenden and the left of McCook was open ground with more woods and undergrowth between McCook and Hurlbut of Grant's army. Small ravines and creeks broke up the ground in front of Crittenden and McCook. The Confederates had placed batteries of artillery on both flanks and in the woods between Nelson and Crittenden and Crittenden and McCook, so that Buell's entire army would come under the fire of the enemy artillery.[5]

Along with the heavy artillery presence in front of Buell's troops Beauregard had placed much of his available forces on his right during the night. Although this made the Confederate right strong for defense that was not the reason the troops were massed on that side of the field. Not knowing that almost all of Buell's army was up and in line Beauregard had originally planned to complete the work of yesterday, sweep the Federals back and take Pittsburg Landing. As it so happened both sides were planning to go on the offensive this morning.[6]

The advantage would be with the Federal army today. Beauregard's troops were dead tired and more than a little discouraged that the slaughter of the day before had settled nothing. Grant's troops were in about the same condition; most of Buell's men were tired from the journey to the field and nobody had been able to sleep during the night. The main difference was obviously the addition of Buell's force and the Confederates were now seriously outnumbered. In addition, Buell's army was intact with its organization complete and its soldiers ready to show what they could do against the enemy that, it seemed to them, had clearly beaten the Army of the Tennessee the day before. Grant had ordered the advance to begin at dawn and everyone was waiting for the orders to move out.[7]

General Buell had tried to survey the terrain in front of his men overnight but the darkness and thick woods limited what he could learn and he later admitted, "It was my misfortune to know nothing about the topography in front." With the ground in question cut up by ravines and clogged with woods and heavy brush the commanders on both sides had a very limited view of the action and there was little Buell could do to guide his army. There would be little room for maneuvering and the battle would degenerate into a fight between small units making attacks and counterattacks until the soldiers on one side or the other gave in, just like the day before.[8]

As soon as it was light enough to move General Nelson ordered his division forward and the fighting soon began. At first Nelson's men had a relatively easy time of it, driving the Confederate pickets back nearly a mile until Buell decided that Nelson had gotten too far out in front and instructed him to halt and wait until Crittenden brought his division up for support on Nelson's right. As it turned out the Confederates had withdrawn from their most advanced position of the night before back to the area of the Federal camps. Soon though, the Federals ran into heavy fire from Hardee's troops, especially Chalmer's brigade, and the concentrated fire from several enemy batteries. The Federal attack on the left stalled and in places Confederate counterattacks pushed them back. About 8 o'clock, Nelson and Crittenden again advanced with Colonel William B. Hazen leading his brigade forward on the right of Nelson's division and capturing one of the Confederate batteries. Soon, however, heavy artillery fire and another enemy infantry assault forced Hazen to abandon his position with heavy losses.[9]

The fighting on his right was the first concrete evidence that General Beauregard was now facing the fresh troops of the Army of the Ohio. This knowledge totally eliminated any possibility of carrying out the original plans of continuing the attack today and finishing off Grant's troops. Instead of completing a glorious victory the Army of Tennessee would soon be fighting for its survival against nearly double its numbers.[10]

Don Carlos Buell (courtesy Library of Congress).

Colonel Ammen's brigade was stationed on the left side of Nelson's division. He reported that his instructions were "as soon as you can see to move, at dawn; find the enemy and whip him." Ammen advanced with Hazen's brigade and ran into the same stubborn resistance after the initial easy start and was checked for a brief period before being assaulted. Colonel Ammen reported, "The attacks of the enemy are frequent and desperate, but our new troops have the coolness of veterans." The left of Ammen's brigade was partially protected by a swamp but with no artillery support and no reinforcements available his troops were slowly being forced back. If Hardee's Confederates could turn the left flank Nelson's entire division would be in grave danger. A potential disaster was narrowly avoided when artillery batteries commanded by Captain John Mendenhall and later Captain William Terrill arrived on the scene and quickly silenced the enemy artillery that was supporting their attack.[11]

The Confederates, however, renewed their attack with even more violence, with "no cessation; no diminution of numbers in our front; no appearance of retreat. The fire is terrible on both sides," and both infantry and artillery were in danger of being overwhelmed. Reinforcements from both Crittenden's division and the 2nd Iowa and 15th Illinois from Grant's army were hurried over to the left and after a tough fight the Confederates were pushed back. The commander of the Sixth Ohio, Lt. Colonel Nicholas Anderson, reported that his regiment was "continually under a hot and heavy fire, supporting for the greater time Terrill's regular battery, and at one time furnishing a company to manage the guns of said battery, its men having been mostly killed or wounded." Continuing the advance Nelson's division pushed the enemy back about eight hundred yards, taking two other batteries aided by the "concentrated fire of Terrill's and Mendenhall's batteries and an attack from Crittenden's division in front."[12]

The back and forth fighting was remembered by two of Buell's soldiers. Private Elisha Stockwell Jr. of the 14th Wisconsin wrote that during the advance "we had lost all formation, and were rushing down the road like a mob." After halting for a rest at the foot of a hill they were soon counterattacked and Stockwell "saw the Rebs coming down hill just like we had." Taking cover behind a tree he began firing but as the enemy approached he looked back to see what the rest of the regiment was doing and "saw the colors going out of sight over the hill." Stockwell quickly joined his comrades as they fell back the way they had come. One of the soldiers in the 41st Ohio remembered that they quickly overcame the Confederate first line but that "the command was inexperienced, and the movement quickly went beyond control in a headlong pursuit." The Ohioans lost their formation and the enemy, "with fresh troops, seized his ground again, driving back the scattered assailants." The fighting on the left continued for hours with first one side then the other launching attacks or being forced back. Eventually, however, Hardee's outnumbered troops were gradually pushed back toward the Federal camps that had been captured the day before.[13]

While Nelson and Crittenden were fighting on the left of Buell's army, on the right General McCook, near the center of the battlefield, had his own problems. McCook's troops were the last to arrive and take their position in line and they began their forward movement later in the morning than Buell's other two divisions. Brig. General L. H. Rousseau's brigade was on the left of McCook's division and they led the advance in driving the enemy from their first lines. However, Rousseau angled a little too far to the right and as he advanced his troops separated from the right of Crittenden's division, leaving a gap that the Confederates were quick to take advantage of. Waves of enemy soldiers came against McCook's left flank and he had to dispatch Colonel August Willich's brigade and the 32nd Indiana, from William Gibson's brigade, to help stem the tide. The rest of Gibson's brigade followed close behind Willich and soon both brigades were engaged in a fierce battle.[14]

McCook's third brigade, commanded by Colonel E. N. Kirk, had just reached the field when they were thrown into the fight to relieve Rousseau's men who had to fall back to replenish their supply of ammunition. While Rousseau was absent the Confederates launched their most desperate attacks in an effort to force their way onto the flanks of Crittenden and McCook. Gibson's left regiment, the 49th Ohio, ended up fighting in several different directions to prevent their position from being overrun. Rousseau hurried his men back to the fight, bringing two regiments from Hurlbut's reserves to help bolster the line. With his flanks secured McCook pushed forward his whole division and drove the exhausted enemy troops back past Sherman's old camp. This would be the last serious Confederate attack against Buell's army. The Confederates remained on the defensive for the rest of the afternoon.[15]

About the same time Nelson's division began to move forward General Wallace opened the fighting on the far right with an artillery duel. Shortly after dawn Wallace instructed his artillery to open fire on an enemy battery stationed on a bluff behind a deep ravine. "From its position and that of its infantry support, lining the whole length of the bluff, it was apparent that crossing the hollow would be at a heavy loss" unless the enemy battery could be forced back or destroyed. Two of Wallace's batteries set up a crossfire on the enemy position and shortly after the Confederates fell back.[16]

Once the way was clear Wallace's men stepped out and the hill was gained "almost without opposition." Wallace got a little too far ahead of the rest of the army and had to wait for them to come up so as not to expose the flanks of his and Sherman's forces. General Sherman said that he was waiting for the sound of General Buell's guns before ordering the advance. Before the real fighting began Sherman had fragments of several regiments move forward and occupy their former camps, which was done amidst light skirmish fire. About 10 A.M. the firing on Buell's front increased dramatically and Sherman decided the time was right for his own troops to move out and attack the enemy. With Wallace on his right Sherman moved slightly toward the left to close on McClernand's right flank. The line was formed facing south with Colonel Ralph Buckland's brigade in front and Colonel Stuart's brigade to the right in the woods. Sherman gave the order and his line "advanced slowly and steadily, under a heavy fire of musketry and artillery."[17]

Moving forward to the road to Corinth Sherman remarked that he witnessed "for the first time the well-ordered and compact columns of General Buell's Kentucky forces, whose soldierly movements at once gave confidence to our newer and less disciplined men." Sherman also saw Willich's troops advance into a strongly defended wooded area, "Then arose the severest musketry-fire I ever heard, and lasted some twenty minutes, when this splendid regiment had to fall back." This wood was about 500 yards east of the Shiloh Meeting-House and according to Sherman, "It was evident that here was to be the struggle. The enemy could also be seen forming his lines to the south."[18]

General McClernand moved out that morning and after adjusting his lines several times and waiting for his artillery to come up and give covering fire he reached his old camp. With his skirmishers out front McClernand "advanced through my camp obliquely to the southwest, thus retaking it." The entire right wing of the Federal army was now advancing and off to McClernand's right, "at the same time Generals Sherman and Wallace were seen advancing in the same direction." McClernand's troops ran up against a log breastwork and the enemy fire was so heavy that the 53rd Ohio was forced to fall back. The right side of McClernand's force was stalled until Colonel C.

Carroll Marsh "opened an oblique fire, which immediately dispersed the enemy in that direction, leaving us in possession of my recaptured camp."[19]

While McClernand was taking back his camp Confederates were moving into the gap between his left and the right of Buell's army, enabling them to attack both flank and front of both forces. McClernand turned his troops to the left and met the advancing enemy in what he described as "one of the severest conflicts" of the entire two days. General Cheatham, whose troops were fighting near the center, under General Polk, described the fighting in his area as "the most hotly contested I have ever witnessed."[20]

At first McClernand drove the Confederates back but enemy reinforcements brought his advance to a standstill: "Our position at this moment was most critical and a repulse seemed inevitable." McClernand requested help from General McCook, who sent over the Louisville Legion from Rousseau's brigade. As McClernand reported, "Extending and strengthening my line, this gallant body poured into the enemy's ranks one of the most terrible fires I ever witnessed. Thus breaking its center, it fell back in disorder."[21]

By mid-day it was obvious that the disparity in numbers was having an effect. Slowly the Confederates were being pushed back, although they fought for every foot of ground, frequently launching local counterattacks that broke temporary holes in the Federal lines. Like the fighting on Sunday, today's battle became a series of small but desperate fights occurring all over the battlefield. A soldier from Wisconsin, James K. Newton, wrote to his parents about what he experienced: "All I know about it is that we drove the rebels & they drove us & then we would drive them again. We were advancing & retreating all the time until afternoon, before we got the upper hand of the Secesh."[22]

Most of the Federal units had experiences similar to that of one of Wallace's new regiments, the 76th Ohio. All day they moved forward though swamp and dense woods, up and down hills and ravines, always receiving enemy fire. They would run to a position then fall down flat as enemy bullets whizzed overhead. "Then up and double quick forward, sometimes filing to the left, then to the right," wrote Charles Miller, "everywhere taking advantage of deviations of the ground to shelter us from the shot and shell, pressing onward while the enemy gradually fell back, contesting every inch of ground."[23]

The Confederate commanders could see that by mid-afternoon they were fighting in a lost cause. One of Beauregard's staff officers, Thomas Jordan, recorded, "Our losses were swelling, and the straggling was growing more difficult to restrain." Around two o'clock Governor Isham Harris, of Tennessee, who had served as a volunteer on General Johnston's staff and continued working for Beauregard, commented that it seemed as if the fighting was going badly and "whether there was not danger in tarrying so long in the field as to be unable to withdraw in good order."[24]

Shortly after talking with the governor Jordan had an opportunity to speak with Beauregard. "General, do you not think our troops are very much in the condition of a lump of sugar thoroughly soaked with water, but yet preserving its original shape, though ready to dissolve? Would it not be judicious to get away with what we have?"

"I intend to withdraw in a few minutes," replied Beauregard.[25]

Even though Beauregard had decided to pull his remaining troops out of the battle it would take time for the orders to filter down to the men on the field. Over on the left of the field about three o'clock General Grant brought two regiments forward and attacked one of the last Confederate positions, breaking their line and forcing them to retreat. Grant later wrote, "I knew the enemy were ready to break and only wanted a little encouragement from us to go quickly and join their friends who had started earlier."[26]

Continuing to advance in the center General McClernand engaged the enemy on his left where he and McCook attacked from front and flank, "driving the enemy in the direction his center and left were already retreating." Falling back the Confederates halted and tried to make a stand but McClernand and McCook again combined to drive them back. McClernand's last fight of the day was in a wood south of the original campsites. The Confederates had stationed several batteries of artillery "which were used with most annoying effect until silenced by McAllister's battery of 24-pounder howitzers." The Federal center followed the retreating Confederates for a while but the artillery engagement was the last real fighting of the day. It was about 4 P.M. and the Federal troops had advanced about three miles. McClernand reported, "So protracted, obstinate, and sanguinary a battle has rarely occurred. In magnitude and importance it is second to but few."[27]

General Wallace reported that even though the fighting in his front was "grand and terrible" the Federal troops within his view prevailed and "about 4 o'clock the enemy to my front broke into rout and ran through the camps occupied by General Sherman on Sunday morning." Over to the left Sherman remembered that earlier "Rousseau's brigade moved in splendid order steadily to the front, sweeping every thing before it," and that after driving the enemy back "at 4 P.M. we stood upon the ground of our original line; and the enemy was in full retreat."[28]

General Beauregard was able to pull most of his army back while localized assaults prevented the Federals from launching an attack that could have been devastating while the army was in motion. Breckinridge moved first, setting up a rearguard position, with the

Pierre G. T. Beauregard (courtesy Library of Congress).

troops on his flanks closing the gap to show a united front. After Breckinridge was safely away Polk's corps fell back, then Hardee and finally Bragg. The retreat was accomplished with little loss and Beauregard claimed, "There was no flurry, no useless haste, among the men or officers; and even the stragglers dropped into line and rejoined their command as they passed." While the rest of the army continued to the rear, Breckinridge set up a strong position near the intersection of the Pittsburg and Hamburg roads, where they had camped Saturday night before the battle began. In addition to successfully withdrawing his army from the field of battle Beauregard commented on a non-event that would be the cause of much consternation in the days following the battle: "No pursuit whatsoever was attempted by the enemy."[29]

There is no question that Grant should have pressed the retreating enemy, but he had very little to chase Beauregard with. Grant's soldiers were exhausted and disorganized and, while technically in overall command of the combined armies, Grant was hesitant to issue orders to General Buell. On Monday evening Grant wrote to Buell saying, "When I left the field this evening my intention was to occupy the most advanced position possible for the night with the infantry engaged through the day," and initiate a pursuit of the enemy with cavalry and reinforcements that were expected to arrive at anytime. "The great fatigue of our men," Grant continued, "would preclude the idea of making any advance to-night without the arrival of the expected re-enforcements." Grant wanted to "feel on in the morning with all the troops on the outer lines" and wait until a sufficient force of cavalry, infantry, and artillery could be organized to make a proper pursuit. Grant was also under orders from General Halleck instructing him not to "advance beyond Pea Ridge, or some point which we can reach and return in a day. General Halleck will probably be here himself to-morrow." Staying within a day's march meant, for all practical purposes, there would be no pursuit.[30]

The simple fact was that Grant's army could not pursue the retreating Confederates and if Buell's could that would be good, but Grant would not order it. Grant was treating Buell more like an equal than a subordinate, which is illustrated in a message on the 8th. General Sherman went out that morning with two tired brigades to verify that the enemy was retreating but didn't get close enough to do anything other than view the abandoned equipment scattered along the roadside. Grant thought that if the Confederates were pressed they might be forced to abandon much of their artillery and other equipment so he inquired of Buell, "Will you be good enough to order your cavalry to follow on the Corinth road and give two or three of your fresh brigades to follow in support."[31]

By allowing Beauregard to fall back without being pursued Grant missed a golden opportunity to deliver a knockout blow to the Army of Tennessee. While it is certainly true that the Federal army was in poor condition, the Confederates were in even worse shape. On the morning of the 8th Braxton Bragg reported to Beauregard while on the road to Corinth:

> Our condition is horrible. Troops utterly disorganized and demoralized. Road almost impassable. No provisions and no forage; consequently everything is feeble.
> It is most lamentable to see the state of affairs, but I am powerless and almost exhausted.
> Our artillery is being left all along the road by its officers; indeed I find but few officers with their men.

>Relief of some kind is necessary, but how it is to reach us I can hardly suggest, as no human power or animal power could carry wagons over this road with such teams as we have.[32]

That same morning General Breckinridge, still in charge of the rear guard, put the situation plainly when he wrote to Bragg, "My troops are worn-out, and I don't think can be relied on after the first volley." Also on the 8th Bragg wrote, "if we are pursued by a vigorous force we will lose all in the rear. The whole road presents the scene of a rout, and no mortal power could restrain it."[33]

In his *Memoirs*, General Grant gives his reasons for not ordering the pursuit that might have destroyed the Army of Tennessee:

>After the rain of the night before and the frequent and heavy rains for some days previous, the roads were almost impassable. The enemy carrying his artillery and supply trains over them in his retreat, made them still worse for troops following. I wanted to pursue, but had not the heart to order the men who had fought desperately for two days, lying in the mud and rain whenever not fighting, and I did not feel disposed to positively order Buell, or any part of his command to pursue. Although the senior in rank at the time I had been so only a few weeks. Buell was, and had been for some time past, a department commander, while I commanded only a district. I did not meet Buell in person until too late to get troops ready and pursue with effect; but had I seen him at the moment of the last charge I should have at least requested him to follow.[34]

Grant was not the kind of commander to hesitate or worry about the feelings of subordinates or his troops when there was a clear opportunity for a crushing blow against the enemy, as he proved over and over during the war. He did follow orders, however, and one factor in not making a serious pursuit of Beauregard's almost defenseless army was contained in a wire from General Halleck on the morning of the 9th: "I leave immediately to join you with considerable re-enforcements. Avoid another battle, if you can, till all arrive. We then shall be able to beat them without fail." That would seem to be pretty clear instructions not to force another fight by attacking the enemy, including their rear guard.[35]

The casualties for what had been the greatest battle ever fought in North America would shock both the North and South. Grant and Buell together lost 1,754 killed, 8,408 wounded, and 2,885 missing, for a total of 13,047. In his report Beauregard puts his total casualties for both days at 1,723 killed, 8,012 wounded, and 959 missing, for a total of 10,694.[36]

The end result of the fighting around Shiloh Meeting-House was a Union victory. They had beaten off a surprise attack and the enemy was forced to retreat. It would take time but as the war continued the significance of turning back this Confederate invasion of Tennessee would become apparent. It had been a close thing and the lack of clear gains coupled with the horrible casualties would bring down a storm of criticism on both commanders and some of their chief subordinates.

8

SHILOH'S AFTERMATH AND SUBSEQUENT CAMPAIGNS

The fighting was over but there was always much to be done in the aftermath of a great battle. The thousands of men who had fled from their commands had to be rounded up and brought back to their units. Thousands of wounded had to be cared for and those that could move be transported north. The officers who had proven they were unfit for command had to be sorted out and sent home. And, worst of all, burial details had to go out and gather up the dead. Judson Bishop of the 2nd Minnesota was on one of those details: "We had to perform the burial of about 4,000 men, gathering them from every part of the battle field." Some died quickly and showed no signs of suffering but for others their pain was evident. When possible the Union dead were identified by comrades and given a little dignity with crudely marked graves. But many of the Federal dead and nearly all the Confederates were unknown, and "they were laid side by side in long pits and were covered, a hundred or more, in one grave."[1]

This battle was over and consistent with his businesslike approach to war Grant was ready to move on. Grant sent a message to Halleck on April 9 informing him that through various sources he had determined "the enemy intend concentrating upon the railroad at and near Corinth all the force possible," even pulling troops away from locations they previously guarded. Lobbying to keep the pressure on the enemy Grant wrote, "I do not like to suggest, but it appears to me that it would be demoralizing upon our troops here to be forced to retire upon the opposite bank of the river and unsafe to remain on this many weeks without large re-enforcements."[2]

Also on the 9th Grant issued orders to put his own house in better order. Most of Grant's troops were still poorly disciplined and relatively untrained in military affairs. Pickets were set up at all roads and approaches to the camps with orders to limit travel in and out of the camps to only those, military and civilian, who held proper authorization. Grant also issued orders to try to improve the sanitary condition in the camps, always a cause of much sickness, and prohibited the indiscriminate firing of weapons, something that the new soldiers enjoyed doing.[3]

While Grant was trying to pull his battered army together General Halleck was on his way to take command of the armies in the field and he would soon be receiving powerful reinforcements. Major General John Pope was headed toward Pittsburg Landing to join forces with Grant and Buell. Pope's army was now available because he had just won an impressive victory on the Mississippi River. Even though the Confederates evacuated the fortress at Columbus in February they were still able to control the flow of shipping on the Mississippi. Just fifty miles downriver was the fort at Island No. 10, with a garrison of about 7,000 men and over fifty powerful guns. General Halleck sent Andrew Foote's fleet of gunboats to shell the fort from the river while Pope's newly created Army of the Mississippi moved in from the west.[4]

The fleet of seven ironclads and ten mortar boats bombarded the Confederate fortifications from long range doing negligible damage. Pope, however, was able to gain control of the riverbank below the island, which meant that the only supply route left open to the fort was through a difficult swamp along the Tennessee shore. During a severe thunderstorm on April 4 the *Carondelet* ran past the guns of the fort with another gunboat following two nights later. With the gunboats providing cover for his troops Pope crossed the river and Island No. 10 was completely cut off from supplies and reinforcements. On April 7 the garrison surrendered and General Pope captured over 5,000 prisoners and all the guns and equipment in the fort. He had achieved a major success with very low casualties. When compared to the slaughter at Shiloh that had apparently negligible results it is little wonder that John Pope won acclaim in the North, and from Halleck.[5]

General Halleck arrived at Pittsburg Landing on April 11 and immediately assumed overall command of all the Federal forces leaving Grant and Buell in command of their respective armies. On the 13th he issued an order thanking the troops and their commanders for the hard-fought victory noting, "The soldiers of the great West have added new laurels to those which they had already won on numerous fields." The next day Halleck wrote to Grant complaining about the condition of his troops: "Immediate and active measures must be taken to put your command in condition to resist another attack by the enemy. Your army is not now in condition to resist an attack. It must be made so without delay." Grant immediately responded with his own orders to improve discipline and drill: "division commanders will see that as many hours per day as is consistent with the health of the men be devoted to drill and that company commanders excuse no soldier from any part of his duties."[6]

On April 21 General Pope arrived at the landing with 30,000 men. Henry Halleck was now in command of a huge force consisting of three separate armies: the Army of the Ohio, commanded by General Buell; the Army of the Tennessee, commanded by Grant; and Pope's Army of the Mississippi. The question now was what would he do with it.[7]

Although the muskets and cannon were silent, the battle with words was just beginning. Long after the event, Grant wrote that the battle of Shiloh "has been perhaps less understood, or, to state the case more accurately, more persistently misunderstood, than any other engagement between National and Confederate troops during the entire rebellion." In General Sherman's opinion, "Probably no single battle of the war gave rise to such wild and damaging reports."[8]

General Grant's refusal to panic after the reverses of Sunday's fighting and, of course, the addition of thousands of Buell's troops, enabled him to turn what might have been a devastating defeat into victory the next day. In the days and weeks immediately after the fighting ended, however, public opinion in the North focused only on the calamity of the first day and the appalling number of casualties. Grant's status as conquering hero quickly fell to that of drunken incompetent. There are several reasons for this swift change in public opinion. Obviously the horribly high number of casualties was a factor, especially in the Midwest. The vast majority of the men killed were buried on the field and in the rest of the North all most people saw were lists of names in newspapers. But, in the Midwest, the thousands of wounded and maimed men who were streaming north from Pittsburg Landing were their sons and husbands, they were real men whose suffering was obvious, and they were very visible. Shiloh was the first of the major battles of the Civil War and the huge number of casualties shocked the public in both the North and South. Soon, unfortunately, after Fredericksburg, Stone's River, and many other bloody battles, the public would get used to the horrible number of casualties that resulted from Civil War battles.

Another source of information that guided public opinion were newspaper reports. Newspaper reporters during the Civil War were a very diverse group. Some tried to do a good job and report accurately on what they saw or heard from reputable sources. Other reporters, many others in fact, simply wrote what they wanted to based on rumor, hearsay, and lies from officers trying to promote themselves or their views, and sometimes they just made up stories their editors wanted to print. Shiloh produced reports that shocked and angered the people back home. General Sherman would later write that it was "publicly asserted at the North" that the army was completely surprised Sunday morning, "that the rebels caught us in our tents; bayoneted the men in their beds; that General Grant was drunk; that Buell's opportune arrival saved the Army of the Tennessee from utter annihilation, etc." Much of this was based on rumors and stories from men who had been the first to run away.[9]

It didn't take long for others to join in the criticism. Many of the officers in the army were prominent in their hometowns and those that had taken to their heels when the fighting broke out had to offer up some excuse, other than they were afraid for their lives. It was easy to say that the army had been surprised because of poor leadership and they could do nothing but follow their men to the rear, trying to rally them to continue the fight at another location.

One way or another the stories and rumors spread until a storm of criticism fell on Grant and some of his officers. That most of these stories were clearly untrue didn't seem to matter much; there was enough that was true to allow people to think that perhaps even the most outrageous stories could be believed.

General Grant had his defenders, however, and they ranged from common soldiers all the way to the top. George W. Squier wrote to his wife in July that he had read "in some of the journals of the day statements that Gen. Grant's army were completely routed, demoralized, and on the point of falling into the hands of the enemy. But that is false. We were not 'whipped,' though driven back." Squier thought that many of these statements were probably made by wounded men who didn't know what they were saying and believed the situation was worse than it really was or "by cowards who left their comrades to face the danger and win or loose the battle as they could and themselves take refuge beneath the riverbank, or by men who wished to detra[c]t from Grant's army." In addition, "Many of the letter[s] were from our sister state Ohio (they doubtless felt mortified at the disgraceful conduct of some of their troops)."[10]

Grant's relations with General Halleck were not negatively affected by the criticism. Halleck had no problem blaming a subordinate when deserved or even just to protect his own reputation. But he stuck by Grant as far as the most damning complaint, that of the army being surprised. On May 2 in a letter to Secretary Stanton, Halleck stated, "The newspaper accounts that our divisions were surprised are utterly false." And on June 15 he wrote, "I am satisfied from a patient and careful inquiry and investigation that all our troops were notified of the enemy's approach some time before the battle commenced." Halleck also informed the secretary that the number of missing was much less than originally reported as many men were just separated from their units and eventually reported in: "There seems to have been a morbid desire on the part of some of our officers to make the loss of their particular commands much greater than it really was." Perhaps this helped to excuse why many of those officers left the field.[11]

Grant also received support from the one man who mattered most, President Lincoln. Journalist and Republican political leader Alexander K. McClure saw that the sentiment in Washington and around the North for Grant's removal "surged against the President from every side, and he was harshly criticized for not promptly dismissing Grant or at least relieving him from his command." In a private meeting with the president, McClure tried to convince him to remove Grant. McClure remembered that Lincoln was silent for a while then said "in a tone of earnestness that I shall never forget: 'I can't spare this man; he fights.' That was all he said, but I knew that it was enough, and that Grant was safe in Lincoln's hands against his countless hosts of enemies."[12] General Grant was not the only army commander to be condemned by the public after the battle. Giving his life bravely leading his men generally exempted Albert Sidney Johnston from any blame for the final results of the battle, but as the number of casualties and how near the Confederates were to a smashing victory became known, General Beauregard came in for serious criticism for not finishing off the desperate Federal army on Sunday. The truth was, however, that the Confederate army was in no condition to continue the fight Sunday evening and if anything Beauregard could have been censored for keeping his disorganized and exhausted troops on the field so they could be beaten the next day.[13]

The terrible fighting at Shiloh was a wake-up call to many in the North who thought the rebellion, given time, would collapse on its own. One of those who had a profound change in their view of the war was Ulysses Grant. "Up to the battle of Shiloh I, as well as thousands of other citizens, believed the rebellion against the Government would collapse suddenly and soon, if a decisive victory could be gained over any of its armies." It seemed to Grant that the victories of Fort Henry and Fort Donelson, the loss of Kentucky and much of Tennessee, and the opening of many miles of the Mississippi River to Federal ships, should have been enough. But when the Confederates were able to form such a large army, not only to hold a defensive line, but "assumed the offensive and made such a gallant effort to regain what had been lost, then, indeed, I gave up all idea of saving the Union except by complete conquest."[14]

By late April it was time for that conquest to continue. Halleck had changed the organization of his force into four parts: right, center, left, and a reserve. Major General George H. Thomas was put in command of the right wing consisting of his own division and the Army of the Tennessee less the divisions of McClernand and Lew Wallace. General Buell commanded the remainder of the Army of the Ohio in the center and General Pope led his Army of the Mississippi on the left wing. McClernand was named commander of the reserve with his and Wallace's divisions. Grant was to command the right wing and reserve and act as second in command of the entire army.[15]

Of course, not everyone was happy with this new arrangement, especially Buell and Grant. Buell complained because his command had been reduced in size and told Halleck, "You must excuse me for saying that, as it seems to me, you have saved the feelings of others very much to my injury." Grant was unhappy since he saw his position as second in command as a mere figurehead with no real work or responsibility. Grant's previous problems with Halleck must have contributed to his feelings of being put on the shelf with a meaningless job and title. It became so bad that Grant was actually packing up his personal belongings in advance of going on leave, from which he did not intend to return, when General Sherman convinced him to stay with the army.[16]

General Halleck either didn't realize how unhappy Grant was or, more likely, had such a low opinion of Grant's ability he didn't care much if Grant left the army. On May 12 Halleck wrote to Grant that he was "very much surprised, general, that you should find any cause of complaint in the recent assignment of commands. You have precisely the position to which your rank entitles you." Halleck was also surprised that Grant could suspect him of trying to injure his subordinate's reputation since for several months "I have done everything in my power to ward off the attacks which were made upon you. If you believe me your friend you will not require explanations; if not, explanations on my part would be of little avail."[17]

The first target of Halleck's massive force, around 90,000 to 100,000 men, was the railroad center at Corinth, Mississippi, where Beauregard had halted his army. By the end of April the Federal army started out on a slow march to Corinth. They only made a few miles a day because General Halleck ordered entrenchments put up at every stop; he was not going to be surprised by a Confederate attack. Of course this also meant that the Federals could do little to force a fight with Beauregard's troops. Grant called the march to Corinth "a siege from the start to the close." Day after day they slowly made their way south, a massive wave of blue that moved irresistibly toward its goal. Halleck was not interested in fighting; his plan was to maneuver Beauregard out of Corinth or, if he had to fight, surround and lay siege to the town with his overwhelming number of troops.[18]

The Confederate high command considered Corinth such an important point that when Beauregard begged for reinforcements with the warning, "If defeated here, we lose the Mississippi Valley and probably our cause," troops were rushed to Corinth from as far away as the Atlantic coast. By far the largest addition was about 15,000 men from Arkansas under the command of Earl Van Dorn. By early May Beauregard had around 60,000 men under his command, although thousands of them were still recovering from wounds received at Shiloh or too sick from the terrible conditions in the town to be effective.[19]

The Confederates in and around Corinth faced more danger from sickness than from Union bullets. There was not enough food for all the troops that had poured into the little railroad town. The water from the wells was so foul and muddy that many of the horses refused to drink it and the men had to hold their noses to get it down. The combination of bad food, bad water, and excessive heat caused thousands of men to come down with dysentery and typhoid. To have any chance to recover the sick had to be transported out of town to farms and villages farther south. Some men were cared for by compassionate citizens and recovered or at least passed in relative comfort, but many hundreds died along the roadside. Beauregard lost almost as many men from sickness at Corinth as were killed in battle at Shiloh.[20]

Despite the loss of so many men to sickness and the obvious disparity in the size of the opposing forces, Beauregard planned to stay and fight. He built up a long line of fortifications north of the town and decided to wait for Halleck to send out small reconnaissance forces that the Confederates could strike quickly and overwhelm. On May 3, Pope pushed a division forward to Farmington, about four miles from Corinth, had a minor little fight and was ordered to pull back. Again on the 8th Pope moved past Farmington and sent two divisions close to the enemy works and again he was ordered to return to the rest of the Federal lines. Both times Beauregard tried to spring a trap with Bragg attacking from the front and Van Dorn coming around to hit the flank. Both times Van Dorn was unable to get into position quickly enough and the opportunity to damage or destroy a modest Union force was missed. Halleck's army continued to move forward, gradually closing in around the town and throwing up earthworks that the Confederates were not strong enough to break.[21]

By late May it was obvious to Beauregard that he would have no chance to successfully attack the Federal forces as Halleck was simply being too careful to give his enemy any opening to exploit. Beauregard called a council of war to discuss the options, of which there were none. It was clear that it would be suicide to launch a major attack against the well-entrenched Federal army. To remain in Corinth would probably bring about the destruction or surrender of the entire army. The unsanitary conditions in the town would only get worse and eventually Halleck could surround the town, cut the lines of retreat, and pound the army into submission. There was only one real choice and that was to abandon Corinth now while the army could still get away to fight another day.[22]

On May 30 the Confederates began to slip out of Corinth. Beauregard organized a brilliant retreat by tricking Halleck into thinking that reinforcements were actually arriving on the trains that were removing his troops to safety. The subterfuge worked so well that on the morning the Confederates were evacuating the town Halleck had his troops in line of battle expecting to be attacked. When the Union troops marched into Corinth they found nothing was left behind; every man and piece of equipment had been removed. Although Halleck had achieved a significant strategic victory, almost bloodlessly, Grant and many other officers were disappointed in the results of the campaign. It was difficult for some to understand "how the mere occupation of places was to close the war while large and effective rebel armies existed."[23]

General Beauregard moved his army about fifty miles south to Tupelo and believed the successful evacuation of Corinth and preservation of his army was as good as a victory. Back in Richmond, however, Jefferson Davis saw things a little clearer and was angered by the loss of such an important rail center. Not long after moving the army to Tupelo, Beauregard took a leave of absence due to ill health and Davis replaced him with an old friend, Braxton Bragg.[24]

After a somewhat reluctant pursuit of the retreating enemy, Halleck reversed his order that formed the different wings of the army and Grant, Buell, and Pope resumed their original commands. Grant was granted permission to make his headquarters at Memphis, the western edge of his district, but far from Halleck who remained in Corinth. At Memphis, Grant found that Southern sentiment was rampant but felt he would soon have the situation under control. He was too optimistic.[25]

Protecting the railroads was of major concern throughout Tennessee. All too often time and money would be spent repairing a road only to see it quickly destroyed by Confederate cavalry or guerrillas. Fighting against organized troops was one thing, and every soldier accepted the risk of battle. But when farmers or store clerks go out at night and shoot guards and burn supplies, that is a different story and a harsh response should be no surprise. Grant issued General Orders, No. 60, on July 3:

> The system of guerrilla warfare now being prosecuted by some troops organized under authority of the so-called Southern Confederacy, and others without such authority, being so pernicious to the welfare of the community where it is carried on, it is ordered that wherever loss is sustained by the Government collections shall be made by seizure of a sufficient amount of personal property from persons in the immediate neighborhood sympathizing with the rebellion to remunerate the Government for all loss and expense of collection.
>
> Persons acting as guerrillas without organization and without uniform to distinguish them from private citizens are not entitled to the treatment of prisoners of war when caught, and will not receive such treatment.[26]

Back in June, General Halleck wrote to Secretary Stanton complaining about all the damage being done to bridges and railroad equipment by guerrillas and Confederate sympathizers: "It will probably take some time to clean out the guerrilla parties in West Tennessee and North Mississippi, and I shall probably be obliged to use hemp pretty freely for that purpose."[27]

On July 11 General Halleck received orders to report to Washington "as soon as he can with safety to the positions and operations within the department under his charge." Finally tired of General McClellan's delays, President Lincoln promoted Halleck to "command the whole land forces of the United States, as general-in-chief." Later, when his shortcomings became obvious, many would wonder why the president entrusted the war effort to Henry Halleck. The fact is, however, that in the summer of 1862 the armies under Halleck's command had produced a nearly unbroken string of victories. These victories, along with his acknowledged ability as an administrator, made him appear to be the perfect choice to take overall command.[28]

Soon after Halleck arrived in Washington he sent Grant instructions authorizing heavy-handed action against Confederate supporters. He wanted West Tennessee and North Mississippi cleared of all organized enemies and, "If necessary take up all active sympathizers, and either hold them as prisoners or put them beyond our lines. Handle that class without gloves, and take their property for public use." In addition Halleck authorized Grant to take all the forage he needed from enemy sympathizers, for "It is time that they should begin to feel the presence of war on our side."[29]

The treatment of civilians in Tennessee at this stage of the war was not particularly harsh; it would get much worse as the war dragged on. For most of the Federal soldiers the South really was like another country. The farms looked different than back home, the people spoke different than back home, and of course, there was silent and sometimes open hostility to the occupying troops. It was not surprising, therefore, that the Federal soldiers began treating the people as foreigners who deserved a bit of rough treatment now and then. And, if the officers did not actually condone this treatment, few tried to stop it.

Still down in Tupelo, where he was reorganizing and refitting his army, General Bragg had received frequent letters and personal visits from prominent Kentuckians who had been assuring him that most of their fellow citizens were loyal to the South and only required the presence of Confederate troops in their state to publicly display that loyalty. Bragg was intrigued by the idea of winning back lost territory for the South and by the end of July began to gradually move his troops north.[30]

Colonel Philip Sheridan was the first to report that the Confederates were on the move. On July 29 he wrote to General Gordon Granger: "The enemy have been and still are moving in large numbers to Chattanooga, via Mobile and Montgomery, concentrating at Rome, Ga." Bragg took a roundabout route toward Chattanooga so as to make use of rail transportation and not exhaust his men in the sweltering summer heat.[31]

General Bragg decided to take bold action while most of the Federal forces were engaged in repairing railroads and garrison duty. After concentrating his forces at Chattanooga, he would march north into Kentucky. Confederate forces under Generals Sterling Price and Van Dorn would keep Grant's troops occupied and Bragg felt that he could maneuver around General Buell, who was busy re-building railroads. If all went as planned Bragg might win back much of the territory that had been lost during the first half of the year.[32]

General Buell had left Corinth in mid–June to move on Chattanooga. The ever-cautious Buell took his time, advancing slowly, repairing the Memphis and Charleston Railroad and battling enemy cavalry raids as his army moved forward. This time, however Buell was a little too cautious and a little too slow and the government was losing patience with him. Halleck wrote on August 12: "I deem it my duty to write to you confidentially that the administration is greatly dissatisfied with the slowness of your operations." Halleck advised Buell that he had already been asked to find someone to replace Buell but had been able to put off any change, so far. Closing with another warning Halleck wrote, "The Government will expect an active campaign by the troops under your command, and that unless that is done the present dissatisfaction is so great your friends here will not be able to prevent a change being ordered."[33]

Taking advantage of the spread out Federal forces Bragg headed north from Chattanooga in mid–August with about 30,000 men and General E. Kirby Smith moved north from Knoxville with about 20,000 troops. After defeating a patched together Union force at Richmond, Kentucky, on August 30, Smith continued his advance and occupied Lexington on September 2 and the state capital of Frankfort the next day. While the Confederate forces were advancing into Kentucky, General Buell decided to defend Nashville.[34]

Also at the end of August there was confusion in the command structure of the

Army of the Ohio. On August 24, Halleck informed Buell that General Thomas, who had just been made commander of the new Department of the Tennessee, would also replace him as the commander of the Army of the Ohio. Thomas, however, refused to accept the command arguing that Buell should remain in command until the current crisis was over. Unknown to both officers was that almost immediately after issuing the order removing Buell from his command the War Department countermanded that order. This confusion over who was in command must have had a negative effect on Buell's subordinate commanders and possibly on his own confidence.[35]

While the Federal army regrouped in Louisville there occurred an incident that would have repercussions beyond the actual event. General William Nelson, who had led Buell's troops onto the field at Shiloh, got into a heated argument with General Jefferson C. Davis. Things got out of hand and Davis shot and killed Nelson in front of many witnesses. Davis had powerful friends and was never prosecuted for murdering a Union general. The loss of General Nelson would be felt in the coming battle.[36]

As Buell's army moved toward Louisville, Bragg had an opportunity to attack the Federal flank, if he moved quickly. Instead, Bragg refused to attack the larger Federal force and wanted to wait until he could combine his and Smith's forces before accepting battle. Smith was still near Lexington and Bragg planned for the armies to meet at Bardstown, which was about thirty-five miles from Louisville. While the troops were converging the two commanders attended the inauguration of Kentucky's new Confederate governor, a purely symbolic gesture that it was hoped would rally popular support to the southern cause. It did not.[37]

While the Confederate commanders were engaged in political showmanship General Buell was finally moving. After receiving message after message from Washington to do something, including a complaint from Halleck that "I fear that here as elsewhere you move too slowly. Bragg in the last two months has marched four times the distance you have," Buell moved his army of about sixty thousand men the first week of October. Bragg's smaller army was spread out between Louisville and Bardstown and a feint by one of Buell's divisions toward Frankfort fooled Bragg into keeping about half his army there. Buell continued advancing with the rest of his army and confronted the other half of Bragg's force, commanded by Bishop Polk, who quickly retreated from the much larger Union force.[38]

Confusion reigned on both sides as Polk took up a defensive position near Perryville and the fighting began on October 8. Phil Sheridan sent his division forward in the morning and drove back the defenders while the rest of the Federal army moved into position. Bragg, still believing that most of the Federal army was near Frankfort, ordered Polk to launch an attack that afternoon. Two veteran Confederate divisions hit two Federal divisions, one of which was composed of new troops, and sent them reeling backward. Meanwhile Sheridan had captured high ground to the northwest and held on despite several assaults, saving the army from being flanked and possibly destroyed.[39]

In his headquarters Buell knew nothing about the back and forth fighting or that he was facing only half of Bragg's army until it was too late in the day to mount a serious assault. Bragg, finally realizing that he was outnumbered nearly two to one, pulled his troops back to unite with Kirby Smith's force. When Buell launched his attack the next morning the enemy was gone.[40]

Nothing really was accomplished by the battle of Perryville other than to increase casualty lists. Both commanders missed opportunities to earn victories through slow movement and mismanagement. The armies stayed close for a few days but neither commander could find an opening to exploit and Bragg soon began to retrace his route back to Knoxville and Chattanooga. Criticized by both the public and government Bragg was called to Richmond but managed to convince President Davis that he had done everything he reasonably could and remained in command of the Army of Tennessee.[41]

General Buell was also roundly criticized for not moving quickly enough to at least harass the Confederates as they retreated. "Neither the Government nor the country," Halleck wired, "can endure these repeated delays. Both require a prompt and immediate movement toward the accomplishment of the great object in view—the holding of East Tennessee." In reply to the dispatches urging him to move faster Buell replied that he could not outmarch his supply lines. Back came a wire from Halleck: "The capture of East Tennessee should be the main object of your campaign. You say it is the heart of the enemy's resources; make it the heart of yours. Your army can live there if the enemy's can." All the orders did no good, Buell just was not the type of general who could lead an army on an important campaign and live off the land while pursuing the enemy. When he revealed that he intended to return to Nashville the government had had enough and Buell was replaced with Major General William S. Rosecrans.[42]

While the campaigning was going on in Kentucky, General Sterling Price led a modest army against the railroad center of Iuka in northern Mississippi. After being rebuffed there, Price joined his remaining troops with those of Earl Van Dorn and on October 3 they attacked the main Federal position at Corinth commanded by General Rosecrans. Both armies numbered a little over twenty thousand men and after two days of terrible fighting the Confederates were thrown back with heavy casualties. It was this victory that propelled Rosecrans into his new command.[43]

9

ROSECRANS TAKES COMMAND

Major General William S. Rosecrans took over the newly named Army of the Cumberland at the end of October. Most of the army was concentrated around Louisville and after a few days of re-supplying the army left for Nashville the first week of November. The army's command structure was reorganized into three wings, or grand divisions: the right was commanded by Major General Alexander McD. McCook; the center by General Thomas; and the left under Major General Thomas L. Crittenden; with the cavalry commanded by General D. S. Stanley.[1]

General Rosecrans was forty-three years old, a native of Ohio who graduated fifth in his West Point class of 1842. He missed serving in the Mexican War and left the army in 1854 to have a go at civilian life where he had modest success at best. When the war began he first served in West Virginia under McClellan and later under his classmate Grant in Mississippi. The victory at Corinth propelled Rosecrans to national attention and promotion to command the Army of the Cumberland.[2]

Rosecrans was generally a genial and relatively friendly person, but had a hair-trigger temper that could put him into a rage in an instant. He also had an unfortunate tendency to speak his mind, to anyone, before thinking through potential consequences. He was almost universally considered an excellent strategist and had an amazing capacity for work, frequently working into the early morning, sleeping for a few hours, and then going back to work. The energy that allowed him to work so much also brought about angry outbursts and serious mood swings, especially when under the enormous pressure of combat. Rosecrans' courage under fire was well known and his men liked and respected him, giving him the nickname "Old Rosey."[3]

With his army concentrated around Nashville it was imperative that the troops be rested and properly supplied. Many of the soldiers were ill and most were badly trained and poorly equipped. These problems had to be addressed before any movement could take place. In addition, the army's supply line was exposed to frequent raids by Confederate cavalry and guerrillas and Rosecrans refused to move until he had built up a large enough reserve of provisions so that if the supply line were cut he would still be able to remain in the field. The Louisville and Nashville Railroad was improved and put into much better working order by the end of November and as Rosecrans reported,

"From November 26 to December 26 every effort was bent to complete the clothing of the army; to provide it with ammunition, and replenish the depot at Nashville with needful supplies."[4]

After only six months in Washington Henry Halleck had apparently forgotten what it was like to campaign in Tennessee in the winter, with rain and mud everywhere, because in early December he began to bombard Rosecrans with requests, quickly followed by demands, that he take action. On December 4 Rosecrans was informed, "The President is very impatient at your long stay in Nashville. If you remain one more week at Nashville, I cannot prevent your removal.... The Government demands action, and if you cannot respond to that demand some one else will be tried."[5]

William S. Rosecrans (courtesy Library of Congress).

Rosecrans was not a man to back down when he believed himself right and he replied to Halleck that same day:

> I have lost no time. Everything I have done was necessary, absolutely so; and has been done as rapidly as possible. If the Government which ordered me here confides in my judgment, it may rely on my continuing to do what I have been trying to — that is, my whole duty. If my superiors have lost confidence in me, they had better at once put some one in my place and let the future test the propriety of the change. I have but one word to add, which is, that I need no other stimulus to make me do my duty than the knowledge of what it is. To threats of removal or the like I must be permitted to say that I am insensible.[6]

The next day Halleck wrote back to Rosecrans with more details. "The President is greatly dissatisfied with your delay.... He has repeated to me time and again that there were imperative reasons why the enemy should be driven across the Tennessee River at the earliest possible moment." Halleck believed that diplomatic pressures were at the root of the president's impatience. It was feared in Washington that Great Britain and France were close to intervention in the war on the side of the Confederacy and it was imperative to show the world that the Federal government was actually winning the war and recovering what had been considered Confederate territory. "You will thus perceive," Halleck continued, "that there is a pressure for you to advance much greater than you can possibly have imagined." Pressure or not, Rosecrans would not advance until he was ready.[7]

About thirty miles southeast of Nashville, in Murfreesboro, Braxton Bragg was happy to let Rosecrans take all the time he wanted before beginning a new campaign. Bragg had asked for and received permission to advance and he moved the army up from Tullahoma in November. Bragg expected Rosecrans to spend the winter in Nashville gathering strength for a spring campaign. In mid–December Jefferson Davis made the long trip from Richmond to inspect the Army of Tennessee and consult with Bragg about future movements. He also succeeded in convincing Bragg to send General Carter L. Stevenson's division, over eight thousand men, to reinforce the army defending Vicksburg. Joseph E. Johnston, recently appointed to overall commander in the west, was opposed to weakening Bragg's army but his advice was ignored.[8]

Bragg had reorganized his army and was able to get authority from Davis to merge Edmund Kirby Smith's Army of Kentucky into his own forces. The new army, now called the Army of Tennessee, was made up of three corps. General Polk commanded one corps with divisions led by Benjamin Cheatham, Jones Withers, and John Breckinridge. General Hardee commanded a corps consisting of divisions commanded by Simon Buckner, soon to be replaced by Patrick Cleburne, and Patton Anderson. Smith's army became a corps with the divisions of Carter Stevenson (soon to leave for Vicksburg) and John McCown.[9]

Since there were no signs that the Federals were going to move before spring Bragg spread his army around to ease the search for food and to protect a wider area. Polk's corps stayed near Murfreesboro and McCown's division was sent to Readyville, about twelve miles east. Hardee's corps was stationed on the Shelbyville and Nolensville pike, about twenty miles southwest between Triune and Eagleville. Bragg also sent most of his cavalry out to do as much damage as possible to Federal communications.[10]

Staying put in the Murfreesboro area and remaining on the defensive was the best policy for Bragg right now. The area around the army was productive farmland and Bragg could get plenty of supplies for his own forces and a surplus to send to other parts of the Confederacy. Also this December the Confederate cavalry was causing trouble in several places. Major General Joseph Wheeler's troopers were providing a solid screen between Nashville and Murfreesboro so that Bragg could rest assured he would not be surprised by any sudden Federal movements. Nathan Bedford Forrest had taken his cavalry west to disrupt railroad communications and Daniel Morgan's cavalry was up north raiding in Kentucky. Bragg had less than 40,000 men at Murfreesboro and was perfectly content to sit there undisturbed through the winter.[11]

By the end of December the Army of the Cumberland had been re-fitted and re-supplied. Rosecrans was aware that Stevenson's division had been sent to Vicksburg and that most of Bragg's cavalry was out raiding in West Tennessee and Kentucky, too far away to assist the main army. Rosecrans decided, "In the absence of these forces, and with adequate supplies in Nashville, the moment was judged opportune for an advance on the rebels."[12]

On Christmas night Rosecrans met with his commanders and gave them the word: tomorrow they marched. With the Confederates spread out as they were Rosecrans developed a plan that would bring all his forces into action. McCook, with three divisions, would advance down the Nolensville Pike toward Triune. Thomas would advance on McCook's right down the Franklin and Wilson pikes and threaten Hardee's right, then move over to Nolensville. Crittenden was to advance down the Murfreesboro Pike toward La Vergne. McCook was to attack Hardee with Thomas to support him if needed. If Hardee was beaten or retreated back to join the rest of Bragg's forces Crittenden was to advance past La Vergne while Thomas attacked the enemy's left and McCook moved around to the rear.[13]

December 26 dawned cold and cloudy and it was soon raining, typical winter in Tennessee. McCook's troops started out right on schedule at 6 A.M. Moving down the Nolensville Pike the Federals quickly ran into Confederate cavalry detachments but Jefferson C. Davis's division, in the lead, easily brushed them aside and by dark he was close to Triune with the remainder of McCook's force a little farther north at Nolensville. General Thomas began his march about an hour after McCook and met no resistance other than the terrible roads.[14]

General Crittenden also had a successful first day as he moved down the Murfreesboro Pike with Colonel Robert Minty's cavalry in the lead. Maybe ten miles out from Nashville they ran into a detachment of Wheeler's cavalry and a sharp but brief fight occurred between the enemy cavalry and Crittenden's lead division, commanded by Brig. General John M. Palmer. Palmer's men ended the first day's march just outside La Vergne and the Confederates pulled back during the night. One of Palmer's men, Corporal Eban Hannaford, of the 6th Ohio, wrote that they marched through "a steady, persistent, pouring rain, whose every component drop seemed to find a malicious delight in splashing in our faces."[15]

It rained all night and the morning of the 27th there was fog so thick that McCook said it "prevented us from seeing 150 yards in any direction." McCook's men moved forward about two miles when they encountered the enemy, this time in force. The fog was still so heavy that "friend could not be distinguished from foe." So McCook called a halt because "I did not deem it prudent to advance until the fog lifted, and I ordered the command to halt until the work could be done understandingly." While the Federal advance was stalled Hardee was able to use the cover of the fog to continue moving east toward Murfreesboro.[16]

While McCook was waiting for the fog to lift General Thomas slowly moved through the mud to the area around Nolensville. Crittenden was instructed to hold his position until McCook reached Triune and did not move forward until about 11 A.M. When they moved through La Vergne Corporal Hannaford noted that the village was "a mass of ruins. Half a dozen of the smaller houses still remained; blackened chimneys standing lone and desolate above gray beds of ashes — significant monuments of the folly and crime of rebellion — told the fate of the rest." Advancing against relatively light resistance Crittenden's men reached Stewart's Creek where they found the only bridge on fire. General Thomas J. Wood reported, "It was a matter of cardinal importance to secure possession of the bridge, as its destruction would entail much difficulty and delay in crossing the stream, and, perhaps, involve the necessity of constructing a new bridge." The 3rd Kentucky charged over the bridge forcing back the enemy rear guard and was able to extinguish the fire and save the bridge.[17]

Around 1 P.M. the fog had lifted enough for McCook to continue his advance.

The afternoon was spent skirmishing with cavalry until they reached the outskirts of Triune where the enemy made a stand on the far side of Nelson's Creek backed by artillery. It was almost dark and with the rain falling heavily and the bridge destroyed McCook halted his troops for the day. The Confederate defenders retired during the evening and General Johnson's division forded the creek and repaired the bridge.[18]

There was little movement on the 28th as McCook sent General Willich out on a reconnaissance mission during which he learned that Hardee had made his way to Murfreesboro. Crittenden pretty much stayed where he was waiting for supplies to be brought forward and Thomas moved forward to Stewart's Creek. Also on the 28th General Bragg began to concentrate his forces in front of Murfreesboro. Bragg reported that being "fully aware of the greatly superior numbers of the enemy it was our policy to await attack."[19]

General Hardee's men arrived during the night of the 27th and the next morning Bragg went to work placing his army in line to wait for Rosecrans' approaching army. General Polk was assigned to the left about two miles from Murfreesboro and west of Stone's River. General Withers' division would be in front with Cheatham in the second line and Breckinridge on the right. General Hardee's troops would form on the right east of the river with Buckner's division in front and Cleburne in support. McCown's division and Jackson's brigade were held in reserve and cavalry guarded both flanks.[20]

There were several problems with this position. The first and most obvious was having the line split by Stone's River. Although the water was currently very shallow if the heavy rains continued it could rise rapidly and divide the army. In addition, there were several points beyond the line that were higher than the Confederate line and if the enemy occupied them, which they surely would, their artillery would have excellent positions to fire on Bragg's troops. It would turn out, however, that Bragg had no intention of staying in this position and waiting for Rosecrans to attack.[21]

The Federal advance continued on the 29th. General McCook moved slowly over bad roads arriving at Wilkinson's Cross-Roads that evening, about five miles from Murfreesboro. Crittenden reported that he halted at dark with Wood and Palmer in line of battle and heavy forces of the enemy in sight, "it was evident they intended to dispute the passage of the river and fight a battle at or near Murfreesborough." During the afternoon Rosecrans received word from General Palmer that he was in sight of Murfreesboro and that the enemy was running. Crittenden received orders to advance one division and occupy the town. General Wood was ordered forward but it was already dark and he protested that it was "hazarding a great deal for very little to move over unknown ground in the night," and suggested that the order be ignored. General Palmer also objected and Crittenden suspended the order until he could check with Rosecrans, who canceled the advance. While this debate over orders was taking place Col. Charles C. Harker's brigade was involved in a sharp skirmish and followed the enemy across the river with Col. Miles S. Hascall's brigade right behind. When word came that the order to advance had been cancelled these troops were brought back as they would have been too exposed where they were.[22]

On the night of the 29th Crittenden posted his troops facing east from McFadden's Ford on the left across the Nashville & Charleston Railroad line and the Nashville

Pike. General Thomas was posted from Crittenden's right south across the Wilkinson Pike. McCook's troops were farther back, west of Overall Creek, well over a mile from the left of Thomas S. Negley's division on Thomas's right flank. Rosecrans called McCook to headquarters after midnight to make sure McCook was aware of the position of the army and how important it was for him to close up on Thomas as early as possible the next morning. Rosecrans was very fortunate that Bragg did not launch an assault on the 29th since most of the Federal troops were just getting into position but the Confederate commander was unaware of the gap between Thomas and McCook.[23]

On the morning of the 30th McCook brought his troops forward with Sheridan's division in the lead. There was some heavy skirmishing between Sheridan's men and McCown until about noon when Sheridan arrived in line and joined with Negley's right. Soon Davis and Richard Johnson brought up their divisions on Sheridan's right and the Federal line was now complete with the left at Stone's River and moving mostly south across the Nashville Pike and the Wilkinson Pike to a wooded area just south of the Wilkinson Cross-Road and near the Franklin Pike.[24]

William J. Hardee (courtesy Library of Congress).

The opposing lines were close enough that each commander knew what the other was doing, at least along the front lines. As McCook came forward and extended the Federal line south Bragg became concerned that his left would be outflanked if Rosecrans decided to launch an attack. Bragg ordered Hardee to bring Cleburne's division over to the left and leave just Breckinridge on the far right of the line and still east of the river. McCown's division was already south of the Franklin Pike and only about three hundred yards from McCook's line. After dark Cleburne brought his troops in behind McCown.[25]

Bragg had decided to attack on his left at first light on the 31st, sending McCown and Cleburne, supported by Gabriel C. Wharton's cavalry, against the right flank of the Federal army. Polk was to begin his attack after the left had swept past the Federal flank and gotten into their rear. Nearly 30,000 men would be assaulting the Federal right and center. Breckinridge would hold his position on the far right to protect the approach to Murfreesboro. Bragg wanted both Hardee and Polk to move their forces with a right-wheel. In other words, with Polk's right as the pivot the Confederates were to swing to the right like a door swinging open. While this might seem like a fine idea to sweep away the enemy troops, under battle conditions this type of movement was very complicated and liable to create confusion among the advancing units.[26]

In an unusual twist, while Bragg was making plans to attack Rosecrans' right, Rosecrans was making plans to attack Bragg's right. During the evening of the 30th Rosecrans was issuing instructions to his wing commanders for an attack at dawn the next day. On the Federal left Crittenden was to send Horatio Van Cleve and Wood's divisions across the river to overwhelm Breckinridge. With a nearly two to one advantage Van Cleve and Wood should be able to smash the Confederate right and swing in behind the rest of their line, trapping Breckinridge between themselves and Thomas. Thomas would advance in the center along the Nashville Pike and McCook was to hold the Confederate left in place so they would not send reinforcements to aid Breckinridge.[27]

General Thomas had informed Rosecrans he had information that it appeared Bragg was going to attack McCook the next morning. Rosecrans discounted this possibility since he expected to launch his attack first. He did, however, caution McCook to refuse, or pull back, his right and face more south to form a perpendicular line to protect his flank. Rosecrans explained to McCook that if he were attacked he had to hold his position, or at worst, fall back slowly making sure to keep the enemy from getting in his rear. Rosecrans asked McCook if he could hold his ground for three hours to which McCook responded, "Yes, I think I can."[28]

On the right of the Federal line McCook had the divisions of Sheridan and Davis in line facing the enemy with Johnson's division in reserve. During the evening General McCook moved his troops bringing Johnson up on Davis' right. On the far right Brig. General Edmund Kirk's brigade moved up slightly to take advantage of some higher ground and August Willich's brigade moved to the right and rear of Kirk facing south "to avoid the possibility of my right being turned by anything like an equal force."[29]

10

SLAUGHTER AT STONE'S RIVER

The last day of 1862 began cold and windy. General McCook's troops were up before dawn and began leisurely cooking their breakfasts. There seemed to be no hurry to prepare for battle since it was well known that the main fighting would be over on the left and all they had to do was hold their ground. Over on the far left Crittenden's men were also up and making their coffee. The battle would begin after they had eaten although a few units were already moving toward the river.[1]

On the far right, General Willich had his brigade ready for battle. Taking cover in a wooded area looking out onto an open field, they were facing south near the intersection of Gresham Lane and the Franklin Pike. But General Kirk's brigade to the left was located in the center of a wood, not on the edge where they could fire more effectively. The angle where the brigades of Willich and Kirk met was at the Franklin Pike.[2]

About 6:30 A.M. McCook's men were surprised to hear gunfire coming from their right. The Federal pickets fired a round or two and then came running back to the main lines, with hordes of Confederates close behind. McCown's division hit the angle where Kirk and Willich were joined. In minutes Kirk's brigade collapsed. They tried to put up a fight, and Kirk even sent the 34th Illinois forward to give time for his artillery to pull back but they were overwhelmed by Brig. General M. D. Ector's Texas brigade and Brig. General Evander McNair's Arkansas brigade. Kirk was wounded and taken prisoner and the survivors of his brigade fled as quickly as they could.[3]

Willich's brigade was hit just as hard as Kirk's and since they were posted toward the south their left flank was exposed when Kirk's men fled. Actually, General Willich was not present when the fighting began; he was conferring with his division commander, General Richard Johnson. Colonel William Gibson of the 49th Ohio was in temporary command and there was little he could do. Gibson reported, "The lines of General Kirk soon yielded to an assault which no troops in the world could have withstood. Most of our field officers were disabled or dismounted by the enemy's fire." Lt. Colonel Charles T. Hotchkiss, commander of the 89th Illinois, reported that his men were making their coffee when firing was heard on Kirk's front, "almost instantly followed by the men of his brigade rushing in confusion and indiscriminately through

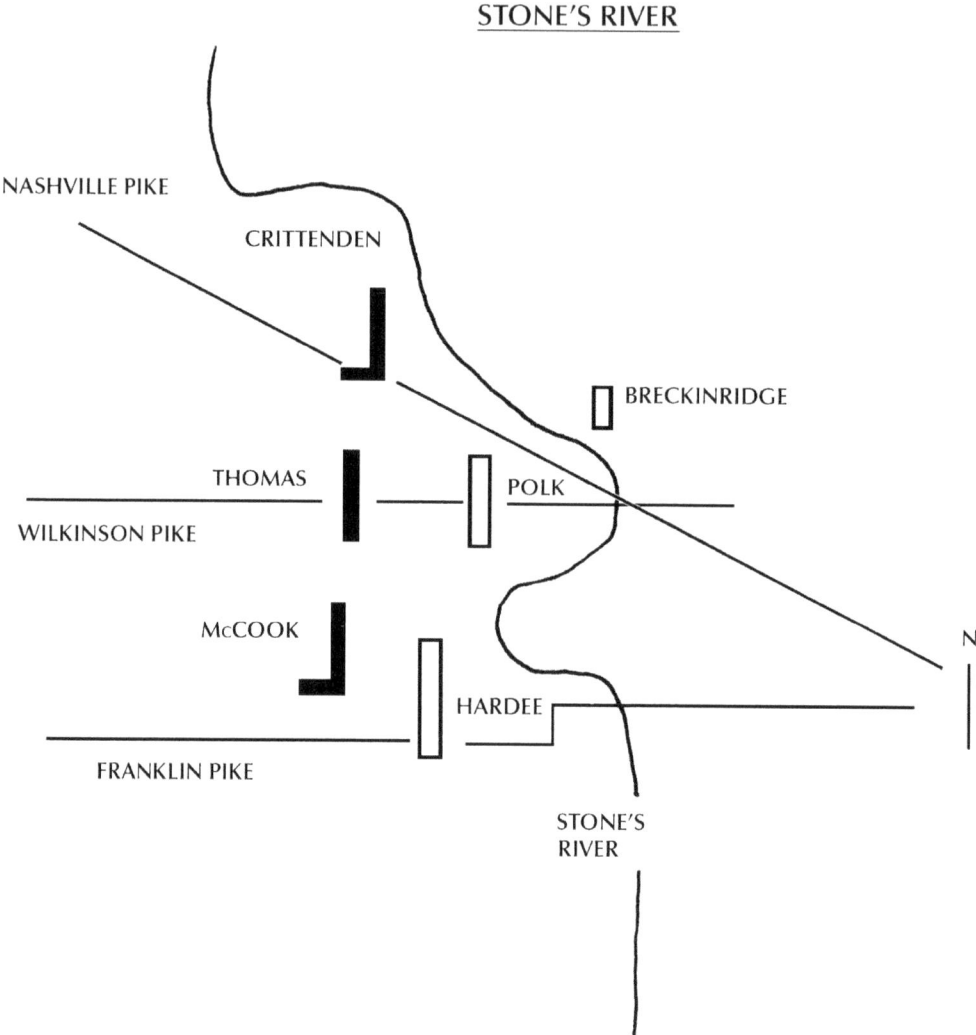

our ranks and over my men, closely followed by a heavy column of rebel infantry." While returning to his brigade Willich's horse was killed and he was taken prisoner. The survivors of the brigade had to flee or be cut off as McCown's troops, with Cleburne right behind, continued forward.[4]

In only about half an hour McCown's troops had achieved a remarkable triumph. Two Federal brigades had been smashed and the right flank and rear of the Federal army lay open and exposed. There was little to stop McCown and Cleburne from rolling up the rest of Johnson's division and hitting Jefferson C. Davis' division in the same manner. The only problem for the Confederates was that McCown's division moved to far to the south and as the broken Federal brigades fled west two of his brigades, commanded by James E. Rains on the outside and Ector in the center, followed them instead of wheeling to the right, as they should have done to keep in formation. General Cleburne's division, following McCown, did pivot to the right as planned and Cleburne soon found "I was, in reality, the foremost line on this part of the field, and that McCown's line had unaccountably disappeared from my front."[5]

Lt. Colonel William Berry's 5th Kentucky was in the reserve of Johnson's division when the front lines were attacked. He was preparing his men to move up when "to my utter amazement, a mass of the enemy appeared, moving obliquely upon my right flank." The reserve regiments tried to swing around to face the onrushing enemy but as Berry reported, "The right of the division was completely crushed in, and I had no connection, consequently no protection, here. It was soon manifest that I must fall back or be isolated."[6]

When Cleburne's troops approached the right of Davis' division they found the going

Patrick Cleburne (courtesy Library of Congress).

much tougher than it had been. The firing on the right had alerted Davis and he quickly moved Colonel Sidney Post's brigade, on the right, back so that it faced the advancing enemy and had an open field in its front. Davis' division was hit as hard as Johnson's had been but his men were more prepared and put up a good fight. Davis reported "the enemy commenced a heavy and very determined attack on both Carlin's and Woodruff's brigades. The conflict was fierce in the extreme on both sides. Our loss was heavy and that of the enemy no less." Soon, however, Colonel William Carlin's right flank came under heavy pressure and he had to withdraw. This uncovered Colonel William Woodruff's flank, forcing him to pull his men back before they were cut off.[7]

Colonel Philemon Baldwin's brigade was Johnson's reserve, positioned a few hundred yards behind Post. They deployed in a field with the front line taking cover behind a rail fence and were joined by some of the remnants of the other brigades of their division. About 7:30 A.M. both Brig. General St. John Liddell and McNair attacked Baldwin's brigade. Liddell's men came across the field in front of Baldwin and were met with a hail of bullets that forced them to take cover in the field. While bullets were flying in the field McNair's troops came up on the left and after pushing aside the remnants of Kirk's and Gibson's brigades began to come in on Baldwin's flank. Liddell's men now rose and moved forward and in minutes Baldwin's brigade fell apart and joined the other Federal fugitives on the way toward the Wilkinson Pike.[8]

Over on the far left of the line Rosecrans had joined Crittenden to observe the attack on Breckinridge. When the fighting began on the right they heard the firing but had no idea how serious it was until the thunder of artillery and crackling of thousands of muskets grew louder and louder. About an hour after the attack began, Rosecrans received information from one of McCook's staff that the right was being violently attacked and assistance was needed. Rosecrans did not know how quickly the far right had collapsed. He later wrote, "Soon after, a second officer from General McCook arrived, and stated that the right wing was being driven — a fact that was but too manifest by the rapid movement of the noise of battle toward the north." With McCown and Cleburne steadily advancing there was a very real possibility that unless a new line was formed and stabilized the entire Federal army was in great danger.[9]

With most of the men from Johnson's and Davis' divisions on their way north Philip Sheridan's division was now the Federal right. As the Union survivors fled toward the Wilkinson Pike McCown's Confederates were right behind. After quickly pushing aside a weak Federal stand in front of the road McCown turned his brigades east to rejoin the main fight. Crowds of Federal soldiers continued on their way north, pursued by Wharton's cavalry and Liddell's infantry. Even if they could be rallied, these Federal troops were already too far away to continue to participate in the battle and Liddell should have left the pursuit to the cavalry. In fact, Liddell pursued the fleeing enemy too far and took his brigade out of the battle for several hours.[10]

After Colonel Woodruff had fallen back General Sheridan had to quickly reposition his units. Brig. General Joshua Sill had been killed and his brigade, now commanded by Colonel Nicholas Greusel, fell back to the Harding farm where they joined Colonel Frederick Schaefer's brigade of Negley's division. The terrain was relatively flat which allowed a good field of fire. When Arthur Manigault's Confederate brigade came forward they ran into a terrible fire from artillery and muskets and were forced to fall back. Colonel Francis Sherman of the 88th Illinois wrote that his men held their fire until the enemy came within one hundred yards then, "like the grass before the scyth of the mower, the ranks of the enemy went down as that volley went crashing and tearing through their ranks." George Maney's brigade came up to support Manigault and they took their time discussing the situation before deciding to advance again with Manigault on the right and Maney to his left.[11]

By this time, about 9 A.M., Cleburne and McCown were moving to Sheridan's right and rear as they approached the Wilkinson Pike. Sheridan realigned his brigades with Colonel George W. Roberts' brigade as the anchor on the original line and Greusel and Schaefer drawn back to meet the enemy coming in from the right. The Federal guns were also repositioned and when Manigault and Maney launched their combined attack, supported now by John C. Vaughn's brigade, they were just as hard hit as the first time, only from different locations. Sheridan succeeded in organizing a solid line of three brigades along one of the best roads on the battlefield, supported by ample artillery. Manigault and Maney advanced and, "suffering and losing many men from the fire on our right which we could not return," they were again forced back.[12]

Sheridan's men were well positioned and probably could have held their lines for quite a while but the fighting on this front was about to take a radical turn. The Confederate brigades that had first attacked the far right had turned back toward the main lines and were now approaching Sheridan's position. Sheridan could see for himself the wave of enemy troops coming down on his division from the right and rear. Forced to again realign his brigades Sheridan swung both Greusel and Schaefer back to a point just north of the Wilkinson Pike where they took a position in a heavily wooded area, forming a near right angle with Roberts who remained south of the Wilkinson Pike. It was a good position with open fields in front of Greusel and Schaefer and limestone boulders at the edge of the wood to provide cover for the men.[13]

After sweeping everything before them so far this morning the victorious Confederates of McCown and Cleburne approached Sheridan's new line from the west and, as Sheridan reported, "one of the bitterest and most sanguinary contests of the day occurred." In a series of attacks that lacked any coordination, first S. A. M. Wood, then Johnson, and finally Lucius Polk advanced against the Federal lines only to face a hailstorm of bullets and artillery fire that forced each brigade back in turn. Manigault also launched another attack against Roberts' brigade, sending his Alabama and South Carolina regiments rushing forward, and was again repulsed with heavy loss.[14]

Cleburne and McCown had been unable to organize a coordinated assault against Sheridan's line so Manigault sought help from the unit to his right. General Patton Anderson's brigade had been waiting all morning for the opportunity to join the fight and they were ready. He sent two of his regiments to help Manigault attack Roberts, but the assaulting force was mowed down by artillery fire. As Anderson reported his "ranks were shattered and broken by grape and canister."[15]

Anderson called up the rest of his brigade and advanced against the Federal artillery by moving through a patch of woods. Heavy fire from the guns pounded the attackers and quite a few were injured by falling branches. When Anderson's men emerged from the woods into a cornfield rifle fire from the brigade of Colonel Timothy R. Stanley ripped into the Mississippians, causing heavy losses. Finally, after courageously advancing about halfway across the field, Anderson's men were compelled to drop to the ground for protection. With almost no cover in the field most of them just tried to lie still and let the bullets fly harmlessly over their heads. Eventually word to fall back was passed along the line and Anderson's brigade withdrew.[16]

A fresh Confederate brigade commanded by Brig. General Alexander P. Stewart now came forward and hit the left side of Sheridan's line. The Federal right flank held on, but shortly after this assault began Colonel Roberts was killed, his next in command was also shot, and the brigade became leaderless. In addition, ammunition was running low and there was none available to replenish the supply. It was time to pull back and save his men from being needlessly sacrificed. While the rest of the division fell back Schaefer's brigade was ordered by Sheridan to "fix bayonets and await the enemy," which they did until they were able to follow the rest of the division. Several pieces of artillery were lost but around 11 o'clock Sheridan's division was able to retire to the northeast and form a new line at the Nashville Pike near the right of Palmer's division.[17]

Lovell H. Rousseau's division of Thomas's command had been in reserve when he received an order from Rosecrans to move forward to the right and rear of Sheridan.

Colonel John Beatty's brigade and Lt. Colonel Oliver H. Shephard's brigade held Rousseau's front line while Colonel Benjamin F. Scribner's brigade deployed to their rear as a second line. Two of General Van Cleve's brigades, Colonel Samuel Beatty's and Colonel James P. Fyffe's, were dispatched to the far right along the pike and Colonel Charles Harker's brigade with James Morton's Pioneers were sent to Rousseau's right. After Sheridan's withdrawal both Rousseau and Negley, to the left, were hit hard in front and flank by brigades from both Cheatham's and Withers' Confederate divisions. McCown's division advanced directly toward the Federals, and his three brigades outflanked their right.[18]

General Rousseau quickly realized it would be impossible to hold his position and decided to withdraw. Shephard's brigade of regulars was engaged in a sharp fight in the trees with Rains' Confederates, but this ended when Rousseau ordered a withdrawal. Scribner's brigade, also engaged, fell back, but John Beatty's men never received the order to retire. Continuing the fight they stopped the advance of Lucius Polk's brigade, which had come up to join the assault. Polk suffered heavy losses, and his attempt to outflank Beatty's right was unsuccessful. Finally realizing that his brigade was fighting alone John Beatty decided that he had to retreat. Pressured by Polk's renewed advance, the Federals scrambled out of the woods and ran across a large open cotton field that bordered the Nashville Pike on the west.[19]

The new line taking shape along the Nashville Pike would be the final Federal position. The retreating was over. As General Rains' men pushed on in pursuit of the Federals they moved into the southern edge of the cotton field. In the distance, about five hundred yards away, along the pike, the Federals were massing troops for their final stand and there were several batteries of artillery stationed on high ground to the left of the field. As Rains advanced the guns immediately opened fire and as the Confederates got closer the Federal infantry began to send volleys of bullets into Rains' lines. General Rains was killed and his troops were forced to fall back and take cover in the woods.[20]

Around noon, General Ector's brigade advanced through the cotton field on the left of Rains' brigade. Ector's Texans ran into large numbers of Federal troops positioned farther up the pike that were well supported by artillery. The Confederates advanced well into the cotton field and engaged Morton's Pioneer brigade and Samuel Beatty's brigade out in the open. With no support on his flanks Ector had to withdraw after a fierce, close-range fight. Samuel Beatty's men and Colonel Fyffe's brigade pursued Ector's men back into the woods. Both Confederate attacks on the new Federal line along the Nashville Pike had been bloodily repulsed and it seemed that finally Rosecrans' right, although it was almost doubled back on the Federal left, was going to hold.[21]

The original Union line was still in place from the Wilkinson Pike, along the west side of McFadden Lane, to the Nashville Pike. Concerned about being attacked on his right by these Federal troops General Cleburne had not advanced too far north after Sheridan fell back. He let his exhausted men take a brief rest in the open field north of the Wilkinson Pike. General Wood's brigade, with only five hundred men left, was sent back to the rear to guard trains, and Johnson's brigade was sent north to find and retrieve Liddell's wayward brigade. Vaughn's brigade and Polk's men followed to Johnson's right. Cleburne knew that the key to winning the battle at this point was finding and getting past the Union right flank to gain the Nashville Pike and cut Rosecrans off from his base.[22]

Near McFadden Lane, Negley's brigades still held out and now Anderson's and Stewart's brigades of Withers' division renewed their attacks. The Confederates had set up several batteries of artillery on high ground east of the lane and these guns poured a concentrated fire on Stanley's brigade, posted on the right. When the brigades of Manigault and Maney advanced on Stanley's flank he was forced to fall back.[23]

Negley's next brigade in line, commanded by Colonel John Miller, was able to hold its position a little longer under the hail of shot and shell, but soon the enemy infantry came up on their right. With his ammunition running out Colonel Miller reported, "The enemy was advancing on my right flank, and on my left, and the fire in front was no less destructive." There was no point in sacrificing his command and it was obvious it was time to pull his men out from this unequal fight. He got the men out safely but lost the artillery since most of the horses had been killed and the ground was too soft for his men to pull the guns out by hand.[24]

The last Federal unit holding the line along McFadden Lane was Brig. General Charles Cruft's brigade of Palmer's division. Around 9 A.M., James Chalmers' Mississippi brigade advanced over an open space of several hundred yards straight at Cruft's men. Chalmers' formation was split by the Cowan house, whose burned ruins stood on a piece of ground directly in front of the brigade. While the right regiments veered off toward the Round Forest at the junction of the Nashville Pike and McFadden Lane, the left wing closed with Cruft's men and a fierce fight took place. Chalmers was wounded and his casualties were too heavy to sustain the fight so after about thirty minutes the survivors fell back. Shortly after Chalmers' men were out of the way Brig. General Daniel Donelson's Tennessee brigade advanced across the same field. Donelson's troops were also split by the house, but he had more success than Chalmers since Stewart's brigade had come forward after forcing back Miller's troops and hit Cruft's right flank forcing him to fall back. Colonel Shephard's regular brigade attacked the advancing enemy, forcing them to halt, allowing the rest of the Federal troops to fall back, and then Shephard also retired.[25]

The climax of the battle was quickly approaching the Round Forest. Colonel William B. Hazen's brigade of Palmer's division had beaten off the attacks of the right portions of Chalmers' and then Donelson's brigades. These were the wings that had veered off from their comrades because of the obstruction caused by the Cowan house. Hazen had to hold this position at all costs because this was the angle where the Federal lines that were almost bent back on each other were joined together. The ground here was only about three feet higher than the surrounding terrain, but it was here that Bragg's attack came to a halt.[26]

About a mile to the north, Cleburne came upon the brigades of Fyffe and Samuel Beatty, who had chased Ector's men and taken position in the southern part of an open field on the west of the Nashville Pike. The woods began sixty yards to their front and stretched southward for hundreds of yards. Colonel Charles G. Harker's brigade of Wood's division had also come forward and was posted to Fyffe's right.[27]

In the early afternoon Cleburne again moved forward, commanding four brigades with Polk, A. J. Vaughn (from Cheatham's division), Johnson, and Liddell in line from the right. Harker's brigade was hit hard on his overlapped right flank and he pulled his men back to a better position on higher ground a couple of hundred yards to the rear. This move exposed Fyffe's right flank and Cleburne's troops were quick to exploit this advantage, overwhelming Fyffe's line. Both Fyffe and Beatty were quickly forced to retreat, and Harker, who was now isolated against four times his number, followed after them.[28]

Cleburne had easily disposed of this last Federal resistance west of the Nashville Pike, but he did not have the strength to follow it up. Rosecrans had extended his line farther northwest along the pike and solid formations of Union troops were standing in the way of any further Confederate advance. Of course, Cleburne still had to try as he continued to follow Hardee's orders to "push the enemy, and, if possible, give him no time to rally or select positions." As the Confederates moved toward the Nashville Pike they ran into heavy artillery fire and long lines of infantry. Cleburne reported, "A report also spread, which I believe was true, that we were flanked on the right. This was more than our men could stand. Smith's brigade was driven back in great confusion. Polk's and Johnson's followed." Cleburne was able to reform his men about 400 yards back at the edge of the woods. Cleburne's, and McCown's men also, had fought magnificently all day but it was now after 3 o'clock and there was a limit to what men could do. General Cleburne reasoned that he had already captured many prisoners and nearly three miles of enemy territory but, "Another repulse, and I might lose all these and cause the demoralization and destruction of my division." He reported the situation to General Hardee, who told Cleburne to stay where he was and let the men rest. With no replacements to continue the drive north the Confederate drive to the Nashville Pike came up just short.[29]

With the halting of the attacks against the Federal right at the Nashville Road the battle had reached its turning point. The only place that Bragg could win the battle now was in the Round Forest. Hardee and Polk's men had accomplished as much as anyone could have asked but the job was not completed and there were not enough Confederates available to finish it. Bragg's only reserve was the division of Breckinridge still east of Stone's River. Bragg had considered using these men in some way all day but rumors of Federal troops moving on the far right held Breckinridge in his place. Bragg did not believe there were significant numbers of the enemy to the right and after reviewing the results of a cavalry reconnaissance in that area, he ordered Breckinridge into action. He was to leave Brig. General Roger Hanson's Kentucky brigade in place and send the brigades of Daniel W. Adams, Joseph B. Palmer, William Preston, and John K. Jackson across Stone's River to join the fight.[30]

Instead of waiting for all of Breckinridge's troops to arrive and making a massive attack on the forest General Polk decided to send these units forward in a series of assaults. The final phase of the battle was about to take place. Colonel Hazen's force still held their ground in the Round Forest with Colonel George D. Wagner's brigade of Wood's division to Hazen's left with his own left near Stone's River, nearly opposite the position occupied by Hanson's brigade and several batteries of artillery.[31]

General Adams' Louisiana brigade was the first to advance as he moved along the Nashville Pike toward the Round Forest. Like the earlier attacks his brigade was divided by the Cowan house and its fences, forcing him to reform after passing the buildings, where his men were met with a hail of rifle and artillery fire. They pushed back the Federal skirmishers but were in turn outflanked when Colonel Wagner counterattacked with two of his regiments. Adams withdrew, leaving over four hundred casualties behind after only thirty minutes of fighting. General Jackson's Georgia and Mississippi regiments went in right after Adams, but they too were mowed down as they advanced and were soon falling back.[32]

By this time, Breckinridge had arrived with Palmer's and Preston's brigades. He was shocked at the terrible casualties suffered by Adams and Jackson, which he blamed on Polk for sending the brigades forward one at a time, and decided to send his last two brigades forward together. General Preston would advance along the same line as Adams and Jackson, a task made even more difficult by having to march over the hundreds of casualties from previous assaults. Colonel Palmer's troops were to slide over to the west, enter the woods on the other side of McFadden Lane, and attack the Round Forest from the south. This was a much more sensible plan than just pounding away in fruitless frontal assaults, but it went bad right from the start. Preston's formation was broken by the Cowan house and its fences, and when they got clear and tried to regroup they were hit by a heavy fire that brought the attack to a halt. Preston led his survivors out of this slaughter pen and into the woods west of McFadden Lane to take cover. Palmer, following his orders, marched into the woods and up to the cotton field west of the Nashville Pike but could clearly see that an attack was pointless so he just stayed in the woods. Breckinridge's division was Bragg's only reserve force and the Confederate army could do nothing more this day.[33]

Except for a few stray flare-ups here and there the fighting came to an end as darkness covered the battlefield. Both armies had fought themselves out but in the end Rosecrans' troops held on to just enough ground to protect the precious supply line. The men of both armies were exhausted and many, especially on the Union side, were scattered and separated from their units. During the night the brigades of John Starkweather and Moses Walker arrived to reinforce the Federal army. Rosecrans met with his corps commanders that night and although they could not agree on a course of action for the morning Rosecrans finally decided to hold his lines and wait to see if Bragg would attack in the morning. If not, Rosecrans would once again advance to attack Bragg's right.[34]

General Bragg was convinced he had won a great victory and sent a message to Richmond: "We assailed the enemy at 7 o'clock this morning, and after ten hours' hard fighting have driven him from every position except the extreme left. Our loss is heavy; that of the enemy much greater." Bragg had won a victory but with Rosecrans still on the field the final outcome had not yet been decided.[35]

11

A Victory of Sorts

When he awoke on New Year's Day of 1863 Braxton Bragg probably believed that Rosecrans' army would begin its retreat back to Nashville and that he, Bragg, would be celebrating a great victory. As it turned out neither of those events occurred as Bragg expected. During the early morning hours Rosecrans had met with his commanders and it was decided that despite the beating it had taken the Army of the Cumberland would hold its position at Stone's River. Rosecrans reported that he ordered provisions and ammunition be sent forward and "on the arrival of which, should the enemy not attack, offensive operations were to be resumed."[1]

Early in the morning Rosecrans made some adjustments to his line. Most significant was that two brigades of Van Cleve's division, now commanded by Samuel Beatty because Van Cleve had been wounded in the foot, crossed over Stone's River on the far left. These brigades commanded by Colonel Samuel Price and Colonel Fyffe splashed across the river and took up a position on a slight hill overlooking McFadden Ford about half a mile from the river with their right on the high ground. In addition, two regiments from Beatty's brigade were positioned, one on each side of the river, to provide support. Rosecrans had received modest reinforcements in the form of Walker's brigade, placed in reserve behind McCook, and Starkweather's brigade, replacing Van Cleve's troops in the main lines. This was the only significant Federal troop movement of the day.[2]

Over in the Confederate lines General Bragg had ordered out skirmishers at dawn to report on the Federal position. Word soon came back to headquarters that the enemy was still there, and based on the improvements made to their positions during the night it appeared they were planning to stay. A little later in the morning Bragg received word from Wheeler and Wharton that large numbers of Federal wagons were heading toward Nashville. Bragg took this to mean that Rosecrans was preparing to withdraw his army but the Federal wagon trains were taking wounded men back to Nashville and out looking for food and forage.[3]

General Bragg held his position during the day except for moving the right of General Polk forward to occupy some empty ground on the west bank of the river. Bragg reported, "Our forces, greatly wearied and much reduced by heavy losses, were held ready to avail themselves of any change in the enemy's position, but it was deemed unadvisable to assail his as then established." The fact is that the Army of Tennessee was in no condition to fight another major battle on January 1. They had fought was well as anyone could have asked the day before but the army was worn out and they just did not have enough men to finish off their adversaries. Both armies had suffered staggering casualties on the 31st and needed to rest and reorganize before resuming anything like normal operations. For most of the day there was scattered skirmish firing and light artillery fire here and there but no real fighting.[4]

On Friday, January 2, Bragg was still searching for a solution to break the deadlock along Stone's River. He knew that Rosecrans had moved troops from his left to support the retreating right on the 31st and that the far Union left might be weak enough to punch through and force a Union retreat. In addition, the troops of Van Cleve's division who had crossed the river and set up a position on the low hill commanded the right of Polk's line and either they had to be removed or Polk had to pull back. If Bragg could regain control of this height artillery could be placed there to fire on the Union forces across the river.[5]

Bragg decided to launch his attack with Breckinridge's troops. Even after the tough fighting at the Round Forest his division was relatively rested and intact compared to the rest of the army. When Breckinridge received his orders he protested vehemently. Even if he was able to drive the Federals from the hill near McFadden Ford, there were other Federal positions on both sides of the river that could pour fire down on his men. The fact was that this was the only chance to salvage a victory and Bragg insisted that his orders be carried out. The assault was scheduled for about 4 P.M., hoping that this would be late enough in the day to prevent any Federal counterattack.[6]

The terrain on the left of the Federal position was relatively flat and open and Federal observers quickly saw the preparations being made for Breckinridge's attack. Colonel Beatty requested and received reinforcements as Colonel William Grose's brigade was sent across the river to a position behind and to the left of Colonel Fyffe. More artillery was also sent to aid Beatty's men and four more brigades and several batteries of artillery were moved to the high ground west of McFadden Ford.[7]

Only about seven hundred yards from the advance Federal positions about 4,500 of Breckinridge's troops assembled for their attack. Colonel Roger Hanson's Orphan Brigade from Kentucky formed on the left with Palmer's brigade, now commanded by Gideon Pillow, of Fort Donelson, to his right. About 200 yards back was another line with Adams' brigade, now commanded by Colonel Randall Gibson, on the left and Preston's brigade on the right.[8]

Right at 4 o'clock Breckinridge's troops stepped out and the attack was begun. Almost immediately they came under fire from the Federal artillery on both sides of the river. Marching through the shot and shell the Confederates kept moving: "The front line had bayonets fixed, with orders to deliver one volley, and then use the bayonet." When they approached to about 100 yards the first Federal line opened a heavy musket fire but Hanson's men kept going despite suffering heavy casualties, including Hanson himself who was mortally wounded. As Pillow's men approached the Federal line they were outflanked on the right by Fyffe's men who poured a heavy fire on them from front and flank. Pillow's men halted and for a while they traded fire with Fyffe's brigade until the second Confederate line closed up and the extra weight forced the Federals back off the high ground.[9]

The second Federal line now advanced to join the fight and both the 19th Ohio and 9th Kentucky poured their fire into the Orphan Brigade. However, part of Hanson's brigade was able to advance on the Ohioans' right flank and they were forced back. Lt. Colonel George H. Cram, commanding the 9th Kentucky, reported that after his support on the right gave way his men were "exposed to a raking fire, which was fast decimating my regiment." Unable to stand alone, they too fled from the charging Confederates. The steady pressure of Breckinridge's men forced the remainder of Beatty and Price's brigades back across the river. Fyffe's brigade fell back to the left and joined Grose's troops on high ground north of the ford.[10]

On the west side of the river General Crittenden could see that Beatty's men were being pushed back. Crittenden's chief of artillery, Captain John Mendenhall, had put together over fifty guns on the left side of the Federal line to cover the brigades on the other side of the river. Now, with those brigades splashing across the river in retreat Crittenden turned to the captain and said "Now Mendenhall, you must cover my men with your cannon."[11]

Almost as soon as Crittenden gave the order the Federal artillery roared and the Confederates pursuing Beatty's retreating men were blasted with shot and shell. Breckinridge's men were stunned by the bombardment and stopped in their tracks. In just a few minutes the Confederate attack had ended and survival was the only thing they cared about. There was nowhere to hide from the artillery fire; the guns were only a few hundred yards away, and grape and canister tore through the Confederate ranks. It was obvious to these veterans that to remain out in the open under this barrage of shot and shell meant certain death. Breckinridge wrote, "I know not how many guns he had. He had enough to sweep the whole position from the front, the left, and the right, and to render it wholly untenable by our force." Soon, first a few at a time, then in groups, Breckinridge's men began to fall back.[12]

When Breckinridge's men began to retreat the Federal infantry on the west side of the river moved forward. Colonel John F. Miller led his brigade across the river and soon Davis, Morton, and Hazen brought

John C. Breckinridge (courtesy Library of Congress).

their brigades across the river to join in the pursuit. Colonel Beatty was able to re-form most of his division and went back across the river to the positions they had recently abandoned. What was left of Breckinridge's division fell back to their original starting point and formed up behind Patton Anderson's brigade, which had been sent to support the attack. During the evening Bragg moved McCown and Cleburne over to the right to make sure Rosecrans could not break through Breckinridge's battered division and get behind the rest of the army.[13]

By now it was dark and the troops east of the river occupied basically the same positions they had before the Confederate assault. Crittenden's corps moved across the river during the night and entrenched their positions. Rosecrans wrote that only the rain and darkness prevented him from pursuing the enemy into Murfreesboro. Breckinridge lost over 1,700 men in the brief attack. Bragg lost his final opportunity to win a victory at Stone's River. He also earned Breckinridge's undying contempt for sacrificing so many of his men in an attack that had little chance of succeeding.[14]

The third of January was a miserable day, cold and wet with rain coming down since early morning. Both armies were fought out and no one was anxious to resume the battle. Rosecrans reported, "The plowed ground over which our left would be obliged to advance was impassable for artillery. The ammunition trains did not arrive until 10 o'clock. It was, therefore, deemed unadvisable to advance." Additional artillery was added to the left so that "the ground could be swept, and even Murfreesborough reached by Parrott shells."[15]

During the early morning hours Braxton Bragg was trying to decide what to do next. Clearly there would be no glorious victory to begin the new year. His army had been decimated and even the senior officers had no enthusiasm for further fighting. Several generals, including Polk, had endorsed a letter advising retreat, but Bragg was not yet convinced. After spending several hours weighing consequences and receiving more negative information, however, the Confederate commander finally made up his mind. In his report Bragg says:

> our forces had been in line of battle for five days and nights, with but little rest, having no reserves.... The necessary consequence was great exhaustion of officers and men, many having to be sent to the hospitals in the rear, and more still were beginning to straggle from their commands. During the whole of this day the rain continued to fall with little intermission, and the rapid rise in Stone's River indicated it would soon be unfordable. Before noon, reports from Brigadier-General Wheeler satisfied me the enemy, instead of retiring, was receiving reenforcements. Common prudence and the safety of my army, upon which even the safety of our cause depended, left no doubt on my mind as to the necessity of my withdrawal from so unequal a contest.[16]

The report that Rosecrans was being reinforced was inaccurate but the rest of Bragg's reasoning was certainly sound. His army was in no condition to launch another attack and if he waited long enough Rosecrans certainly would. There would be no reinforcements coming to Bragg's aid but Rosecrans could and would be reinforced soon. In addition, with the river rising if Bragg postponed his decision much longer part of the army might be cut off and unable to fall back. He really did not have much of a choice but to save his remaining troops for another fight. In a conference of corps commanders before noon Bragg informed them of his decision to pull out.

About 10 P.M. that night, General Breckinridge began the movement back to Shelbyville. The rain had turned the roads into mush and the exhausted men could do little more than put one foot in front of the other as they marched. Around midnight Bragg left Murfreesboro and it was not until dawn that the rear of the army led by McCown and Cleburne headed south. The weary Confederates marched all day on the 4th and finally reached Shelbyville the next day. The march continued until they reached the new base at Tullahoma a few days later.[17]

Back at Stone's River the Federal army was unaware that the Confederates had withdrawn until the afternoon of the 4th. A single brigade sent forward to investigate was able to find only cavalry pickets. Bragg's army was gone. Exhibiting excessive caution Rosecrans did not send any large numbers of troops forward until the next day when Negley's division moved into Murfreesboro. About the only thing they found in the town were many hundreds of wounded Confederates who were too ill to be moved. A few cavalry patrols were sent out to scout beyond the town but as Rosecrans reported, "farther pursuit was deemed unadvisable." The Federal army had suffered about the same number of casualties as had Bragg's and considering the poor condition of the roads and the exhaustion of the men Rosecrans had no intention of moving past Murfreesboro.[18]

In a dispatch to General Halleck on the 4th, Rosecrans reported, "the enemy is in full retreat. We shall occupy the town and push the pursuit to-morrow with the center. Will not, probably, be prudent to advance the army very far until communications shall be open to Nashville." And on the 5th Rosecrans wrote to Secretary Stanton: "God has crowned our arms with victory. The enemy are badly beaten and in full retreat. We shall press them as rapidly as our means of traveling and subsistence will permit."[19]

In another telegram to Halleck on the 5th Rosecrans neglected to mention how close the army came to disaster, "We have fought one of the greatest battles of the war, and are victorious. Our entire success on the 31st was prevented by a surprise of the right flank; but have, nevertheless, beaten the enemy, after a three-days' battle." Also that same day Rosecrans received a wire from President Lincoln, "God bless you, and all with you! Please tender to all, and accept for yourself, the nation's gratitude for your and their skill, endurance, and dauntless courage."[20]

The news of a Union victory was received with mixed feelings in the North. A victory was always good news but the cost was staggering and the recent Union defeat at Fredericksburg and Sherman's repulse near Vicksburg dampened public enthusiasm. In the South the joy that followed Bragg's initial dispatch claiming victory was replaced with depression a few days later when the news of the army's retreat became known. In Richmond, J. B. Jones wrote that after the initial excitement "we are all down again."[21]

Considering the terrible losses it is difficult to consider Stone's River much of a victory. But Rosecrans did achieve a great deal that was not at first obvious. First, and foremost, Stone's River prevented any further realistic possibility that the Confederacy could ever retake Kentucky or Tennessee from Union control. In addition, there would be no enemy interference with Grant's campaign against Vicksburg the coming spring. President Lincoln saw these advantages and later that year, when Rosecrans fell from favor the president wrote him, "I can never forget, whilst I remember anything, that about the end of last year, and beginning of this, you gave us a hard-earned victory which, had there been a defeat instead, the nation could scarcely have lived over."[22]

Each army suffered about thirteen thousand casualties at Stone's River, close to one-third of the men engaged. The armies had fought themselves into exhaustion at Stone's River and both Rosecrans and Bragg would take several months to rest and regroup their armies before they were able to actively campaign again.[23]

On January 11 from the new headquarters at Tullahoma, in an apparent effort to deflect some of the flood of criticism leveled at him, the always-unpopular Braxton Bragg wrote to several of his top subordinates asking them to confirm that they were the ones who first suggested the army retreat from Murfreesboro. Bragg wrote:

> Finding myself assailed in private and public by the press, in private circles by officers and citizens, for the movement from Murfreesborough, which was resisted by me for some time after advised by my corps and division commanders, and only adopted after hearing of the enemy's re-enforcements by large numbers from Kentucky, it becomes necessary for me to save my fair name, if I cannot stop the deluge of abuse, which will destroy my usefulness and demoralize this army.[24]

This unusual request could be considered as trying to set the record straight; unfortunately Bragg opened the door to yet more criticism when he also wrote, "I shall retire without regret if I find I have lost the good opinion of my generals." Most of the officers contacted did admit they had suggested the army fall back but Bragg also received several comments about his ability to continue to lead the army. Breckinridge wrote that while his brigade commanders "entertain the highest respect for your patriotism, it is their opinion that you do not possess the confidence of the army." Patrick Cleburne wrote back that although he and his brigade commanders were united in "personal regard for yourself, in a high appreciation of your patriotism and gallantry," they too believed that Bragg had lost the confidence of the army. An even more blunt reply came back from Hardee, who said, "Frankness compels me to say that the general officers, whose judgment you have invoked, are unanimous in the opinion that a change in the command of this army is necessary." Hardee assured Bragg that he and the other generals had the "highest respect for the purity of your motives, your energy, and your personal character; but they are convinced, as you must feel, that the peril of the country is superior to all personal considerations."[25]

After the generals informed Bragg of their lack of confidence in his ability to command the army General Polk wrote to President Davis on February 4, "My opinion is he had better be transferred." Davis had previously remarked that he could use someone with Bragg's organizational skills in Richmond and Polk suggested that Bragg's "capacity for organization and discipline, which had not been equaled among us, could be used by you at headquarters with infinite advantage to the whole army." For whatever reason, however, Davis took no action and Bragg remained in command of the Army of Tennessee.[26]

12

SPRING 1863

After Bragg retreated from Stone's River he established a fortified position about thirty miles south at Shelbyville. Soon after this camp was established, however, Bragg had a change of mind and, leaving Polk's corps to defend Shelbyville, he moved the remainder of the army about twenty miles farther southeast to Tullahoma. The main line of the Nashville and Chattanooga Railroad ran through here and it was imperative to keep control of this supply line. Bragg made it the army's headquarters and built fortifications manned by Hardee's troops.[1]

The dissention in the high command of the Army of Tennessee exploded out into the open after Bragg received a vote of no confidence from his generals. When Jefferson Davis learned of Bragg's ill-advised letter to his commanders and the universal dissatisfaction with their commanding general, Davis ordered Joseph E. Johnston to investigate the situation. Gen. Johnston was to decide if Bragg should remain in command.[2]

Johnston was not especially happy with his mostly administrative position as commander of the western theater; he wanted to command an army in the field, and he had the authority to remove Bragg if he felt it was necessary. With Bragg out of the way Johnston would be the logical choice to be the new commander but getting the command in such a manner would leave a bad taste in the mouths of almost everyone involved and Johnston was a little too honorable to ruin a man's career to satisfy his own desires.

In late January General Johnston arrived in Tullahoma and quickly discovered firsthand how unpopular Braxton Bragg was with most of his subordinate commanders. The troops, however, were well fed, well disciplined, and their morale was high. All things considered the army was in pretty good condition considering the terrible battle it had recently fought. To an unbiased observer it seemed that at least some of the generals who did the most complaining about Bragg's handling of the army were the same officers who had less than stellar performances at Stone's River. In addition, while the execution might not have gone as well as it could have Johnston found that Bragg's overall strategy was sound under the circumstances he was faced with. After a thorough review of the situation Johnston ended up recommending that Bragg continue as commander of the Army of Tennessee.[3]

President Davis was not particularly pleased with Johnston's recommendation and continued his efforts to get Johnston to take over the army. But, as Johnston wisely pointed out, any officer who replaced Bragg should be from outside the army and not someone who had anything to do with removing Bragg. The only other available officer of high enough rank and with experience commanding an army in the field was General P. G. T. Beauregard. Davis and Beauregard disliked each other personally and were political foes so Davis never seriously considered taking that drastic step. Davis would not let the matter alone, however, perhaps because Polk kept complaining. In March the president ordered Bragg to Richmond to consult with the government and instructed Johnston to take over command of the army while Bragg was away. Seeing through this less than subtle ploy Johnston informed Davis that Bragg was caring for his wife, who was too ill to be left alone, which she was. So Bragg remained in Tullahoma. The next month General Johnston became ill and after that the Vicksburg campaign heated up and Johnston was needed where he was. After all the scheming and maneuvering by his subordinates and his president to remove him the final result was that Braxton Bragg retained the command of the Army of Tennessee.⁴

Joseph E. Johnston (courtesy Library of Congress).

During the months after Stone's River, while the opposing armies regrouped, Bragg significantly strengthened his defenses. The Confederate army was spread out with Polk's corps positioned on the left in the well-fortified positions around Shelbyville, watching the southern end of Guy's Gap. To the right Hardee was stationed around the village of Wartrace, about fifteen miles north of Tullahoma. From here Hardee had to cover three more gaps through which the enemy could advance: Bell Buckle, Liberty, and Hoover's. These four gaps were the most practical way and most direct routes through the difficult terrain between Murfreesboro and Tullahoma. As important as it was for the Confederates to control these gaps to prevent the Federals from pouring through them Bragg also had to watch for a move around either of his flanks where the terrain was not as hostile. General Wheeler's cavalry was posted on the far right near McMinnville and General Forrest's troopers guarded the left flank of the army around Columbia. These cavalry units had to perform a duel function: watch for any enemy movements and also to assist in gathering supplies that had to be drawn from ever increasingly distant sources.[5]

To the north in Murfreesboro, General Rosecrans faced multiple problems in deciding where and how to advance on Bragg's forces. Guy's Gap was the largest and most easily accessible of the routes south; unfortunately it was also the best defended and Rosecrans had no interest in assaulting the strong defenses at Shelbyville. For reasons of supply it would be best to stick close to the Nashville and Chattanooga Railroad using Bell Buckle Gap or Liberty Gap, but that would take the Federal forces straight into Hardee's position near Wartrace. Hoover's Gap was the route farthest from Bragg's main forces but it was narrow and easily defended by a relatively small force. Hoover's Gap was also the farthest away from Murfreesboro and if Rosecrans decided to use this route he would need to leave a reasonably large force behind to guard against Bragg's swinging around behind the advancing Federal army and cutting their supply lines or even recapturing Murfreesboro.[6]

Rosecrans could avoid the gaps altogether and take his army east from Murfreesboro through a desolate area known as the Barrens then turn south to McMinnville, coming in on the right flank of the Confederate lines. However, this route was farther away from the railroad than was prudent and the countryside contained little in the way of food or forage. The roads from Murfreesboro to McMinnville and then to Tullahoma were poor and Rosecrans would have to depend on a long and tenuous supply line, easily broken by bad weather or enemy raiders.[7]

Considering all the potential problems along with the possible benefits it would appear that the best route to get at the enemy would be to go around to the southwest. The terrain was better and food and forage more easily obtained from the surrounding countryside. In addition, the Nashville & Decatur Railroad could be used to transport supplies, if it were repaired. As always, however, there was a problem. Bringing his army around by this route brought Rosecrans no closer to the ultimate objective of Chattanooga and his supply base of Murfreesboro would again be open to an attack by Bragg unless sufficient forces were left behind which, of course, would weaken the advancing force.[8]

Despite the difficulties that Rosecrans would have to overcome no matter what route he moved by, the Federal commander did have some advantages. First was that Rosecrans had the luxury of picking and choosing where he would strike while Bragg had to defend everywhere at the same time. Another advantage Rosecrans had was that he was receiving excellent intelligence about the various routes he might use and about Bragg's numbers and the deployment of the Confederate forces. The Federal cavalry had done a good job of scouting the area and information was constantly coming into Federal headquarters from intelligence operatives and loyal civilians.[9]

The Army of the Cumberland had undergone a major re-organization after Stone's River. Most of the commanders were still with the army but their units were scrambled around. General Thomas now commanded the Fourteenth Corps, General McCook commanded the Twentieth Corps, and General Crittenden the Twenty-first Corps. In addition to these three infantry corps a new, smaller unit, the Reserve Corps, was established under the command of Major General Gordon Granger. The cavalry was under the command of Major General David S. Stanley.[10]

Alexander McCook graduated from West Point in 1852 and had remained in the regular army until the war broke out. He was only thirty-two years old but had been a corps commander since before the battle at Perryville. The McCook family was well known during the Civil War with seventeen of its members serving the Union cause. Thomas Crittenden was forty-four and the son of the distinguished United States senator from Kentucky, John J. Crittenden, who had worked so hard to prevent the war. There were two Crittendens fighting in the war, Thomas and his brother George, who wore a gray uniform. Thomas was a lawyer who had served in the Mexican War and, like McCook, had several months of experience as a corps commander.[11]

With the coming of spring and the improvement in the weather came more and more messages from Washington urging Rosecrans to take action, then demanding that he take action, and finally threatening him if he did not take action. As in the period before Stone's River they made little impression on the strong-willed general. As quickly as Washington sent Rosecrans dispatches to take action he returned dispatches requesting more of everything. When Rosecrans was given command of the Army of the Cumberland what President Lincoln was hoping for was that he was getting a commander with the drive of Ulysses Grant. But with all the delays and excuses for not moving forward it was beginning to appear as if Rosecrans was more like Don Carlos Buell. All the president really wanted from a general was that he be willing to put up a fight.

On March 8 Rosecrans wrote to Quartermaster-General Montgomery Meigs to let him know that a larger supply depot was needed in Nashville, "a very large one." "Time is precious," Rosecrans stated. "If we fail, it will be in the management of our transportation, and consequent failure to get supplies." On March 25 General Halleck wrote to Rosecrans, "It is exceedingly important at the present time that you give the enemy in your front plenty of occupation." The same day Rosecrans responded with, "I do not think it prudent or practicable to advance from this position until I am better or differently informed."[12]

Also in March, General Halleck foolishly resorted to what was plainly bribery to get some action against the enemy. He sent out a dispatch to his army commanders saying, "There is a vacant major-generalcy in the Regular Army, and I am authorized to say that it will be given to the general in the field who first wins an important and decisive victory." At that time in the war the rank of major general was the highest available and the vast majority of major generals held that rank in the volunteer service. When the war ended those that stayed in the army would revert back to their previous and much lower rank. A commission as a major general in the Regular Army meant a guaranteed future. General Grant and most of the other possible candidates pretty much ignored Halleck's offer, but not the outspoken Rosecrans. On March 6 he responded by writing to Halleck that as an officer and an American citizen he felt degraded "to see such auctioneering of honor. Have we a general who would fight for his own personal benefit, when he would not for honor and the country? He would come by his commission basely in that case, and deserve to be despised by men of honor." Of course, this reaction did not help Rosecrans in his dealings with the high command in Washington.[13]

The main Union objective in the west during the spring of 1863 was the capture of the fortress city of Vicksburg, Mississippi, and the opening of the Mississippi River to New Orleans. Putting pressure on Bragg's army so that he was unable to send reinforcements to Vicksburg could play an important part in achieving that objective. Rosecrans, however, refused to move his army an inch until he was satisfied it was ready.

By the end of April, General Grant had been able to get his army below Vicksburg and on the same side of the river. The Confederate government responded by transferring about five thousand troops that were originally being sent to reinforce Bragg's army to Vicksburg instead. In addition the authorities in Richmond pressed Bragg to part with some of his troops. Bragg did not put up much of a fight and soon General Breckinridge and his division were on their way to Mississippi. This was a clever move by Bragg as it made him look good to his superiors and rid himself of one of the major troublemakers in his command.[14]

The Federal authorities were just as anxious to aid Grant's efforts to take the riverfront city. Clearly an advance by Rosecrans would be a major help but even as late as May he was not ready and the administration was losing patience. On May 28 President Lincoln wrote to Rosecrans: "I would not push you to any rashness but I am very anxious that you do your utmost, short of rashness, to keep Bragg from getting on to help Johnston against Grant." Rosecrans responded as if the president's message was a mere annoyance, "Dispatch received. I will attend to it."[15]

Less than a week later General Halleck took the gloves off and on June 2 he sent Rosecrans what was basically an ultimatum: "All accounts concur that Johnston is collecting a large force against General Grant, a part of which comes from Bragg's army. If you can do nothing yourself, a portion of your troops must be sent to Grant's relief." This was not just a threat because Halleck had recently sent Grant thousands of men from Ambrose Burnside's Army of the Ohio. Rosecrans was not convinced, however, but before he replied to Halleck he decided to confer with his commanders, and all of them backed Rosecrans' position that the time was not yet right for an advance.[16]

The messages continued to flow between Murfreesboro and Washington and it appeared that the general in chief simply had no control over one of his subordinates. On June 11 Halleck wrote, "I deem it my duty to repeat to you the great dissatisfaction that is felt here at your inactivity." On June 16 Halleck again asked Rosecrans to get going: "Is it your intention to make an immediate movement forward? A definite answer, yes or no, is required." Pushing his luck to the limit Rosecrans answered, "In reply to your inquiry, if immediate means to-night or to-morrow, no. If it means as soon as all things are ready, say five days, yes."[17]

The reason for all the effort and concern expended by both governments in Middle Tennessee was the small mountain town of Chattanooga. With less than three thousand inhabitants this little town seemed an unlikely place to be the cause of so much death and material expense as had been and would be spent. What made Chattanooga so important were the railroads. After Richmond and Atlanta, this small town that occupied a valley in the mountainous region just north of the Georgia border, was the most important rail center the Confederacy still controlled. Chattanooga was at the southern end of the Virginia & Tennessee Railroad that ran through Knoxville and all the way to Richmond, allowing for relatively quick transportation of food and troops between the two vital areas. The Western & Atlantic Railroad ran from Chattanooga through Dalton, Georgia and then to Atlanta and other points south. The Nashville

& Chattanooga road ran west from Chattanooga through the mountains to Stevenson, Alabama, where it turned north and headed to Nashville. At Stevenson it connected with the Memphis & Charleston Railroad that ran west to the Mississippi River. The railroads that ran through Chattanooga connected almost every important point in the Confederacy east of the Mississippi.[18]

General Rosecrans had been given freedom to "select, without restriction, his own line of operation by which to reach Chattanooga." The only request from Washington was that he attempted to "connect his left, so far as practicable, with the army of General Burnside." Burnside was also ordered to keep his right as close as possible to Rosecrans' left "so that if the enemy should concentrate upon either army, the other could move to its assistance." As it turned out Rosecrans and Burnside never got anywhere near each other during the entire campaign. Finally, after months of preparation, the long and bloody road to Chattanooga began shortly after midnight on June 24 when Rosecrans sent the long awaited announcement to Washington, "The army begins to move at 3 o'clock this morning."[19]

13

A Campaign of Maneuver

General Rosecrans actually had already started his troops moving on June 23. General Granger's Reserve Corps began the fifteen-mile march to Triune, hoping to convince Bragg to keep Polk's troops in the fortifications at Shelbyville waiting for an attack that was not coming. While Granger was advancing on the far left of the Confederate lines General Palmer started his division of the 21st Corps, and a brigade of cavalry, on a march to the southeast, around the far right of Bragg's lines, toward the village of Bradyville. Bragg had only cavalry patrols in this area and Palmer could easily push through the gap and move into the Barrens. Once through the gap Palmer could move directly on Manchester, in the rear of the Confederate army.[1]

During the evening of the 23rd, after Granger and Palmer had moved out, Rosecrans explained his plan of campaign to his corps commanders: George Thomas, Alexander McCook, and Thomas L. Crittenden. Rosecrans had not divulged his plans and none of the corps commanders were aware of what he had in mind until this conference. He informed them that Granger's advance was a feint to convince Bragg that the Federal army was going to swing around west of Shelbyville, where Bragg believed they would come from. With Polk manning the works at Shelbyville, Hardee's forces would have little support. Rosecrans was hoping that Bragg would believe that Palmer's move around the Confederate right was the feint that was supposed to distract him from Granger. Rosecrans was using two false moves to keep Bragg busy enough to not notice that the real attack was coming from yet another direction.[2]

General McCook's troops were to come up behind Granger and then move east through Liberty Gap and advance on Hardee's center. Granger would continue to threaten Shelbyville and take control of the roads in the area. General Thomas, meanwhile, was to march three divisions down the Manchester Pike to Hoover's Gap on Hardee's right. A mounted infantry brigade commanded by Colonel John T. Wilder, and equipped with new Spencer repeating rifles giving them tremendous firepower, would lead the way and clear any enemy forces out of Hoover's Gap. If all went as planned Hoover's Gap would be under Federal control that night. General Crittenden was instructed to leave one division in Murfreesboro as a reserve then move forward on the left, join Palmer and wait for further orders. After the rest of the planned movements were under way Crittenden would then be ordered to advance on the Confederate right. What had begun as a limited move to distract Bragg would be turned into an opportunity to turn the Confederate right flank.[3]

Right on schedule the lead elements of Rosecrans' army moved out on the morning of the 24th. As happened so often the weather played a part in the coming campaign. Shortly after the army began to move it began to rain, and it continued to rain for the next two weeks, and not just a pleasant summer rain but, as one Union soldier described it, "no Presbyterian rain, but a genuine Baptist downpour."[4]

Colonel Wilder quickly moved his mounted infantry and in a few hours he was in front of Hoover's Gap. A thin line of Confederate cavalry picketed the opening to the gap and Wilder's men hit them so quickly that they had no time to man the works in the gap. Realizing that a relatively small enemy force could hold up the entire advance in the narrow gap Wilder pushed on through to the other end and Hoover's Gap was under Federal control. Whether Wilder could hold it until infantry support, which was about six miles to the rear, arrived was another matter.[5]

Not far from the gap was the camp of a Confederate brigade commanded by Brig. General William B. Bate. In civilian life Bate had risen from steamboat clerk to successful politician. He joined the Confederate army as a private and through connections and talent rose to command a brigade, which he would be leading into battle for the first time today. Bate's brigade was part of a division commanded by recently promoted Major General Alexander P. Stewart. A classmate of Rosecrans at West Point Stewart had been a professor at West Point and the University of Nashville. He opposed slavery and secession but went along with his home state of Tennessee and was a capable commander. Like Bate, this campaign would be the first time leading his new command in battle.[6]

General Bate was well aware of the importance of holding Hoover's Gap and rushed his men forward to push aside what he believed to be a small cavalry force. Wilder was so far ahead of his infantry support that the commander of Thomas's lead division, Joseph Reynolds, sent orders for Wilder to fall back and wait until he arrived. Wilder also knew how important it was to hold on to the gap so he stayed put and got his men under cover as best as possible. Bate sent his men forward, head-on into a withering fire from Wilder's repeating rifles that decimated the Confederate lines. Bate tried again from different directions and the result was the same. With no hope of dislodging Wilder from Hoover's Gap, Bate pulled back and not long afterward Reynolds' infantry arrived and Hoover's Gap was securely in Federal hands. Due to delays in getting organized and bad information the rest of Stewart's division did not arrive at the gap until nearly sundown, too late to be of any use.[7]

About six miles west of Hoover's Gap General McCook's column approached Liberty Gap. The lead division was commanded by Brig. General Richard W. Johnson, who elected to stop at the entrance of the gap to wait for the rest of his support. The gap was defended by only two Confederate regiments and McCook saw that if he moved quickly he could gain control of the gap before significant enemy reinforcements had time to come forward. General Willich's brigade moved forward and flanked the defenders out of their positions. With the support of another of Johnson's brigades Liberty Gap was soon cleared of the enemy and before dark they had pushed out well in front of the southern entrance.[8]

While the other commands were making good time General Crittenden was having problems advancing over bad roads made worse by the rain as he moved toward Manchester on his way to Bragg's right flank. Over on the right of the Federal army Guy's Gap was held by artillery supported by cavalry. Colonel Robert Minty's cavalry brigade drove the defenders out of the gap and all the way back to near Shelbyville.[9]

At the end of the first day the Federal strategy was working about as well as could be hoped. The execution of Rosecrans' plan by his commanders and their men was flawless. All three of the gaps were in Union hands and Rosecrans' superior numbers could now be used to good effect. Bragg had simply been taken by surprise. He probably should have had more men defending the gaps, especially the ones on his right, but that would have impeded his ability to concentrate the army to defend Tullahoma. The fact is that Rosecrans moved much faster and with more precision than anyone could have expected. While Bragg was contemplating how to stop all the various columns coming at him the weather gave him exactly the thing he needed most, time.

The constant rain had turned the roads into swamps. Crittenden was unable to reach the position assigned to him for the 24th and Thomas could not make his movement to the left in anywhere the time allotted. Colonel Francis T. Sherman of the 88th Illinois wrote home on the 28th that when it first began to rain it was "hailed as a blessing in laying the dust," but since then the rain has "proved to be almost intolerable. The dust was allayed and became muddy, from that to mud, from mud to slosh, slosh to an almost impassable quagmire, and still it rains. I never saw anything like it." It became so bad that moving the army was nearly impossible and most of the movements scheduled for the 25th were delayed.[10]

Part of the problems facing General Bragg was his inability to obtain current information about what his enemy was doing. The cavalry arm of the Army of Tennessee was one of its worst handicaps. Many of the horses were underfed and in poor condition, the discipline among the men was almost non-existent and the cavalry commanders themselves were part of the problem. Joseph Wheeler was a recent West Point graduate but had little experience in command and exhibited little interest in the everyday work of the cavalry such as intelligence gathering. John Morgan had made his reputation as a raider, and that was about all he and his men were good for. Just before the campaign began he ignored his orders and set out on a raid that would eventually land him in prison in Ohio. Nathan Bedford Forrest could be an excellent commander when he wanted to, as long as his orders did not conflict with what he wanted to do. Earl van Dorn would have been a good man but he got too friendly with a married woman and was killed by her husband. Concerning Bragg's cavalry General Arthur Manigault later wrote: "It often appeared to me that many of our failures or misfortunes arose from our lamentable deficiency in this branch of the service."[11]

Overall Bragg's cavalry could not be depended on to keep him informed of the far-flung movements of Rosecrans' army. When the Army of the Cumberland stopped on the 25th Bragg had time to develop a response to the Federal advance if he had accurate information. Bragg was unaware that there was only one division advancing against his left and he did not know that Crittenden was on the far right. If the Federal advance had not been held up by the rain Bragg very possibly would have been overwhelmed before he had a chance to consolidate his army.[12]

On June 26 Thomas sent four divisions forward against Stewart, who rapidly fell back to the southwest, toward Wartrace. Thomas then sent three of his divisions to continue pressing Stewart back and Reynolds' division headed south toward Manchester. The Manchester Pike cut through the rugged country at the edge of the Barrens and climbed up to the plateau through a narrow, winding ravine, a perfect place for an ambush. Reynolds sent Wilder's brigade around the hills to flank any enemy positions but surprisingly there were none. The Confederates had missed another golden opportunity to delay the enemy advance and Reynolds' division moved on unmolested.[13]

Also on the 26th Bragg was in Shelbyville meeting with Polk to discuss what they could do to stop or at least delay Rosecrans. By now Bragg realized that Granger's force was just a decoy and he had developed a plan to derail the Federal advance. Bragg wanted Polk to make a night march with his corps going north up the Murfreesboro Pike and then swing around to the northeast and attack the Federal troops near Liberty Gap from the rear while Hardee moved out of his works and came at them from the front. Trapped between the two assaults this portion of Rosecrans' army could very well be destroyed or at least scattered and made ineffective for some time. Polk, of course, objected to the plan for several reasons but Bragg insisted that the move be carried out. As it turned out, Bragg had to cancel the attack because Hardee apparently failed to understand what Bragg intended to do.[14]

It was fortunate for Rosecrans that Bragg could not get his generals to follow his orders because he had ordered McCook to pull back from Liberty Gap and move to the left to take advantage of Thomas's breakthrough at Hoover's Gap. Had Polk made the attack Bragg wanted he could have caught McCook from behind while on the march. In addition, with McCook gone, Polk would have been closer to the Union base at Murfreesboro than any of Rosecrans' larger units. But, as would happen again, the distrust between the senior officers of the Army of Tennessee caused them to lose the chance to damage the enemy.[15]

There was another reason that Hardee was not interested in leaving his fortifications to attack McCook: he was planning to retreat. On the evening of the 24th Hardee was already planning to fall back and instructed Stewart, "If hard pressed tomorrow, you will fall back gradually toward Wartrace," which is what Stewart did do when Thomas advanced in force. When Bragg learned that Stewart had fallen back he realized that there was no time to implement any moves against Rosecrans from the present positions. Early on the 27th Bragg pulled his army back and by late afternoon they were safely within the works around Tullahoma.[16]

On Sunday, June 28, with most of Bragg's troops in and around Tullahoma, the majority of Rosecrans' men were to the northeast around Manchester. Crittenden was still slowly working his way through the mud several miles north and Rosecrans decided to wait until all his forces were together before moving on. He did, however, send Wilder on a raid to cut the railroad behind the Army of Tennessee.[17]

The next day, the 29th, Bragg informed his commanders that the army had fallen back far enough and they would make their stand at Tullahoma. As usual, Polk and Hardee disagreed with Bragg's decision and in a meeting that afternoon Polk brought up a number of imaginative reasons why it would be unwise to remain in Tullahoma.

Mostly they were concerned about being cut off from their supplies in Chattanooga and then being forced to retreat to the southwest. This would leave Chattanooga open to capture and expose Georgia to invasion. Polk proposed to fall back toward Chattanooga to protect their supply line.[18]

During the last day of June both armies were getting organized for what appeared to be a major battle around the fortifications of Tullahoma. Rosecrans made plans to assault the Confederate lines and spent most of the day looking for weak points. Bragg spent most of the day reflecting on what Polk and Hardee had told him the day before and speculating on what other moves Rosecrans might have in motion to cut off the Army of Tennessee from its base at Chattanooga. Bragg made up his mind about 3:00 P.M. and issued orders to abandon Tullahoma that night. The next morning, July 1, the Army of the Cumberland formed in line of battle and advanced on the Confederate works, which they found empty to the undoubted relief of everyone from Rosecrans on down to the lowest private.[19]

Once Bragg had his army on the move away from Tullahoma he had to decide where to make his next stand. At first he issued orders to set up a position about eight miles to the southeast behind the Elk River, but Bragg was already beaten physically and mentally. On the evening of July 1 he changed his mind and continued heading toward Chattanooga. Passing one good position after another Bragg could not decide where or even if he should stop to face the enemy. By the 4th of July the lead units of the Army of Tennessee were crossing the Tennessee River and by the evening of the seventh the exhausted troops ended their march and camped around Chattanooga.[20]

General Manigault later wrote: "From the moment of our leaving Shelbyville, we had nothing but hard marching and a most fatiguing time of it. The weather was very warm, and much rain fell." On July 1 Colonel Sherman wrote home that "One thing is certain: all that part of this state from which the Rebs expected to draw large supplies is lost to them.... The Confederacy has received a blow from which it will never recover."[21]

Rosecrans sent three divisions after the retreating Confederates but delays at Elk River because of destroyed bridges and the weather slowed the pursuit. General Sheridan's was one of these divisions and there was no commander more aggressive but the most he could do was exchange light fire with Confederate cavalry protecting their rear. After a few days Rosecrans called his troops back and the army settled down to rest and bring up badly needed supplies.[22]

Rosecrans could be justly proud of what would be known as the Tullahoma Campaign. From his new headquarters in Winchester Rosecrans reported: "Thus ended a nine days' campaign, which drove the enemy from two fortified positions and gave us possession of Middle Tennessee, conducted in one of the most extraordinary rains ever known in Tennessee at that period of the year." The campaign was a masterpiece of planning and execution. Even Confederate General Manigault was impressed as he wrote that the campaign "was, I think, the most brilliant of the war." Although the Confederates still controlled Chattanooga and East Tennessee "yet all the most fertile and more wealthy portion of the state was lost to us."[23]

In contrast to the Federal commander, General Bragg made a very poor showing. Once again, however, the entire fault was not his alone. The defensive positions around

Tullahoma were about as good as could be done under the circumstances. His plan to attack the Federal flank from Shelbyville and cut their supply line might have produced significant results if Polk and Hardee had cooperated. And here was the main problem, Bragg simply could not get his subordinates to do what he wanted them to do. The relations among the high command of the Army of Tennessee were so poisoned that nothing positive could be done. And this was filtering down to the troops who had done a great deal of fighting and suffering with nothing to show for it. Morale in the army was getting worse and Rosecrans' provost marshal reported that over 1,600 enemy soldiers were captured during the campaign, with over 600 coming in voluntarily.[24]

Back in Washington Rosecrans' campaign was viewed as a first step in a larger campaign to clear all of Tennessee and take Chattanooga. With the victories at Gettysburg and Vicksburg the Confederacy was reeling. Now was the time to strike, and strike hard. President Lincoln, Secretary Stanton and General Halleck all wanted Rosecrans to continue the campaign as soon as possible. By the middle of July, however, Rosecrans, as he did after Stone's River, decided to stay put and gather up his strength, stockpile supplies, and make plans for the next campaign to be launched sometime in the future. President Lincoln was still adamant about liberating East Tennessee and he wrote to a resident there, "I do as much for East Tennessee as I would, or could, if my own home and family were in Knoxville." Soon the pressure began to build for Rosecrans to take action.[25]

On August 4 General Halleck wired Rosecrans: "Your forces must move forward without further delay. You will daily report the movement of each corps till you cross the Tennessee." As earlier in the year Rosecrans was not going to be forced into making any move he was not ready for. After consulting with and receiving the support of his generals Rosecrans wired back to Halleck on the 6th: "My arrangements for beginning a continuous movement will be completed, and the execution begun, by Monday next." Rosecrans wanted to wait until he had enough supplies to last sixty days of hard campaigning in the mountains where food and forage was scarce. He also complained "to obey your order literally" would put the troops in a dangerous position on narrow mountain roads "where they would not be able to maneuver as exigencies may demand, and would certainly cause ultimate and probable disaster." Rosecrans ended his message with a show of his convictions: "If, therefore, the movement which I propose cannot be regarded as obedience to your order, I respectfully request a modification of it, or to be relieved from the command."[26]

Rosecrans' hesitancy to move forward until he was ready was in part due to the fact that he faced the daunting task of crossing the Cumberland Plateau in order to strike a blow at the enemy. This mountainous region was about thirty miles wide with nothing but rugged terrain, bad roads, and almost no food and fodder over the entire area. It was not too difficult to imagine his army being stuck in this desolate region while the enemy blocked the few narrow passages. It was imperative, as far as Rosecrans was concerned, for his army to be as self-sufficient as humanly possible while crossing the mountains. In order to obtain the huge amounts of supplies needed for the coming campaign the Nashville and Chattanooga Railroad had to be put back into service to Tullahoma and Winchester, and this of course took time.[27]

General Bragg faced some of the same problems as Rosecrans, but from the opposite side. It would probably be best to form his defense along the top of the plateau. But the same problems of supply that concerned his counterpart also worried Bragg, especially since the defenders might have to remain at their positions for quite a while. In addition, the sheer length of the area to defend was prohibitive. Almost 150 miles of front would have to be covered. Cavalry could be used to give warning of approaching enemy forces but Bragg wanted to use his horsemen on the flanks. As bad as it might be for Rosecrans to break through the mountains it would be much worse if he were able to move around one of the flanks and get behind Bragg.[28]

As if Bragg didn't have enough to worry about, up in Kentucky Ambrose Burnside was threatening to move into East Tennessee with the new Army of the Ohio. This would threaten Knoxville and the important East Tennessee & Virginia Railroad. Even worse was the possibility of Burnside continuing down toward Chattanooga and either joining Rosecrans or combining in an attack from different directions. The only thing Bragg could do was to move a large force to the northeast of Chattanooga to prevent being overwhelmed by both Union armies.[29]

While Rosecrans was exchanging dispatches with Washington, down in Chattanooga General Bragg was working to improve his chances in the coming campaign. At first it was suggested from Richmond that Joseph Johnston's forces be transferred to Bragg's command to launch a surprise attack on Rosecrans' inert army around Winchester. Bragg considered it but the difficulty of crossing the intervening mountains, especially if the Federals discovered the movement and put up a fight in the narrow passes, caused him to reject the idea. At least Bragg was given authority to put General Buckner's command in east Tennessee under his command to summon if needed.[30]

By the middle of August Rosecrans was preparing to move again, this time the goal would be the ultimate prize in Tennessee: Chattanooga. One of Rosecrans' aides, Lt. Henry Cist, wrote later that "Brilliant campaigns without battles, do not accomplish the destruction of an army. A campaign like that of Tullahoma always means a battle at some other point." The lowly lieutenant was absolutely correct and Chattanooga was worth fighting for. For the Union it was the door that led to the Deep South and for the Confederacy it opened onto Middle Tennessee and Kentucky.[31]

Rosecrans began the campaign for Chattanooga on August 16, the same day Burnside began moving toward Knoxville. Like the movement to Tullahoma Rosecrans devised a complicated strategy to maneuver Bragg out of Chattanooga while avoiding a major battle as much as possible. The main thrust of the campaign was to get the army below the Tennessee River, concentrate near Bridgeport and Stevenson, and cut Bragg's communications with Atlanta. If successful Bragg would be cut off from help and caught between Rosecrans and Burnside, exactly what Bragg feared most.[32]

Hoping to conceal his intentions as long as possible Rosecrans advanced on a wide front from Winchester to McMinnville. The terrain posed even more of a problem than it had during the movement to Tullahoma. In addition to confusing Bragg, Rosecrans had to spread his army out to avoid getting bunched together going through the narrow gaps in the mountains. General Crittenden advanced directly on Chattanooga, along the railroad between Sand and Raccoon Mountains southwest of the city. Once past the mountains he could move into the valley below the western side of Lookout Mountain and move along the northern base of Lookout along the river right to Chattanooga.[33]

Thomas would move his corps along several narrow roads over Sand Mountain, advance through Lookout Valley and across the mountain using Stevens Gap, over twenty miles south of Crittenden. General McCook would be even farther south by going through Winston's Gap, over forty miles from the Tennessee. Once across Lookout Mountain McCook was to continue southeast to Alpine, Georgia. With his army so spread out Rosecrans was taking a risk that one or more of the corps could be attacked by a much larger Confederate force and his army destroyed piece by piece.[34]

General William Hazen had command of an advance force of four brigades that was moving from place to place trying to appear larger than they really were. On August 21 Colonel Wilder was on a reconnaissance along the river opposite Chattanooga when he decided to stop and send some artillery shells into the Confederate lines outside the city. Bragg happened to be visiting his wife at a hospital in Ringgold, Georgia, that day. When he was informed of the shelling he hurried back to his army in case an attack was coming. At his headquarters he learned that there was a great deal of Federal activity to the north where it appeared Rosecrans might be trying to link up with Burnside. It was determined that the Federal troops in the Sequatchie Valley and further upstream would make an attempt to attack the isolated Buckner and then join together with Burnside to fall on Chattanooga. Buckner had already abandoned Knoxville and was stationed about thirty-five miles northeast of Chattanooga. Bragg sent reinforcements to Buckner and shifted more of his infantry in that direction. He also pulled out the one division that had been stationed near Bridgeport. The army was soon concentrated between Chattanooga and Buckner, above the city, waiting for the Federal attack. But Rosecrans was nowhere to be found.[35]

Rosecrans' strategy had once again worked to perfection. While Bragg and the majority of his army were waiting for an attack north of Chattanooga, leaving the river below the city unguarded, Rosecrans began crossing the Tennessee at several places. General Sheridan put up a bridge across the river at Bridgeport and General Reynolds seized Shellmound, Tennessee, and began crossing in boats. Two more crossings were established farther away from Chattanooga and by the 30th Rosecrans had all four crossing sites in operation. Crittenden was brought down to join the rest of the army, leaving Hazen's force behind to cause as much confusion as possible. By September 4 Rosecrans had his army across the river except for Granger, who was to remain behind in charge of the rail center at Stevenson.[36]

Rosecrans now began his move to cut the Western & Atlantic Railroad that brought Bragg's supplies up from Atlanta and force him to retreat. But in order to reach the railroad Rosecrans would have to cross three heights. First was Sand Mountain, which could be crossed only by a few bad roads, beyond which lay a narrow valley and then the formidable and much higher Lookout Mountain. There were only a few places where wagons could cross Lookout and these were simply narrow gaps in the solid palisades that crowned the mountain, narrow, winding, and altogether terrible routes. Missionary Ridge was the last barrier and compared to Lookout Mountain it was easy, with several real gaps that the army and its wagons could use.[37]

Bragg had to do something because as Rosecrans noted, "As a prudent commander, Bragg could not afford to leave us forty miles south of his position, to get quietly down and concentrate between him and Atlanta." Unfortunately, Bragg was not sure what to do since he was unsure of what Rosecrans meant to do. After learning that the Federals had crossed the river south of Chattanooga Bragg realized he could not allow them to just march east and cut his supply lines but he did not have enough troops to hold Chattanooga and face Rosecrans at the same time. In addition, the information Bragg was receiving was sketchy at best and he was naturally hesitant to abandon Chattanooga if the enemy movement to the south was actually just a diversion.[38]

By September 7 however, Bragg had received enough information to prove that the majority of Rosecrans' army was indeed south of the city and heading east. This convinced Bragg that he had to abandon Chattanooga and take his army south to meet the threat to his supply lines. Orders were issued for the army to leave the city on the morning of the 8th. Early that morning the Army of Tennessee began marching south from Chattanooga on the road to La Fayette, Georgia, which the lead units reached that night.[39]

Rosecrans kept his army moving and by the 8th Crittenden had arrived southwest of the city at Wauhatchie, Thomas had his front division on the crest of Lookout Mountain, and McCook was less than twenty miles south. During the afternoon the dust rising from the La Fayette Road could be seen from Lookout and by evening Rosecrans received word that Chattanooga was his, all he had to do was walk in and take it. Now, however, Rosecrans wanted more than to just force Bragg from one more position; this time he wanted Bragg's army. Rosecrans had been getting information from prisoners, deserters, and civilians that Bragg's army was so demoralized that they would probably run all the way to Atlanta.[40]

On the afternoon of September 9 General Crittenden sent his lead division forward to take control of Chattanooga and with the rest of his corps continued onto Rossville, about five miles south of the city. The rest of the army was to continue after the fleeing Confederates. Rosecrans wanted to do more than just follow Bragg's army; he wanted to catch and destroy it.[41]

14

A Fight Is Coming

September 9, 1863, should have been a day of great rejoicing for the men of the Army of the Cumberland. The capture of Chattanooga was the culmination of a campaign that had begun on the cold dark morning of December 26. They had made terrible sacrifices at Stone's River, and marched in all kinds of conditions from cold and rainy to hot and dusty, struggling up and down narrow mountain roads; so much blood and treasure had been spent to reach this goal, and now it was theirs. As it turned out, however, few of the Union soldiers were anywhere near Chattanooga.

Early on the 9th, General Rosecrans issued new orders that would change the spread out flanking movement into the pursuit of an apparently broken enemy. As far as Rosecrans could tell the Confederates were running away in a headlong retreat and all he had to do was catch up to them and start hauling in prisoners.[1]

Rosecrans' army was well positioned to trap or attack Bragg's army depending on which route they took. General Thomas, whose corps was in the center of the Union force, was about twenty miles southwest of Chattanooga at Steven's Gap. Thomas was to head southeast through McLemore's Cove and over Pigeon Mountain. Continuing on through Dug Gap on the east side of the mountain Thomas was to march for La Fayette, Georgia, which would put him on the road from Chattanooga to Rome. If Bragg were retreating on this road Thomas could block him until reinforcements arrived. General McCook's corps was about twenty miles southwest of Thomas and heading southeast toward Alpine and Summerville in Georgia. If Bragg were heading for Ringgold and then Dalton both McCook and Thomas would be in position to attack his flank while on the march. McCook was ordered to "Attack him whenever you can reach him with reasonable chances of success." General Crittenden was to leave one brigade in Chattanooga and press the retreating enemy column from behind. If Rosecrans were really lucky he might catch Bragg's army stretched out on the road and hit him from rear and flank. The possibilities were dazzling.[2]

The normally cautious Rosecrans had seemingly thrown caution to the wind. The even more cautious George Thomas had suggested that the spread out army be drawn back to Chattanooga which, after all, was the objective of the campaign, to regroup and re-supply before setting out on another campaign, the difficulty of which no one could know. Rosecrans rejected this idea out of hand; he was not interested in anything but pursuing what was believed to be an already beaten enemy. He wrote to Halleck the evening of September 9: "Chattanooga is ours without a struggle, and East Tennessee is free. Our move on the enemy's flank and rear progresses, while the tail of his retreating column will not escape unmolested." After all the delays and excuses for not taking the offensive this new attitude from Rosecrans was very welcome in Washington. The only problem was that Rosecrans' confidence was based on a serious misunderstanding of the situation.[3]

The truth was that not only was General Bragg not making a panicky retreat, he was concentrating his army behind Pigeon Mountain at La Fayette only about twenty-five miles from Chattanooga. General Buckner's 8,000 troops had just recently joined Bragg's army and he was ready to take advantage of the opportunity Rosecrans had presented. And opportunity there was; Bragg could not have asked for much more. With the three Federal corps spread out at least twenty miles from each other in mountainous terrain they could not possibly support each other. At La Fayette, Bragg was within striking distance of all of them and could concentrate most of his force against them one at a time.[4]

General Bragg's first target would be George Thomas. General Negley had brought his division down the eastern slope of Lookout Mountain and moved into McLemore's Cove. Negley had over five thousand men and was well in advance of the rest of Thomas's corps, and he had no idea how much danger he was in. Bragg developed an excellent plan to crush Negley between two columns and, if successful, the remainder of Thomas's corps would be at his mercy. Once Thomas was disposed of Bragg could deal with the widely separated corps of McCook and Crittenden one at a time. A smashing victory was clearly within Bragg's grasp. All he had to do was get his army to cooperate.[5]

Late on the 9th Bragg sent out orders that should result in the destruction of Negley's division. Up at Lee and Gordon's Mill, about thirteen miles north of La Fayette, Major General Thomas C. Hindman, who had been brought east from Arkansas, received orders for his division to immediately move toward McLemore's Cove. At the same time Bragg had sent orders to Lt. General Daniel H. Hill to send Cleburne's division west from La Fayette to join Hindman in the attack. This joint force would "move upon the enemy, reported to be 4,000 or 5,000 strong." Hit from front and flank by superior numbers the destruction or capture of Negley's division was about as sure as anything could be in war.[6]

As it turned out, however, the good fortune that gave Bragg this golden opportunity was about to run out. In reply to his orders General Hill replied "the movement required by him was impracticable, as General Cleburne was sick, and both the gaps [Dug and Catlett's] had been blocked by felling timber." Hindman had moved quickly and by the morning of the 10th was just a few miles from Negley's flank. Now he halted his troops and decided to wait. Bragg was not about to pass up this chance to destroy an entire Federal division so about eight o'clock in the morning he issued orders for General Buckner, who was also stationed near Lee and Gordon's Mill, to follow Hindman and "execute without delay the order issued to General Hill." Buckner had his troops on the road soon after receiving his orders and joined Hindman late that afternoon. Hindman was the ranking officer and took command of the combined force but it was too late in the day to do anything more than send out scouts.[7]

14. A Fight Is Coming

General Hindman was a native of Tennessee who had served with distinction in the Mexican War. He had been a congressman from Arkansas before the war and had seen both good and bad times as a Confederate officer. Mostly he was stubborn and like too many officers in the Army of Tennessee would sometimes ignore orders he didn't agree with. Buckner felt pretty much the same way and the two generals decided that Bragg's plan could not work so they decided to do nothing other than send a message to Bragg asking him to revise the orders.[8]

During the afternoon Confederate headquarters began to receive reports that Rosecrans was pulling his scattered troops closer and the Confederate advantage might soon be gone. Bragg sent two more messages to Hindman during the evening emphasizing how crucial it was for him to act quickly. At 6 o'clock: "Crittenden's corps marched from Chattanooga this morning in this direction, and that it is highly important that you should finish the movement now going on as rapidly as possible." Another dispatch at 7:30 P.M. was even more emphatic: "The enemy is now divided. Our force at or near La Fayette is superior to the enemy. It is important now to move vigorously and crush him." The effect of these dispatches was negligible.[9]

General Hindman had been sending messages of his own, mostly explaining why he could not make the attack. In messages to both Hill and Bragg he expressed concern about possible enemy troops coming up from behind:

> Whether the main body has moved or not I am yet unable to determine, but hope to learn to-night. If it has, our attack ought and will be made. If it has not, my force will probably be insufficient, and I will be attacked in rear from Stevens' Gap while attacking the column going east.

In another dispatch to Bragg, Hindman proposed instead of attacking Negley's single division that the army should turn against Crittenden coming down from Chattanooga.[10]

This is not at all what Bragg wanted. Making a frontal assault against Crittenden would only result in large casualties and drive the Federals back into Chattanooga. The whole purpose of Hindman's flank attack was to confuse and disrupt Negley's division by cutting off his avenue of retreat before the troops from La Fayette came into action. Bragg was getting more and more frustrated as the day went by and by evening decided to move his headquarters to La Fayette, "to secure more prompt and decided action in the movement ordered," arriving at about 11:30 P.M. Bragg soon learned that Cleburne was feeling just fine and when Bragg instructed him to have his troops clear the obstructions in Dug Gap and move forward to take part in the operation the tough Irishman was only too happy to obey.[11]

Soon after arriving at La Fayette, Bragg received the message from Hindman, quickly rejected any idea of changing his plan and sent back both verbal and written orders. Hindman was advised that Crittenden was moving down from Chattanooga and that General Polk had been ordered to send a division to cover his rear. The orders could not be any clearer: "General Bragg orders you to attack and force your way through the enemy to this point at the earliest hour that you can see him in the morning. Cleburne will attack in front the moment your guns are heard." Bragg also ordered Walker's Reserve Corps to join Cleburne's division at Dug Gap to add more weight to the assault. If Bragg could only get his subordinates to obey orders an important victory was there, just waiting to be taken.[12]

Early on the morning of the 11th Bragg rode out to Dug Gap to join Cleburne who had spent the night clearing the way into McLemore's Cove. Cleburne already had pushed two brigades through the gap and they were "waiting the opening of Hindman's guns to move on the enemy's flank and rear." And they waited and waited. The morning passed and then early afternoon and still no attack from Hindman. "Most of the day was spent in this position, waiting in great anxiety for the attack by Hindman's column. Several couriers and two staff officers were dispatched at different times urging him to move with promptness and vigor."[13]

At 3 P.M. Bragg was practically imploring Hindman to do something, "Time is precious. The enemy presses from the north. We must unite or both must retire. The enemy is small force in line of battle in our front, and we only wait for your attack." Bragg did not want to send Cleburne's troops forward alone because he knew only too well that a frontal assault would be bloody, and that without Hindman's attack Negley would simply fall back to safety.[14]

About the same time Bragg composed his final message to Hindman, that general was sending his own dispatch to the army commander stating he had information that 11,000 Federal soldiers were closing in on his position. He also wrote that he believed the force he was supposed to attack was larger than his own and that "Generals Buckner and Anderson concur, and they also agree with me that any farther advance would be imprudent." This decision was based upon the belief that their rear was insecure and Hindman decided to "retire by Catlett's Gap to La Fayette. The orders are now given."[15]

While Bragg was trying to get his generals to carry out his orders, the Federal forces finally realized the dangerous position they had put themselves in. On the morning of the 11th General Absalom Baird's small division came forward to support Negley. It also finally became apparent to Negley that he had marched himself into a perfect location to be trapped and by afternoon the signs of Confederate forces in his front and rear were so obvious that he decided to fall back from McLemore's Cove to Stevens' Gap. As Negley was withdrawing his skirmishers exchanged fire with Hindman's and the firing triggered Cleburne's advance, which at this point accomplished nothing. Negley was able to withdraw with minor casualties and one of the Confederates' most promising opportunities of the campaign was lost.[16]

A furious Bragg accompanied Cleburne as his troops moved forward and when Hindman rode up the confrontation must have been unpleasant to say the least. No commanding general could have done much more than Bragg had. His orders had been clear and specific and more than enough troops were provided to accomplish the mission. Hindman simply refused to obey his orders. General William L. Martin, commanding a cavalry division observing McLemore's Cove, was near Hindman through much of the 11th. He later wrote "Certainly an attack could have been made by General Hindman by 11 o'clock, and probably sooner. The delay was inexplicable to me." Martin knew that Hindman's troops were in good position to attack "and were eager to do so; I cannot now, nor did I then understand why he failed to move." Brigadier General Arthur Manigault later wrote that Hindman had been given an opportunity for striking a serious blow to the enemy and distinguishing himself but "he was not up to the work, it being far beyond his capacity as a general." So much time was wasted in forming lines and conferring with other generals that "the whole affair proved a miserable failure, although had there been a proper man to manage for us, I have little doubt but that a most brilliant success would have been achieved."[17]

Information that Bragg had not retreated as far and as quickly as originally believed had been coming in to Federal headquarters since Sept. 10 but Rosecrans still believed he was chasing a demoralized enemy and was skeptical of the new information. When it became clear that Bragg had retreated down the road to La Fayette, Rosecrans ordered Crittenden to advance to Ringgold and send scouts toward Lee and Gordon's Mill. Reports from Crittenden and Thomas showed that significant enemy forces were near Lee and Gordon's Mill and also in the vicinity of La Fayette. The size of the forces that had almost trapped Negley were unknown but the fact that they were there and ready to fight must have given Rosecrans cause for concern.[18]

On the 12th Crittenden moved toward Lee and Gordon's Mill and the remaining two divisions of Thomas's corps, John M. Brannon and Reynolds, closed up with Baird and Negley. Thomas's entire corps was now together and in good position covering Stevens' Gap at the foot of Lookout Mountain. By now the sheer volume of information from reconnaissance and civilian sources convinced Rosecrans that he was facing a reinforced enemy that was concentrated near the center of his far-flung army, and able to attack either flank before help could arrive. As Rosecrans later wrote, "Our fate now depended, first upon prompt concentration, and next, on our choosing our own battleground, where our flanks would be protected."[19]

Although the debacle at McLemore's Cove was not the kind of situation that Bragg would get over in a day he was determined to take advantage of the still widely separated Union forces, and he was soon given another chance to do just that. General Crittenden had already sent Colonel Harker's brigade of General Wood's division on toward Lee and Gordon's Mill and on the 11th he ordered Wood to take his other brigade to support Harker. Crittenden's other two divisions were in Ringgold and on the morning of the 12th they too were marching down the La Fayette road. When Bragg learned from his cavalry that there was but a single Federal division at Lee and Gordon's Mill, well out in front of the rest of their corps he quickly saw that he had been given another opportunity to strike a telling blow.[20]

On the evening of the 12th General Bragg sent instructions to Polk to head toward Lee and Gordon's Mill and attack Wood's division: "This presents you a fine opportunity of striking Crittenden in detail, and I hope you will avail yourself of it at daylight to-morrow. This division crushed, and the others are yours. I shall be delighted to hear of your success." To make sure there could be no doubt as to the outcome of a fight Bragg also ordered Walker and Hindman to quickly move up to support Polk's troops.[21]

Undoubtedly the recent lack of aggressiveness by his commanders weighed on Bragg's mind and at 8 P.M. he sent another dispatch to Polk instructing him "to attack at day dawn to-morrow." And even later that evening Bragg tried to push his subordinate toward taking action: "The enemy is approaching from the south, and it is highly important that your attack in the morning should be quick and decided. Let no time be lost."[22]

All Bragg's orders and entreaties were useless, however, as Polk was convinced his commander was wrong. At 8 P.M. Polk had sent a dispatch back to headquarters in which he stated that he had "the whole of Crittenden's corps, with Wilder's cavalry brigade, confronting me and moving in line of battle," in addition to an unknown number of enemy troops in reserve. Not willing to take any chances Polk also asked for significant reinforcements in the form of Buckner's corps and stated: "I am, therefore, clearly of the opinion that you should send to me additional force, so as to make failure impossible, and great success here would be of incalculable benefit to our cause."[23]

By now General Bragg was probably beside himself with frustration but he quickly agreed to Polk's request and Buckner's troops were ordered north. Bragg wrote to Polk informing him that Buckner would be there in the morning and "He was promptly ordered not to defer his attack, his force being already numerically superior to the enemy, and was reminded that his success depended upon the promptness and rapidity of his movements."[24]

On the morning of the 13th Bragg rode up to Lee and Gordon's Mill to personally view the situation and see if anything could be done to salvage some sort of victory. What he found was Bishop Polk sitting in his works waiting for a Federal attack that was never coming. In fact, Crittenden realized that he was too exposed and brought his corps together, pulling back to the west side of Chickamauga Creek. Once again Bragg saw a victory slip out of his fingers because of subordinates who were so unhappy with him as commanding general that they didn't trust his judgment or because they stubbornly believed they knew better and simply refused to obey his orders.

Bragg didn't press the issue and pulled his army together on the east side of Chickamauga Creek holding the crossing at Lee and Gordon's Mill and extending several miles north. By this time Braxton Bragg was physically and mentally exhausted. He had gotten little sleep the last several days, spending most nights traveling or reading the multitude of reports coming into headquarters. In addition, for a man like Bragg, who had a reputation as a disciplinarian, the apparent breakdown in the command structure of his army would have been especially discouraging. There was another reason why Bragg didn't want to bring on any major action at this time. He had recently received word that the promised reinforcements from Virginia would be arriving shortly.[25]

Back on September 9, the same day Chattanooga was evacuated, Lt. General James Longstreet, and about 12,000 of the best soldiers in the Army of Northern Virginia, began the long journey that would bring them to the banks of Chickamauga Creek. The direct, and much shorter route, through Knoxville had been broken by General Burnside, so these troops would have to travel about nine hundred miles through Virginia, North and South Carolina, and Georgia.[26]

The length of the trip was bad enough but the condition of the Southern railroads by the summer of 1863 made the journey much worse. The South had few facilities to construct or repair railroad equipment and as rails and rolling stock wore out many lines became undependable if not dangerous. There were sixteen different railroads involved in the movement and many were short and ended abruptly without connecting to another line. In several places the troops had to unload from the trains when one railroad line ended and march to where the next line began. Even with all the difficulties involved in transporting so many troops and their equipment over so great a distance the movement went relatively smoothly. By the 18th the leading brigades were joining the Army of Tennessee.[27]

Since the middle of August the number of available troops in both the Army of the Cumberland and the Army of Tennessee had changed greatly. Rosecrans started the campaign with a large numerical superiority but with all the troops left behind to guard important points and the casualties and usual loss through illness his army had shrunk considerably. Meanwhile Bragg had been receiving reinforcements from all across the Confederacy. Besides Buckner's troops brought down from Knoxville, Joe Johnston had sent 9,000 men in two divisions, commanded by John C. Breckinridge and W. H. T. Walker, from Mississippi. Not long after these men arrived two more brigades totaling 2,500 men also came east. Taking into consideration Longstreet's troops it was likely that Bragg would have a slight numerical edge on the Federal army, a very unusual situation for a Confederate commander. But Bragg needed to make use of his army before Rosecrans was able to bring his scattered troops together.[28]

After missing the opportunity to attack Crittenden's isolated division on the 13th, Bragg returned to La Fayette in the afternoon. He held a conference with the corps commanders the next day giving them the latest intelligence on the position of the Federal army. It was believed that McCook was still down at Alpine, Thomas near McLemore's Cove and Crittenden had concentrated in the vicinity of Lee and Gordon's Mill. One of Bragg's critics was General Daniel Hill, who felt that while the scattered enemy forces might present opportunities they also caused problems. Hill thought that Bragg was faced with a difficult situation "due, doubtless, to his uncertainty about the movements of his enemy, and to the certainty that there was not that mutual confidence between him and some of his subordinates that there ought to be between the chief and his officers to insure victory." Of course, Hill was one of those subordinates that contributed to the difficult situation.[29]

Once it was established that the main body of Bragg's army was near the center of his scattered forces Rosecrans made every effort to pull his army together. General McCook was instructed to leave two brigades to guard Dougherty's Gap at Pigeon Mountain about ten miles southwest of La Fayette, and bring the rest of his corps over Lookout Mountain and join with General Thomas as quickly as possible. Unfortunately McCook was unfamiliar with the mountain roads and ended up marching about twice as far as he needed to, going up and down the mountains before reaching Thomas's right on the 18th.[30]

When McCook's corps arrived in position General Thomas moved his corps to the left to close up with Crittenden, who was ordered to move back from Lee and Gordon's Mill with his right closed up with Thomas, where they remained until McCook was able to close up. By the evening of the 17th all three Union corps were within supporting distance of one another. Rosecrans issued orders for the entire army to move to the northeast, along Chickamauga Creek, in an effort to cover the La Fayette road to Chattanooga. Rosecrans' army was protected from a frontal assault by the steep banks of the creek, crossable only at a few bridges and fords. He was gradually moving sideways toward Chattanooga and if nothing were done to stop or delay it the Army of the Cumberland would soon be out of danger. Even with an advantage in numbers Bragg could not hope to successfully besiege the Army of the Cumberland unless it was severely damaged; he had to act before they reached Rossville.[31]

Braxton Bragg was well aware that as the Union army crept northward his options were dwindling. What Bragg needed to do was fairly obvious: turn the Federal left flank and get between them and Chattanooga. How to accomplish this was the problem since the constantly moving Federal army presented a moving target that was difficult to get a fix on. With Chickamauga Creek between the armies they were far enough apart that the occasional cavalry contacts didn't supply enough information to determine troop locations as both armies moved north. Bragg had to make sure he didn't walk into a trap as the Federals almost did, twice.

On the evening of the 16th Bragg issued orders for an advance that would bring Buckner and Walker, with Polk on their left, well north of Crittenden's position but at least a mile east of Chickamauga Creek. The only way to cut Rosecrans off from Chattanooga was to cross the creek above Lee and Gordon's Mill to cut the roads that led back to Chattanooga. As the armies moved north this plan was scrapped the next day. General Crittenden had moved a bit south in order to link up with Thomas, and now his left flank, and that of the entire army, rested at Lee and Gordon's Mill with cavalry patrolling the area to the north.[32]

At this point in the campaign the keys to victory were two roads that went back to Chattanooga from the vicinity of Lee and Gordon's Mill. The La Fayette road went straight north from Lee and Gordon's Mill for about 5 or 6 miles where it turned left and crossed Missionary Ridge at Rossville Gap before descending into the village of Rossville and then down along Chattanooga Creek and into the city. It was a relatively good road for the standards of the day. There was another road, nowhere as good, known as the Dry Valley Road. It ran west of the La Fayette Road along the eastern side of Missionary Ridge for about 2 or 3 miles north of Lee and Gordon's Mill, then it veered to the west crossing the ridge at McFarland's Gap and ran into Rossville. It was imperative that the Army of the Cumberland held these two roads. They provided a supply route from Chattanooga and an escape route back to the city if necessary.[33]

Even though Missionary Ridge was smaller than Lookout Mountain the only way over or through the rough terrain was to use the various gaps. The southern end of the ridge lay in McLemore's Cove where Chickamauga Creek runs to the east and Chattanooga Creek to the west. When Rosecrans moved his troops north he decided to stay east of the ridge and west of Chickamauga Creek and use the La Fayette Road or, if necessary, the Dry Creek Road. Bragg's final plan was to attack north of Lee and Gordon's Mill where the two roads were less than a mile apart. This was the best spot to cut Rosecrans' communications with Chattanooga. Further north where the Dry Valley Road turns west there would be too much territory to try to control in order to cut both roads. If Bragg waited until the Federals got close to Roseville, where the roads met again, his own supply line would be in danger.[34]

There was one more road that Bragg had to control for his assault to be a real success. The La Fayette Road and the Dry Valley Road were connected by the Dyer Road, which ran west toward McFarland's Gap. Federal troops that were north of the Dyer Road had a relatively safe route on the Dry Valley Road to retreat back to Chattanooga, but those south of the Dyer Road could be cut off and captured or dispersed to escape as best they could. In order to effectively destroy the Army of the Cumberland Bragg would have to trap it south of the Dyer Road or, if necessary, force it below the road.[35]

At first Bragg planned to cross Chickamauga Creek close to Lee and Gordon's Mill, but as the armies moved north it became apparent that Rosecrans would be able to cover the crossings in that area. Early on September 18, Bragg once again revised his plan and decided to send troops over four miles to the northeast to Reed's Bridge. This bridge was to be captured and held by a division under Brig. General Bushrod R. Johnson supported by Forrest's cavalry. During the day a portion of Longstreet's force commanded by Major General John Bell Hood would be arriving at Catoosa Station to join Johnson's troops and Hood would take over command. At the time this move was conceived it was believed that there was only a scattering of Federal cavalry that far north.[36]

The rest of Bragg's plan consisted of crossing the creek at several places. About two miles south from Reed's Bridge General Walker's Reserve Corps was to cross at Alexander's Bridge. In addition, about two miles east of Lee and Gordon's Mill, General Buckner's corps would cross the creek at Thedford's Ford. Bragg expected Federal infantry to oppose these movements so he instructed Johnson to turn south after securing Reed's Bridge and push aside the defenders at the other crossings. At the same time as the crossings were being made General Polk would threaten to launch an attack at Lee and Gordon's Mill to keep as much of Rosecrans' army in position as possible.[37]

As happens so often with units from different commands there were problems and delays for Johnson's men as they advanced from Catoosa Station. Near Pea Vine Creek he ran into Colonel Minty's Federal cavalry who had been out gathering information along the left flank of the army. Minty had heard the trains carrying Longstreet's troops arriving and early that morning found Confederate troops advancing on several roads. After sending out couriers to warn the closest infantry units Minty attempted to slow Johnson's advance about 11 A.M.[38]

Colonel Minty harassed Johnson's column with great effectiveness. Lightning quick cavalry charges were combined with infantry musket fire, then he quickly fell back to repeat the tactics. Time after time Johnson had his troops form into line to attack an enemy who didn't wait around to be attacked. Eventually, though, Minty could not keep Johnson's much larger force from advancing and by about 3 P.M. Reed's Bridge was in Confederate hands and several thousand enemy troops were filing across to the west bank of Chickamauga Creek, well beyond the left flank of Rosecrans' army.[39]

Farther south things were going worse for Bragg. Buckner's and Walker's troops had marched into a traffic jam when they both tried to use the same road to reach their respective crossing points at Thedford's Ford and Alexander's Bridge. After they got this straightened out and continued forward Walker ran into a detachment of Colonel Wilder's cavalry defending the opposite side of Alexander's Bridge. The cavalrymen sent clouds of bullets across the creek from their repeating rifles. Walker soon gave up trying to dislodge them and went looking for another crossing. He found one about a mile and a half downstream and by late afternoon Walker was able to flank Wilder's troopers out of position. Buckner had an easier time of it at Thedford's Ford and during the evening the rest of Bragg's army, except for three divisions, crossed over to the west side of Chickamauga Creek.[40]

Near Lee and Gordon's Mill, General Crittenden could see the clouds of dust being raised by Polk's troops as they maneuvered on the opposite side of the creek. Later that afternoon he received word from Colonel Wilder that he could not keep the enemy from crossing to the west side of the creek. Faced with an unknown force in his front and enemy troops moving on his flank Crittenden moved only a single division over to his left. Fortunately Wilder's troopers and darkness brought a halt to the Confederate advance, now under the command of General Hood, only a mile from the end of Crittenden's line.[41]

On the 18th it became quite clear to Rosecrans "that the enemy was moving to our left," and it became imperative for the Army of the Cumberland to also continue moving to its left. General Crittenden was ordered to move his command north of Lee and Gordon's Mill with both Thomas and McCook following to keep the line together. General Granger, currently near Rossville Gap, was instructed to send a brigade down the La Fayette road as far as the road to Reed's Bridge. Late in the afternoon Rosecrans decided that the fighting along the creek proved that Bragg was getting more aggressive and that the Union left was the place of most danger. A drastic step was needed to protect the route to Chattanooga.[42]

Protecting the left was of paramount importance so Rosecrans ordered Thomas to leave Negley's division near the creek south of Lee and Gordon's Mill and march the rest of his corps north, using the Dry Valley Road and a small country road, to the La Fayette Road near Kelly's farm. Thomas's men pulled out of their position in the center of the army and moved behind Crittenden's corps, with McCook moving up to close on Crittenden. Thomas's already tired men made a miserable night march over dusty roads lit by only an occasional bonfire. Early on the 19th General Baird's division reached Kelly's farm and had a brief rest while the rest of the corps came up. As unpleasant as it was for the men Thomas's move probably saved the Army of the Cumberland from total disaster. Rosecrans didn't know it yet but his left was now past the flank of Bragg's army and his troops also controlled the Dyer Road and the connection to the Dry Valley Road. With roads heading both north and west the Federal army was reasonably safe from being cut off from their base at Chattanooga. Bragg's only hope of the decisive victory that he and the Confederacy needed was to drive Thomas's corps south of the Dyer Road.[43]

As the sun was coming up on September 19 most of the Army of Tennessee was on the west side of Chickamauga Creek, but all the maneuvering of the last days had disrupted the army's organization. General Forrest's cavalry was posted on the right flank at Reed's Bridge with Walker's corps on his left and then Cheatham's division of Polk's corps further left. Continuing to the left was General Hood, commanding Longstreet's troops that had arrived so far, and then Buckner's corps northwest of Lee and Gordon's Mill. Still on the east side of the creek were Cleburne's division of Hill's corps at Tedford's Ford, Hindman's division at Lee and Gordon's Mill, and Breckinridge's division of Hill's corps on the left. Wheeler's cavalry was stationed on the far left guarding the upper fords across the creek.[44]

Rosecrans' army was also in new positions with three of Thomas's divisions now on the left flank: Reynolds near the Widow Glenn's house, Baird and Brannon covering the roads from Alexander's and Reed's bridges, with Negley south at Crawfish Springs. General Crittenden's corps was posted around Lee and Gordon's Mill, and McCook now near McLemore's Cove in reserve.[45]

The wooded and broken terrain prevented both commanding generals from learning the current position of their opponent. The last information Bragg had was that the left of Rosecrans' army was around Lee and Gordon's Mill. With most of his army north of the mill Bragg believed he was in position to smash Rosecrans' left flank and a magnificent victory would be his. Early on the 19th, however, news arrived at headquarters from Forrest that large numbers of Federal infantry were north of Bragg's right flank, suddenly it appeared as if victory might turn into disaster for the Army of Tennessee.[46]

15

CHICKAMAUGA—FIRST DAY

At dawn on September 19 the two armies faced each other over a line of several miles. During the night General Rosecrans had been able to reposition his army to prevent the Confederate forces from cutting him off from the Federal base at Chattanooga. General Thomas's divisions made an exhausting night march around behind the Federal army and came up on the left in the early morning hours. It was this area, the left of the Federal line, that would be the focus of both commanders and the scene of the heaviest and most protracted fighting in the coming battle.[1]

Colonel Daniel McCook, younger brother of General McCook and commander of one of General Granger's brigades, was on a reconnaissance the evening before and reported to Thomas that he had run into a lone Confederate brigade on the west side of Chickamauga Creek. McCook had burned Reed's Bridge, which was the nearest way back over the creek, and he believed the enemy brigade could be trapped if rapid action was taken. Thomas ordered General Brannan to take two brigades and find and destroy this wayward enemy unit.[2]

What McCook had evidently stumbled upon was Nathan Bedford Forrest's cavalry screening the rear of the Confederate troops that had crossed over the creek the day before. About 9:30 A.M. Brannon ran into Forrest's men, who were dismounted, and the fight began. Outnumbered, Brannan quickly brought up the rest of his division. Forrest received reinforcements as Bragg sent a brigade from General Walker's division forward and soon after Walker's entire division. The fighting soon increased in intensity and began to spread.[3]

By ten o'clock the battle was on as both Rosecrans and Bragg rushed their troops forward to the rapidly expanding battle lines. Bragg got his army into position west of the creek with Walker's corps on the right, Hood and Johnson's divisions to the left and Buckner about one mile below Lee and Gordon's Mill, with Cheatham's division in reserve. Rosecrans had Thomas defending the crucial left flank with McCook's corps on his right and Crittenden was brought closer in from Lee and Gordon's Mill. All day the lines would go back and forth as the Army of the Cumberland fought desperately to retain control of the La Fayette Road.[4]

One of the major problems that both armies had to contend with was that the terrain in the area could hardly be worse ground on which to conduct a major battle. General Thomas reported that in his front, from the La Fayette Road east to Chickamauga Creek, the ground was "undulating and covered with original forest timber, interspersed with undergrowth, in many places so dense that it is difficult to see 50 paces ahead." Sometimes units as large as brigades had deadly little fights where they seemed to be on their own. The heavy woods covering many areas of the battlefield concealed troops from friend and foe alike. Many times during the battle units would be engaged in savage fighting isolated from support that might be nearby but unable to make their way through the dense woods and undergrowth. Many Civil War battles were fought in similar terrain but what made Chickamauga a more difficult battle for the generals was that both armies were constantly sliding north and rearranging their units so that it was almost impossible for the commanders to know the positions of their opponents, and frequently their own troops.[5]

Colonel John Croxton's brigade was in the lead when Brannan met Forrest's men on the Federal left. At first Croxton pushed back the Confederates but as Walker's men came forward and joined with Forrest the Confederate resistance grew stronger and Thomas ordered General Baird to advance to support Brannan. Baird moved forward, united his troops with Brannan's and "drove the enemy steadily before him for some distance, taking many prisoners." Soon, however, Baird learned that there were enemy forces advancing on his right. Baird tried to reform his lines to meet this new threat but before the troops were able to complete their realignment, "the enemy, in overwhelming numbers, furiously assaulted Scribner's and King's brigades, and drove them in disorder."[6]

General Baird's right was attacked by two brigades of General Liddell's division. Generals Daniel Govan and Edward Walthall struck hard and quickly began to roll up the Union right. The Federal retreat soon turned into a rout as Liddell's men pushed Baird and Brannan back. Liddell pressed his advantage but after advancing several hundred yards he ran into another line of Federal troops that overlapped his force on both flanks. General Richard Johnson, from McCook's corps, had arrived to reinforce Thomas. Brannan was able to reorganize his troops and together, Brannan and Johnson quickly put an end to Liddell's advance. Shortly after his arrival on the scene Johnson struck the left of Walthall's brigade and Liddell pulled his troops back before they could be overwhelmed.[7]

Around eleven o'clock Bragg had ordered General Cheatham to move forward to assist Liddell but he did not arrive until the Federal reinforcements had already taken control of the field. Cheatham's division of about seven thousand men struck Johnson's right flank hard and drove his men back "with heavy loss," as Cheatham reported, "to the distance of about three-fourths of a mile, where he took shelter behind his breastworks, and, assisted by the arrival of heavy re-enforcements, checked the farther advance of my line."[8]

While this back and forth fighting was going on General Thomas received more reinforcements when one of his own divisions, commanded by Joseph Reynolds, and John Palmer's division of Crittenden's corps arrived on the scene. Thomas put together a powerful line with Johnson on the left then Palmer and Reynolds forming to the right. As soon as this line was formed "they advanced upon the enemy, attacking him in flank and driving him in great disorder for a mile and a half." Brig. General Otho Strahl, commanding one of Cheatham's brigades, reported that as he was moving to the right to close up with the rest of the division "the enemy met the front of my column with a murderous and destructive fire, enfilading nearly the whole of my line," and forcing Strahl to fall back before he was cut off from the rest of Cheatham's division. The Confederates fell back until they reached a strong defensive position between Reed's and Alexander's bridges. With reinforcements at hand and more on the way, General Thomas instructed Brannan and Baird to move over to the far left to reorganize their commands and protect the left flank.[9]

General Cheatham reported that his division had been fighting for about two hours "without support on my right or left," and his men were exhausted. After halting the Federal advance at his new position Cheatham made no attempt to advance against the much larger enemy force and wrote that he "deemed it prudent, therefore, to simply hold my position and await the arrival of re-enforcements."[10]

Throughout the morning most of the fighting took place on the northern end of the battlefield as the Confederates tried to advance far enough to gain control of the La Fayette Road. The fighting had been gradually moving south, however, and by midafternoon the battle was raging in previously quiet areas. In an attempt to provide a little relief for his right flank, Bragg ordered Major General Alexander Stewart to advance with his division.[11]

Stewart moved in on the left of Cheatham and when he advanced he came in on the right flank of Palmer's division. Colonel William Grose's brigade was stationed on Palmer's right and they bore the brunt of Stewart's attack. Palmer tried to move two other brigades, commanded by Charles Cruft and John Turchin, to Grose's assistance but soon they too were fighting for their lives. Palmer reported, "For ten minutes or more our men stood up under this fire, and then the enemy charged them and bore them back. It seemed as if nothing would prevent a rout." Colonel Cruft sent two regiments to support Grose but they found their comrades on the right "overpowered and giving way, stubbornly, under a most impetuous attack by overwhelming numbers, with its supporting lines on the right wholly gone." Fortunately for Palmer's men they had not received the full force of the Confederate attack since Stewart's objective was to break through the Federal lines to cut the La Fayette Road.[12]

Shortly after pushing Palmer's right out of the way Stewart's troops smashed into two brigades of Van Cleve's division from Crittenden's corps. Van Cleve had just arrived to support Palmer's right when Stewart's men came forward through the woods. One after another Stewart's brigades threw themselves at the Federal lines. Brig. General Henry Clayton commanded a newly formed brigade that had not seen action before. Clayton led his men forward into the woods and bushes and an hour later, after losing about four hundred men, they fell back to replenish their ammunition. John C. Brown moved his brigade forward to replace Clayton and he reported moving through "an unbroken forest, rendered the more difficult of passage by the dense undergrowth." Between the woods, the smoke of the battle and smoke from burning trees and bushes, Brown said it was "impossible to distinguish objects 20 paces in advance.[13]

General Brown pressed the attack and although "volley after volley of musketry in quick succession swept my men by scores at every discharge," they drove the Federal defenders from their front line. Continuing to move forward Brown's men soon came upon another enemy line posted on a low ridge and supported by artillery. Briefly checked by "showers of canister" Brown's men regrouped and advanced again, driving the Federal troops out of their position and over the ridge.[14]

Like Clayton before him, Brown's brigade suffered heavy casualties, and Stewart relieved him, sending forward his third brigade. Brig. General William Bate's brigade "was brought up and received by the enemy with as hot a fire as had successively greeted Clayton and Brown. Attacking, however, with their usual impetuosity they drove the enemy back." The situation near the center of the Federal line had developed into a serious problem for Rosecrans because Stewart's troops now separated Thomas from the rest of the army. But it was about to get much worse. As Bate's brigade continued to surge forward Stewart brought up Clayton's brigade again and the combined force drove Van Cleve's men back past the La Fayette Road. Here was a real disaster in the making with Thomas isolated and the main route to Chattanooga broken.[15]

An indication of just how close Bragg came to winning a decisive victory on the afternoon of the 19th can be seen in Rosecrans' report: "The roar of musketry in our center grew louder, and evidently approached headquarters at Widow Glenn's house, until musket balls came near and shells burst about it. Our center was being driven." Fortunately General Negley had previously been ordered to leave Crawfish Springs and bring his division north to act as a reserve. Negley was stationed near headquarters when Stewart's men punched their hole in the lines and he sent two brigades commanded by William Stoughton and William Sirwell to stem the flood of enemy troops coming in on Thomas's right and rear. Coming up on the right of Stewart's force Negley's brigades hit the Confederate's flank and after a relatively brief fight Stewart pulled his men back to the east side of the La Fayette Road.[16]

While Stewart was forcing his way through the Federal lines John Bell Hood and Bushrod Johnson moved forward a little to the south on Stewart's left. It was already after four o'clock when Hood and Johnson approached the La Fayette Road and ran into the division of Jefferson C. Davis, who had been sent forward from McCook's corps. After crushing the brigade of Colonel Hans Heg, Hood appeared to be headed for the rear of the Federal army when McCook's other division, commanded by Philip Sheridan, and Thomas Wood's division from Crittenden's corps came up and joined the fight.[17]

General Wood had just arrived on the scene and was discussing the situation with Davis when they saw the survivors of Colonel Heg's brigade running out of the woods and across the La Fayette Road. Wood, like many Federal commanders, saw that "it was evident a crisis was at hand. The advance of the enemy, before which these men were retiring, must be checked at once, or the army would be cut in twain." Wood sent Colonel George Buell's brigade forward to check the advancing enemy when "it was struck by a crowd of fugitives and swept away." Buell rallied his men, moved forward, was driven back again by a combination of fleeing Federal soldiers and the heavy fire from the enemy. Once again Buell rallied his brigade and retook their previous position at the edge of an open field. The Confederates advanced again but this time a portion of Colonel Carlin's brigade and one of Philip Sheridan's brigades came up and together they repelled the enemy assault.[18]

Shortly before sunset the relatively fresh divisions of Wood, Sheridan, Davis, and Negley combined to push Stewart, Hood and Johnson away from the La Fayette Road almost back to their original lines. Most of the exhausted Federal troops probably thought that the battle was over for the day as it was nearing dark and it appeared that both armies were too weary to continue the fight until morning, but they were mistaken.[19]

General Patrick Cleburne had been stationed on the south end of Bragg's line for most of the day but around 3:00 P.M. he received orders to take his division to the right of the army. After Cleburne's men made a difficult six-mile march General Cheatham reported that about "6 P.M. the division of Major General Cleburne arrived on the field, and with my command was ordered by Lt. General Polk to attack the enemy at once." It was nearly dark when, with Cleburne on the right and Cheatham to his left, the Confederate right advanced hitting "first Johnson and then Baird in a most furious manner."[20]

General Cleburne reported that as soon as he moved forward "the enemy, posted behind hastily constructed breastworks, opened a heavy fire of both small-arms and artillery. For half an hour the firing was the heaviest I had ever heard." This heavy firing, however, did not do as much damage as might be expected since, in the dark, no one could discern targets and both sides fired at the muzzle flashes of the other. While Cleburne and Cheatham were assaulting these breastworks from the front, Hill came in from the far right with artillery and General Willich, commanding the 1st brigade of Johnson's division, reported, "A shower of canister and columns of infantry streamed at once into our front and both flanks. My two front regiments were swept back to the second line."[21]

After more than an hour of deadly fighting Cleburne and Cheatham were able to force the Federals back several hundred yards nearer the La Fayette Road but despite heavy losses they could not achieve a breakthrough. About 7:30 P.M. Thomas was able to stabilize his lines and Cheatham received orders to end the attack and keep his men in line during the night.[22]

After almost an entire day of furious and deadly fighting neither army really achieved much of anything that was worth the heavy cost paid by both. Bragg had not been able to take and hold the La Fayette Road and the most Rosecrans could claim was that his army held its ground. The Federal troops got little rest that night as they worked hard to cut down trees and "threw up temporary breastworks of logs,

John Bell Hood (courtesy Library of Congress).

and prepared for the encounter which all anticipated would come off the next day." The men were exhausted and, although it was still early fall, Thomas J. Doughman of the 89th Ohio remembered, "It was a cold night that will never be forgotten by any who was on that field. Chilled to the bone and fatigued beyond endurance." Also during the night Thomas learned that Baird was not able to stretch his division far enough to the left to cover Reed's Bridge so Thomas requested General Negley's division be sent "to take position on Baird's left and rear, and thus secure our left from assault."[23]

During the evening Rosecrans brought his corps commanders to his headquarters at the Widow Glenn's house to give them instructions for the fighting that was sure to come in the morning. General Thomas would, of course, remain in his position on the left with his line east of the all-important La Fayette Road. The reinforcements sent to him during the day would remain under his command. General McCook was to hold his advanced positions as long as possible then close on Thomas and swing back his right to protect that flank. General Crittenden's two divisions were to be held in reserve near where Thomas and McCook's lines met so he could send reinforcements in either direction when needed. Bragg would almost certainly continue to pound away at the left and Rosecrans wanted his commanders to be ready to move quickly to protect the lifeline to Chattanooga.[24]

Not too many miles away from Rosecrans' headquarters, Braxton Bragg also called together his commanders to give them his instructions for the next morning. General Longstreet would arrive during the night with two more brigades. In an unusual move, Bragg divided the army into two commands: Polk on the right and Longstreet, who did not actually arrive in camp until 11 P.M. and did not join his troops until daylight, on the left. The bulk of Bragg's forces were positioned between Chickamauga Creek and the La Fayette Road pretty much parallel with the road. Bragg's plan was to again concentrate on the Federal left to break the connection with Chattanooga. Polk was to attack on the far right at dawn and then "take up the attack in succession rapidly to the left. The left wing was to await the attack by the right, take it up promptly when made, and the whole line was then to be pushed vigorously and persistently against the enemy throughout its extent."[25]

About 8:00 P.M. Rosecrans had sent a message to General Halleck:

We have just concluded a terrific day's fighting, and have another prospect for to-morrow. The enemy attempted to turn our left, but his design was anticipated, and a sufficient force placed there to render his attempt abortive. The battle-ground was densely wooded and its surface irregular and difficult. We could make but little use of our artillery. The number of killed is inconsiderable; that of our wounded very heavy. The enemy was greatly our superior in numbers. Among our prisoners are men from some thirty regiments. We have taken 10 cannon and lost 7. The army is in excellent condition and spirits, and by the blessing of Providence, the defeat of the enemy will be total to-morrow.[26]

16

Chickamauga— Second Day

At dawn of September 20 Braxton Bragg had expected to hear the thunder of artillery and the crackling of musket fire coming from the right side of his army. What he did hear early that morning was silence. Bragg reported, "With increasing anxiety and disappointment I waited until after sunrise without hearing a gun, and at length dispatched a staff officer to ascertain the cause of the delay and urge him to a prompt and speedy movement." Still there was no attack. Around 7 o'clock Bragg received a message from General Polk saying, "I am this instant in receipt of my first communication from General Hill, who informs me that he will not be ready to move for an hour or more, because his troops are receiving rations." It seems that Hill's supply wagons had gotten lost the night before and his men had nothing to eat. Hill would begin the attack "as soon as he is prepared for it."[1]

As the sun slowly rose in the sky Bragg was getting more and more frustrated. Finally he decided to ride over to the right to see for himself what was holding up the attack: "Proceeding in person to the right wing, I found the troops not even prepared for the movement." General Polk refused to accept the blame for the delay by saying that the orders had been sent to General Hill "in proper time, that he fully expected a prompt and ready compliance with it, and was himself in the saddle at the appointed time, expecting momentarily to hear the battle commence on the right." Polk had sent a staff officer to hurry Hill up and later rode to Hill's headquarters himself. Polk found Hill's men cooking their breakfasts and was informed by Hill that his men had not eaten the night before and needed to eat before going into battle. Polk ordered Hill to make the attack immediately whether his men had been fed or not. General Manigault later wrote, "In this manner, four precious hours or more were lost, any one of which was of more value at that time than two or perhaps three at a later period of the day."[2]

Bragg wasn't sure which of his subordinates was at fault for the delay, so he blamed them both. In fact, the general commanding had good reason to be upset, not only because once again his orders had been ignored. It was important to launch the assault as early as possible because, as he observed, "the ear was saluted throughout the night with the sounds of the ax and falling timber as the enemy industriously labored to strengthen his position by hastily constructed barricades and breastworks." This delay

16. Chickamauga — Second Day

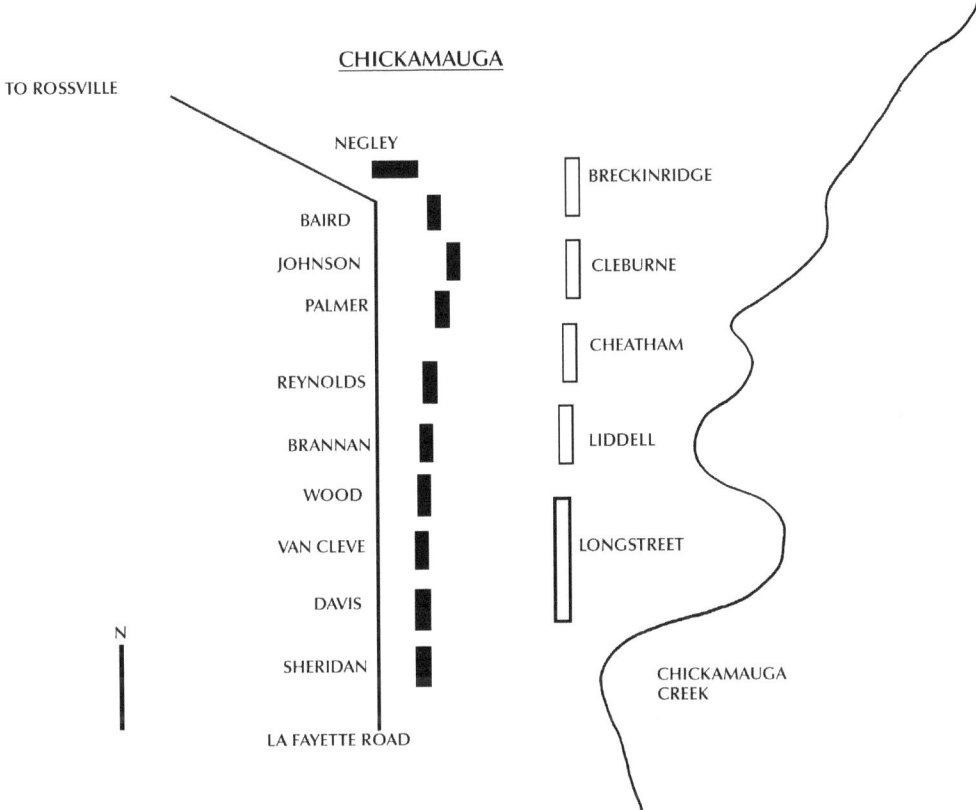

turned out to be an important factor in the coming battle. During the early morning hours General Rosecrans was still transferring troops to Thomas on the left and the Federal troops already in line were improving their protection as much as possible. Had the assault been launched on time the left of the Army of the Cumberland would have been much less prepared to receive the blow than they were hours later.[3]

General Rosecrans was up early that morning making a personal tour of his lines. The Federal formation began about four hundred yards east of the La Fayette Road. General Thomas had a mixed bag of units under his command due to yesterday's hurried and sometimes confused attempts to send reinforcements to the left. General Baird's division of Thomas's corps was on the far left of the army, next to him and to the south were Johnson's division of McCook's corps, Palmer's division of Crittenden's corps and another of Thomas's divisions, commanded by Reynolds. Thomas's command was bent back toward the road at both ends. Continuing south were two more of Thomas's divisions commanded by Brannan and Negley, with two of McCook's divisions, commanded by Sheridan and Davis, on the southern end of the line. Two of Crittenden's divisions, Wood and Van Cleve, were in reserve with cavalry units at each end of the line.[4]

Believing that Thomas's position at the north end of the line would receive most of the enemy's attention again today, shortly after sunrise Rosecrans instructed General Negley to pull his troops out of the line and move north to reinforce Thomas.

General McCook was ordered to provide troops to fill Negley's place in the line. McCook was slow to move and Rosecrans changed his orders so that Crittenden, who was also slow in moving up, would replace Negley. Negley's reserve brigade left for Thomas's front first but it was not until after 9:00 A.M. that Negley was finally relieved so he could move the remainder of his division to the left.[5]

As Bragg's troops waited for the battle to begin nerves began to fray. General Manigault wrote that as the early morning hours passed it was so quiet that it seemed "as though no human being was within miles." Along with thousands of other men Manigault was waiting to move out against the enemy when "suddenly and just as we began to breathe more freely, and the intense suspense began to wear off, the report of a distant gun at the extreme right of our line sounded in our ears, followed by another and another."[6]

It was about 9:30 A.M. when Breckinridge's troops stepped off and shortly after Cleburne's men joined the attack. On the far left of Thomas's line John Beatty had just gotten his brigade into a line that was pulled back nearly perpendicular to Baird's division to cover the left flank when his men were struck by two of Breckinridge's brigades and forced back. Benjamin Helm's brigade of Breckinridge's division and Lucius Polk's brigade of Cleburne's division ran straight into the Union breastworks and were repulsed with heavy casualties, including General Helm. General Baird reported that while the enemy was assaulting his troops on the left "they likewise assailed Starkweather furiously in front, to crush that portion of our line," but Baird's line held firm.[7]

General Cleburne reported that Breckinridge was already advancing when he received orders to advance on his left. As his troops moved forward Cleburne's right "encountered the heaviest artillery fire I have ever experienced. I was now within short canister range of a line of log breastworks, and a hurricane of shot and shell swept the woods from the unseen enemy in my front." Cleburne's line came to a halt less than two hundred yards from the Federal line and could go no farther.[8]

The two brigades of Breckinridge's division that had gotten around Thomas's far left, commanded by Daniel Adams and Marcellus Stovall, were able to advance all the way to the La Fayette Road. Determined to keep the Federal escape route open Thomas sent his reserve, consisting of the brigades of General Willich and Colonels Ferdinand Van Derveer and Grose, to retrieve control of the road. In a fierce struggle Adams was wounded and captured and the two Confederate brigades suffered so many casualties that they had to fall back out of the fighting altogether.[9]

Farther down the line Cleburne's left and Cheatham's division struck Johnson, Palmer, and Reynolds with equal ferocity but the breastworks that the Union soldiers were busy erecting during the night proved their worth. General Johnson reported, "I have not heard heavier musketry during the war than we had for one hour, when the enemy was handsomely repulsed in great confusion, leaving the ground literally covered with their dead and dying." Thomas reported that for two hours the enemy kept coming forward "making assault after assault with fresh troops, which were met by my troops with a most determined coolness and deliberation." With the Confederate attacks against Thomas's lines accomplishing nothing the fighting on this end of the battlefield died down for a while after 11:00 A.M.[10]

The inability of Polk's wing to push Thomas back forced Bragg to change his strategy of attacking the Federal flanks and launch an assault against the center of Rosecrans' lines. About 11:00 A.M. General Stewart and then General Walker sent their men forward only to be bloodily repulsed by Reynolds and Brannan. Shortly after this attack General Longstreet assembled his own and Buckner's corps for a frontal attack on the Federal center. While the Confederates were preparing, whatever good luck Rosecrans might have had so far during the battle deserted him. About 11 o'clock Wood received a message from Rosecrans that he should "close up on Reynolds as fast as possible, and support him." One of Rosecrans' staff officers had noticed that Brannan's troops were not in line and that Reynolds' flank was exposed so Rosecrans ordered Wood to move to his left to support Reynolds. As it turned out Brannan was in position just a little further back.[11]

General Wood dutifully obeyed the order and began to pull his men out of the line and move around behind Brannan toward Reynolds' position, creating a real hole in the line. Wood reported that he advised General McCook of his move and asked McCook to "close up his command rapidly on my right to prevent the occurrence of a gap in our lines." With his troops moving to the left Wood rode forward to find his new position when he met General Thomas who informed Wood that Reynolds needed no help. However, Thomas needed all the help he could get on the far left and sent Wood to support General Baird on the end of the line, Thomas taking responsibility for changing Wood's orders.[12]

Fortune was not just smiling on James Longstreet that day, she was laughing out loud. With General Hood in the lead the left wing of Bragg's army struck the Federal line right at the gap created by Wood's withdrawal. The Confederates poured through the gap in the Federal line like a flood, destroying everything in their wake. Brannan was hit in front and in the right flank simultaneously and his division swung back like a door. The last of Wood's brigades, commanded by Colonel Buell, was just pulling out when the Confederates struck and as he stated, "My own little brigade seemed as if it were swept from the field." On the right Jefferson C. Davis was moving up to fill in the line when his men were struck in front and in the left flank. The fighting was brief but fierce; Davis' position was "little better than an outpost and perfectly untenable against the overwhelming force coming against it. Nothing but precipitate flight could save my command from annihilation or capture."[13]

Sheridan and Van Cleve were in the process of moving two brigades from each of their divisions to the left to assist Thomas when the center was struck. Van Cleve's troops were totally disrupted by Brannan's men as they retreated from the line. Sheridan was able to get his two brigades into the fight but they were soon overwhelmed and had to fall back. Sheridan's men and other scattered units tried to make a stand along a ridge but were soon driven back to the La Fayette Road, where they joined with other scattered units to make another stand on a nearby ridge.[14]

On the far right Colonel Wilder's mounted infantry briefly held on but with the rest of the right side of the army heading to the rear he soon withdrew to avoid being cut off. General Rosecrans was on the right side of the line when Longstreet struck and he tried to bring Sheridan's men in on the enemy flank as they advanced but as he wrote, "It was too late. The crowd of returning troops rolled back, and the enemy advanced." Rosecrans sent word to the scattered units to rally at a ridge behind the Dry Valley Road. Sheridan reached the Dry Valley Road but found the Confederates pursuing and he was unable to join Thomas and ended up falling back all the way to Rossville. The right side of the Army

James Longstreet (courtesy Library of Congress).

George H. Thomas (courtesy Library of Congress).

of the Cumberland was shattered. Some units stopped in a futile attempt to delay the enemy but most of the troops kept heading north toward Rossville and with them went Rosecrans, McCook, and Crittenden, all the way to Chattanooga. The last information Rosecrans received from Thomas was that the left was being pressed hard and reinforcements were needed. Perhaps the general commanding assumed that the battle was lost and the best thing to do was to reach Chattanooga and prepare the city for an attack by Bragg's victorious army.[15]

On the left side of the battlefield, however, the fight was not nearly over. Thomas reported that around two o'clock one of his aides was scouting the area behind the lines where firing was heard when he saw large formations of enemy soldiers approaching the rear of Reynolds' lines. Colonel Harker of Wood's division moved his brigade over onto a hill and connected with Brannan's division and units of Beatty's and Stanley's brigades from Negley's division. General Wood brought up more of his division and joined Brannan on the crest of the hill. Thomas's line now took on the appearance of a horseshoe with his right bent back along Snodgrass Hill. Soon this newly formed line was being hit by enemy troops and the battle continued.[16]

Longstreet's corps, led by Stewart and Bate had come around to the right after breaking the Federal center and right. Again and again Longstreet's men went forward only to be thrown back by the stubborn resistance of Thomas's right. With the rest of the Union army beaten and falling back to Rossville it was left to George Thomas to save the army from total defeat by holding his position. General Rosecrans reported, "The fight on the left after 2 P.M., was that of the army. Never, in the history of this war at least, have troops fought with greater energy and determination." The magnificent defensive stand of his men that afternoon earned General Thomas the nickname "The Rock of Chickamauga."[17]

Around 2:00 P.M. it appeared as if Longstreet finally had total success within his grasp. The Federals on the right were exhausted and ammunition was running low. Although the Confederates had been taking heavy casualties in their attacks they were also doing serious damage to Thomas's units and the defenders were gradually weakening. It was about this time that Longstreet was able to get two brigades past the Federal right and it was just a matter of time before they would be slamming into the rear of Thomas's lines. Just when it looked like Longstreet was about to land another crushing blow help for the beleaguered Union troops came from a most unexpected source.[18]

About five miles north of Thomas's position General Gordon Granger knew there was a battle going on and about 10:30 A.M. he could see the dust raised by thousands of men and could hear the sound of battle which, as Granger reported, "was momentarily increasing in volume and intensity on our right, in the direction of General Thomas's position." From these sounds Granger was convinced that Thomas was under heavy attack "and fearing that he would not be able to resist their combined attack, I determined to go to his assistance at once." Granger's chief of staff, Major J. S. Fullerton, remembered that the general had been ordered to hold his position near Rossville to protect the far left and keep the road open to Chattanooga, "at all hazards." Shortly after eleven o'clock, however, Granger had heard enough and told Fullerton, "I am going over to Thomas, orders or no orders."[19]

General Granger was soon on the road south with the brigades of Brig. General Walter Whitaker and Colonel John Mitchell, under the immediate command of Brig. General James B. Steedman. Colonel McCook's brigade was left behind to protect the road. Although Granger was technically disobeying his orders under the circumstances Rosecrans was not displeased when he reported that Granger, "with the instinct of a true soldier and a general, hearing the roar of battle on our left, and being beyond the reach of orders from the general commanding, determined to move to its assistance."[20]

As General Steedman led his troops down the road they were struck by some light shelling as they approached the battle zone but Granger's force arrived safely and he reported to Thomas about 1:30 P.M. Thomas immediately sent Steedman to support Brannan's right on Snodgrass Hill where the Federal line was about to be flanked by J. B. Kershaw's and Bushrod Johnson's Confederates. To the right of Brannan, Granger could see the enemy forming on a ridge and in a gorge through which they could move around past the right flank and attack Brannan's rear. This was where help was needed the most and Steedman, without hesitating, seized the flag of one of his regiments and led his men forward. "With loud cheers they rushed upon the enemy, and, after a terrific conflict lasting but twenty minutes, drove them from their ground, and occupied the ridge and gorge. The slaughter of both friend and foe was frightful."[21]

Charles Partridge of the 96th Illinois remembered that as they approached the enemy "there came the pattering of shots, like the first drops of a shower, then the ragged tearing shots of an irregular skirmish volley; then the constant deafening roar, as regiment after regiment took up the deadly work." The blue-clad men continued on over logs and boulders, down one hill and up the slope of another to the crest of the ridge. "The noise was terrible. The enemy was but from six to ten rods in our front and through the smoke and bushes we could hardly see a man although their guns belched forth their terrible fire seemingly right in our faces."[22]

Now that Steedman had the ridge he had to keep it. The casualties had been terrible, about 20 percent of his 3,500 men had been killed or wounded and the enemy still wanted that ridge just as much as the Federals did. There was about a half-hour lull before Longstreet's troops returned. This time troops from the divisions of Lafayette McLaw, Hindman, and Bushrod Johnson attacked the ridge with as much fury as had been shown early in the day. Steedman's troops held their positions despite the savage attacks. As Granger observed, "Our whole line was continually enveloped in smoke and fire." The Confederates were beaten back after about thirty minutes of severe fighting but as Steedman reported, "in a few minutes he renewed the attack with increased force." Longstreet's veterans hurled themselves at the Federal lines with the knowledge that if they could break through the battle would be over. But Granger's and Brannan's men held firm. Charles Partridge later wrote, "I cannot describe those terrific charges and countercharges, as the rebels again and again sought to drive us back."[23]

Still determined to take Snodgrass Hill and get into Thomas's rear, General Longstreet requested reinforcements from Bragg but was informed there were none available. It was late afternoon when Longstreet once again sent his men forward against the Federals on the ridge. Colonel William Stoughton, commanding Stanley's brigade after that officer was wounded, reported: "The enemy was in heavy force, and fought with the most determined obstinacy. As fast as their ranks were thinned by our fire they were filled by fresh troops. They pressed forward and charged up to our lines."[24]

The fighting on the left continued unabated and up on the ridge the Federals were running out of ammunition. Granger had brought 95,000 extra rounds with him, but this had been distributed to the other Federal units fighting on Snodgrass Hill. The cartridge boxes of the dead and wounded had been emptied and just before dark Granger reported that his men "had not a round of ammunition left." Soon the Confederates came on again and, "With fixed bayonets our troops gallantly charged them and drove them back in confusion." Shortly after dark Granger's men fell back to another ridge just behind the one where the fighting had been going on. About 7:00 P.M. Granger received orders to fall back to Rossville while covering the retreat of the other units. Granger reported that the fighting at Snodgrass Hill cost him 1,733 men.[25]

On the left side of Thomas's line around Kelly Field there was little fighting during the early afternoon. Thomas reported that General James Garfield, Rosecrans' chief of staff, arrived at his position about 4:00 P.M. It was then that Thomas received the first accurate information about the disaster to the rest of the army. Shortly after this Thomas received a dispatch from Rosecrans instructing him to "assume command of all the forces, and, with Crittenden and McCook, take a strong position and assume a threatening attitude at Rossville." Thomas decided he would try to hold his position until dark, then retire.[26]

When Garfield arrived on the scene he sent a dispatch to Rosecrans to update him on the situation: "General Thomas holds nearly his old ground of this morning. I think we may in the main retrieve our morning disaster. I never saw better fighting than our men are now doing. If we can hold out an hour more it will be all right."[27]

Also about 4:00 P.M., General Hill was given command of the Confederate forces on the right and he resumed the fight. On the right of Hill's lines, Breckinridge and Walker advanced their troops against light opposition until they came to the La Fayette Road. Over on the left Cleburne moved his artillery forward to pound the Federal breastworks. Generals Baird and Johnson, who were stationed on the left of Thomas's line, received orders to fall back toward Rossville about 5:00 P.M. Baird reported that when he received the order it appeared "to be the signal for another attack, the most violent of all, upon my portion of the line. This time the enemy used artillery, and concentrated the fire of three batteries upon us, while his infantry pressed on with the utmost vigor."[28]

Some units from Breckinridge and Walker were able to get across the La Fayette Road but fortunately for Thomas's troops General Reynolds' column was just coming up and Turchin's brigade swung into line and drove the enemy back. Turchin's men, supported by Colonel Milton S. Robinson's brigade and General Willich's brigade of Johnson's division, took a position to protect the road. Orders were sent out for the army to begin the movement and most of the units on the right were able to pull out with little trouble. On the left, however, Johnson, Baird and Palmer were attacked just as they began to pull back. There was some confusion in Palmer's division but overall the Federal troops were able to withdraw without serious loss. Thomas's forces made the march to Rossville unmolested and defensive positions were immediately set up at Rossville Gap and along Missionary Ridge.[29]

Before the fighting had come to an end a flurry of telegrams began coming out of Chattanooga. Rosecrans wrote to Burnside at 5 P.M. informing him that the army had "met with a severe disaster. The extent of it is not yet known. If you are near enough to join us, do so at once." Assistant Secretary of War Charles Dana, an observer assigned to the army wrote, "My report today is of deplorable importance. Chickamauga is as fatal a name in our history as Bull Run."[30]

Rosecrans also sent a preliminary report of the battle to General Halleck:

> We have met with a serious disaster; extent not yet ascertained. Enemy overwhelmed us, drove our right, pierced our center, and scattered troops there. Thomas, who had seven divisions, remained intact at last news. Granger, with two brigades had gone to support Thomas on the left. Every available reserve was used when the men stampeded.[31]

At 8:40 P.M. General Garfield sent Rosecrans a dispatch from Rossville: "On the whole Generals Thomas and Granger have done the enemy fully as much injury today as they have suffered from him." The enemy attacks on the left had all been repulsed but he was unable to estimate how much loss was incurred on the right. Apparently Garfield did not truly understand how badly the rest of the army had been beaten because he optimistically wrote: "The rebels have, however, done their best to-day, and I believe we can whip them to-morrow. I hope you will not budge an inch from this place, but come up early in the morning, and if the rebs try it on, accommodate them."[32]

General Thomas was instructed to hold his position at Rossville until nightfall then fall back to Chattanooga. On the morning of the 21st things were looking much better for the Army of the Cumberland. Thomas had remained at Rossville Gap and along Missionary Ridge in case the Confederates tried to pursue but other than some skirmishing there was no serious fighting. Thomas could not stay too long at Rossville, however, because Bragg could outflank his force and cut them off from Chattanooga, so that evening Thomas withdrew and joined the rest of the army in Chattanooga.[33]

At the time and for many years later General Bragg was criticized for not pressing the retreating Federal army. There were seemingly very good reasons why Bragg did not immediately set out after the fleeing Union army; clearly his men were exhausted from two days of terrible fighting and there were thousands of dead and wounded to care for. General Hill felt that with all the things that had gone wrong, some of which involved him, "The great blunder of all was that of not pursuing the enemy on the 21st. The day was spent in burying the dead and gathering up captured stores." With the Federal troops still disorganized and spread out on the road to Chattanooga on the morning of the 21st Hill wrote, "Forrest sent back word to Bragg that 'every hour was worth a thousand men.' But the commander-in-chief did not know of the victory until the morning of the 21st, and then he did not order a pursuit."[34]

General Bragg defended his decision not to immediately press Rosecrans in his report: "Any immediate pursuit by our infantry and artillery would have been fruitless, as it was not deemed practicable with our weak and exhausted force to assail the enemy, now more than double our numbers, behind his entrenchments."[35]

President Lincoln offered Rosecrans words of support in a message sent just after midnight: "Be of good cheer. We have unabated confidence in you and in your soldiers and officers. In the main you must be the judge as to what is to be done." The president suggested that Rosecrans fortify his position and wait for Burnside to arrive and informed him that reinforcements were on the way from Grant's army but exactly where they were was unknown. The president assured Rosecrans, "We shall do our utmost to assist you." Also on the morning of the 21st Lincoln wrote to Burnside: "Go to Rosecrans with your force without a moments' delay."[36]

The president showed that he understood the strategic importance of Chattanooga as well as anyone in a message to Halleck on the 21st:

> I think it very important for General Rosecrans to hold his position at or about Chattanooga, because if held from that place to Cleveland, both inclusive, it keeps all Tennessee clear of the enemy, and also breaks one of his most important railroad lines. To prevent these consequences is so vital to his cause that he cannot give up the effort to dislodge us from the labor, expense, and hazard of going farther to find him and also giving us the advantage of choosing our own ground and preparing it to fight him upon.

Lincoln wanted to leave the details to Rosecrans and to let him know that at this time all that was expected of the general was to stay where he was and occupy Chattanooga. The president continued with, "If he can only maintain this position without more, the rebellion can only eke out a short and feeble existence, as an animal sometimes may with a thorn in its vitals."[37]

Another telegram that went to Washington on the 21st was from Rosecrans to President Lincoln:

16. Chickamauga — Second Day

After two days of the severest fighting I ever witnessed our right and center were beaten. The left held its position until sunset. Our loss is heavy and our troops worn down. The enemy received heavy re-enforcements Saturday night. Every man of ours was in action Sunday and all but one brigade on Saturday. We have no certainty of holding our position here.[38]

Also on September 21 Bragg wrote to General Cooper in Richmond:

The enemy retreated on Chattanooga last night, leaving his dead and wounded in our hands. His loss is very large in men, artillery, small-arms, and colors. Ours is heavy, but not yet ascertained. The victory is complete, and our cavalry is pursuing. With the blessing of God our troops have accomplished great results against largely superior numbers.[39]

It would have been difficult for General Bragg not to notice that after two days of terrible fighting trying to cut Rosecrans off from Chattanooga the final result of the battle was to force the Federal army back into the city.

17

CHATTANOOGA UNDER SIEGE

By September 22 the Army of the Cumberland was back in Chattanooga. Within a few days Bragg's troops took up commanding positions in the hills and mountains around the town and, for all practical purposes, put the city under siege. On the 23rd Rosecrans wired President Lincoln, "We hold this point, and I cannot be dislodged except by very superior numbers and after a great battle." He then went on to ask for reinforcements from Kentucky.[1]

Inside the fortifications of Chattanooga the Army of the Cumberland was relatively safe from attack by Bragg's army. The real danger they faced was starvation and then a humiliating surrender. It took no military genius to see that the army was trapped and the officers and men must have wondered how they were going to survive. Few of the men could have known it at the time but far to the east in Washington and far to the west in Vicksburg, events had already been set in motion that would decide the ultimate fate of the army and the city.

In mid–September General Halleck was busy sending telegrams to Vicksburg and other commands in the west ordering that troops be sent to reinforce Rosecrans against attack from Bragg and Johnston. On September 13, Halleck had sent a wire addressed to Grant or Sherman, whichever one of them was available, saying, "All of General Grant's available forces should be sent to Memphis, thence to Corinth and Tuscumbia, to co-operate with Rosecrans." On both September 13 and 14 Halleck also wired General Hurlbut in Memphis telling him to send all his available troops east to assist Rosecrans and to forward these orders to Sherman.[2]

General Burnside, in Knoxville, was much closer to Rosecrans than Grant's army and he too received appeals to send reinforcements to the Army of the Cumberland. On the 14th Halleck wired, "There are reasons why you should re-enforce General Rosecrans with all possible dispatch. It is believed that the enemy will concentrate to give him battle. You must be there to help him." And the next day Burnside received another wire from Halleck saying that Washington had information "that three divisions of Lee's army have been sent to re-enforce Bragg. It is important that all the troops in your department be brought to the front with all possible dispatch, so as to help General Rosecrans."[3]

Unfortunately Grant knew nothing of all this. He had gone to New Orleans to confer with General Nathaniel P. Banks about future movements. While there Grant suffered a severe leg injury when his horse fell and he had been incapacitated in New Orleans for several weeks. On September 22, now back in Vicksburg but still bedridden, Grant finally began receiving the messages that Halleck had sent to Vicksburg and Memphis over a week before. Communications during the Civil War were frequently unreliable and this was one of those times. There was direct telegraph communication between Washington and Chattanooga so that it only took hours for messages to go back and forth. Farther west, however, messages had to travel by wire, by steamboat, and sometimes by courier before reaching their final destination.[4]

Grant immediately recalled one of James McPherson's divisions commanded by General John Smith that had been sent to Arkansas and redirected it toward Memphis. Sherman, who was camped near Vicksburg with four divisions, was also notified to send one of his divisions to Vicksburg and then to Memphis and he had General Peter Osterhaus' division moving that evening. The next day Sherman arrived at Grant's headquarters and by then more information was available. Realizing the severity of the situation Grant ordered Sherman to take the divisions of Giles A. Smith and John Corse, join up with the other two divisions already on the way to Memphis, take command of the entire force and lead them east to reinforce Rosecrans.[5]

During the march east Sherman's little army was to move along the Memphis & Charleston Railroad as far as Athens, Alabama. Between the rival armies going back and forth and Confederate raiders much of this road had already been destroyed and Sherman's men would have to make repairs as they went. This would slow down Sherman's progress, but it was necessary so that once he reached Athens "we should not be dependent on the roads back to Nashville, already overtaxed by the demand of Rosecrans's army." In the end all the activity in Vicksburg and Memphis meant little as the battle Grant's troops were supposed to help fight was already over by the time they started.[6]

Back around Chattanooga the campaign and battle at Chickamauga was being analyzed and criticism of both commanders began almost as soon as the last shots were fired. Clearly, Rosecrans lost the battle but that wasn't the worst of it. His incessant delays in moving the army and then boasting of the near bloodless victories he achieved in maneuvering Bragg out of first Tullahoma and then Chattanooga only came back to haunt him after losing one of the bloodiest battles of the entire war. Worst of all, however, was the fact that Rosecrans left the field while the fighting was still going on and the army's best efforts of the battle, Thomas's magnificent defensive stand, occurred after the commanding general had ridden away believing that all was lost. No one questioned Rosecrans' personal courage but it appeared that the shock of the battle had left him dazed.

Despite the fact that his army was the clear victor complaints against Bragg continued unabated. The real problem he had was that the battle could have been the beginning of something much greater, but the opportunity was unfulfilled. A more vigorous pursuit during the Federal retreat might have decimated the Army of the Cumberland. Also, after Rosecrans' army reached Chattanooga, Bragg might have made a bold push across the Tennessee River to cut the Federal supply lines and force a quick surrender rather than settle down for a siege. After the war, James Longstreet, one of Bragg's most vocal critics, wrote, "Our last opportunity was lost when we failed to follow the success at Chickamauga and capture or disperse the Union army."[7]

It is, of course, always easier to know what should have been done long after the event. The fact is that the Army of Tennessee lost nearly one-third of its fighting men at Chickamauga, a devastating loss for any army, and the day after the battle the survivors were in no condition to make any kind of active pursuit. Rosecrans had lost about the same percentage of his army but they were done moving and could now regroup in relative safety. Bragg's army had nowhere near enough wagons and animals to mount a cross-country march, which meant that he had to stay close to the Western & Atlantic Railroad that brought supplies up from Atlanta. And, even if they could manage to solve the problem of supplies, the only way the Confederates could get across the Tennessee was by swimming or wading as they had no pontoon boats and the bridges across the river had been destroyed.[8]

Besides, there didn't appear to be any reason to press the Federals at the moment as they weren't going anywhere. Rosecrans' army was not strong enough to fight its way out of Chattanooga. The supply situation for the Federal army was bleak and would be getting worse as time passed. From Bragg's point of view it seemed as if the smart thing to do was just wait until the Army of the Cumberland was starved into surrender.

Shortly after the battle Bragg relieved both Polk and Hill from their commands, hardly a surprise considering their constant refusal to follow orders. The complaining and lack of confidence in Bragg by his subordinates continued, however, and in a message sent directly to Confederate secretary of war Seddon, Longstreet concluded: "I am convinced that nothing but the hand of God can save us or help us as long as we have our present commander." The temperamental General Forrest simply refused to serve under Bragg anymore and returned to an independent command.[9]

In addition to the backstabbing that was going on in the high command, the Army of Tennessee had its own problems with receiving and distributing supplies. Provisions were brought to the army on a single-track railroad from Atlanta. This road, and the Confederate commissary system in general, had never really been able to fulfill all the needs of the army. Now, with the thousands of men who had been brought in from other areas, the supply system was totally inadequate. In addition, to restrict the Federal ability to supply Chattanooga, Bragg had his army spread out on a line over eight miles long from Lookout Mountain to the north end of Missionary Ridge. Getting supplies through such rugged terrain was difficult at best and shortages soon became the rule. The Confederate troops were also suffering from morale problems. Even though they had just won a hard fought victory the defeats at Gettysburg and Vicksburg that summer were ominous signs that the war was not going well for the Confederacy. These defeats, coupled with the lack of confidence in Bragg that had begun to work its way through the ranks from the commanders to the private soldiers and the lack of sufficient supplies cast a gloom over the Army of Tennessee.[10]

That gloom, along with the criticism from subordinate generals, had once again reached Richmond and once again Jefferson Davis was forced to take action. On October 6, the Confederate president left Richmond on a special train for the long trip to the headquarters of the Army of Tennessee. Arriving on the 9th he first met with Bragg to hear his side of the situation during which Bragg offered to resign but Davis didn't want that, at least not now. The next step was a meeting with Davis, Bragg, and the army's senior generals. This mass meeting turned out to be an exceptionally bad idea when Davis asked each of the subordinate generals to voice their opinion of their commander. It must have been a very embarrassing situation for all parties as the generals, one by one, gave their reasons why Bragg should go. Whether or not their concerns were fair, or even true, the obvious consensus was that Bragg had lost the confidence of his highest-ranking subordinates.[11]

To allow this situation to continue and probably deteriorate further could potentially destroy the effectiveness of the Army of Tennessee. Davis had to do something, but what? Being a former military man, the idea of promoting one of the generals who had tried to bring down their commander was out of the question as far as Davis was concerned. One possibility was to return General Beauregard to command of the Army of Tennessee. Beauregard, however, was busy defending Charleston and as Davis had already relieved the hard to get along with Creole from this command once before he had little interest in making this move. Another possibility was Joseph Johnston, who certainly commanded the respect of the officer corps. Davis didn't particularly like Johnston either and besides he blamed Johnston's lack of action for the loss of Vicksburg. In the end there really was no viable option available but to leave Bragg in command. In an attempt to ease the situation a little Davis approved the removal of Polk and Hill and brought Hardee back to replace Polk. Braxton Bragg and his generals would have to find a way to work together to finish the job started at Chickamauga.[12]

Before returning to Richmond, Davis made another ill-fated suggestion. It was clear that Bragg and Longstreet, probably Bragg's main detractor, would never get along. With the Army of the Cumberland trapped in Chattanooga it must have seemed like a good idea at the time to send Longstreet and two of his divisions to attack General Burnside, recapture Knoxville, and open the Virginia and Tennessee Railroad to the east. The Confederate positions around Chattanooga seemed so strong that even with the loss of about one-fourth of his army Bragg should have no trouble holding those positions until the Union troops were starved into surrender. His work done, Davis returned to Richmond leaving behind an army that was still unhappy and would soon be significantly reduced in numbers.[13]

While the Confederacy was doing what little it could to assist the Army of Tennessee, the Federal government responded to calls of help from Chattanooga. Once the immediate shock and despair from the defeat was past Rosecrans settled down to defend Chattanooga as best he could. Assistant Secretary Dana wrote to Secretary Stanton on September 23 that Rosecrans was "determined to fight it out here at all hazards." But he would need help, and quickly.[14]

Washington's response was quick and substantial. Major General George Meade, commander of the Army of the Potomac, was ordered to send two of his corps to Washington immediately. Naturally he picked two units that were a little undersized and had earned a less than stellar reputation: Oliver Otis Howard's 11th Corps and Henry Slocum's 12th Corps. To command this force Major General Joseph Hooker was brought back to active duty. Of course, the Federal army, like its Confederate counterparts, had many conflicts between commanders. One of the more serious was that Slocum detested Hooker on both a military and personal level and at first tried to resign rather than serve under him. Somehow the high command worked out an agreement that allowed Slocum to have little or no personal contact with Hooker and the two corps began their journey west.[15]

The power of the Union was now impressively put on display. The War Department pulled together a huge array of Federal, railroad, and state executives and employees to cooperate together in a major effort to rush Hooker's command to Chattanooga. Only forty-eight hours after Dana's request for reinforcements was received the first trains carrying Hooker's command left Washington. Just four days later they reached Louisville and in twelve days two army corps, with their artillery and baggage, were in Bridgeport, Alabama, thirty miles from Chattanooga. This was a truly amazing feat for the times. It is possible to argue that the movement of Longstreet's corps from Virginia to Chickamauga was an even bigger accomplishment because the Confederacy had much less to work with. However, the point should be noted that the Confederacy strained all it had to move Longstreet while the North had the resources to repeat their troop movement over and over. Here was one more instance where the vast difference in the industrial might between the North and the South made itself felt.[16]

Even while Hooker's troops were arriving in the vicinity of Chattanooga the fate of the city and its garrison was still uncertain. Part of the problem was Rosecrans himself. Normally he had a good mind for strategy and had always made sound plans in previous campaigns. And, although he was careful to complete his plans and have everything ready before acting, when he did take action he was decisive and resolute. Since the battle at Chickamauga, however, Rosecrans was displaying none of these qualities and had simply become ineffective as an army commander.

In addition, Assistant Secretary Dana reported to Secretary Stanton that, "The general organization of this army is inefficient and its discipline defective," and, "our condition and prospects grow worse and worse." In another telegram Dana commented, "Amid all this, the practical incapacity of the general commanding is astonishing, and it often seems difficult to believe him of sound mind. His imbecility appears to be contagious, and it is difficult for any one to get anything done."[17]

An ineffective commander was bad enough but the real problem facing the Army of the Cumberland was simply that it was stuck in an exceptionally poor location. Chattanooga is situated on the south bank of the Tennessee River where it makes a turn west. The town is at the northern end of a valley, about five or six miles wide, through which runs Chattanooga Creek. The eastern side of the valley is formed by Missionary Ridge, which rises from three to six hundred feet above the valley floor in a mostly northeast to southwest direction, meeting the Tennessee River east of the city. South of the city forming the west side of the valley is the towering Lookout Mountain, nearly one thousand feet high. As the Tennessee passes Chattanooga the river forms a hairpin curve first heading south then quickly turning back north running along the base of Lookout Mountain leaving only enough room for a single track of the Memphis and Charleston Railroad and a narrow road. The northern part of Lookout Mountain is very steep and rugged ground that rises until it reaches a gentle slope with a narrow band of cultivated fields that extend to near the summit where a vertical palisade of more than thirty feet crowns the mountain.[18]

Braxton Bragg's army made good use of the high ground around Chattanooga by starting their fortifications on the north end of Missionary Ridge and extending them south along the crest. The line of works continued west across Chattanooga Valley to Lookout Mountain, which was also fortified. They also had troops in the valley west of Lookout Mountain and further west on Raccoon Mountain and down to the river so as to cover the road along the north bank of the river. There was also a line of Confederate works in Chattanooga Valley that ran from east of the city down to Lookout Mountain. In addition to the main position on top of Missionary Ridge there was a line of works along its base with rifle pits dug in several locations on the slope of the ridge. The creek that ran through the valley was pretty much the dividing line between the armies and both sides had pickets stationed at frequent intervals.[19]

From inside Chattanooga the Confederate positions looked unassailable and Bragg had every reason to believe that hunger would soon force the Army of the Cumberland to surrender. The Federals had been short of supplies since occupying Chattanooga and there was no good way to bring provisions into the city. Above the city the river was virtually closed by Confederate guns, preventing supplies from being sent in by steamers. The large base at Bridgeport was the logical place from which to re-supply Chattanooga but that too had been taken out of the picture. When the Federals withdrew into Chattanooga, Rosecrans unfortunately withdrew one of his brigades that had been stationed on the northern end of Lookout Mountain. When Bragg's army came up Longstreet was quickly sent to occupy this important position, virtually putting the city under siege although it was nowhere near actually surrounded.[20]

Under normal conditions all the supplies for the Army of the Cumberland came down by rail from Nashville to Stevenson, Alabama, where the Memphis & Charleston Railroad ran up to Bridgeport. From there supplies could easily be moved either by river, rail, or a narrow road past Lookout Mountain and then north into Chattanooga, but now this route was closed by the Confederate guns on the mountain. There was also another road that ran along the north side of the Tennessee from Bridgeport, which was also made unusable by the Confederate guns on Lookout Mountain. The only way left to supply the city was by wagon train moving west of the river through the Sequatchie Valley and over Walden's Ridge coming into Chattanooga from the north. This was a long and very difficult route estimated at between sixty and seventy miles over absolutely terrible mountain roads. From Bridgeport the first part of the route went north around the curve of the Tennessee to Jasper, which was the easy part. From Jasper the route went northeast about twenty miles through the valley of the Sequatchie River. The road then headed back southeast across Walden's Ridge where the road was not much more than a narrow mountain trail. The army could not be supplied by this route during good weather and once winter arrived the roads would be impassable.[21]

For the men in Chattanooga the situation became worse as the days passed and on October 2, Rosecrans formally placed the army on two-thirds rations, but many units were already well below that. Charles Briant, of the 6th Indiana, wrote: "The supplies became so short that parts of crackers and corn, dropped in handling the packages, were eagerly seized and eaten, to stay the demands of hunger ... and no one knew how it would ultimately end." Another soldier noted that the short rations, tattered clothing, and wet and cold weather "were telling fearfully on the men, whose sunken cheeks and spiritless manner gave token that their powers of endurance were being greatly tried. Sometimes they were so weak that they tottered and staggered like old men." William Hartpence, of the 51st Indiana, remembered how pitiful it was to see soldiers following the few supply trains that came into the city "holding their hats under the wagon to catch whatever might fall; following forage wagons for squares with the hope that an ear of corn, or a few grains even, might be jolted out."[22]

"On October 15", Dana wrote, "the troops were on half rations, and officers as they went about where the men were working on the fortifications frequently heard the cry of 'Crackers!'" Dana also noted that during this time "General Rosecrans seemed to be insensible to the impending danger; he dawdled with trifles in a manner which scarcely can be imagined." It seemed that nothing could get done; the officers and men were ready to take whatever action was needed to relieve their desperate situation but no orders came forth from headquarters. "I never saw anything which seemed so lamentable and hopeless," Dana continued. "Our animals were starving, the men had starvation before them, and the enemy was bound to make desperate efforts to dislodge us." Still Rosecrans took no action, spending "that part of the time which was not employed in pleasant gossip to the composition of a long report to prove that the Government was to blame for his failure on the 20th."[23]

Something had to be done, and soon. The barren country north of the Tennessee, which was the only direction Federal foragers could go, could furnish no supplies for the city. Every item of food and other supplies had to travel over the narrow and winding roads from Bridgeport. Some of the hills were so steep that the weight of the army wagon itself was about all the starving mules could pull. Often half or more of the precious supplies had to be thrown away so that the remainder could get through. To make the situation even worse, rain turned the already terrible roads into rivers of mud so soft that wagons would sink up to their axles. One of General Granger's staff wrote that, "In one instance, a wagon having sunk till its bed rested on the mud, the driver did not, as usual, beat his mules and swear; he simply sat on a rock by the wayside, looked at the wretched animals, and *cried*."[24]

The lack of supplies was causing problems for Rosecrans outside of Chattanooga as well. Rosecrans had planned on retaking Lookout Mountain when reinforcements arrived, thus solving the supply problem. Hooker's two corps were just thirty miles away but they could not be used because the supply problem was so serious that if they were brought to the vicinity of Chattanooga the combined army would probably starve before the supply line could be opened. Rosecrans and his staff developed several other plans to break the noose around the city's neck but no action was ever taken.[25]

By mid–October Rosecrans' luck had just about run out. There was no disputing the fact that Rosecrans had badly miscalculated Bragg's intentions, lost a battle, and had gotten his army trapped and facing starvation in Chattanooga. In addition, Dana's frequently critical reports and Rosecrans' own lack of action had brought about a loss of confidence in him back in Washington. However, as frequently happened during the Civil War, there were political considerations that had to be taken into account when the government dealt with military matters. Rosecrans was a very popular Ohioan who supported the Republican candidate for governor in that state. Removing him before the October 9 election could have serious political repercussions for the party in Ohio and nationally.[26]

After the Republican candidate won the election it would have been safe to relieve Rosecrans but President Lincoln continued to support him in gratitude for his loyalty and hoped that he would find a way out of the situation at Chattanooga. On October 16, however, a message arrived from Chattanooga making it clear that some sort of action had to be taken. Dana wrote that the situation had deteriorated to the point where he believed "Nothing can prevent the retreat of the army from this place within a fortnight, and with a vast loss of public property and possibly of life, except the opening of the river."[27]

That same day in a cabinet meeting the highest-ranking members of Lincoln's administration voted for a change of commanders for the Army of the Cumberland. The president, however, had decided on a different way to achieve the same goal. There were three departments involved in the most important areas of the west: the Cumberland, Ohio, and Tennessee. The commanders of those departments were Rosecrans, Burnside, and Grant. The president decided to create the Military Division of Mississippi, incorporating all three departments with Grant in overall command, leaving the decision about what to do with Rosecrans up to him.[28]

Secretary Stanton had apparently seen what was coming and had already sent orders to Grant on October 3: "It is the wish of the Secretary of War that as soon as General Grant is able he will come to Cairo and report by telegraph." With the normal delay in forwarding messages Grant did not received this order until the 10th and, although still in pain from his leg injury, he immediately started for Cairo.[29]

Grant and his staff arrived in Cairo on the 16th, and wired Halleck that he was awaiting further orders. A reply came back the next morning directing Grant to "immediately proceed to the Galt House, Louisville, Ky., where you will meet an officer of the War Department with your orders and instructions." Grant's staff and headquarters personnel and equipment were to accompany him. Grant left within two hours and as his train was pulling out of Indianapolis it was stopped for the "officer of the War Department" who couldn't wait in Louisville and had come further west to meet with Grant as soon as possible.[30]

It turned out that the War Department official was the secretary of war himself who joined Grant on his train. As they rolled over the countryside toward Louisville, Stanton informed Grant of the creation of the Military Division of the Mississippi and Grant's assignment to command this vast area from the Alleghenies to the Mississippi, except for Louisiana. The three armies involved had never been under one command and it was expected that this new arrangement would result in closer cooperation and coordinated movements between them. Grant's first job, however, was to solve the problem of the Army of the Cumberland at Chattanooga. The administration was afraid that Rosecrans was not up to the job and Grant was shown two sets of orders: "One order left the department commanders as they were, while the other relieved Rosecrans and assigned Thomas to his place." Grant wasn't particularly friendly with either man, but Rosecrans had been a difficult subordinate the previous fall in Mississippi and Grant did not hesitate to accept Thomas as the new commander of the Army of the Cumberland.[31]

After arriving in Louisville Grant and Stanton spent the day together exchanging news and considering possible options for future movements. That evening Grant and his wife Julia, who had accompanied him from Cairo, went out for a social visit with some local friends. During the course of the evening Stanton received a more pessimistic than usual message from Dana saying that it appeared as though Rosecrans was preparing to abandon Chattanooga. This turned out to be inaccurate but Stanton obviously could only go by the information he received. Near panic, the secretary tried to find Grant, even sending hotel guests out to look for him. When Grant returned to the hotel about eleven o'clock he found the secretary pacing the floor of his room in great distress. After Grant read the telegram from Dana the general "immediately wrote an order assuming command of the Military Division of the Mississippi, and telegraphed it to General Rosecrans." In a separate communication Grant then sent Rosecrans a copy of the order assigning Thomas to the command of the Army of the Cumberland.[32]

In a telegram to Thomas, Grant wrote to "Hold Chattanooga at all hazards. I will be there as soon as possible." Grant also requested an update on the supply situation in the city. Later that day came the reply from Thomas: "Two hundred and four thousand four hundred and sixty-two rations in store-houses; ninety thousand to arrive tomorrow, and all the trains were loaded which had arrived at Bridgeport up to the 16th — probably three hundred wagons." Rosecrans added, "I will hold the town till we starve." The defiant tone of the last sentence sounded good but the numbers told a different story. The reality was that there were only five days' rations on hand with two more on the way. Since it took at least eight days to make the journey from Bridgeport to Chattanooga the situation was indeed desperate.[33]

Grant later admitted: "I appreciated the force of this dispatch later when I witnessed the condition of affairs which prompted it. It looked, indeed, as if but two courses were open: one to starve, the other to surrender or be captured."[34]

It was imperative that Grant reach Chattanooga as quickly as possible. Leaving Julia with relatives in Louisville he headed to Nashville on the 20th then proceeded south on the Nashville & Chattanooga Railroad to Stevenson, Alabama, where it connected with the Memphis & Charleston to Bridgeport. At Stevenson on the evening of the 21st, Grant met with General Howard, whose corps was stationed around Bridgeport, ten miles from Stevenson. Howard was a pious man and a good Christian who abstained from alcohol and had lost an arm fighting in Virginia. He was considered a good soldier although his corps had acquired a reputation as being unreliable. Given another chance in the west Howard would make the most of it. What Howard found was not the victorious general depicted in the newspapers but a man "in size small, in color pale at that time, in manner remarkably quiet and retiring."[35]

While Howard was meeting with Grant a messenger from General Hooker, who had his headquarters in Stevenson, arrived and announced that Hooker would be happy to entertain Grant at his headquarters and offered to provide transportation for the commanding general. As Howard describes it Grant gave no sign of annoyance but politely told the messenger, "If General Hooker wishes to see me, he will find me on this train." Not long after General Hooker appeared in person, courteously paying his respects. Howard felt that this was "General Grant's method of asserting himself where he thought a general who had had large commands and considerable self-assertion might be seeking an ascendancy over him."[36]

Grant received another visitor that evening, General Rosecrans, who was heading north. After receiving the news that he had been relieved, Rosecrans quickly turned the army over to Thomas and quietly left Chattanooga before the men in the ranks were aware of the fact that they had a new commander. Grant and Rosecrans did not get along and it must have been an uncomfortable meeting. Rosecrans explained the situation at Chattanooga and informed Grant of plans to alleviate the supply problems that had been developed but not yet set in motion. The meeting was cordial enough and Rosecrans was soon on his way to forced retirement. Grant's later comments about this brief meeting tell much about his opinion of Rosecrans, who had "made some excellent suggestions as to what should be done. My only wonder was that he had not carried them out." After Rosecrans departed Grant's train continued on to Bridgeport where he spent the night at Howard's headquarters.[37]

Early on the morning of October 22 Grant and his escort began the journey to Chattanooga. Grant was still on crutches and had to be lifted onto his horse. Grant now got a firsthand look at what the wagon trains had to go through to get supplies to the army in Chattanooga: "There had been much rain, and the roads were almost impassable from mud, knee-deep in places, and from wash-outs on the mountain sides." Grant's party, traveling on horseback through heavy rain and cold mountain wind, needed two full days to make the trip, arriving at General Thomas's headquarters on the night of the 23rd.[38]

Apparently the reception Grant received at Thomas's headquarters was only slightly less chilly than the weather outside. Grant and Thomas were not at all friendly toward one another, possibly because of Thomas being given command of Grant's army during the summer after Shiloh. Whatever the reason, after initial greetings both men ended up sitting in front of the fireplace, not saying a word, a pool of water forming under Grant's chair as water dripped from his soaked uniform. Colonel James Wilson, one of Grant's staff, finally mentioned to Thomas that the commanding general might like something to eat and some dry clothes, which Thomas's staff quickly provided. Colonel Horace Porter, who was then working for Thomas but would later join Grant's staff, remembered things a little differently. Grant had a light dinner and had been offered a change of clothing but he preferred to just sit in front of the fire in quiet contemplation. Whichever version is true, Grant spent the night at Thomas's headquarters. During the evening many of the general officers came by and briefed Grant on the situation in and around Chattanooga. Particularly impressive was General William F. Smith, whom Grant had known at West Point, and his plan to break the Confederate stranglehold on the city.[39]

18

GRANT GOES TO WORK

On the morning of October 24 Assistant Secretary Dana sent a telegram to Secretary Stanton notifying him that "Grant arrived last night, wet, dirty and well." The new commanding general had indeed arrived wet and dirty but he was not particularly well. Grant still had serious pain in his leg from the fall in New Orleans and the rough trip from Bridgeport only made it worse. In a wire to Halleck, Grant complained that the trip from Bridgeport had been made "over the worst roads it is possible to conceive of, and through a continuous drenching rain." He was still on crutches, "and had to be carried over places where it was not safe to cross on horseback." One positive thing came out of this ordeal: Grant saw firsthand that it would be impossible to maintain the army in Chattanooga unless another supply route was opened, and opened quickly.[1]

Early the next morning Grant, Thomas, and Smith, accompanied by staff officers, took a ride to inspect the terrain to the north of town. They crossed to the north side of the Tennessee and rode out to Brown's Ferry, about three miles north of Lookout Mountain. The Confederate pickets on the opposite side of the river could clearly see this group of enemy officers but did not fire on them. Grant later commented that, "I suppose, they looked upon the garrison of Chattanooga as prisoners of war, feeding or starving themselves, and thought it would be inhuman to kill any of them except in self-defence." [2]

The reason for this morning's ride was so Grant could see the terrain for himself; only so much can be learned from maps. The key to the Federal supply problem in Chattanooga, and any later movements in the vicinity, was the course of the Tennessee River around the city. As the river passes the city it turns south for a couple of miles until it runs past the northern end of Lookout Mountain. Making a sharp turn at Moccasin Bend, the river then flows back north creating a narrow piece of land called Moccasin Point. Flowing north for several miles the river passes the city and curves around to the west around the northern end of Raccoon Mountain and then turns southwest toward Bridgeport.[3]

The really important part of all this is that there was a narrow road running across Moccasin Bend that was hidden by woods from the Confederates on Lookout Mountain. This road began directly across the river from Chattanooga and ran just over a mile to a place called Brown's Ferry. On the other side of the river from Brown's Ferry was a gap in Raccoon Mountain that led back to the river at Kelley's Ferry, which could be easily reached from Bridgeport. General Smith proposed forcing the Confederates away from Raccoon Mountain, and putting up a pontoon bridge between Brown's Ferry and Chattanooga. This would provide a much shorter and easier route from Bridgeport to Chattanooga, thus ensuring sufficient supplies for the army.[4]

The obvious reason why this route had not already been opened was that Bragg's Confederates controlled the south side of the river from Lookout Mountain around Moccasin Bend and north to Raccoon Mountain. However, General Longstreet, the Confederate commander in this area, had concentrated most of his forces on Lookout Mountain, and the territory along the west side of the river and north to Raccoon Mountain was weakly held by scattered units. There was only one company of infantry guarding the gap opposite Brown's Ferry.[5]

General Smith's plan to open a new supply line contained three distinct parts, all of which had to work in order for the entire plan to succeed. The first, and most daring, part was to send a brigade of infantry in pontoon boats down the river and around Moccasin Bend during the dead of night. If this force could get through undiscovered by the Confederate pickets they would land on the shore opposite Brown's Ferry and take control of the eastern end of the gap in Raccoon Mountain. At the same time another brigade would cross Moccasin Point to Brown's Ferry on the same road Grant's party had just used. The boats that had transported the amphibious force would be used to build a pontoon bridge across the river and the land force would soon be able to join their comrades on the west side of the river to secure the road through Raccoon Mountain to Kelley's Ferry. Artillery positioned on the eastern bank would cover the landing party from across the river. If these two brigades could make it to the west side of the river there were nowhere near enough enemy troops on Raccoon Mountain to prevent them from accomplishing their mission.[6]

While the weakness of the Confederates around Raccoon Mountain should allow the surprise night attack to succeed there could be no doubt that both Longstreet and Bragg would see what the Federals were trying to do and quickly respond by sending large forces from Lookout Mountain toward Raccoon Mountain. This is where the Brown's Ferry route gained in importance. Once the pontoon bridge was in place the Federal troops in Chattanooga would be much closer to the scene than the Confederates on Lookout Mountain. Grant could reinforce his troops much faster than Longstreet could send forces to oppose them.

The third part of Smith's plan was perhaps the most important to ensure success. Anticipating a Confederate move toward Raccoon Mountain, Smith wanted to make use of Joe Hooker's divisions that were just sitting around Bridgeport and Stevenson. One of Hooker's divisions was guarding the railroad back to Nashville but the other three would be enough to accomplish the job Smith had in mind. Hooker could cross the Tennessee at Bridgeport and simply follow the railroad north. He would arrive at Wauhatchie, on the eastern side of Raccoon Mountain about four miles south of Brown's Ferry. Hooker's force would basically form a barrier from Wauhatchie to the river to prevent any Confederate force from Lookout Mountain from disrupting the new supply route.[7]

This was "Baldy" Smith's plan and it appeared to offer a quick solution to the Federal army's most vexing problem. Smith had already received approval from General Thomas to begin preparations. In fact the project had been originally conceived under General Rosecrans, but he did not act on it. Smith had established a sawmill along the river and was busily turning out wood for the boats. All that was required was Grant's approval to proceed and that the project be given priority for men and material. Grant immediately told Thomas and Smith to move ahead as quickly as possible, leaving the details in their capable hands.[8]

General Smith was given command of his operation and while preparations continued Grant had to take care of another serious situation. He had received a telegram from General Halleck saying that over 20,000 men had been detached from the Army of Northern Virginia and were on their way to Tennessee and that Grant would have to prevent Bragg from moving into East Tennessee. This report turned out to be totally inaccurate but Grant had to accept it as fact and make preparations to meet this new enemy.[9]

East Tennessee was full of Union supporters who had been suffering under Confederate rule. Gaining control of this area had been one of President Lincoln's pet projects since the beginning of the war. Unfortunately the problems of difficult terrain and lack of supplies had made invading and holding the region a low priority for the Federal commanders in the area. However, all that had changed during the past summer. Rosecrans's campaign that maneuvered Bragg out of Tennessee provided the opening, and Ambrose Burnside had brought his small Army of the Ohio down through Kentucky and took the city of Knoxville and the surrounding area.

Burnside was facing two problems as he tried to consolidate his gain. The first was that the lack of provisions was just as bad as everyone thought it would be. Burnside reported his "men had been on half rations from the moment of their arrival in East Tennessee." The Second problem facing Burnside was that his troops were spread out far and wide from Knoxville, mostly to cover more territory in the search for food. He also had to defend the city of Knoxville and the Cumberland Gap and it was simply not possible to assemble a significant force and march to Chattanooga to assist Rosecrans. There was also the fact that to abandon East Tennessee so soon after the loyal citizens had declared their support for the Union would have been a terrible move politically, to say nothing of the reprisals that would probably have been visited upon the citizens by Confederate sympathizers. So in the end Burnside stayed where he was with an army too big to feed itself and too small to defend itself. Grant was willing to assist Burnside if he could but on the 26th he was forced to admit "Thomas's command is in bad condition to move, for want of animals of sufficient strength to move his artillery, and for want of subsistence."[10]

What Grant was really concerned about, at least more than East Tennessee, was the possibility of an independent Confederate force getting past Burnside and approaching Chattanooga. About twenty-five miles east of Chattanooga the town of Cleveland lay on the railroad that connected to Atlanta. From there a Confederate army could head north toward Nashville and cut the supply line of the Army of the Cumberland, which would force the disastrous retreat that Grant had been sent to prevent. With the forces in Chattanooga unable to move the only other Federal troops that could prevent such a Confederate advance were Sherman's, and he was still slowly making his way east along the Memphis & Charleston Railroad, making repairs as he marched.[11]

On October 24 Grant sent an urgent message to Sherman, who at that time was just east of the Mississippi and Alabama border at Bear Creek:

> Drop everything east of Bear Creek and move with your entire force toward Stevenson until you receive further orders. The enemy are evidently moving a large force toward Cleveland, and may break through our lines and move on Nashville, in which event your troops are the only forces at command that could beat them there. With your forces here before the enemy cross the Tennessee we could turn their position so as to force them back.[12]

In a message to Halleck on the 26th Grant informed the general in chief of Smith's plan saying, "If successful, and I think it will be, the question of supplies will be fully settled." He also reported the fact that if a Confederate force moved up the river "our artillery horses are not in a condition to enable us to follow, and neither is our larder," and that Sherman's orders had been changed "with a view of having his forces in a position to use if the enemy should attempt this move." Grant also promised that he would "also endeavor to get the troops in a state of readiness for a forward movement at the earliest possible day." This last statement was the key to the strategic situation in Tennessee. Certainly Grant had been sent to Chattanooga to save the Army of the Cumberland but that was only the first step. Grant was given this new command because he was a fighter and his job would not be complete until Bragg was driven out of Tennessee and the way to the Deep South, and Atlanta, was open to invasion. But before any of this could occur the new supply route had to be opened and the attack was set to begin on the morning of October 27.[13]

General Smith needed fifty pontoon boats and two larger flat boats to transport the amphibious force around Moccasin Point. Brigadier General William B. Hazen was chosen to lead the assault and the landing party of 1,500 men would be taken from his brigade. The rest of Hazen's brigade would join the brigade of Brigadier General John B. Turchin, who would command the force moving overland to Brown's Ferry. The commanders did an excellent job of preparing for the assault. Turchin's men carried extra lumber so they could quickly build the pontoon bridge as soon as Hazen was done with the boats. In addition, axes were provided so the men in the landing party could cut down trees to provide defensive works and fires were prepared along the shoreline so Hazen's force could have some idea where they were while floating down the river in the darkness.[14]

The movement began about one o'clock on the morning of the 27th. Hazen's men were awakened and quietly loaded into the boats on the Chattanooga waterfront. They left behind anything that might make noise, such as bayonets and tin cups, taking only rifles and ammunition along with a few axes in each boat. The entire trip around Moccasin Point and back to Brown's Ferry was about nine miles, nearly seven of which were in full view of Confederate pickets. If they were discovered there was enough Confederate artillery in the area to blow the boats out of the water.[15]

About three o'clock the boats pushed off into the river. The boats were rowed until the first Confederate picket fire was sighted then they pulled over toward the right bank and let the current of the river carry them along. The men had been told how important it was to keep silent and there was only one real problem that occurred during the trip. A muffled shout went up as they were passing Lookout Mountain. An officer in one of the lead boats had been swept overboard by a tree branch jutting out from the water. The men in his boat thought they would never see him again but luckily he was picked up by one of the boats in the rear.[16]

While Hazen's men were floating along on the river General Turchin's column crossed the pontoon bridge at Chattanooga and marched across Moccasin Point to Brown's Ferry bringing three batteries of artillery under Major John Mendenhall. It didn't take them long to arrive at their designated position and they quietly waited in the woods for Hazen's men to arrive.[17]

Other than the man going overboard Hazen's men had a nerve-wracking but uneventful trip. The moon had been out at first but there was heavy cloud cover and fog and mist on the river. Around Moccasin Point they floated, sometimes seeing the enemy pickets gathered around their campfires. Hazen had hoped to arrive at the landing site before it got light and once again luck was with him. In the lead boat was Lieutenant Colonel James C. Foy of the 23rd Kentucky and it was his job to take the first men ashore and secure the landing place. It was still just barely dark when the last of the signal fires was passed and suddenly Hazen shouted, "Pull in Col. Foy; pull in! pull in!"[18]

Colonel Foy's boat immediately turned and made for shore. As soon as they came to a stop his men went running ashore and straight up the bank. It all happened so quickly that the Confederate pickets barely had time to let go a shot and then run back into the hills. Men from the other boats swarmed up the bank and forming their companies branched out to the right and left to secure the landing area. As the troops moved forward to the higher ground behind the riverbank the boats that carried them were already heading across the river to get Turchin's men. Hazen noted that the men disembarked from the boats and moved forward so quickly and that everyone did their job so well that "the entire crest was occupied, my skirmish lines out, and the axes working, before the reinforcements of the enemy, a little beyond the hill, came forward."[19]

As the Federal troops moved inland to take possession of the mouth of the valley the sounds of fighting began to increase. It was just barely light enough to see and the situation was confusing but Hazen's men continued to move forward. The Confederates in the area were from Lafayette McLaw's brigade of Longstreet's corps and they would not be pushed away without putting up some kind of fight. There was some confused fighting in the hazy light on the hills but Hazen's men were able to start cutting down trees and building defensive positions. By 5:30 A.M. General Smith was able to report, "We hold the crest."[20]

During the early morning hours the Confederates launched several uncoordinated attacks on the Federal positions on the high ground but these were easily repulsed and by the time full daylight arrived Turchin's men were landing. Later in the day the pontoon bridge to Brown's Ferry was completed and Mendenhall's artillery was brought across the river and the Federal positions were secure. At 3:30 P.M. General Smith reported, "This place cannot be carried now." Federal losses were less than forty men and they had control of their end of the valley. As an extra precaution General Thomas sent Brigadier General W. C. Whitaker with his brigade to Brown's Ferry in case General Smith's troops needed reinforcements but this extra manpower wasn't needed. So far everything had gone as planned, and now it was up to General Hooker to do his part.[21]

General Hooker began his movement around dawn on the 27th, about the same time Hazen's men were securing their positions in the hills above the river. Crossing the Tennessee at Bridgeport, General Howard led the Eleventh Corps consisting of two divisions commanded by Adolph von Steinwehr and Carl Schurtz. Behind Howard was John Geary's division of the Twelfth Corps. They had a relatively uneventful march along the railroad at the base of Raccoon Mountain, across Lookout Valley and past Wauhatchie. They brushed aside a few small bodies of Confederate skirmishers and by late afternoon the head of Howard's corps had arrived about a mile from Brown's Ferry. General Geary's small division, only about 1,500 men, was left about three miles behind at Wauhatchie to guard the rear. By the evening of the 28th all the facets of "Baldy" Smith's plan had come together beautifully; in fact few, if any, Civil War movements went as smoothly.[22]

By the time the Confederate commanders realized what was happening there was little they could do to stop the Federal movements. There had been plenty of time for the Confederates to prepare a defense against what had just happened but the feuding between Bragg and his subordinates, especially Longstreet, once more came into play. Longstreet was responsible for the Confederate left, from Chattanooga Creek, past Lookout Mountain to the Tennessee River on the other side of Raccoon Mountain. Even though he was well aware that Hooker's force was camped just across the river around Bridgeport, Longstreet concentrated his troops on the northern end of Lookout Mountain and in the valley to the east facing Chattanooga. No Confederate troops were posted in Lookout Valley or on Raccoon Mountain until October 9, when Bragg ordered Longstreet to send troops to those areas. Even now there were only two regiments assigned to set up skirmish lines that would be totally inadequate to prevent any sizable Union force from advancing along the route Hooker had just taken.[23]

In a normal situation between a commander and his subordinate Bragg probably should have seen this lack of preparation and brought it to Longstreet's attention. However, in the Army of Tennessee relations between the generals was anything but normal. Bragg had given Longstreet a remarkable degree of independence with his command. Possibly because of Longstreet's reputation as Lee's right hand man Bragg believed his subordinate knew what he was doing. It is also possible that because Longstreet exhibited such obvious distain for his commanding general that Bragg simply wanted to avoid the inevitable clash whenever they were together. Whatever problems existed between Bragg and Longstreet it must have been obvious to them that if the Federals were allowed to consolidate their gains and open a new supply route the Federal troops in Chattanooga could no longer be starved into submission or retreat.

Longstreet set up an attack on Hooker's troops for the night of October 28. The attack was to be made by three brigades under Brigadier General Micah Jenkins and one brigade commanded by Brigadier General Evander Law. Jenkins was ordered to "hold the point designated for General Law with a sufficient force, while a portion of his command moved up the road and captured or dispersed the rear guard." If the attack succeeded Jenkins could, "if time and circumstances favored it" move forward and attack Hooker's main body and endeavor to drive the enemy across the river; but if the latter should appear inexpedient, to recross the mountain before daylight." The assault was scheduled for 10 P.M. but the usual delays in moving troops at night caused a delay until midnight. Jenkins sent one of his brigades to join Law on some hills along the road between the main Federal force and Geary. Colonel John Bratton's brigade was to make the attack on Geary's camp with another brigade waiting on Law's left to support Bratton if needed.[24]

John Geary had been sensible enough to take precautions against a surprise attack when he made camp. His troops slept in line, fully dressed with weapons nearby. There had been some picket line firing before 11 P.M. but it died down and the men tried to go back to sleep. Between midnight and one A.M., however, Bratton's Confederates hit the Federal camp hard, but Geary's men were ready. The Confederates were stopped in their tracks and both sides settled down to a tough fight in the darkness lit only by the flash of muskets. As Geary reported:

> Charge after charge was made, each with redoubled effort upon our left, which they seemed determined to force, but each time the enemy's lines were hurled back under the unintermitting fire, both from infantry and artillery, that like a wall of flame opposed them.[25]

Back at Brown's Ferry the sounds of the battle quickly roused the rest of Hooker's command. General Howard remembered that he had just gotten up when a message from Hooker arrived: "Hurry, or you cannot save Geary. He has been attacked." Howard felt that Hooker was "quite anxious, as might be expected." In fact, Hooker had good reason to be anxious, as he was the one that left Geary stranded three miles away with no support. Orders quickly went to Howard and General Schurz, to start at once to Geary's aid. The surprise of the attack combined with the darkness and the haste to send aid to Geary produced confusion in Hooker's camp and caused delay and duplication of orders.[26]

As quickly as they could form ranks Howard's troops set out on the road to Wauhatchie but soon ran into General Law's Confederates positioned on hills overlooking the road where they were stationed to prevent reinforcements from reaching Geary. A deadly little fight ensued with Howard's men charging the slopes of the hills over and over, only to be thrown back by Law's tough

Oliver O. Howard (courtesy Library of Congress).

veterans. Learning of this second battle Hooker ordered more troops forward but in the confusion did not realize that these were the same units he had ordered to Wauhatchie.[27]

Down at Wauhatchie, Geary's men continued to hold their position although "the contest raged with vehemence along the whole line." On Geary's left the 137th New York "fought the over-reaching right of the enemy by part of them fighting back to back with the other part." After several hours of hard fighting the Confederates began to pull back about 3:30 A.M., and the battle was over. But the controversy was just beginning. General Law says he received a report about three o'clock that the Wauhatchie attack had failed and saw no reason to sacrifice his men needlessly so he pulled back. Longstreet, however, reported that Bratton was making good progress until Law abandoned his position, allowing reinforcements to join Geary. The bad blood between the Confederate commanders would continue and even increase in intensity. On the Federal side, Hooker condemned General Schurz in his report for not following orders. He was later cleared of any wrongdoing since the problem lay in the fact that in the confusion Hooker sent conflicting orders to Schurz, giving him two different assignments at the same time.[28]

Longstreet would later say that he did not use a larger force in the Wauhatchie attack because "they could not be reinforced, as the enemy's Moccasin batteries commanded the only road across the mountain." In addition to this somewhat feeble excuse he did not want to take troops out of their "proper positions in the line of investment for that purpose" because "to have done so would have broken our line and exposed the whole army." Since at this time the troops in Chattanooga could barely move let alone launch an attack, and the Confederates knew this, it is hard to see what Longstreet's troops would have been exposed to.[29]

The Federal position at Brown's Ferry was now safe and the opening of what would be known as the "cracker line," named after the hardtack crackers that were a staple of the soldier's diet, could proceed. On the evening of October 28 Grant had wired Halleck in Washington:

> General Thomas's plan for securing the river and south side road hence to Bridgeport has proven eminently successful. The question of supplies may now be regarded as settled. If the rebels give us one week more time I think all danger of losing territory now held by us will have passed away, and preparations may commence for offensive operations.[30]

Braxton Bragg was not aware of it yet but his army had just been put on the defensive.

The opening of the new supply line affected the common soldiers in more ways than just eliminating the prospect of starvation. A soldier in the 41st Ohio wrote: "What of the relief to the men of the Union army? It was beyond description. The depression which had lasted from the days at Chickamauga was gone. The troops felt as if they had been in prison, and were now free."[31]

In his *Memoirs* Grant wrote about the changes at Chattanooga:

> In five days from my arrival in Chattanooga the way was open to Bridgeport and, with the aid of steamers and Hooker's teams, in a week the troops were receiving full rations. It is hard for any one not an eye-witness to realize the relief this brought. The men were soon reclothed and also well fed; an abundance of ammunition was brought up, and a cheerfulness prevailed

not before enjoyed in many weeks. Neither officers nor men looked upon themselves any longer as doomed. The weak and languid appearance of the troops, so visible before, disappeared at once. I do not know what the effect was on the other side, but assume it must have been correspondingly depressing.[32]

One of Bragg's soldiers who felt the depression Grant wondered about was Lieutenant Joshua K. Callaway of the 28th Alabama who wrote to his wife on November 1: "I am almost dead to see you and be with you. My patience is worn entirely out with the war. I am perfectly miserable; but God knows if I could see any prospect for peace, even a year hence, I could manage to bear it. But I see no prospect for it even ten years hence. The Lord help us!" Lieutenant Callaway was killed on November 25.[33]

On a lighter note, as soon as the Brown's Ferry route was opened Grant began looking over the Confederate lines to see where they might be vulnerable. One morning along Chattanooga Creek where the pickets of both armies were separated only by the stream he left his escort behind to approach the shore without attracting attention. Horace Porter related that a Federal picket recognized Grant as he approached, and gave the customary cry, "Turn out the guard — commanding general!" The Confederates across the creek evidently heard this and one of them cried out, "Turn out the guard — General Grant!" The Confederate's comrades decided to play along and promptly formed up facing the Federal shore, and, exhibiting the mutual respect the fighting men of both sides had for their opponents, presented arms. Grant unhesitatingly returned the salute by lifting his hat to his countrymen and enemy.[34]

19

NOTHING TO DO BUT WAIT

The opening of the "cracker line" removed the threat of actual starvation for the Army of the Cumberland but General Grant still had other serious problems to overcome before he would be able to make any offensive movements and they all seemed to do with transportation. The railroads that brought provisions down from Nashville to Bridgeport and then to the Chattanooga area were simply wearing out from overuse. Grant would later report that even with the opening of the Brown's Ferry route, "The capacity of the railroad and steam-boats was not sufficient, however, to supply all the wants of the army, but actual suffering was prevented."[1]

On November 1 Grant sent a message to J. B. Anderson, the superintendent of military railroads in Nashville explaining what was required: "Send thirty, and if possible more, cars through to Stevenson and Bridgeport daily, loaded with rations." Anderson was told to send any and all supplies that the quartermaster's department could furnish and Grant expected "the road should be run to its utmost capacity, and should there be at any time spare cars, load them with rations or forage and send them through. On no account fail to send the thirty cars daily loaded with rations." Illustrating the need for more railroad transport Grant told Colonel C.L. Kilburn, the chief commissary officer in Louisville, that "cars can also be taken from the Louisville road" to bring supplies south.[2]

Another, and more serious, problem was that the Army of the Cumberland was virtually immobilized. The thousands of horses and mules that pulled artillery, wagons and ambulances were so weak that most were basically useless. In a message to the War Department, Montgomery C. Meigs, quartermaster general of the army, who was in Chattanooga to inspect the operations of his department, wrote that he believed it would take three months for the animals to regain enough strength before they would be useful again. "They should be returned to Louisville for this purpose. Hard work, exposure, short grain, and no long fodder have almost destroyed them." John Rawlins, Grant's chief of staff, also noted how the condition of the army's animals affected its ability to conduct operations. In a letter to James McPherson, in Vicksburg, Rawlins wrote: "Owing to the difficulties of getting forward supplies and the poverty of the animals, a forward movement from here, before spring, is exceedingly problematical."[3]

The railroads were the key to everything. Virtually all the supplies that came down from Nashville traveled on the single track of the Nashville & Chattanooga Railroad that joined the Memphis & Charleston at Stevenson, which then ran to Bridgeport. It was already difficult to move enough provisions down this one line to supply the Army of the Cumberland, and the demands for just about everything an army needed to operate were going to increase dramatically. Grant was well aware that when Sherman's force arrived it "made an additional army, with cavalry, artillery, and trains," which would have to draw its supplies from Nashville. In addition, "All indications pointed also to the probable necessity of supplying Burnside's command in East Tennessee, twenty-five thousand more, by the same route. A single track could not do this."[4]

There was a possible solution to this problem but it would not be easy. About seventy miles west of Stevenson, Alabama, there was another railroad line, the Nashville & Decatur, that ran about one hundred miles from Nashville to Decatur, Alabama, where it intersected the Memphis & Charleston, which then continued to Stevenson and Bridgeport. By utilizing this road the amount of supplies that could be brought into the area around Chattanooga could be increased dramatically. Unfortunately, the tracks from Nashville to Decatur ran through an area with numerous rivers and streams and as Grant later wrote, "All the bridges over these had been destroyed, and the rails taken up and twisted by the enemy. All the cars and locomotives not carried off had been destroyed as effectually as they knew how to destroy them." Putting the road back into operating condition would be a massive undertaking.[5]

There was also a shortage of railroad engines and cars, so much so that Grant began taking cars from wherever he could find them. On November 3 Grant wrote to General McPherson to send without delay "all the locomotives at Vicksburg with the exception of two and all the cars with the exception of ten. Let the locomotives and cars be the best you have. They are required for immediate use."[6]

To rebuild the Nashville & Decatur Grant chose Brigadier General Grenville Dodge, who "besides being a most capable soldier, was an experienced railroad builder." Sherman was ordered to send Dodge and his division to take over the railroad line and restore it to working order as quickly as possible, a daunting task. There were shortages of everything from track to cars to bridge material but Grant gave this project the highest priority and personally intervened to hurry things up. He ordered Anderson, in Nashville, to expedite the ordering of bridge building materials and to send down several prefabricated bridges from Louisville. Since it would take too long to get new rails from the manufacturers, Grant had troops tearing up small branch lines around Tennessee and Kentucky that weren't being used and shipping the rails to General Dodge's work gangs. It really was a remarkable effort but the entire one hundred miles of railroad was put into working condition forty days after Dodge received his orders.[7]

With the supply situation in Chattanooga improving Grant was able to devote more attention to Burnside's situation in Knoxville. By the first week of November it had become clear that the twenty thousand or more troops that were supposed to be moving into Tennessee from Virginia were not coming, which removed the threat of losing Knoxville by force. But as Grant knew "Burnside was in about as desperate a condition as the Army of the Cumberland had been, only he was not yet besieged." Knoxville was nearly one hundred miles from the nearest supply base and any Union controlled railroad was farther away. "East Tennessee still furnished supplies of beef, bread and forage, but it did not supply ammunition, clothing, medical supplies, or small rations, such as coffee, sugar, salt and rice." Nothing could be done for Burnside, however, until the second railroad line was opened and Sherman's troops arrived. Braxton Bragg, however, inconveniently refused to wait.[8]

Now that the Brown's Ferry supply line was open and safe from disruption Bragg could see that the opportunity of achieving a relatively bloodless victory by starving the Army of the Cumberland out of Chattanooga was gone and his other options were limited. An all-out assault against the well-fortified city was out of the question as the chances of success were small and the casualties would almost surely be unacceptable. To retreat would be to admit failure, destroy what was left of the army's morale, and, after the slaughter at Chickamauga, end Bragg's military career. Just as unacceptable would be to sit on the heights around Chattanooga and wait for Grant to build up his strength and eventually launch an attack at a time and place of his choosing.

It appeared to Bragg that the best opportunity lay in making a movement toward Knoxville. This would provide more protection for his supply line and the East Tennessee & Georgia Railroad, which went through Knoxville and then all the way into southwestern Virginia, increasing the sources for supplies. In addition, there were several thousand Confederate troops under Major General Samuel Jones in southwest Virginia guarding salt works and lead mines in the area and these troops might be tapped for reinforcements or a combined move against Knoxville. But what might be the best reason of all to make the move, at least for Bragg, was the opportunity to get rid of James Longstreet.[9]

When Jefferson Davis had made his visit to Bragg's headquarters in early October one of the subjects that was discussed was sending Longstreet to attack Burnside in Knoxville. General Lee wanted his right-hand-man to return to the Army of Northern Virginia and sending Longstreet to Knoxville would bring Lee's troops that much closer to Virginia. It was also hoped that by threatening President's Lincoln's precious East Tennessee Grant would be forced to send troops from Chattanooga, or Sherman's force when it arrived, to reinforce Burnside.[10]

On November 4 Bragg ordered Longstreet to take his command, consisting of McLaw and Hood's divisions, and move toward Knoxville in order to "drive Burnside out of East Tennessee first, or better, to capture or destroy him." Longstreet began leaving the works on Lookout Mountain the next day with about fifteen thousand men. Grant learned of Longstreet's departure quickly enough but admitted, "The situation seemed desperate, and was more aggravating because nothing could be done until Sherman should get up."[11]

When the high command back in Washington learned that Bragg was sending troops to attack Burnside they rained telegrams on Grant urging him "to do something for Burnside's relief; calling attention to the importance of holding East Tennessee; saying the President was much concerned for the protection of the loyal people in that section, etc."[12]

Grant tried to get action and on the 7th he ordered Thomas to attack the northern end of Missionary Ridge "with all the force you can bring to bear against it, and, when that is carried, to threaten, and even attack, if possible, the enemy's line of communications between Dalton and Cleveland." If Thomas could carry the northern end of Missionary Ridge his troops could move out past the mountain and break the railroad between Dalton, Georgia, and Cleveland, Tennessee. This was Longstreet's lifeline and most of Bragg's provisions also came through Dalton; any threat to either area should force Longstreet's return.[13]

The desperate nature of Grant's order comes through when he wrote that the troops were to carry four days of rations in their haversacks and told Thomas that if horses were not available "to move the artillery, mules must be taken from the teams or horses from ambulances; or, if necessary, officers dismounted and their horses taken. The movement should not be made one moment later than to-morrow morning." Grant informed Halleck of his orders for the attack and wrote to Burnside confidently telling him that the attack "must have the effect to draw the enemy back from your western flank." Grant then went on to give Burnside suggestions as to what action to take if the Confederates failed to cooperate by withdrawing.[14]

It turned out, however, that General Thomas had to inform Grant that his order could not be carried out at that time. The animals of the army simply could not move all the wagons and artillery that would be needed. Even if there were enough of them mules would probably panic at the first sound of gunfire and officers' horses were not strong enough to pull guns. Even if they could break through the lines on Missionary Ridge without wagons to carry provisions and ammunition the army could not travel far enough to complete the mission of severing the Confederate supply route. An embarrassed Grant had to wire Halleck the next day that "General Thomas cannot make the movement telegraphed yesterday for several days yet." And he informed Burnside that his relief would have to wait until Sherman's forces arrived.[15]

This was probably the most frustrating period of the war for Grant. In sending away Longstreet and two divisions of infantry Bragg had given the Federal army a golden opportunity, and Grant was unable to take advantage of it. The Army of the Cumberland was stuck where it was and for the time being nothing could be done about it. Two weeks later Grant was still upset. In a message to Halleck on November 21 he wrote: "I have never felt such restlessness before as I have at the fixed and immovable condition of the Army of the Cumberland. General Meigs states that the loss of animals here will exceed 10,000. Those left are scarcely able to carry themselves."[16]

Finally, on November 13, there was some good news for Grant and the army in Chattanooga; General Sherman's troops had reached Bridgeport. His army of about 17,000 men had made a miserable march. Moving slowly through the mountains on narrow, muddy roads they seldom had enough to eat and day after day they were pelted by cold rain. After reaching Bridgeport Sherman decided his men had gone hungry long enough and ordered that the supply wagons should follow behind each division. This made it easier to feed the men but at the same time the wagons got stuck in the muddy roads and the entire column was slowed to a crawl.[17]

It would take a day or two for Sherman's entire force to come up so he rode into Chattanooga to meet with Grant on the 14th. To say that Grant was pleased to have his old friend, and his troops, under his command again would certainly be an understatement. When Sherman arrived at headquarters he and Grant greeted each other like old friends rather than commander and subordinate. Grant, Thomas, and Sherman spent much of the evening casually discussing the situation until they arrived at a plan to deal with the Confederate army around Chattanooga.[18]

The next morning the generals went out to make a survey of the surrounding area in person. Sherman noted the Confederate positions on Missionary Ridge and the works on Lookout Mountain and could easily see the enemy pickets walking their posts. Sherman could not help but remark, "'Why,' said I, 'General Grant, you are besieged'; and he said, 'It is too true.' Up to that moment I had no idea that things were so bad." During this reconnaissance the generals learned that there were good roads from Brown's Ferry that Sherman could use to move north behind a series of hills that would hide his movement from the enemy. It would be difficult, at least for a while, for Bragg to learn if Sherman was heading toward Knoxville or staying at Chattanooga. In addition to the hidden roads it was also discovered that the northern end of Missionary Ridge was lightly manned. Sherman went back to his troops on the 16th and work began to implement the attacks.[19]

Grant later wrote that he had already completed his basic plans for the coming battle before Sherman's troops arrived and that only the date to begin the move was left open. It was decided that Lookout Mountain was not all that important and Hooker was ordered to send Howard's corps up to the hills opposite Chattanooga. The rest of Hooker's force was to move into Chattanooga Valley. The crucial role was left to Grant's trusted friend, Sherman, who was to cross the Tennessee at Brown's Ferry and move behind the hills where he would be out of sight of the Confederates on Missionary Ridge. General Smith had 116 pontoon boats waiting in the North Chickamauga, about seven or eight miles east of the city. At night one of Sherman's divisions would board these boats and float down to the Tennessee where a few boats were to head for the mouth of the South Chickamauga a few miles past the city, and lay a bridge across the river. The rest of the division would land on the south shore opposite the north end of Missionary Ridge and establish their position. The boats could then be used to ferry the rest of Sherman's force across the river. Sherman would then assault the lightly defended north end of Missionary Ridge threatening the railroad in Bragg's rear.[20]

Originally Hooker was to cross from Lookout Valley, where he was protecting the supply line, over the northern end of Lookout Mountain to Chattanooga Valley then move south of the Confederate lines to Rossville. From there Hooker could move north threatening Bragg's rear and left flank. Grant later changed his mind because "the passage over the mountain was a difficult one to make in the face of an enemy" and he "was perfectly willing that the enemy should keep Lookout Mountain until we got through with the troops on Missionary Ridge." The plan was changed so that when the battle began Hooker's force could be better used by following Sherman's route to Chattanooga and then moving out to the right toward Rossville. When it came time to launch the attack, however, Hooker's orders were changed back to the original plan because the river was so high that the Brown's Ferry crossing was not safe.[21]

Grant felt that Thomas's troops were demoralized from their defeat at Chickamauga and weakened from the time spent on short rations in Chattanooga. He wanted General Thomas to form his troops in front of Missionary Ridge to draw attention away from the flanks where the real assaults would take place. After the battle was joined Thomas's men could either help out on the flanks or make a demonstration against the enemy works in the center of Missionary Ridge. Grant's plans were flexible enough to take into consideration what Sherman found when he actually reached the northern end of Missionary Ridge and what steps Bragg might take in response.[22]

In addition to making plans to defeat the Confederates at Chattanooga, East Tennessee and Burnside were always on Grant's mind. As soon as he learned Sherman had arrived at Bridgeport Grant wrote to Burnside informing him of this development and asking if he could hold Longstreet in check until Sherman got up and Grant was able to "force the enemy back from here and place a force between Longstreet and Bragg." On the 17th Grant told Burnside that he was "doing exactly what appears to me right. I want the enemy's progress retarded at every foot all it can be, only giving up each place when it becomes evident that it cannot be longer held without endangering your force to capture." In another message Grant told Burnside of the specifics of the plan to attack Bragg, advising him that since Sherman's advance troops were just reaching Bridgeport it not be until the 19th at the earliest that the attacks would begin and again inquiring if Burnside could hold out till then.[23]

As it turned out Burnside was not in as much danger as was previously believed. For some reason Longstreet halted his march at Loudon until the 13th. Grant believed that since this was the end of his railroad connections "it is probable he was directed to remain there awaiting orders. He was in a position threatening Knoxville, and at the same time where he could be brought back speedily to Chattanooga." Longstreet later wrote that his troops had been delayed because of lack of rail transportation. Whatever the reason it gave the Federals a little breathing room.[24]

Sherman began moving his troops up from Bridgeport on Tuesday, November 17, and he quickly learned that Grant's original timetable could not be met. It started raining and it continued to rain for two days. The roads turned to mud and Sherman's army could not move much faster than a crawl. If this wasn't bad enough the heavy rain made the river rise which damaged the pontoon bridge at Brown's Ferry.[25]

The head of Sherman's column did not arrive at Brown's Ferry until the 20th, and most of the troops were still strung out far behind. Sherman sent General Hugh Ewing's division south to create a diversion by appearing to move on Lookout Mountain. Grant wanted Sherman to begin his assault on the north end of Missionary Ridge the next day. Word had come that a battle was raging at Knoxville, communication with Burnside had been cut off and Grant was anxious to begin, but it was not physically possible. Grant had to change his orders again, changing the day of the assault to the 22nd, ordering Thomas to also move on that day. But, as Grant recorded "the elements were against us. It rained all the 20th and 21st. The river rose so rapidly that it was difficult to keep the pontoons in place."[26]

During the next two days Sherman crossed his men over the river as quickly as the weather would allow. At this point he was in full view of the Confederates on Lookout Mountain but once across the river the troops were hidden from view by the hills. Sherman then moved behind the hills up to a point on the other side of the river from the north end of Missionary Ridge. Grant had to postpone the assault until Sherman was ready, which now looked like it would not be until Monday, November 23.[27]

Thomas was concerned that the delay would allow the Confederates to discover

Sherman's movements. On Sunday, the 22nd, he urged Grant to again change Hooker's orders so that he would attack Lookout Mountain, which should draw attention and perhaps men away from the north and center of Missionary Ridge. By now, however, Hooker's force was a grab bag of different units. Howard's divisions had gone north to cooperate with Sherman, and only John Geary's division remained of Hooker's original four divisions. Joining Hooker was Charles Cruft's division of Granger's corps that had been sent to assist in opening the cracker line and one of Sherman's divisions commanded by Peter J. Osterhaus that had been stranded on the south side of the river when the Brown's Ferry bridge fell apart. None of these units had ever worked together before but even if they did not actually capture Lookout Mountain an attack there would make a useful diversion.[28]

Back on November 20 Grant had received an unusual letter from Bragg: "As there may still be some non-combatants in Chattanooga, I deem it proper to notify you that prudence would dictate their early withdrawal." Whatever Bragg's intentions were, this note worried no one. Grant "understood that this was a device intended to deceive; but I did not know what the intended deception was." Charles Dana was even more specific, "Of course, we all knew this was a bluff." Two days later, however, a Confederate deserter let it be known that Bragg was going to retreat and that same day it was learned that two Confederate divisions, Cleburne's and Buckner's, had pulled out of the lines and were headed toward Knoxville. Even though Bragg must have known about the Federal troop movements he was so sure of the strength of his works that he was willing to further reduce his strength. Bragg also felt that Grant would detach some of his forces to support Burnside but up to this point there was no proof of any Federals troops leaving the Chattanooga area.[29]

Grant decided it was time to move, "I determined, therefore, to do on the 23d, with the Army of the Cumberland, what had been intended to be done on the 24th." Early on the 23rd Grant ordered Thomas to make a demonstration to see if the Confederates were pulling out or not. He also sent orders to Hooker that if Osterhaus was unable to cross the river by the next morning he should place himself under Hooker's command and the entire force under Hooker should attack Lookout Mountain. By then Sherman would be able to launch his assault in the north and both ends of the Confederate line would be under attack, with Thomas waiting for an opportunity to attack in the center.[30]

One of the strong points in the Federal line was Fort Wood, located opposite the center of Missionary Ridge about two miles away. About halfway between the Federal lines and the Confederate lines at the base of the ridge was a lightly manned Confederate advance line on a chain of low hills, Orchard Knob being the highest, a rough hill about one hundred feet high that stuck out from the relatively flat surface of the valley. Another reason to pick Orchard Knob as the target was that Grant did not want to draw attention to either of the enemy's flanks, where the real attacks were to be made.[31]

General Thomas may have been slow to act but when he did it was with overwhelming strength. Four divisions were massed in front of the Federal lines in plain sight of the Confederates. General Granger's two divisions were formed in the center with Sheridan on the right and Wood on the left, extending almost to Citico Creek.

Palmer's corps was brought up for support with Johnson's division on Sheridan's right. In addition, Thomas stationed Howard's corps behind the center of the line just in case. Over twenty thousand men formed up in straight lines with flags waving and bayonets glistening in the sun. The scene looked the way war was supposed to look, colorful and heroic, the way the men who enlisted in 1861 thought war would be like and not the horror they had learned was the reality. The Confederates on the heights looked down on the mass of blue thinking they were forming for a grand review.[32]

The signal was given about 1:30 P.M. and the perfectly aligned wave of blue moved forward. Only now did the Confederate pickets and those in the rifle-pits along Orchard Knob and the other hills realize they were being attacked. They began firing into the Federal lines but they were too few to stop the massive force coming down on their positions. From the heights of Missionary Ridge artillery fire came down on the Federal lines but it was too late. There were some crumbled heaps of blue dotting the field and some ambulances came hurrying back with wounded but Thomas's men continued on. The Confederate pickets were easily brushed aside as Wood's men pressed forward to Orchard Knob. General Willich's brigade moved up the hill and pushed the defenders from the summit as Hazen's brigade captured the hill to the right. Sheridan's men overran the enemy lines to the right of the hills and in about an hour Thomas's troops had control of the entire line. The attack happened so quickly that Bragg had no chance to send reinforcements to make a real fight of it and the surviving Confederates scurried back to the first line of works at the base of Missionary Ridge.[33]

Quartermaster General Montgomery Meigs, who was visiting from Washington, wrote to Secretary Stanton that the enemy had no idea that an assault was coming until Thomas opened fire: "Prisoners assert that they thought the whole movement was a review and general drill, and then it was too late to send to their camps for reinforcements, and they were overwhelmed by force of numbers. It was a surprise in open daylight."[34]

Later in the afternoon Thomas moved Howard's troops up on Wood's left, artillery was brought up and the works on the hills were improved. The fight itself was a small affair, about two hundred casualties on each side. But the move was much more important than it might appear to be. Clearly Grant learned that Bragg was still firmly planted on the heights. Even more important was that the Federal lines were now much closer to Missionary Ridge, an important consideration for a future assault. In addition, the attack on his center caused Bragg to pull Walker's division off Lookout Mountain to strengthen his center and right, significantly weakening the defense on Lookout Mountain.[35]

While the capture of Orchard Knob significantly improved the Federal position it also forced Bragg into making some decisions that had the potential to materially aid the Confederates. Bragg could now see that Grant was getting ready to launch a major offensive, probably very soon. Bragg felt confident that his positions were strong but nevertheless he immediately recalled Cleburne and Buckner's divisions. As it turned out most of Buckner's troops were too far away but one of his brigades and all of Cleburne's troops were able to return — very important additional manpower, as it would turn out. In addition, with Thomas threatening the center of the Missionary Ridge area Bragg ordered that fortifications be built along the crest of the ridge. Previous to this there were only rifle pits at the base of the ridge. It would seem like a major lapse in judgment not to have already entrenched on the crest but because of limited access it was difficult to supply troops along the top of Missionary Ridge for any length of time. Now that a battle looked imminent Bragg could delay no longer.[36]

While Thomas's men were capturing Orchard Knob, Sherman was struggling to get his men up to Brown's Ferry and across the river. The pontoon bridge was broken several times during the day but by the evening of the 23rd Sherman was in position to cross the river north of Chattanooga and head for the northern end of Missionary Ridge.[37]

20

LOOKOUT MOUNTAIN

The morning of November 24 was cold, rainy, and miserable. South of Chattanooga fog and low clouds obscured most of Lookout Mountain. Union major general Joseph Hooker was perfectly contented with the dismal weather. Originally his part in the coming battle was to have been a relatively minor one: provide a diversion and try to get in the rear of the Confederate army after General Sherman began the main movement on the northern end of Missionary Ridge. Now, mostly due to circumstances beyond his control, Hooker had the opportunity to play a major role in the battle and redeem his military reputation that had been so badly damaged by Stonewall Jackson and Robert E. Lee at Chancellorsville the previous spring.[1]

Lookout Mountain had lost much of its strategic importance after the supply route through Brown's Ferry had been opened at the end of October. The Confederate supply lines ran behind Missionary Ridge and the capture of Lookout Mountain would do little to bring about, Grant's ultimate objective, the destruction of Bragg's army. But, with the addition of Osterhaus to Hooker's command Grant decided that three divisions were too large a force not to give them something meaningful to do. On the night of the 23rd Grant sent orders that if Osterhaus, who was still in the vicinity of Brown's Ferry, could not get across the river by 8 A.M. he was to join Hooker, who was then ordered to attack Lookout Mountain.[2]

Hooker might have been pleased at the opportunity to conduct a real assault

Joseph Hooker (courtesy Library of Congress).

instead of just a diversion, but the idea of trying to wrest control of that huge rock from veteran Confederate soldiers would have made anyone take time to pause and consider the difficulty of the task. The terrain facing Hooker's troops was steep and heavily wooded rising about two-thirds of the way up the mountain where it leveled off to form sort of a shoulder where a few houses and small farms were located. Above this shoulder the mountain rises steeply again until it turns into a sheer rock palisade for the last fifty feet or more to the summit. The palisade runs around the north end and for miles back along both sides of the mountain. The very top of the mountain is a plateau that forms a point above the river and widens to about two miles as it moves south.[3]

It was on the shoulder of the mountain that the Confederates had placed their main defensive positions. Earthworks, reinforced with logs, had been built across the steep northern end of the mountain and continued down both the east and west sides. General Hooker reported that along this mostly level ground "a continuous line of earth-works had been thrown up, while redoubts, redans, and pits appeared lower down the slope, to repel an assault from the direction of the river." Along the flanks of the mountain "were rifle-pits, epaulements for batteries, walls of stone, and abatis to resist attack from either the Chattanooga or Lookout Valleys."[4]

There were two groups of Confederate defenders on Lookout Mountain. On the shoulder two brigades of Cheatham's division were stationed where they could command the slope below. The Confederate defenders on the western slope were from Walthall's Mississippi Brigade. Part of his brigade faced west, downhill toward the creek, and he also had a thin line on his left stretching back to the palisade to protect that flank. Along the lower slopes a picket line was established from Lookout Creek around the north end of the mountain to Chattanooga Creek on the east side. On the level top of the mountain two brigades of Stevenson's division were guarding against Federal attempts to reach the top through gaps in the palisade, and to support artillery that had been positioned on the crest to shell the Federal works in Chattanooga, without much success.[5]

Around daybreak General Geary brought his division and Walter Whitaker's brigade of Cruft's division down past Wauhatchie under cover of the fog. Turning sharply to the east they forded Lookout Creek about 8:30 A.M., capturing forty-two defenders. The rest of Cruft's division moved to seize two damaged bridges over the creek near the railroad to effect a crossing for themselves and Osterhaus' division. Grose's brigade drove the Confederate skirmishers from the bridge and immediately started making repairs. The fighting at the bridge brought Confederate defenders down from the mountain and into their works along the railroad which, as Hooker reported, "enabled them, without exposure, to sweep, with a fire of musketry, the field over which our troops would be compelled to march for a distance of 300 or 400 yards."[6]

Concern about heavy casualties and waiting for news of Geary's troops caused some delay but about 10:30 A.M. Hooker decided it was time to make a move. Cruft was instructed to leave two regiments to continue working on the bridge and send the rest of Grose's brigade about half a mile up the creek to construct another bridge and then join Geary's troops when they approached along the slope. Hooker also established several batteries of artillery to fire on the enemy positions in the valley and along the slopes of the mountain.[7]

While Cruft and Osterhaus were engaged in making their way across the creek Geary continued his move south. The clouds and mist hid the Federals from view as they moved up the valley until they were well past the Confederate positions. They then turned left and began the difficult climb up the side of the mountain. Whitaker's brigade was in the lead driving back the Confederate pickets as they ascended the slope. Upon reaching the palisade Whitaker then turned north with his right flank near the palisade and joined with Geary's troops below forming a line that stretched over the shoulder and down the mountain side facing north.[8]

Once Geary had his men in line they began to sweep forward across the western face of Lookout Mountain. The ground was difficult to move over and one of Whitaker's men, Isaac C. Doan, of the 40th Ohio, later wrote that they were frequently "descending into ravines that furrow the slope, climbing the opposite bank with infinite labor." The Federals made slow but steady progress and Doan also wrote, "We make up for lack of speed, with yells, while the opposite mountain sends back the echoing battle cry, until the rebels afterward captured said they thought there was a million of us."[9]

General Walthall only had one regiment covering his left and they were no match for Geary's force. As Geary's line swept across the slope heading north, Osterhaus and Cruft were still contending with the enemy in their front. About 11:30 A.M. the troops at the creek finished their bridge and Osterhaus and Grose's troops began to flood across to engage Walthall's men, supported by artillery from Moccasin Point. Grose joined his troops to the extreme left of Geary's line as they continued to move across the face of the mountain. The fighting here grew more serious but the Confederates were holding on when suddenly the left flank of Walthall's line was struck by a wave of blue clad men. The Confederates were pushed back into their main works which Geary describes as "covering the whole plateau in front of the left of my right and my center, formidable in natural defense and seemingly impregnable with rocks, stone, and earth breastworks, surrounded by tangled slashings."[10]

Walthall tried to hold his lines on the west side instead of pulling back to the much stronger position on the northern end of the mountain. He also brought forward his reserve regiment in piecemeal fashion, which did nothing to slow the mass of Union soldiers coming at his troops. Geary reported that his men were "full of animation and enthusiasm" and despite fire from enemy troops hidden in gorges and from the crest above they "made a sudden and vigorous assault." Colonel David Ireland's brigade along with the 29th and 111th regiments from Pennsylvania "hurled themselves upon their flank with furious effort. Our fire was delivered in continuous volleys while hotly pressing upon and encompassing the camp." The Mississippians fought bravely but, attacked from the front and flank by overwhelming numbers, the Confederate line gave way. "The ardor of our men," Geary reported, "surprised and stultified the enemy, and we punished him severely in his irresolution." The Federal troops steadily pushed Walthall's stubborn survivors back until they reached the northern slope around noon.[11]

On the northern end of the mountain the going became much more difficult for the Union troops. The slope was steeper and littered with boulders with narrow but deep little gullies scattered here and there. It was on the shoulder of the northern end of the mountain that the Confederates had built their strongest defensive works, intending to make a stand here to prevent any Union force from moving around the mountain into Chattanooga Valley. On the shoulder at the point of the north end of the mountain was the farm of Robert Cravens. It was here that the Confederates planned to halt any Federal advance. The ground had been fortified with rifle pits and stone walls and a couple of pieces of artillery were strategically placed on the grounds of the once peaceful farm.[12]

Walthall rallied the remaining troops from his brigade to defend the ground around the farm and General John Moore's brigade came up into position on the right to defend the line from Craven's house down the slope. Once again the Confederates tried to put up a fight and once again they were flanked out of their positions. The Federal troops closest to the palisade came down upon Walthall's left flank and in the center, around the Craven house, Geary's men attacked relentlessly. The Federal troops jumped over logs, climbed boulders, sometimes crawling over the rough terrain, but they kept coming, cheering as they advanced. The Confederate artillery was all but useless in the confusing melee and the gunners eventually joined the fight on the lines. Moore tried to hold the blue tide back but when Walthall's troops broke for the rear he could not hold his position without being flanked and possibly trapped on the side of the mountain, and Moore's troops also fell back around the end of the mountain or down into the valley below.[13]

All morning the Federal troops down in Chattanooga heard the firing on Lookout Mountain. Because of the location of the fighting and the fog and low clouds, however, they could not see anything. As the morning wore on into afternoon the sounds of battle came closer and closer, and increased in intensity as the fighting became heavier on the northern end of the mountain around the Craven farm. The crack of muskets and the roar of artillery echoed between the mountains and to the men between Lookout Mountain and Missionary Ridge it sounded as if a huge battle was being waged, but all they could do was stare at the fog and smoke from the battle and wonder what was going on.[14]

One of Thomas's men, Major James A. Connolly, wrote to his wife that while the men were waiting for some news of what was happening, "All eyes are turned toward the Mountain, and the stillness of death reigns among us in the valley, as we listen to the sounds of battle on the other side of the Mountain while all was quiet as a Puritan Sabbath on our side of it." Suddenly, the wind blew away the clouds and smoke and fog and for a very brief moment the sun shone on the mountain and the soldiers of the Army of the Cumberland were astonished by what they saw.[15]

Around the slope of Lookout Mountain came hundreds and hundreds of Confederates, in full retreat. Close behind them came line after line of blue-coated soldiers with rifle barrels glistening in the sun and flags flying. Thousands of Thomas's soldiers exploded with joy, cheering, throwing their caps in the air, bands began to play all across the Federal lines, and the artillery roared in salute. Major Connolly wrote, "Oh! Such a cheer as then went up in the valley! Manly cheeks were wet with tears of joy." The celebrating lasted only a short time as the clouds soon hid the sun and the fog covered the mountain, but the men in Chattanooga knew they had seen victory and now they wanted to join in.[16]

It was now early afternoon and the fighting had shifted to the eastern side of Lookout Mountain as Hooker's troops pursued the Confederates around the mountain's northern end. Soon, however, the Confederates were able to form another line and the retreat ended. Geary reported that "about 500 yards beyond Craven's house, and in front of the mountain road, the enemy, already reported, appeared in heavy force." From the summit of the mountain Stevenson, who wasn't able to participate in the battle so far because of the angle of the slope, sent down part of his force to reinforce Walthall's surviving troops. With a brief rest and re-supplied with ammunition the Confederates were able to form a line that extended all the way up the slope to the palisade, eliminating the ability of the Federals to flank their position as they had been doing. The Confederates "made several charges within a very short time, and were as often repulsed to their original line."[17]

By one o'clock the fog had closed in heavier than before, it began to rain again and Hooker decided it was impractical for his exhausted men to try to continue advancing. The Federal troops had accomplished everything that could have been expected. The enemy had been swept off the western and northern slopes and enough of the eastern side had been taken to command the Confederate works in Chattanooga Valley. The Confederates, however, were not finished. Geary reported that around "1 o'clock the enemy made an assault in force upon my left," which was beaten back. Still later in the day, about three o'clock, "the enemy were observed massing a force under the cliff of the extreme right held by Cobham." This threat was also quickly broken up and the serious fighting was over. There was some scattered firing through the night and both sides kept up their guard. Geary's men "suffered considerably from the intensely cold winds that swept around the mountain sides," but even though they were tired and cold "many expressed their impatience for the coming of day that the attack might be renewed." They had tasted victory, it was sweet, and they wanted more.[18]

From the Confederate point of view the fighting on Lookout Mountain had been a debacle. General Stevenson took over the command of all the Lookout Mountain forces after Hardee had been transferred to the right. Stevenson did not have time to get acquainted with the terrain or the defensive positions around the mountain since it was already dark when he took command and the fighting began at first light the next day. Most of the fighting along the slopes was done by Jackson's troops, who put up a good fight but had no real chance against Hooker's overwhelming numbers. Bragg was unhappy with the performance of his commanders on Lookout Mountain, blaming Stevenson for not using all the troops at his disposal, but since he knew the heights had lost their importance he was not willing to make a major effort to hold the mountain.[19]

A few hours before Hooker's assault on Lookout Mountain and on the other end of the Federal lines General Sherman put into motion what was supposed to be the principal part of Grant's plans to defeat Bragg's army. About two o'clock in the morning Sherman watched as Brig. Gen. Giles A. Smith's brigade was loaded into pontoon boats waiting along the shore of North Chickamauga Creek. They quietly floated along into the Tennessee and proceeded downriver until about 2:30 A.M. when they came to a landing area on the south bank above the mouth of the South Chickamauga Creek where two regiments landed and captured the Confederate pickets. The rest of Smith's brigade continued down the Tennessee to a point below the Chickamauga where the leading boats pulled to their left and Smith's men began splashing ashore. The few Confederate pickets on duty were quickly captured and soon the boats were headed back to the opposite shore for more troops. By sunrise two division of Sherman's army, nearly eight thousand men, had been transported across the river and were entrenching their positions. Like Hooker at Lookout Mountain, Sherman was assisted by the dark, gloomy skies and misty rain that made it difficult for Confederate lookouts on the heights to see what was going on below them. In addition to the help from nature Sherman's troops were covered by over fifty pieces of artillery set up by Thomas's chief of artillery, General Brannan, the previous night, on the low hills which had hidden Sherman's men from view.[20]

By the time it was light "Baldy" Smith and his engineering troops arrived and began to assemble the boats that ferried Sherman's men across the river into a pontoon bridge. In addition to the bridge across the Tennessee, another bridge was built over Chickamauga Creek that connected Sherman's main force with the troops that had landed above the creek. Once again Smith and his engineers performed wonders. An impressed Sherman later wrote, "I have never beheld any work done so quietly, so well, and I doubt if the history of war can show a bridge of that extent (viz. 1,350 feet) laid down so noiselessly and well in so short a time."[21]

While the troops secured their positions on the far shore and the engineers worked on the bridge Sherman's third division was ferried across the river by the small steamboat *Dunbar*. Surprisingly there was no Confederate attack to drive the small beachhead into the river, only occasional picket firing and a small amount of artillery fire from Missionary Ridge, too far away to be very accurate. About noon, General Howard arrived directly from Chattanooga with a brigade of his corps after marching up the left bank. Not long after Howard came up the pontoon bridge was completed and Jefferson C. Davis's division crossed over to the left shore. Sherman's operation had gone amazingly smoothly and by early afternoon he had a dozen brigades and batteries of artillery solidly established on the left bank of the Tennessee. In addition, he could be quickly reinforced, if necessary, by the bridge across the river and the overland route from Chattanooga along the left bank.[22]

Everything seemed to falling into place just as planned. Sherman need only march over and seize the northern end of Missionary Ridge and then advance along the crest driving in the flank of Bragg's army. The hills forming the end of the ridge were about a mile and a half away over lightly rolling terrain with no obvious impediments. About one o'clock, Sherman gave the order to move forward. Three divisions, under the overall command of Major General Frank P. Blair, advanced in three columns. Morgan L. Smith led his division along Chickamauga Creek, with John E. Smith in the center and Hugh Ewing on the right. Davis' division stayed behind to guard the bridge and provide a reserve force. The fighting was mostly heavy skirmishing as Captain S. H. M. Byers, of the 5th Iowa, described it: "All the afternoon we maneuvered and fought for position, chasing the enemy off one high hillspur only to find him better intrenched behind another."[23]

By 3:30 P.M. the Federals had taken a hill that was supposed to be the north end of Missionary Ridge and another smaller hill, in advance of that. Just ahead, not quite a mile away, was Sherman's objective, a huge pile of rock known as Tunnel Hill. The tunnel through the mountain connected Chattanooga with the railroad running east, and Bragg's supply line. It was now too late in the day to continue the advance so Sherman halted his men and dug in for the night. The Confederates launched a weak attack around 4:00 P.M. but were thrown back leaving Sherman to better fortify his position and bring artillery up to the top of the hill.[24]

General Sherman believed that his forces now occupied the end of Missionary Ridge and he notified Grant that he was in a good position to assault Tunnel Hill in the morning. Grant sent back orders for Sherman to "attack the enemy at the point most advantageous from your position at early dawn to-morrow morning (25th instant)." In addition to Sherman's attack, "General Thomas has been instructed to commence the attack early to-morrow morning. He will carry the enemy's rifle-pits in his immediate front, or move to the left to your support, as circumstances may determine best."[25]

With Sherman rolling up Bragg's right flank, Thomas hitting him head on, and Hooker coming in around the other end of the Confederate line, victory appeared assured. Unfortunately, as often happens in war, appearances really were deceiving. Sherman's troops were not actually where he thought they were. After all the time spent studying maps and the personal trips made by all the top generals at Chattanooga to view the ground in person they had gotten it wrong. Sherman had not occupied the end of Missionary Ridge but was on a hill that was separated from the ridge proper by a steep valley. Not only was this not a good place to begin his attack in the morning it was an exceedingly bad one. General Bragg finally saw what was coming and sent the just returned Patrick Cleburne over to hold Tunnel Hill and the surrounding hills. Cleburne's troops began arriving late in the afternoon and spent the night preparing a series of tough defensive positions. Early the next morning they were reinforced by troops that had been moved over from Lookout Mountain.[26]

The slope and crest of Missionary Ridge is littered with numerous ravines, small dips in the ground, and knobby little knolls. In other words, the terrain was difficult for an army to advance over but excellent to defend. The crest of the ridge was narrow enough so that a modest number of men could defend it against a much larger force.

Cleburne, arguably Bragg's best division commander, had his men set up heavy log barricades on the slopes so they could defend the ridge from their front and both flanks. Strategically placed artillery covered all the ground from which the Federals could approach.[27]

Back at Confederate headquarters, Bragg along with Hardee and Breckinridge met to discuss the situation. Apparently Hardee was concerned that the rising water in Chickamauga Creek could cut off the army's retreat and suggested that it might be better to evacuate the area now. Bragg and Breckinridge disagreed, feeling that despite the loss of Lookout Mountain they still held a superb defensive position. Let Grant smash his army against Missionary Ridge; if the Confederates could not hold this position where else could they make a stand? For the next day Bragg placed Hardee in overall command of the northern sector of the ridge and sent reinforcements so that about half the army would be defending about one-third of the ground. Breckinridge, with the other half of the available forces, would be in charge of defending the rest of Missionary Ridge, opposite Thomas's men.[28]

In Chattanooga that evening Grant wired the news of the day's fighting to General Halleck:

> The fight to-day progressed favorably. Sherman carried the end of Missionary Ridge, and his right is now at the tunnel, and left at Chickamauga Creek. Troops from Lookout Valley carried the point of the mountain, and now hold the eastern slope and point high up. I cannot yet tell the amount of casualties, but our loss is not heavy.

Of course Grant was mistaken in Sherman's location. Early the next morning came responses form Halleck and President Lincoln offering congratulations but also making sure that Burnside was always on Grant's mind. The president wrote, "Well done. Many thanks to all. Remember Burnside." Halleck wrote, "I congratulate you on the success thus far of your plans. I fear that General Burnside is hard pressed, and that any further delay may prove fatal. I know that you will do all in your power to relieve him."[29]

Grant already knew what he wanted to do on the 25th: more of the same. His orders were for Sherman to continue his advance along the ridge and roll up the Confederate right flank. Hooker was ordered to move at dawn and clear out any enemy troops left on Lookout Mountain then cross Chattanooga Creek and attack the left of Bragg's line on the ridge. If the end of the ridge was unoccupied then Hooker was to move toward Rossville and get behind the enemy forces on Missionary Ridge. Thomas was to wait in front of the center of Missionary Ridge until it could be determined if he should attack the rifle pits in his front as a diversion to assist Sherman's assault or to move to his left and join in on the attack with Sherman's men.[30]

21

MISSIONARY RIDGE

The battle for control of Missionary Ridge on November 25 consisted of several very distinct and separate assaults. The first, and the one that Grant expected to produce victory, was Sherman's attack on the northern end of the ridge. Sherman's assignment was to roll up the right flank of the Confederate army and push them away from the roads that led to their supply line. General Thomas in the center and General Hooker over by Lookout Mountain were relegated to the roles of assisting Sherman, if he even needed any help, and mopping up the retreating enemy, respectively. This certainly looked like a good plan on the night of the 24th. However, early the next morning it became clear that not everything was going to unfold as planned.

About daybreak on the 25th another of those events that helped to create the legend of the battles around Chattanooga occurred. Over on the northern end of Lookout Mountain eight daredevils from the 8th Kentucky Infantry scaled the nearly sheer face of the palisade and planted a large American flag on the very top that could be seen for miles. When the flag was unfurled the Federal troops down in the valley burst out with cheers. Isaac Doan of the 40th Ohio remembered that as he joined in the cheering "the whole mountain side resounded with huzzahs of joy and triumph. It is no derogation to the manhood of soldiers whose valor had been fully proved, to say, that the tears of joy coursed down many a war-worn face." Up on Lookout Mountain, General Geary's men joined in the celebration, "the enthusiasm," he reported, "was such as can only emanate from hearts of patriots, overflowing with gratitude for a great and signal victory."[1]

General Grant learned early that morning that Sherman had not in fact advanced as far as first believed. In another change of orders Hooker was instructed to come down from Lookout Mountain, crossing the creek and valley, and move forward to Rossville. He would then be in position to operate against the Confederate left and rear. Up on Missionary Ridge General Bragg was repositioning his troops in preparation for the coming attack. Two divisions commanded by Cheatham and Stevenson had been transferred from Lookout Mountain to reinforce the right along the ridge. They had marched most of the night and at dawn, and for hours after, troops were still moving along the summit of the ridge, clearly visible from the Federal lines below. During the previous night General Cleburne had pulled his men back a little to somewhat better positions and by morning his line was ready to dispute the Federal advance from whatever direction they might come.[2]

Sherman's men began their advance at daylight with Brig. General John M. Corse's brigade in the lead. The skirmishers moved out slowly and carefully since no one was sure exactly where the enemy was. It didn't take them long to find out as they were soon under musket and artillery fire from the heights in their front. Moving down into the valley between the Federal lines and the Confederate positions was bad enough, but it was much worse going up the opposite side. Cleburne's skillfully placed troops were fortified on the slopes and crest of the first hill and farther back, where the ground was higher, was another set of works. The Confederates were able to fire from several directions on the advancing Federals and the sounds of battle were loud and continuous for much of the morning. As Sherman observed, "The line advanced to within about 80 yards of the intrenched position, where General Corse found a secondary crest, which he gained and held." Corse called for and received reinforcements but "the space was narrow and it was not well to crowd the men, as the enemy's artillery and musketry fire swept the approach to his position."[3]

The fighting got progressively heavier as Sherman's men slowly advanced and it took several hours before they were able to force their way to a point from where the real attack could be launched. The top of the ridge was not wide enough for any more troops than Corse's brigade. Corse was supported by part of Morgan L. Smith's division on the east base of the ridge and three brigades led by Colonel John M. Loomis on the west side. The fighting intensified as Corse moved forward and "a severe contest ensued, lasting more than an hour, gaining and losing ground." Corse drove his men right up to the Confederate works and in a few places there was hand-to-hand fighting. The lines moved back and forth with each side sometimes gaining a temporary advantage only to lose it in a counterattack, but Cleburne's men held.[4]

Captain S. H. M. Byers of the 5th Iowa wrote that all morning the sounds of fighting echoed among the hills around Missionary Ridge. "The battle raged for over an hour for the possession of a single hill-crest." Neither side could gain an advantage; the enemy was dug in and had the advantage of position in the higher ground. "So close were they, and so protected behind rifle-pits, logs, and bowlders, that they could throw stones on the assaulting column and do almost as much harm with them as with bullets."[5]

One of Corse's commanders, Colonel Charles C. Walcutt of the 46th Ohio, described one of the many charges his troops made that day:

> The advance was sounded, and the several lines rushed over the brow of the hill under a most terrific fire. Being in easy canister and musket range, it seemed almost impossible for any troops to withstand it, but so eager were the men to take the new position that they charged through it, all with a fearlessness and determination that was astonishing.[6]

Patrick Cleburne was everywhere that morning, skillfully moving his men around the hill to launch a counterattack to retrieve a lost position then encouraging the men at another position to hold firm under multiple assaults. The fighting on the Federal right was fierce and "swayed backward and forward for some time." Confederate artillery above the tunnel was brought to bear on this part of the field and the Union troops were unable to close on the enemy's positions. Each side settled down to heavy skirmish firing from behind what cover they could find. On the left, however, Corse's men were able to use the abandoned Confederate works and the woods for protection. At one point they charged Charles Swett's battery on the hill but "the artillerymen stood bravely to their guns under a terrible cross-fire, and replied with canister at short range." Just as the Federals were approaching the artillery position Brigadier General J. A. Smith launched an attack with part of Colonel Roger Mills' regiment and Hiram Granbury's Seventh Texas. At the same moment Morgan L. Smith's Federal troops to the north poured a heavy fire into the attackers who were quickly driven back to seek cover behind the abandoned Confederate works. General Smith was gravely wounded leading this charge and Colonel Granbury assumed command of his brigade.[7]

In the attack on the Confederate battery the Federal fire was so deadly that all its officers and so many men were killed and wounded that Granbury had to detail some of his infantrymen to help man the battery that was now commanded by the senior surviving gunner, a corporal. Corse's men fought just as stubbornly, hanging on to some of their positions despite ferocious enemy attacks and constant musket and artillery fire. General Corse was wounded in one of the charges and finally, around noon, his men pulled back for a breather, Colonel Walcutt taking over the command from Corse. For most of the rest of the afternoon both sides pretty much held their positions, exchanging musket fire.[8]

So far Sherman's troops had done a lot of hard fighting with nothing to show for it. He went up to the front to see for himself what could be done and what he saw was not encouraging. It turned out that the terrain was not at all what had been expected. The narrow crest of the hill limited the number of troops that could be sent against the Confederate positions and the rough ground provided Cleburne's men with the best possible positions from which to beat back the Federal assaults. Sherman decided it was time to consider alternatives. Instead of slogging it out along the crest, which was going nowhere, he could shift the focus of the attack to either the northwest slope facing Chattanooga or the opposite side of the ridge on the northeast. Since Sherman was unfamiliar with the terrain on either side and there was no obvious benefit in choosing one side

William T. Sherman (courtesy Library of Congress).

or the other he apparently decided on the northwest simply because it would be easier to bring up reinforcements to that side of the ridge. There were plenty of Federal troops that could not be used because of the lack of room on the ridge so supporting another assault from a different direction would not pose a problem.[9]

About one o'clock Sherman launched the assault on Tunnel Hill from the northwest. Colonel Loomis led two brigades up the slope and they ran into the same tough defense that held the crest. Loomis' men didn't quite make it up to the crest when they had to take shelter behind trees, logs and boulders. This position was a bit precarious as Loomis was "threatened on my entire front and left flank by the enemy coming down the hill-sides and the road." The fighting on the western slope was similar to that along the crest with both sides keeping up a heavy fire but unable to dislodge their opponent. Just under the crest the Federals opened fire in the direction of a Confederate battery only about twenty-five yards away. Cleburne reported, "Tier after tier of the enemy, to the foot of the hill and in the valley beyond, supplied this fire and concentrated the whole on a space of not more than 40 yards, till it seemed like one continuous sheet of hissing, flying lead."[10]

The fighting surged back and forth on the slopes and around a farm near the mouth of the tunnel. The farm changed hands several times with both sides using the buildings for cover until they were finally set on fire. Cleburne's hard-pressed men were bolstered by the Lookout Mountain troops when General Alfred Cumming's brigade of Stevenson's division and General George Maney's brigade of Walker's division arrived and were immediately put into supporting positions. After nearly two hours of terrible fighting in which neither side could gain an advantage Lt. Colonel E. Warfield told Cleburne that "our men were wasting ammunition and becoming disheartened at the persistency of the enemy, and proposed a charge down upon them with the bayonet." The always-aggressive Confederate commander quickly agreed.[11]

In mid-afternoon Cleburne assembled a force near the tunnel gorge and moving under cover of the ground and heavy brush they attacked Loomis' troops on the western slope. The Confederates, Sherman reported, "suddenly appeared on the right and rear of this command. The suddenness of the attack disconcerted the men, and, exposed as they were in the open field, they fell back in some disorder to the lower edge of the field and reformed." However, even as the Confederates were pursuing in hope of driving the Federals off the ridge they "were caught in flank by the well-directed fire of one brigade on the wooded crest" and quickly were forced to halt the chase and take cover. This fire came from Walcutt's men who had seen the Confederates following Smith's retreating men and "poured into the enemy volley after volley, that sent him running to his works." It was now about three o'clock and Sherman was clearly not going to win his expected victory.[12]

While Sherman's men were bravely trying to make their was across Missionary Ridge from the north, down in Chattanooga the fighting could be heard, and in some cases, seen by both troops and generals. Once again Grant had to modify his plans. Realizing that Sherman was not going to just roll up the Confederate flank as expected and witnessing the back and forth fighting on the western slope of J. E. Smith's brigades, Grant ordered Thomas to send a division to reinforce Sherman. Earlier in the day two divisions of General Howard's corps were sent to reinforce Sherman and now General

Absalom Baird's division was detached from the right of Orchard Knob and marched behind the lines over to the north end of the ridge only to learn that Sherman had plenty of men. It was not a lack of manpower that was keeping Sherman from fulfilling his part of the battle plan, it was the difficult terrain and the tough Confederate defenders. With Sherman unable to defeat Cleburne's stubborn troops and push across the crest of the ridge Grant sent word to General Hooker to attack the southern end of Missionary Ridge. Hopefully coming at Bragg's army from both ends would cause them to crack, or at least weaken the center to reinforce the flanks, opening up the possibility for an attack on the center by Thomas.[13]

Over on the far right of the Federal position General Hooker was having his own problems completing his assignment. During the night General Bragg had pulled the remaining troops off Lookout Mountain to bolster the defenses of Missionary Ridge. They had burned the bridge over Chattanooga Creek and obstructed the road as much as possible. Hooker started early in the morning and with Osterhaus' division in the lead the column reached the destroyed bridge over Chattanooga Creek, about three-fourths of the way to Rossville Gap, around noon. The recent rains had raised the level of the creek to the point that it was unfordable, so Hooker had to wait until the bridge was rebuilt. In the meantime troops of the 27th Missouri rigged a narrow and unstable footbridge that allowed the men to cross in single file, basically one at a time. Osterhaus had his men working feverishly on the bridge but it was not until well after 3 o'clock that Hooker was able to continue his march toward Rossville. As Grant explained, "Thus was lost the immediate advantage I expected from his forces. His reaching Bragg's flank and extending across it was to be the signal for Thomas's assault of the ridge."[14]

Once General Osterhaus got his infantry over Chattanooga Creek, they quickly moved forward and after a brief fight troops from General Charles R. Woods' brigade on the right and Colonel James Williamson's brigade on the left flanked the Confederates out of the gap, capturing artillery, ammunition and provisions that had been stored there. After the bridge was completed and Hooker was able to bring up the rest of his force and the artillery he set about moving north along Missionary Ridge. Spreading his forces out Hooker advanced with Osterhaus "parallel with the ridge on the east, Cruft on the ridge, and Geary in the valley, to the west of it, within easy supporting distance," and began to roll up the Confederate defenders.[15]

Those Confederate defenders, General Stewart's division, tried to use the old Federal works on the ridge but as Hooker reported: "Such was the impetuosity of our advance that his front line was routed before an opportunity was afforded him to prepare for a determined resistance." Many of the Confederate fugitives ran down the eastern slope in an effort to escape and ran right into the lines of Osterhaus' troops. Some who tried to escape on the west side of the mountain were captured by Geary's men. Most of the enemy troops, however, continued the fight on the top of the ridge by falling back to a second defensive line. These stubborn Confederates were soon routed, and the fight turned into a chase with occasional stops to exchange fire. Hooker reported: "Whenever the accidents of the ground enabled the rebels to make an advantageous stand, Geary and Osterhaus, always in the right place, would pour a withering fire into their flanks, and again the race was renewed." This type of running fight continued until evening "when those of the enemy who had not been killed or captured gave way, and in attempting to escape along the ridge, ran into the arms of Johnson's division, of the Fourteenth Corps, and were captured."[16]

All morning long Grant had seen "column after column of Bragg's forces moving against Sherman" and this constant transfer of enemy troops to the north may have given the impression that Sherman was heading for an embarrassing defeat. Although he had been unable to force his way across the ridge he had plenty of troops and they were almost as well dug in as their opponents, it was very unlikely that he could have been pushed off the northern end of the ridge. But the day was slipping by and it was becoming obvious that, despite the heroic efforts of his men, Sherman's assault was going nowhere. Hooker was too far away to have any effect on the battle, and Grant was getting concerned. "Sherman's condition was getting so critical that the assault for his relief could not be delayed any longer."[17]

At the Union headquarters on Orchard Knob General Grant had been waiting for news that Sherman had broken through the Confederate lines on the north end of Missionary Ridge and captured Tunnel Hill, and he was still waiting for that news at three o'clock in the afternoon. It was time to go at Bragg from still another direction. The smashing victory Grant had been expecting to achieve by attacking both ends of Missionary Ridge seemed to be slipping away. Sherman's assault from the north was stalled and on the southern end of the ridge General Hooker had also been delayed and it was now too late for his force to make a significant contribution. For most generals the situation would have brought despair and resignation to the fact that the operation had failed. Fortunately for the Union Ulysses Grant was not like most generals.

Grant was well known for his calm demeanor, especially in times of crisis. But behind his stoic expression his mind was constantly at work; if one plan didn't succeed there was always another one to take its place. Grant was a realist and knew there was usually more than one way to achieve a goal, or win a battle. Ok then, Grant probably thought, Sherman's part of the operation did not work out as expected and Hooker was not going to sweep across the ridge from the south, Thomas still had over 20,000 men right in front of the center of the enemy's position.

Originally the Army of the Cumberland was supposed to provide a diversion to draw attention away from Sherman and perhaps join in the mopping up after the Confederate lines had been broken at both ends. It was never part of Grant's plan to make an all-out assault on the center of Missionary Ridge. It looked suicidal. Between Orchard Knob and the base of the ridge there was a mile or more of partly wooded but mostly open ground, perfect for artillery to fire on massed troops as they marched. Along the base of the ridge the Confederates had positioned a line of rifle pits with felled trees for several hundred yards out in their front to slow the progress of an attacker, and keep them under fire longer. As troops approached the rifle pits they would be hit by musket fire from the front and flanks along with artillery fire from the crest. The ridge here is about five or six hundred feet high and about half way up the steep slope was another line of works, not yet finished but still a serious obstacle considering the rough terrain. Finally, the crest of the ridge was lined with infantry and artillery. Most of the

Confederate commanders felt the position was so strong that the Federals would not dare make a serious attempt to take the center of the ridge.[18]

On Orchard Knob, directly across from the center of the Confederate position on Missionary Ridge, General Thomas had four divisions lined up and waiting for orders. On the left was Baird's division, then moving to the right were the divisions of Wood and Sheridan with Johnson on the far right, over twenty thousand men altogether. In mid-afternoon Grant made his decision, Thomas was ordered to move forward his entire force "and carry the rifle-pits at the foot of Missionary Ridge, and when carried to reform his lines on the rifle-pits with a view to carrying the top of the ridge."[19]

Sending Thomas's troops up against the center of Missionary Ridge was not really as desperate a gamble as it might have seemed. Grant had seen with his own eyes all the troops that Bragg had sent to the right to stop Sherman's assault. It was very possible that the Confederate center had been weakened enough so that Thomas might be able to break through. It also would have occurred to Grant that an attack on Bragg's center might force him to bring troops back from his right thereby increasing the chance that Sherman might still break through along the crest of the ridge. Here were two opportunities to drive the Confederates from their position and Grant was willing to gamble that one of them would work. Which one didn't matter; only the results mattered to Grant.

22

AN IMPOSSIBLE VICTORY

It always took some time for orders to filter down from commanding general to the lower ranks and Grant was growing impatient when he turned to ask General Thomas what was taking so long for the assault to begin. Grant was surprised to see General Wood standing next to Thomas engaged in conversation. Grant "spoke to General Wood, asking him why he did not charge as ordered an hour before. He replied very promptly that this was the first he had heard of it, but that he had been ready all day to move at a moment's notice." Grant instructed Wood to go back to his division and begin the assault at once. Another possible reason for the delay was that General Granger spent quite a bit of time aiming and firing the guns of a nearby battery of artillery instead of preparing his corps for the attack.[1]

Between 3:30 and 4:00 P.M., the signal to advance was given, six guns fired in rapid succession. The sound of cheers reverberated through the air as the men of the Army of the Cumberland moved out in front of Orchard Knob and formed their ranks. Thomas was sending four divisions, about 23,000 men, and they looked like a sea of blue over a mile wide. Like the attack on Orchard Knob two days before the army appeared to be forming for a review, rank upon rank in neat rows, muskets shining in the afternoon sun, flags waving, an altogether awe-inspiring example of the grandeur of war.[2]

Chattanooga was one of the few Civil War battles where both sides could see almost the entire field and the Confederates on the ridge had a clear view of the Federal troops forming their ranks. Even though they would soon be doing their best to kill and maim each other the Confederates must have marveled at the magnificent spectacle made by their blue clad enemy. This was the way war was supposed to be, the soul-stirring splendor that made men forget the dirt and the hunger and the blood. It is also quite likely that more than a few of the men on the ridge were beginning to wonder if they could stop this juggernaut.

They would find out soon enough as the massive Federal formation surged forward. The Federals had a little cover as they passed through the narrow wooded area near Orchard Knob but once they moved into the open the artillery on the crest of the ridge opened up with a tremendous roar. There were upwards of fifty guns stationed along the crest and they filled the air with deadly shot and shell. Major James Connolly wrote that when the Confederate artillery opened fire "the very heavens above us seemed to be rent asunder; shells go screaming over our heads, bursting above and behind us." An soldier from the 41st Ohio later wrote that the opening blast of artillery fire was "stunning; but in a moment it was plain that no harm was being done. Rather, a feeling of new confidence came upon the men as they moved on, always too fast for the Confederates' depressing of their pieces."[3]

Depending on their position in the advancing line once past the wooded areas the Federal troops had between 500 to 700 yards of open ground to cover in front of the rifle-pits at the base of the ridge. Waiting for them were approximately nine thousand Confederate defenders and there is some question as to whether they should have even been there. Ever since General Bragg realized he was going to have to fight a defensive battle to remain in control of Missionary Ridge the vast majority of time and effort was spent on strengthening the flanks. Only after Thomas took Orchard Knob was much attention paid to the defenses in the center. Neither Bragg nor John C. Breckinridge, who was in command of the center of the Confederate line, had been too concerned about an attack up the steep and rugged slope in the center of Missionary Ridge.[4]

After losing Orchard Knob the Confederates rushed to improve the defenses on the center of the ridge but it was too late and mistakes were made. Among the more serious problems was that the artillery had been placed on the very top of the ridge rather than a little lower on the military crest, which gave a better field of fire. From where they were located the guns could not be depressed far enough to sweep the entire slope and there were many areas where attackers were safe from artillery fire. In addition to the problem of artillery placement the layout of trenches and fortifications was haphazard, at best. When work began on the fortifications along the crest some of the subordinate commanders pulled their troops from the rifle pits at the base and brought them up to the crest. In other sectors, however, a line of works was built halfway up the ridge making it difficult to form a solid defensive front. Also, the troops in the second line would have to fire over the heads of their comrades below and if the works at the base were lost the retreating Confederates would be right in the line of fire of the men in the second line. Overall the Confederate defenses in the center of Missionary Ridge were haphazard, at best, and it appeared as if Bragg was counting on the difficulty of the terrain to be his biggest ally. Whatever deficiencies there were in the Confederate defenses it was too late to do anything about it now; Thomas's men were on their way and they looked unstoppable.[5]

Alfred G. Hunter of the 82nd Indiana remembered that as his regiment advanced toward the base of the ridge and "The enemy soon opened a most terrific artillery fire from the ridge, yet it did but little injury as we advanced so rapidly that they could not get proper range upon us, the missiles falling behind us tearing up the earth."[6]

The Federal lines moved quickly over the open ground brushing aside the Confederate pickets. In minutes they worked through the felled trees and pushed on toward the enemy rifle pits. Bullets were flying everywhere and there were many crumpled figures in blue on the ground behind the charging troops, but they pressed on. Here and there a few defenders broke and ran but most stayed and kept up their fire. The blue horde came closer and closer until they reached their objective. Henry Aten of the 85th Illinois remembered a "moment of death and terror" as the Federals swept into the trenches. In some spots the defenders quickly took flight up the ridge like "bees from a hive," Grant thought. Apparently Breckinridge had given orders for the troops at the base of the ridge to fire one volley and then retire up the slope to the more defensible works but not all were notified. One of the defenders on the crest, W. J. Worsham of the 19th Tennessee, watched as his comrades who made it out of the rifle pits tried to climb up the slope "through a shower of bullets that plowed the ground and skinned the trees all around them." Many did not make it to safety. The defenders who stayed and fought were quickly overwhelmed from the front and sides as the Union troops spread out among the works and the survivors became prisoners.[7]

The front lines of Federals occupied the trenches but there was hardly room for the entire attacking force. They caught their breath, congratulating themselves and each other for the victory and surviving it and then they did something that, as much if not more than the battle above the clouds on Lookout Mountain, brought about the legend of Chattanooga. Once the retreating Confederates had scrambled to safety the defenders began to rain bullets and shells on the Federals occupying the rifle-pits. A soldier in the 41st Ohio wrote, "The infantry on the Ridge had opened a severe fire, and the artillery, by firing obliquely down the face of the steep slope, was able to be effective. Both arms together made the firing hot." William Calkins of the 104th Illinois remembered that "their musketry was telling rapidly on our ranks in the rifle pits below," and that it "would be death to stay there." And General Sheridan reported "the enemy had now changed from shot and shell to grape and canister and musketry. The fire was terrific." [8]

Grant's orders had been that after taking the rifle pits Thomas's troops were to reform their lines, "with a view to carrying the top of the ridge." This was a bit ambiguous, and there was confusion among men and officers as to whether they were to continue up the slope. L. G. Bennett of the 36th Illinois later wrote that the heavy fire coming down on the men meant they could not stay where they were for very long; they must retreat or advance: "To retreat was out of the question, after such a success, and over such a plain, and yet there were no orders to advance."[9]

The generals had much the same problem. General Baird, on the far left, said he was told by an aide from General Thomas "that I would be following his wishes were I to push on to the summit." On the right side of the Federal line General Johnson said he had been ordered to stay in touch with Sheridan's division. Sheridan was not sure what he was supposed to do and just before the attack was launched sent an aide back to get positive orders from General Granger. It wasn't until Sheridan's men were already in the rifle pits that one of Granger's aides brought news that "the original order was to carry the first line of pits, but that, if in my judgment, the ridge could be taken, to do so."[10]

In the center, Wood said, "The goal for which we had started was won. Our orders carried us no farther. We had been instructed to carry the line of intrenchments at the base of the ridge and there halt." Even within Wood's division there was no consensus of what to do. August Willich reported that it was not until after the battle that he learned they were supposed to stop at the base of the ridge. But, he also reported that "it was evident to every one that to stay in this position would be certain destruction and final defeat ... every one saw instinctively that the only place of safety was in the enemy's works on the crest of the ridge." Another of Wood's brigade commanders,

William Hazen, said, "On commencing the advance, the thought of storming Mission Ridge had not entered the mind of any one, but now the necessity was apparent to every soldier of the command." General Wood could also see that there was no option but to head up the ridge as "the intrenchments were no protection against the enemy's artillery on the ridge. To remain would be destruction — to return would be both expensive in life and disgraceful."[11]

If the Federal soldiers in the rifle pits at the base of Missionary Ridge could not stay where they were and they would not go back, there was only one other thing they could do, and they did. The legend is that these thousands of soldiers simply decided on their own that they were going to charge to the top of the ridge. Instead it is pretty clear that the men were ordered, or rather led, up the mountain by their officers. During the Civil War it was not uncommon for a commander in the field to override a superior's orders based on what was happening at the scene of the fighting, and the base of Missionary Ridge was just such a place.

It probably began with some individual soldiers who decided to move out of the rifle pits on their own, especially when they could see that the rocks and gullies on the slope provided more protection against the enemy fire than sitting in the open. Then a colonel or perhaps even a captain told his men to make for a ravine or crop of rocks where the Confederate fire could not reach them. First small groups, then larger groups and finally regiments and brigades left the rifle pits and began to climb the rugged slope. Some units moved forward because they had been ordered to stay aligned with another unit and when their neighbor moved up they followed. General Hazen wrote, "Giving the men about five minutes to breathe, and receiving no orders, I gave the word forward, which was eagerly obeyed." Some of Sheridan and Willich's men had already started up and, all of a sudden, it seemed as if the entire army was making its way up the steep slopes of Missionary Ridge. Lt. Col. Robert Kimberly of the 41st Ohio wrote, "Once the ascent was begun, however, the men came together, for the gullied and broken face of the Ridge afforded shelter not to be found on the level ground below." Mr. Dana told Secretary Stanton that he believed Sheridan and Wood gave the order to assault the crest "because the men were not to be held back, dangerous as the attempt appeared to military prudence. Besides, the generals had caught the inspiration of the men, and were ready themselves to undertake impossibilities."[12]

Back on Orchard Knob, Grant, Thomas, and the army commanders could see everything although they were not sure they could believe what they were seeing. Dana wrote in his report that when he saw the thousands of men snaking their way up the ridge it seemed "as awful as a visible interposition of God." General Granger's Chief of Staff, J. S. Fullerton, later wrote about the reaction to the unauthorized advance. "Grant quickly turned to Thomas, who stood by his side, and I heard him angrily say: 'Thomas, who ordered those men up the ridge?' Thomas replied, in his usual slow, quiet manner: 'I don't know; I did not.' Grant then turned to General Granger asking, 'Did you order them up, Granger?' 'No,' said Granger; 'they started up without orders. When those fellows get started, all hell can't stop them.'"[13]

When the Federals had first advanced to the base of the ridge they kept their tight military formation until they were almost on top of the Confederate works. Now, as they moved up the steep slope of Missionary Ridge they looked more like a mob than an army. The men went up in groups of regiment size or smaller, usually with a flag at the head and the men trailing back on each side in a V-formation. Anything resembling a formal line of battle was impossible on the steep and broken slope. There were quite a few narrow roads or trails weaving back and forth across the face of the ridge and these provided a relatively sheltered route to the top. Many men took advantage of the small gullies and ravines that littered the ground, hopping from one to another for protection from the hail of gunfire coming down from the crest. Captain Tilmon D. Kyger of the 73rd Illinois wrote in his diary that he and his men moved up the face of the ridge "from tree to tree, from stump to stump, and from log to log."[14]

Looking at the steep and rugged slope of the ridge from the ground it was easy to understand why the Confederates were confident they could hold it. The steepness of the slope was, however, a two-edged sword. There were many spots where the angle of the slope provided shelter from the Confederate fire, giving the attackers a place to take a brief rest before continuing up toward the top. Also, the bullets were not just coming down the ridge; they were flying in both directions. When the Confederate riflemen wanted to fire on the advancing enemy they frequently had to stand up above their parapets to compensate for the angle of the slope, making them excellent targets silhouetted against the sky.

These few benefits Thomas's men received from the terrain made their task only a little less impossible. The Federals advancing up Missionary Ridge probably outnumbered the defenders by about two to one and that's not counting the survivors from the rifle pits. Not really much of an advantage for Civil War assaults against a fortified position on a steep height. All through the ascent the Federals were suffering heavy casualties. Color-bearers had an especially short life span since they were almost always out in front of their unit. The troops making the assault up the ridge suffered about 20 percent casualties but their courage and desire kept them going. General Willich noted that "many men fell down exhausted in climbing up under the enemy's fire, some fainted, but irresistible was the general advance." John Hartzell of the 105th Ohio remembered that many trees had been cut down "so forming as abatis over which we made slow progress. We just crowded over and under and through, and made headway slowly but surely." And Ephraim Wilson of the 10th Illinois thought the roar of the artillery and thousands of muskets sounded like "the very heavens above and earth beneath were at eternal war with each other."[15]

On the top of Missionary Ridge, General Bragg and his men must have begun to wonder just how impregnable their position was. Despite the difficult terrain and the bullets and shells filling the air the Federal troops kept moving up the slope, past the partially built line of works near the center of the slope and getting dangerously close to the crest. Major James Connolly wrote his wife he and his men slowly climbed up the ridge "mostly on hands and knees, amid a terrible storm of shot, shell and bullets," and after driving the enemy from their works on the mountain side, "on our gallant boys went, officers and men mingled together, all rank forgotten, following their old flag." Up on the crest was W. J. Worsham who nervously watched these men in blue as they got closer and closer to his position: "The ridge where we were was quite steep but the enemy came on, crawling up the steep ascent like bugs, and were so thick they were almost in each other's way."[16]

On the top of Missionary Ridge the critical moment was rapidly approaching. Bragg had ordered Hardee to bring troops from the right back to the center to shore up the thin lines on the crest. One of the defects of the Confederate position was that the top of the ridge was so narrow and broken up with small knobs and ravines that there was little room to maneuver or pull back and create another defensive line if necessary. The Confederates had to stop the Federal assault at the edge of the crest or all was lost. The Union troops were now so close to the summit that the artillery was almost useless as the guns could not be depressed enough. Some of the desperate artillerymen began to light the fuses of their shells and just roll them down the slope hoping to do what damage they could.[17]

The most forward of the Federal troops were now nearing the summit. Both Generals Willich and Hazen had to struggle to keep up with their men and just below the crest their troops, now hopelessly intermingled, stopped for a brief rest. John Hartzell wrote that as he reached the top there was a position that had been built up with logs and leveled off with dirt. "On it were two field guns which were being worked industriously, but could not be depressed enough to do us much harm. We all began to cluster up against this log pen like a swarm of bees on a limb."[18]

After just a momentary pause to get their breath the men in blue went up and over. Pandemonium broke out on the crest of Missionary Ridge. Muskets were fired at point-blank range then used as clubs. Confederate artillerymen fought hand to hand with the infantry flooding over their works. After a brief pause under the artillery position John Hartzell and his comrades made their move: "All at once, without orders, we burst up over the logs onto the gun platform. It was hand to hand fighting, and the 'devil take the hindmost.' The gunners stood to their guns like heroes, and the musket butts were pitted against sweat sticks and rammers."[19]

All along the crest the Confederate lines were breached almost simultaneously. Sheridan's troops went over the works with their fiery little general right beside his men. In front of the 24th Wisconsin eighteen-year-old Lieutenant Arthur MacArthur grabbed the flag and led his regiment over the top shouting, "On Wisconsin," which would earn him a Congressional Medal of Honor. Toward the northern end of the

Philip H. Sheridan (courtesy U.S. Military History Institute).

works two Fourteenth Corps brigades led by Colonels Turchin and Van Derveer, with the 2nd Minnesota in front, threw themselves over the enemy works and captured an entire battery of artillery intact after a brief hand-to-hand fight.[20]

The story was the same all along the crest of the ridge. A few groups of Confederates stood and fought but after the first initial shock of the assault most that could get away did. As panic and fear set in the Confederate officers tried to regain control, at times cursing and then imploring, but it was too late. General Bragg did his best to rally the men. He rode back and forth along the crest practically begging his men to hold firm and continue the fight, but it was useless. The Confederates were already beaten in their minds, their morale shattered by too many defeats and failures, too many days with not enough food, and too much time spent looking down at the thousands of troops in blue and seeing them relentlessly turn their once dismal situation around and impose their will on the Army of Tennessee.[21]

As the Federals took control of the summit they began to understand the enormity of what they had accomplished. Missionary Ridge was theirs, the enemy was broken and thousands of enemy soldiers were fleeing down the eastern side of the ridge as fast as they could go. Dead and wounded men lay everywhere, more clad in gray than blue. The fear and exhaustion of the victors quickly gave way to frenzied joy. Some men jumped up and down shouting as loud as they could or danced around like children, while others exhausted and stunned by what they had done fell to the ground and wept in joy and gratitude for surviving. Nixon B. Stewart of the 52nd Ohio remembered that "cheer after cheer, rang like bells, through the valley of the Chickamauga. Men flung themselves, exhausted, on the ground. They laughed, they wept, they shook hands and embraced each other.... It was as wild as a carnival." Major Connolly saw "dead and wounded rebels under our feet by hundreds, cannon by scores scattered up and down the ridge with yelling soldiers astraddle them, rebel flags lying around in profusion, and soldiers and officers completely and frantically drunk with excitement." John Hartzell summed it up when he wrote, "Such a scene of wild exultation. We had accomplished that which, for more than two months, we had looked upon as an impossibility."[22]

It was getting dark by now but despite all the celebrating the fighting wasn't quite done yet. On the eastern slope of Missionary Ridge Confederate troops were running as fast as their weary legs could carry them, throwing away muskets, blankets and anything else that might slow them down. Teams of horses pulled artillery pieces much too fast down the narrow, winding roads, the drivers more concerned about capture than crashing. The fugitives who headed south along the ridge had the worst luck of all; they ran into Hooker's troops coming north from Rossville and were captured in droves.[23]

On the other end of the Confederate line things went much better for Bragg's survivors. Before the crest was lost General Hardee had sent orders to Cleburne, still defending the northern end of the ridge against Sherman's troops, to bring all the men he could spare to reinforce the center. The Confederate lines were shattered beyond repair before Cleburne could reach the center positions but he was able to form a line across the ridge facing south. Here he was able to shelter the fugitives from the center and protect his own command from being attacked from the rear.[24]

Even though the assault up Missionary Ridge was not as spontaneous as the legends made it out to be, it was something very special. Mr. Dana told Secretary Stanton, "The storming of the ridge by our troops was one of the greatest miracles in military history." He added an honest observation: "No man who climbs the ascent by any of the roads that wind along its front can believe that men were moved up its broken and crumbling face unless it was his fortune to witness the deed."[25]

After dark Hardee and Cleburne set up a line across the ridge just south of Tunnel Hill. Using the darkness to conceal their movements they pulled the remainder of their troops off the northern end of the ridge and headed for safety. Cleburne set up a rear guard to cover the retreat.

Most of the Federal forces were much too exhausted and units too badly mixed up to make any effective pursuit, except for Phil Sheridan. That evening the tough little general sent two brigades down the opposite side of Missionary Ridge where they ran into an enemy defensive position anchored by artillery about a mile from the ridge. Sending part of his force around the flank he drove the defenders, capturing several pieces of artillery and quite a few prisoners. Continuing down the slopes Sheridan swung around to the left toward the railroad near Chickamauga Station.[26]

Sheridan learned that Patrick Cleburne and many of the men who had fought on the northern end of the ridge were still forming the Confederate rear guard. He realized that if he could take the railroad station Cleburne might be cut off from the rest of Bragg's retreating army and be destroyed or at least badly damaged. Sheridan also realized that he would need more troops to go up against Cleburne's force so he rode back to Missionary Ridge to get help. Both Grant and Thomas had by now returned to Chattanooga and General Granger, the highest ranking officer in the area, had gone to bed. Sheridan explained the situation and tried to convince Granger to help him take advantage of this opportunity but Granger refused to give Sheridan any additional troops. Finally, Granger told Sheridan to continue his movement and if he ran into any serious opposition support would be sent. Sheridan returned to his troops and near midnight they pushed the Confederate rear guard across the creek and approached to about half a mile of Chickamauga Station, where Sheridan decided he needed reinforcements before advancing any further and running into Cleburne's troops. Sheridan even staged a fake battle by having his troops fire into the air to convince Granger to send help but no more troops came and Sheridan finally gave up for the night, camping where he was. Cleburne was able to get away the next morning and the chance to severely damage the only undefeated force of the Army of Tennessee was missed.[27]

As in most Civil War battles the number of casualties suffered by each side, especially the Confederate losses, is not always easy to calculate or accurately reported. Grant, in his official report, states that for the entire series of battles at Chattanooga the Federals suffered 757 killed, 4,529 wounded, and 330 missing, for a total of 5,616. General Bragg gave no reliable casualty figures in his report but later figures show 361 killed, 2,160 wounded, 4,146 missing, for a total of 6,667. Clearly the Federal losses in killed and wounded were much higher because they were doing most of the attacking against well- fortified enemy positions. Another telling bit of information is that during the period when Grant was in command at Chattanooga the official returns say that 6,142 Confederates became prisoners of war. This high number of Confederates who were captured or deserted gives some idea of the failing morale of the common soldier in the Army of Tennessee.[28]

General Grant's gamble had paid off handsomely. In fact his instincts were correct since the attack in the center did force Bragg to pull troops from in front of Sherman; it was just too late to take advantage of this development. Gaining control of Missionary Ridge was the key to breaking the Confederates' hold on Chattanooga. And control of Chattanooga was the key to all of central Tennessee. With Federal forces occupying the ridge there could be no more serious enemy threats to Chattanooga. All of central Tennessee was now open to Union movements and the way to send relief forces to Knoxville was also open. More importantly controlling Chattanooga and the heights around the town would open the way for further Federal advances into the Deep South, especially toward Atlanta.

23

AFTER CHATTANOOGA

The day after the battle, November 26, was America's first official national Thanksgiving Day. Back in October President Lincoln had issued a proclamation asking the nation to set this day aside to give thanks to God for the Union victories at Gettysburg and Vicksburg and the continued growth and prosperity of the nation even with civil war raging. As telegraph wires carried news of the victory at Chattanooga out across the nation there really was a reason to be thankful, at least in the North.[1]

Ulysses Grant was as politically aware as any Union general and he certainly knew of the importance President Lincoln placed on East Tennessee. During the next few days and weeks this knowledge would influence Grant's decisions and cause him to take actions he would not otherwise have taken without the pressure of politics. Even before the fighting at Chattanooga was completed Grant had issued orders for General Granger to move his corps to relieve Burnside at Knoxville as soon as Bragg was defeated. Those orders were still in effect on the evening of the 25th, when Grant decided that Burnside could wait a day or two. As Grant wrote to Sherman, "On reflection, I think we will push Bragg with all our strength to-morrow, and try if we cannot cut off a good portion of his rear troops and trains." The opportunity to do more damage to the fleeing Confederate army was just too good to ignore so the pursuit of Bragg was continued in the hope of at least damaging his rear forces.[2]

Throughout the day of the 26th Federal troops, led by General Hooker, pursued the fleeing Confederates. The weather had become ugly with rain turning the roads into mud, slowing the infantry and making it almost impossible for wagons to move at all. The men were bone-weary from the fighting and many had still not fully regained their strength from the weeks of short rations. To make the pursuit even more difficult the Confederate rear guard, commanded by Patrick Cleburne, did all they could to delay the Federal troops by obstructing roads and burning bridges. Still, even with all these problems, Hooker's troops were able to pick up a moderate number of Confederate prisoners and some artillery pieces. If they could just catch up to the rear of Bragg's army there was still a chance to inflict some major damage.[3]

General Hooker did catch up to Bragg's rear guard at a place called Ringgold Gap where the Western & Atlantic Railroad, which Bragg's army had been following south, cut its way through the mountains. Cleburne decided this was the place to make a stand and he could not have chosen a better location. Hooker's troops reached the gap early on the 27th and although he had no artillery and was unfamiliar with the terrain Hooker decided to strike before the Confederates could get too well dug in. The exhausted Federal troops attacked Cleburne's well-placed men again and again, and each time they were thrown back with heavy casualties. By the end of the day the Confederate wagons and artillery were beyond the reach of the Union forces and Cleburne fell back to join the rest of the army.[4]

Grant realized that nothing further could be gained and called off the pursuit, besides he still had Burnside to worry about. "Had it not been for the imperative necessity of relieving Burnside, I would have pursued the broken and demoralized retreating enemy as long as supplies could have been found in the country." As Hooker learned, however, the enemy was not as broken as Grant believed. Bragg continued south until he reached Dalton, Georgia, where he stopped and regrouped the Army of Tennessee, staying in that vicinity through the winter.[5]

General Grant had already made arrangements to send Granger's corps to Burnside's relief but during the pursuit of the retreating enemy Grant had told Thomas not to start Granger until he received further orders. Grant was concerned that Bragg might turn around and join up with Longstreet's troops to make a combined attack on Knoxville. When Grant reached Ringgold, however, he was convinced that "the retreat was most earnest," and that there was nothing to fear from Bragg's army in the immediate future. On the 27th a staff officer was sent back to Chattanooga to inform Thomas to start Granger's force toward Knoxville at once.[6]

Grant returned to Chattanooga on November 29 and to his surprise found that Granger had not yet begun his march to Burnside's relief. "Finding that Granger had not only not started but was very reluctant to go, he having decided for himself that it was a very bad move to make," Grant decided to send Sherman instead. That same day Grant wrote to Sherman that Granger was still being sent to Knoxville "but I have lost all faith in his energy or capacity to manage an expedition of the importance of this one. I am inclined to think, therefore, I shall have to send you." Sherman was to move as quickly as possible and take from Granger's force whatever troops he needed. "In plain words, you will assume command of all the forces now moving up the Tennessee, including the garrison at Kingston, and from that force organize what you deem proper to relieve Burnside." Any troops Sherman did not need should be sent back to Chattanooga.[7]

Grant's confidence in his subordinate shows as he added to the orders, "I leave this matter to you, knowing that you will do better acting upon your discretion than you could trammeled with instructions." Grant also added that the last report received from Burnside indicated that he had only enough rations to last until December 3.[8]

As it turned out Burnside didn't really need as much help as it was believed. Longstreet did not press Burnside very hard and the Federal commander had pulled his troops inside the fortifications around Knoxville. On November 29 Longstreet launched an assault that was easily repulsed with heavy losses. After learning of Bragg's defeat at Chattanooga Longstreet pulled his troops out of the area around Knoxville and moved over fifty miles to the northeast, causing no more trouble. Sherman's force came within fifteen miles of Knoxville on December 5, when he received word that Longstreet had left the area. Granger, and his corps, was left in Knoxville to protect the city and surrounding area while Sherman brought his own troops back to Chattanooga and active campaigning in the region was ended.[9]

On December 8, Grant received a wire from President Lincoln:

> Understanding that your lodgment at Knoxville and at Chattanooga is now secure, I wish to tender you, and all under your command, my more than thanks, my profoundest gratitude for the skill, courage, and perseverance with which you and they, over so great difficulties, have effected that important object. God bless you all.[10]

While all this was going on Braxton Bragg was down in Dalton wondering how it all went so wrong. In his official report Bragg was unable to account for the loss of Missionary Ridge: "A panic which I had never before witnessed seemed to have seized upon officers and men, and each seemed to be struggling for his personal safety, regardless of his duty or his character." Bragg believed, as did almost everyone else, that the position on the ridge was practically invulnerable and "the position was one which ought to have been held by a line of skirmishers against any assaulting column." The courage of the Federal troops who climbed that ridge in the face of the heavy Confederate fire should not be underestimated but as Bragg pointed out "those who reached the ridge did so in a condition of exhaustion from the great physical exertion in climbing, which rendered them powerless, and the slightest effort would have destroyed them." The only excuse he could offer was that his troops "had for two days confronted the enemy, marshaling his immense forces in plain view, and exhibiting to their sight such a superiority in numbers as may have intimidated weak-minded and untried soldiers." But, as Bragg pointed out, "our veterans had so often encountered similar hosts" that considering the strength of the position he had no doubt that his men would stand firm.[11]

On December 1, along with his official report, Bragg sent a letter to Jefferson Davis. In it he honestly admitted "the disaster admits of no palliation, and is justly disparaging to me as a commander. I fear we both erred in the conclusion for me to retain command here after the clamor raised against me." Bragg offered his resignation, which Davis accepted.[12]

The campaign for Chattanooga was over, as was the fight for control of Tennessee. The second half of 1863 was disastrous for the South. The Federal victory at Gettysburg and Grant's capture of Vicksburg, opening the Mississippi and cutting off the western states were, each by itself, a disaster and usually looked upon as the turning point of the war. The loss of Chattanooga would prove to be just as real a calamity for the Confederacy. The states of Kentucky and Tennessee were now permanently under Federal control. With control of the river and the mountain passes in and around Chattanooga the Federal armies now had direct routes into the heart of the Deep South. Alabama and Georgia were now open to invasion and a little over 100 miles away, right down the line of the Western and Atlantic Railroad, lay Atlanta, without which the Confederacy could not survive.

One of the Federal army's more pressing needs at Chattanooga was to improve the railroad service. Even though the siege had been broken and provisions were freely coming into the city there was still not enough food coming in for all the troops and animals to have full rations. Grant was upset at the slow pace of improvements and after complaining to Quartermaster General Meigs, the War Department's superintendent of military railroads, Colonel D. C. McCallum, and over three hundred construction workers were dispatched to improve the railroad system. Colonel J. L. Donelson, the Army of the Cumberland's quartermaster, had once called the Nashville & Chattanooga line "a rickety, stringer-tie, dilapidated affair, never worth much before the rebellion, and well used up supplying Bragg," and it had not been improved in the last few months. McCallum and his men went to work with a vengeance and by mid-January, for the first time, the road was open to Chattanooga and supplies were pouring in. Grant wanted to make Chattanooga the main supply depot for any further movement south. Huge warehouses were built and for most of the winter supplies of all types were accumulated for future campaigns.[13]

The only thing left to do at the end of 1863 was to remove Longstreet from East Tennessee where he had gone into camp after abandoning the siege of Knoxville. Longstreet was not actually doing anything but the presence of enemy troops in the region was a cause of concern both to Grant and in Washington. On December 17, Grant wrote to Halleck that he would soon go to Nashville and Louisville to see for himself if there was anything that could be done to force Longstreet out of Tennessee entirely. Grant wrote that he wanted any enemy troops removed "so as to be able to select my own campaign in the spring instead of having the enemy dictate it for me."[14]

Grant soon learned, however, that very little could be done to force Longstreet back to Virginia. General Burnside became ill and gave up his command. His replacement re-injured an old wound and could not function. Finally Grant gave the command to General John M. Schofield, who had been in command of St. Louis. Schofield was young and energetic but the lack of food, animals to draw the wagons and artillery, and a shortage of almost everything meant that no movement could be made for at least two months. So Longstreet stayed where he was throughout the winter.[15]

The war was going to be prosecuted differently from now on. In a few months Ulysses Grant would become the only lieutenant general in the army. He would take over as general in chief, replacing Halleck, who became The Army's chief of staff. Sherman would take Grant's job in the West; and both he and Grant knew that was where the war would be decided. Now that the Union had control of Tennessee, the very heart of the South was open to invasion. It was only a matter of time before the Confederacy would be cut up and defeated and the nation would finally be at peace again.

CHAPTER NOTES

Chapter 1

1. Larry Shapiro, ed., *Abraham Lincoln — Mystic Chords of Memory* (New York: Book-of-the-Month-Club, 1984), 72.
2. Steven E. Woodworth, *This Grand Spectacle: The Battle of Chattanooga* (Abilene, TX: McWhiney Foundation Press, 1999), 15.
3. Stephen D. Engle, *Don Carlos Buell: Most Promising of All* (Chapel Hill, NC: University of North Carolina Press, 1999), 99.
4. Thomas Lawrence Connelly, *Army of the Heartland: The Army of Tennessee, 1861–1862* (Baton Rouge: Louisiana State University Press, 1967), 3–7.
5. James B. McPherson, *Battle Cry of Freedom, The Civil War Era* (New York: Oxford University Press, 1988), 359.
6. Stephen D. Engle, *Struggle for the Heartland: The Campaigns from Fort Henry to Corinth* (Lincoln, NE: University of Nebraska Press, 2001), 30; Henry Coppee, *Life and Services of Gen. U. S. Grant* (Chicago: Western News Company, 1868), 35; McPherson, 394.
7. Engle, *Struggle*, 30; Coppee, 35; McPherson, 394.
8. Engle, *Struggle*, 20–21; McPherson, 394; Engle, *Buell*, 117; Coppee, 74; United States War Department, *War of the Rebellion: A Compilation of the Official Records of the Union and Confederate Armies*, Volume 16, Part 1 (Washington, DC: Government Printing Office, 1880–1901), 51–59
9. Engle, *Struggle*, 20–21, 30; McPherson, 394; Engle, *Buell*, 130.
10. McPherson, 393–94; John Fiske, *The Mississippi Valley in the Civil War* (Boston: Houghton, Mifflin, 1900), 53.
11. McPherson, 393–94; Fiske, 53.
12. Engle, *Struggle*, 30.
13. Coppee, 37; McPherson, 393; Lew Wallace, "The Capture of Fort Donelson," *The Century*, December 1884: 286–87.
14. Coppee, 37–38; McPherson, 393; Fiske, 52; H. Allen Gosnell, *Guns on the Western Waters: The Story of River Gunboats in the Civil War* (Baton Rouge: Louisiana State University Press, 1949), 46.
15. Coppee, 37; Stanley F. Horn, *The Army of Tennessee* (Norman, OK: University of Oklahoma Press, 1968), 57.
16. Engle, *Struggle*, 47; *Official Records*, Volume 7, 845.
17. *Official Records*, Volume 7, 845.
18. Ibid., 524–25.
19. McPherson, 395; *Official Records*, Volume 7, 526.
20. *Official Records*, Volume 7, 527.
21. *Official Records*, Volume 7, 527–28.
22. Bruce Catton, *Grant Moves South* (Boston: Little, Brown, 1960), 116–17; *Official Records*, Volume 7, 528–29.
23. *Official Records*, Volume 7, 535.
24. Ibid., 532.
25. Ibid.
26. Ibid., 533.
27. Engle, *Buell*, 152; *Official Records*, Volume 7, 528–29.
28. Engle, *Buell*, 154; *Official Records*, Volume 7, 578–79; Engle, *Struggle*, 43.
29. Nancy Scott Anderson and Dwight Anderson, *The Generals — Ulysses S. Grant and Robert E. Lee* (New York: Wings Books, 1994), 53–58, 68, 121–22.
30. Ulysses S. Grant, *Personal Memoirs of U. S. Grant*, Volume 1 (New York: Charles L. Webster, 1885), 249–50; McPherson, 395–96; Anderson, *The Generals*, 197–98.
31. Catton, *South*, 118–19; *Official Records*, Volume 7, 533–34; Grant, *Memoirs*, Volume 1, 285.86.
32. Catton, *South*, 119; Grant, *Memoirs*, Volume 1, 285–86.
33. *Official Records*, Volume 7, 561; Grant, *Memoirs*, Volume 1, 286; Engle, *Struggle*, 40.
34. Catton, *South*, 103; McPherson, 393; John G. Nicolay and John Hay, "Abraham Lincoln: A History, Tennessee and Kentucky," *The Century*, August 1888: 577.
35. McPherson, 392–93; Nicolay, "Tennessee," 577; *Official Records*, Volume 7, 565.
36. *Official Records*, Volume 8, 509–10.
37. Ibid.
38. Catton, *South*, 129–30; Nicolay, "Tennessee," 577.
39. Engle, *Struggle*, 40; Grant *Memoirs*, Volume 1, 287.
40. *Official Records*, Volume 7, 120–21.
41. Ibid., 121.
42. Coppee, 40; *Official Records*, Volume 7, 121.

43. *Official Records*, Volume 7, 572; Catton, *South*, 130–31.
44. *Official Records*, Volume 7, 575.
45. *Ibid.*, 121–22.
46. *Ibid.*, 575, 577.
47. *Ibid.*, 574, 576, 578–79.
48. *Ibid.*, 581.

Chapter 2

1. Catton, *South*, 138; Henry Walke, "Operations of the Western Flotilla," *The Century*, January 1885: 426–27.
2. Walke, 426–27; Coppee, 42; Catton, *South*, 139.
3. Coppee, 41; Catton, *South*, 139; Grant, *Memoirs*, Volume 1, 291.
4. Coppee, 41; Grant, *Memoirs*, Volume 1, 291.
5. Grant, *Memoirs*, Volume 1, 291–92; Coppee, 41.
6. John Y. Simon, ed., *The Papers of Ulysses S. Grant*, Volume 4 (Carbondale, IL: Southern Illinois University Press, 1972), 147.
7. Simon, 149.
8. *Official Records*, Volume 7, 125.
9. *Ibid.*; Coppee, 42–43.
10. Catton, *South*, 141–42; *Official Records*, Volume 7, 139–40.
11. Grant, *Memoirs*, Volume 1, 292; Catton, *South*, 142–43.
12. Walke, 428.
13. *Official Records*, Volume 7, 122; Walke, 428–29.
14. *Official Records*, Volume 7, 123–24; Walke, 431; Jesse Taylor, "The Defense of Fort Henry," *Battles and Leaders of the Civil War*, Volume 1, Robert Underwood Johnson and Clarence Clough Buel, eds. (New York: Thomas Yoseloff, 1956), 371; William Preston Johnston, *The Life of Gen. Albert Sidney Johnston* (New York: Da Capo Press, 1997), 431.
15. *Official Records*, Volume 7, 136.
16. Taylor, 371.
17. *Official Records*, Volume 7, 124.
18. *Ibid.*, 125.
19. Grant, *Memoirs*, Volume 1, 294–95.
20. *Official Records*, Volume 7, 599.
21. *Ibid.*, 153–55.
22. *Ibid.*, 124.
23. Catton, *South*, 150–51; *Official Records*, Volume 7, 595.
24. *Official Records*, Volume 7, 130–31.
25. Steven E. Woodworth, *Jefferson Davis and His Generals: The Failure of Confederate Command in the West* (Lawrence, KS: University Press of Kansas, 1990), 79–80; *Official Records*, Volume 7, 861; McPherson, 397–98.
26. *Official Records*, Volume 7, 594.
27. *Ibid.*, 599
28. Catton, *South*, 149–50; *Official Records*, Volume 7, 594.
29. *Official Records*, Volume 7, 600, 603–04.
30. *Ibid.*, 604; Grant, *Memoirs*, Volume 1, 298.
31. *Official Records*, Volume 7, 604; Grant, *Memoirs*, Volume 1, 296, 298.
32. *Official Records*, Volume 7, 605; Coppee, 48.

Chapter 3

1. Grant, *Memoirs*, Volume 1, 298–99; Coppee, 49–50; Wallace, "Fort Donelson," 292.
2. Grant, *Memoirs*, Volume 1, 299; Catton, *South*, 155.
3. Wallace, "Fort Donelson," 288–89; Coppee, 50–51; Walke, 431–32.
4. Wallace, "Fort Donelson," 288–89; Coppee, 50–51; Walke, 431–32.
5. Woodworth, *Jefferson Davis*, 80; Coppee, 51–52.
6. Walke, 432–33; Catton, *South*, 155–56.
7. Grant, *Memoirs*, Volume 1, 300; *Official Records*, Volume 7, 172.
8. *Official Records*, Volume 7, 172–73, 205–06, 212–13.
9. *Ibid.*; H. Robert Ferrel, ed., *Holding the Line: The Third Tennessee Infantry 1861–1864* (Kent, OH: Kent State University Press, 1994), 18.
10. Henry I. Smith, *History of the Seventh Iowa Veteran Volunteer Infantry During the Civil War* (Mason City, IA: E. Hitchcock, Printer, Binder, 1903), 42; Coppee, 53–54; *Official Records*, Volume 7, 174, 185.
11. Ferrell, 21–22.
12. Coppee, 55; Wallace, "Fort Donelson," 295.
13. *Official Records*, Volume 7, 613.
14. Simon, Volume 4, 211.
15. *Official Records*, Volume 7, 613–14.
16. Fletcher Pratt, *Civil War on Western Waters* (New York: Henry Holt, 1956), 59–60.
17. Wallace, "Fort Donelson," 299; *Official Records*, Volume 7, 166; Walke, 435; Gosnell, 68.
18. *Official Records*, Volume 7, 166; Walke, 435. Gosnell, 68.
19. *Official Records*, Volume 7, 159; Grant, *Memoirs*, Volume 1, 305.
20. *Official Records*, Volume 7, 268.
21. *Ibid.*, 268, 281–82; Coppee, 57–58.
22. Jeffrey L. Patrick, ed., *Three Years With Wallace's Zouaves: The Civil War Memoirs of Thomas Wise Durham* (Macon, GA: Mercer University Press, 2003), 70.
23. Grant, *Memoirs*, Volume 1, 304–05; Wallace, "Fort Donelson," 302; Catton, *South*, 163–64.
24. W. S. Morris, et al, *History 31st Regiment Illinois Volunteers* (Carbondale, IL: Southern Illinois University Press, 1998), 35.
25. Wallace, "Fort Donelson," 301; *Official Records*, Volume 7, 189; Coppee, 58–59.
26. *Official Records*, Volume 7, 189; Wallace, "Fort Donelson," 301–02; Coppee, 58–59.
27. Wallace, "Fort Donelson," 303; Coppee, 59; Catton, *South*, 165–66.
28. Wallace, "Fort Donelson," 303–04; Coppee, 60–61; Catton, *South*, 165–66.
29. Wallace, "Fort Donelson," 304.
30. Grant, *Memoirs*, Volume 1, 307.
31. *Official Records*, Volume 7, 618.
32. Grant, *Memoirs*, Volume 1, 307–08.
33. Wallace, "Fort Donelson," 305–06; Patrick, 72.
34. Wallace, "Fort Donelson," 306–07; Coppee, 61.
35. Wallace, "Fort Donelson," 307; Catton, *South*, 170–71; Coppee, 61.
36. *Official Records*, Volume 7, 283.
37. John H. Brinton. *Personal Memoirs of John H. Brinton: Civil War Surgeon, 1861–1865* (Carbondale, IL: Southern Illinois University Press, 1996), 120; Coppee, 63.
38. Brinton, 120–21; Coppee, 64.
39. *Official Records*, Volume 7, 283.

40. *Ibid.*, 269, 283.
41. *Ibid.*, 269–70; Catton, *South*, 176; McPherson, 401.
42. Ira Blanchard, *I Marched with Sherman: Civil War Memoirs of the 20th Illinois Volunteer Infantry* (San Francisco: J. D. Huff, 1992), 49.
43. Patrick, 74.
44. *Official Records*, Volume 7, 160.
45. Brinton, 129–30; *Official Records*, Volume 7, 161.
46. Catton, *South*, 175; Brinton, 129; *Official Records*, Volume 7, 161.
47. Catton, *South*, 177–78.
48. *Official Records*, Volume 7, 625.
49. *Ibid.*, 160.
50. Blanchard, 50.

Chapter 4

1. *Official Records*, Volume 7, 161.
2. Catton, *South*, 181; Brinton, 142; *Official Records*, Volume 10, 62.
3. *Official Records*, Volume 7, 626; Catton, *South*, 182.
4. *Official Records*, Volume 7, 629.
5. Coppee, 74; *Official Records*, Volume 7, 422–23, 629; Catton, *South*, 184.
6. *Official Records*, Volume 7, 422–23; Coppee, 74.
7. *Official Records*, Volume 7, 424, 648.
8. *Ibid.*, 594; Catton, *South*, 186–87.
9. *Official Records*, Volume 7, 595.
10. *Ibid.*, 628, 637.
11. *Ibid.*, 632–33.
12. Catton, *South*, 188; *Official Records*, Volume 7, 641, 647.
13. *Official Records*, Volume 7, 645–46.
14. *Ibid.*, 648.
15. *Ibid.*, 648, 655.
16. *Ibid.*, 652.
17. Grant, *Memoirs*, Volume 1, 318–19; *Official Records*, Volume 7, 662–63.
18. Catton, *South*, 190–91; *Official Records*, Volume 7, 666.
19. Grant, *Memoirs*, Volume 1, 320.
20. *Official Records*, Volume 7, 670; Catton, *South*, 192.
21. Grant, *Memoirs*, Volume 1, 321.
22. Fiske, 64–65; Johnston, *Albert Sidney*, 496–97.
23. McPherson, 402–03; Fiske, 64–65.
24. McPherson, 405–06; Johnston, *Albert Sidney*, 496.
25. G. P. T. Beauregard, "The Shiloh Campaign, Part I," *The North American Review*, January 1886: 9.
26. William Preston Johnston, "Albert Sidney Johnston and the Shiloh Campaign," *The Century*, February 1885: 619.
27. Catton, *South*, 193.
28. *Official Records*, Volume 7, 655, Volume 52, Part 1, 217; Catton, *South*, 193–94.
29. *Official Records*, Volume 7, 674.
30. *Ibid.*, 674–75.
31. Catton, *South*, 194–95; *Official Records*, Volume 7, 645–46.
32. *Official Records*, Volume 7, 679–80.
33. *Ibid.*, 680.
34. *Official Records*, Volume 10, Part 2, 3.
35. *Ibid.*, Part 2, 6–7.
36. *Ibid.*, Part 2, 4–5.
37. Catton, *South*, 202; *Official Records*, Volume 10, Part 2, 15.
38. *Official Records*, Volume 10, Part 2, 15.
39. *Ibid.*, 21.
40. *Ibid.*, 22.
41. *Ibid.*, 22.
42. *Ibid.*, 13–14.
43. *Ibid.*, 30.
44. *Ibid.*, 32, 36; Grant, *Memoirs*, Volume 1, 328.
45. *Official Records*, Volume 7, 683.
46. *Ibid.*, 683–84.
47. *Official Records*, Volume 10, Part 2, 62–63.
48. Grant, *Memoirs*, Volume 1, 327–28.
49. Brinton, 148.
50. John G. Nicolay and John Hay, "Abraham Lincoln: A History, The Mississippi and Shiloh," *The Century*, September 1888: 666; J. F. C. Fuller, *The Generalship of Ulysses S. Grant* (New York: Da Capo Press, n. d.), 98; Catton, *South*, 210.
51. William T. Sherman, *Memoirs of W. T. Sherman, Written by Himself* (New York: Charles L. Webster, 1891), 256.
52. Grant, *Memoirs*, Volume 1, 330–31.
53. Sherman, *Memoirs*, Volume 1, 261.
54. *Official Records*, Volume 10, Part 2, 41.
55. *Ibid.*, 46, 49, 52; Fuller, 100.
56. *Official Records*, Volume 10, Part 2, 51; Fuller, 100.
57. *Official Records*, Volume 10, Part 2, 55; Fuller, 100.
58. *Official Records*, Volume 10, Part 2, 62

Chapter 5

1. William S. Rosecrans, "Corinth," *The Century*, October 1886: 903; Beauregard, "Shiloh, Part I," 20.
2. Johnston, "Shiloh Campaign," 618; McPherson, 406; Beauregard, "Shiloh, Part I," 19.
3. Catton, *South*, 214; *Official Records*, Volume 7, 899–900.
4. Fiske, 70–71.
5. Fiske, 71; Woodworth, *Jefferson Davis*, 90–94.
6. Beauregard, "Shiloh, Part I," 19; G. P. T. Beauregard, "The Shiloh Campaign, Part II," *The North American Review*, February 1886: 159.
7. Charles P. Roland, *Jefferson Davis's Greatest General: Albert Sidney Johnston* (Abilene, Texas: McWhiney Foundation Press, 2000), 54–55; Nicolay, "Mississippi and Shiloh," 667.
8. Steven E. Woodworth, *Six Armies in Tennessee: The Chickamauga and Chattanooga Campaigns* (Lincoln, NE: University of Nebraska Press, 1998), 7; Peter Cozzens, *This Terrible Sound: The Battle of Chickamauga* (Urbana, IL: University of Illinois Press, 1992), 3.
9. Beauregard, "Shiloh, Part I," 20–21; McPherson, 336, 367; Woodworth, *Jefferson Davis*, 95.
10. *Official Records*, Volume 10, Part 1, 385; Johnston, "Shiloh Campaign," 619.
11. Beauregard, "Shiloh, Part I," 22–23.
12. *Official Records*, Volume 10, Part 1, 385; Thomas Jordan, "Notes of A Confederate Staff-Officer at Shiloh," *The Century*, February 1885: 630; Beauregard, "Shiloh, Part II," 159–60.
13. *Official Records*, Volume 10, Part 1, 385–86; Jordan, 630.

14. John Kent Folmar, *From That Terrible Field: Civil War Letters of James M. Williams, Twenty-first Alabama Infantry* (Tuscaloosa, AL: University of Alabama Press, 1981), 54; William C. Davis, *Diary of A Confederate Soldier: John S. Jackman of the Orphan Brigade* (Columbia, SC: University of South Carolina Press, 1990), 29–30.
15. *Official Records*, Volume 10, Part 1, 385–86.
16. Beauregard, "Shiloh, Part II," 161–62; *Official Records*, Volume 10, Part 1, 463–64; Jordan, 631.
17. Johnston, "Shiloh Campaign," 621–22.
18. *Official Records*, Volume 10, Part 1, 386, 567–68; Beauregard, "Shiloh, Part II," 164.
19. Johnston, "Shiloh Campaign," 620–21; Larry J. Daniel, *Shiloh: The Battle That Changed the Civil War* (New York: Simon & Schuster, 1997), 119.
20. Ulysses S. Grant, "The Battle of Shiloh," *The Century*, February 1885: 597; Sherman, *Memoirs*, Volume 1, 257.
21. Grant, *Memoirs*, Volume 1, 338–39; Thomas B. Van Horne, *History of the Army of the Cumberland*, Volume 1 (Cincinnati: Robert Clarke, 1875), 104–05; Daniel, *Shiloh*, 109.
22. Grant, *Memoirs*, Volume 1, 334, 338; *Official Records*, Volume 10, Part 1, 112.
23. Warren Olney, "The Battle of Shiloh, With Some Personal Reminiscences," *Overland Monthly and Out West Magazine*, June 1885: 578; Sherman, *Memoirs*, Volume 1, 257.
24. Grant, *Memoirs*, Volume 1, 332–33, 358.
25. Grant, *Memoirs*, Volume 1, 334; *Official Records*, Volume 10, Part 2, 91.
26. *Official Records*, Volume 10, Part 2, 93–94.
27. *Ibid.*, Part 1, 89, 330–31.
28. Lucius W. Barber, *Army Memoirs of Lucius W. Barber, Company "D," 15th Illinois Volunteer Infantry* (Chicago: J. M. Jones Stationery and Printing Co., 1894), 48.
29. William W. Cluett, *History of the 57th Regiment Illinois Volunteer Infantry* (Princeton, NJ: T.P. Streeter, 1886), 17–18.

Chapter 6

1. Wilber F. Crummer, *With Grant at Fort Donelson, Shiloh and Vicksburg* (Oak Park, IL: E. C. Crummer, 1915), 55; Blanchard, 53.
2. Lot D. Young, *Reminiscences of A Soldier of the Orphan Brigade* (Louisville, KY: Courier-Journal Job Printing Company, 1918), 26; John W. Carroll, *Autobiography and Reminiscences* (Henderson, TN: n.p., 1898), 22.
3. Johnston, "Shiloh Campaign," 622.
4. *Official Records*, Volume 10, Part 1, 282.
5. *Ibid.*, 278; Victor Hicken, *Illinois in the Civil War* (Urbana, IL: University of Illinois Press, 1991), 57.
6. *Official Records*, Volume 10, Part 1, 278, 280.
7. Sherman, *Memoirs*, Volume 1, 258.
8. Hicken, 56; *Official Records*, Volume 10, Part 1, 264.
9. John A. Bering and Thomas Montgomery, *History of the Forty-eighth Ohio Vet. Vol. Inf.* (Hillsboro, OH: Highland News Office, 1880), 20.
10. *Official Records*, Volume 10, Part 1, 581.
11. *Ibid.*, 258.
12. McPherson, 409; Grant, *Memoirs*, Volume 1, 343.
13. Hicken, 58; *Official Records*, Volume 10, Part 1, 133.
14. Blanchard, 54; *Official Records*, Volume 10, Part 1, 133.
15. Hicken, 59; *Official Records*, Volume 10, Part 1, 116.
16. *Official Records*, Volume 10, Part 1, 116–18; Olynthus B. Clark, ed., *Downing's Civil War Diary by Sergeant Alexander G. Downing, Company E, Eleventh Iowa Infantry* (Des Moines, IA: Historical Department of Iowa, 1916), 41.
17. Olney, 582.
18. Coppee, 88.
19. Julie A. Doyle, John David Smith, and Richard M. McMurry, eds., *This Wilderness of War: The Civil War Letters of George w. Squier, Hoosier Volunteer* (Knoxville, TN: University of Tennessee Press, 1998), 10–11.
20. Hicken, 62; *Official Records*, Volume 10, Part 1, 278.
21. Grant, *Memoirs*, Volume 1, 334–35; *Official Records*, Volume 10, Part 2, 95.
22. *Official Records*, Volume 10, Part 1, 184–85, Volume 10, Part 2, 95.
23. *Ibid.*, Volume 52, Part 1, 232.
24. *Ibid.*, Volume 10, Part 1, 181.
25. Grant, "Shiloh," 595; *Official Records*, Volume 10, Part 1, 185.
26. *Official Records*, Volume 10, Part 1, 185; Catton, *South*, 225–26.
27. *Official Records*, Volume 10, Part 2, 95.
28. Johnston, "Shiloh Campaign," 624.
29. Grant, *Memoirs*, Volume 1, 343.
30. A. L. Conger, *The Rise of Grant* (Freeport, NY: Books for Libraries Press, 1970), 246–47.
31. *Official Records*, Volume 10, Part 1, 278–79; Hicken, 62.
32. W. J. Worsham, *The Old Nineteenth Tennessee Regiment, C. S. A.* (Knoxville, TN: Press of Paragon Printing Company, 1902), 37, 39; Daniel E. Sutherland, ed., *Reminiscences of a Private: William E. Bevens of the First Arkansas Infantry, C. S. A.* (Fayetteville, AR: University of Arkansas Press, 1992), 71.
33. *Official Records*, Volume 10, Part 1, 465–66.
34. *Ibid.*, 438–39.
35. Blanchard, 55–56.
36. Davis, 32.
37. Beauregard, "Shiloh, Part II," 172.
38. Hicken, 60–61.
39. *Ibid.*; Marion Morrison, *A History of the Ninth Regiment Illinois Volunteer Infantry, With the Regimental Roster* (Carbondale, IL: Southern Illinois University Press, 1997), 33–34.
40. Olney, 585–86; Hicken, 63; Johnston, "Shiloh Campaign," 626.
41. Johnston, "Shiloh Campaign," 627; Beauregard, "Shiloh, Part II," 171.
42. *Official Records*, Volume 10, Part 1, 119; Catton, *South*, 232; Olney, 587.
43. Grant, *Memoirs*, Volume 1, 340.
44. James C. Thrall, "Letter From Captain James C. Thrall," *Southern Historical Society Papers*, January 1879: 46; Hicken, 64.
45. Hicken, 64; *Official Records*, Volume 10, Part 1, 149.
46. *Official Records*, Volume 10, Part 1, 279.

47. Hicken, 64; Coppee, 90–91; Beauregard, "Shiloh, Part II," 173.
48. *Official Records*, Volume 10, Part 1, 323; Beauregard, "Shiloh, Part II," 172–73.
49. Robert L. Kimberly and Ephraim S. Holloway, *The Forty-first Ohio Veteran Volunteer Infantry in the War of the Rebellion, 1861–1865* (Huntington, WV: Blue Acorn Press, 1999), 21–22; *Official Records*, Volume 10, Part 1, 324, 333.
50. Grant, "Battle of Shiloh," 600.
51. Don Carlos Buell, "Shiloh Revisited," *The Century*, March 1886: 753–54; *Official Records*, Volume 10, Part 1, 292; Grant, *Memoirs*, Volume 1, 344.
52. Grant, *Memoirs*, Volume 1, 344–45.
53. Coppee, 90–91; *Official Records*, Volume 10, Part 1, 550–51.
54. Beauregard, "Shiloh, Part II," 173–74; S. H. Lockett, "Controversies in Regard to Shiloh: A Staff Officer's Account of the Attack and Withdrawal," *The Century*, March 1886: 783; *Official Records*, Volume 10, Part 1, 467.
55. *Official Records*, Volume 10, Part 1, 339; Sherman, *Memoirs*, Volume 1, 273.
56. Grant, "Battle of Shiloh," 602.
57. Grant, "Battle of Shiloh," 601–02; Coppee, 90.
58. *Official Records*, Volume 10, Part 1, 170; Grant, "Battle of Shiloh," 595; Henry B. Carrington, "Major General Lew Wallace at Shiloh," *The Bay State Monthly*, March 1885: 331.
59. *Official Records*, Volume 10, Part 1, 170, 181–82; Grant, *Memoirs*, Volume 1, 351; Coppee, 91.
60. Grant, "Battle of Shiloh," 601–02.
61. Grant, *Memoirs*, Volume 1, 348; McPherson, 410; Sherman, *Memoirs*, Volume 1, 273.
62. *Official Records*, Volume 10, Part 1, 506.
63. Cluett, 22; Daniel McCook, "The Second Division at Shiloh," *Harper's New Monthly Magazine*, May 1864: 829.
64. Grant, *Memoirs*, Volume 1, 348–49.
65. Beauregard, "Shiloh, Part II," 174.
66. *Official Records*, Volume 10, Part 1, 467; Connelly, *Army of Heartland*, 170–71.
67. *Official Records*, Volume 10, Part 1, 384.
68. *Ibid.*, 387.
69. Catton, *South*, 242.

Chapter 7

1. Charles C. Briant, *History of the Sixth Regiment Indiana Volunteer Infantry of Both the Three Months' and Three Years' Services* (Indianapolis: Wm. E. Burford, Printer and Binder, 1891), 102–03.
2. Grant, *Memoirs*, Volume 1, 350; Van Horne, 109–10.
3. Beauregard, "Shiloh, Part II," 175, 177.
4. *Official Records*, Volume 10, Part 1, 583.
5. *Ibid.*, 293–94.
6. Van Horne, 111–12.
7. Catton, *South*, 244; Beauregard, "Shiloh, Part II," 177; Van Horne, 109.
8. Buell, 779; Gerald J. Prokopowicz, *All For the Regiment: The Army of the Ohio, 1861–1862* (Chapel Hill, NC: University of North Carolina Press, 2001), 102.
9. Grant, *Memoirs*, Volume 1, 349; *Official Records*, Volume 10, Part 1, 294, 324; Van Horne, 109–11.
10. Beauregard, "Shiloh, Part II," 176.
11. *Official Records*, Volume 10, Part 1, 335–36; Van Horne, 112–13.
12. *Official Records*, Volume 10, Part 1, 336, 339, 294; Van Horne, 112–13.
13. Byron R. Abernathy, ed., *Private Elisha Stockwell, Jr. Sees the Civil War* (Norman, OK: University of Oklahoma Press, 1958), 19; Kimberly, 23.
14. *Official Records*, Volume 10, Part 1, 295; Van Horne, 113.
15. *Official Records*, Volume 10, Part 1, 295; Van Horne, 113–14.
16. *Official Records*, Volume 10, Part 1, 170.
17. *Ibid.*, 170, 251; Sherman, *Memoirs*, Volume 1, 267.
18. Sherman, *Memoirs*, Volume 1, 267; *Official Records*, Volume 10, Part 1, 251.
19. *Official Records*, Volume 10, Part 1, 119.
20. *Ibid.*, 119–20, 441.
21. *Ibid.*, 120.
22. Stephen E. Ambrose, ed., *A Wisconsin Boy in Dixie: The Selected Letters of James K. Newton* (Madison, WI: University of Wisconsin Press, 1961), 15.
23. Stewart Bennett and Barbara Tillery, eds., *The Struggle for the Life of the Republic: A Civil War Narrative by Brevet Major Charles Dana Miller, 76th Ohio Volunteer Infantry* (Kent, OH: Kent State University Press, 2004), 28.
24. Jordan, 633–34.
25. Jordan, 634.
26. Grant, *Memoirs*, Volume 1, 350–51.
27. *Official Records*, Volume 10, Part 1, 120.
28. *Ibid.*, 173; Sherman, *Memoirs*, Volume 1, 268.
29. Beauregard, "Shiloh, Part II," 178; *Official Records*, Volume 10, Part 1, 388.
30. *Official Records*, Volume 10, Part 2, 96–97.
31. *Ibid.*, 98.
32. *Ibid.*, 398–99.
33. *Ibid.*, 400.
34. Grant, *Memoirs*, Volume 1, 354–55.
35. *Official Records*, Volume 10, Part 2, 99.
36. *Ibid.*, Part 1, 108, 395.

Chapter 8

1. Judson W. Bishop, *The Story of a Regiment: Being a Narrative of the Service of the Second Regiment Minnesota Veteran Volunteer Infantry in the Civil War of 1861–1865* (St. Paul, MN: Regimental Association, 1890), 54.
2. *Official Records*, Volume 10, Part 2, 88–100.
3. *Ibid.*, 100.
4. McPherson, 415; Gosnell, 71; Walke, 439.
5. Walke, 439, 442–43; McPherson, 415.
6. *Official Records*, Volume 10, Part 2, 105–06, 109, 130.
7. Grant, *Memoirs*, Volume 1, 371.
8. *Ibid.*, 369–70; Sherman, *Memoirs*, Volume 1, 272.
9. Sherman, *Memoirs*, Volume 1, 272; Catton, *South*, 253–54.
10. Doyle, 19.
11. *Official Records*, Volume 10, Part 1, 99.
12. Alexander K. McClure, *Abraham Lincoln and Men of War-Time* (Lincoln, NE: University of Nebraska Press, 1996) 195–96.
13. McPherson, 414; Connelly. *Army Heartland*, 168.

14. Grant, *Memoirs*, Volume 1, 368.
15. *Ibid.*, 371–72.
16. *Official Records*, Volume 10, Part 2, 144; Sherman, *Memoirs*, Volume 1, 283.
17. *Official Records*, Volume 10, Part 2, 182–83.
18. Grant, *Memoirs*, Volume 1, 376–77.
19. *Official Records*, Volume 10, Part 2, 440; McPherson, 416; Beauregard, "Shiloh, Part II," 181.
20. Douglas Hale, *The Third Texas Cavalry in the Civil War* (Norman, OK: University of Oklahoma Press, 1993), 110–11; Beauregard, "Shiloh, Part II," 181.
21. Grant, *Memoirs*, Volume 1, 377–78; Beauregard, "Shiloh, Part II," 182.
22. Beauregard, "Shiloh, Part II," 182–83; Grant, *Memoirs*, Volume 1, 379–80.
23. Beauregard, "Shiloh, Part II," 183; Grant, *Memoirs*, Volume 1, 380–81.
24. Beauregard, "Shiloh, Part II," 183–84; McPherson, 417.
25. Grant, *Memoirs*, Volume 1, 385; Catton, *South*, 281.
26. *Official Records*, Volume 17, Part 2, 69.
27. *Ibid.*, Volume 16, Part 2, 14.
28. *Ibid.*, Volume 17, Part 2, 90.
29. *Ibid.*, Volume 17, Part 2, 150.
30. David Urquhart, "Bragg's Advance and Retreat," *Battles and Leaders of the Civil War*, Volume 3, Robert Underwood Johnson and Clarence Clough Buel, eds. (New York: Thomas Yoseloff, 1956), 600.
31. *Official Records*, Volume 17, Part 2, 132.
32. Urquhart, 600; Catton, *South*, 300.
33. *Official Records*, Volume 16, Part 2, 314–15.
34. Urquhart, 600; McPherson, 516–17.
35. *Official Records*, Volume 16, Part 2, 539; Richard O'Connor, *Sheridan the Inevitable* (New York: Konecky & Konecky, 1993), 70.
36. O'Connor, 78–79.
37. McPherson, 518; Urquhart, 601–02.
38. Urquhart, 602. *Official Records*, Volume 16, Part 2, 530; McPherson, 518–19.
39. McPherson, 519.20; O'Connor, 81–82.
40. O'Connor, 81–82; McPherson, 520.
41. Urquhart, 603; McPherson, 520.
42. *Official Records*, Volume 16, Part 2, 638, 626.
43. Grant, *Memoirs*, Volume 1, 416–17; McPherson, 522–23.

Chapter 9

1. William S. Rosecrans, "The Campaign for Chattanooga," *The Century*, May 1887: 129.
2. Woodworth, *Six Armies*, 9.
3. Cozzens, *Terrible Sound*, 7–8; Bruce Catton, *Grant Takes Command* (Boston: Little, Brown, 1969), 30.
4. *Official Records*, Volume 20, Part 1, 189.
5. *Ibid.*, Part 2, 117–18.
6. *Ibid.*, 118.
7. *Ibid.*, 123.
8. Urquhart, 603–04; *Official Records*, Volume 20, Part 2, 453.
9. Earl J. Hess, *Banners to the Breeze: The Kentucky Campaign, Corinth and Stones River* (Lincoln, NE: University of Nebraska Press, 2000), 186.
10. Hess, 187; John Fitch, *Annals of the Army of the Cumberland* (Philadelphia: J. B. Lippincott, 1864), 382; *Official Records*, Volume 20, Part 1, 189.
11. *Official Records*, Volume 20, Part 1, 189, 422; Horn, *Army of Tennessee*, 192–93.
12. R. W. Johnson, *A Soldier's Reminiscences in Peace and War* (Philadelphia: J. B. Lippincott Company, 1886), 203–04; *Official Records*, Volume 20, Part 1, 189.
13. *Official Records*, Volume 20, Part 1, 189–90; Fitch, 382–83.
14. Hess, 187–88; *Official Records*, Volume 20, Part 1, 190.
15. Hess, 187–88; *Official Records*, Volume 20, Part 1, 190; Eban Hannaford, "In the Ranks at Stone River," *Harper's New Monthly Magazine*, November 1863: 809.
16. *Official Records*, Volume 20, Part 1, 253; Hess, 190.
17. Hannaford, 810; *Official Records*, Volume 20, Part 1, 190, 458–59.
18. *Official Records*, Volume 20, Part 1, 253–54.
19. *Ibid.*, 184, 663.
20. Hess, 190–91.
21. *Ibid.*, 191.
22. *Official Records*, Volume 20, Part 1, 190–91, 254, 448; Gilbert C. Kniffin, "The Battle of Stone's River," *Battles and Leaders of the Civil War*, Volume 3, Robert Underwood Johnson and Clarence Clough Buel, eds. (New York: Thomas Yoseloff, 1956), 613.
23. Hess, 192–93.
24. *Official Records*, Volume 20, Part 1, 372; Fitch, 389–90.
25. Hess, 193–94; *Official Records*, Volume 20, Part 1, 664.
26. Hess, 193–94; Bruce Catton, *Never Call Retreat* (Garden City, NJ: Doubleday, 1965), 40; *Official Records*, Volume 20, Part 1, 664.
27. Fitch, 392–93; Hess, 194; *Official Records*, Volume 20, Part 1, 192.
28. *Official Records*, Volume 20, Part 1, 192.
29. *Ibid.*, 255; Kniffin, "Stone's River," 615.

Chapter 10

1. Catton, *Never Retreat*, 41.
2. *Official Records*, Volume 20, Part 1, 255; Hess, 197.
3. Hess, 199; *Official Records*, Volume 20, Part 1, 255.
4. *Official Records*, Volume 20, Part 1, 304–05, 310.
5. *Ibid.*, 844.
6. *Ibid.*, 341.
7. *Ibid.*, 264.
8. *Ibid.*, 255; Hess, 200, 202.
9. *Official Records*, Volume 20, Part 1, 193.
10. Hess, 203.
11. Hess, 205; C. Knight Aldrich, *Quest for a Star: The Civil War Letters and Diaries of Colonel Francis T. Sherman of the 88th Illinois* (Knoxville, TN: University of Tennessee Press, 1999), 22.
12. *Official Records*, Volume 20, Part 1, 348–49, 734; Kniffin, "Stone's River," 620; R. Lockwood Tower, ed., *A Carolinian Goes to War: The Civil War Narrative of Arthur Middleton Manigault, Brigadier General, C. S. A.* (Columbia, S. C.: University of South Carolina Press, 1983), 57.
13. Hess, 206; O'Connor, 92; *Official Records*, Volume 20, Part 1, 350.
14. *Official Records*, Volume 20, Part 1, 349; Hess, 206; O'Connor, 92.

15. Tower, 57; *Official Records*, Volume 20, Part 1, 764.
16. Hess, 206–07; *Official Records*, Volume 20, Part 1, 421.
17. O'Connor, 93–94; *Official Records*, Volume 20, Part 1, 349; Kniffin, "Stone's River," 621.
18. Kniffin, "Stone's River," 623–24; *Official Records*, Volume 20, Part 1, 193, 378; Fitch, 295.
19. *Official Records*, Volume 20, Part 1, 383; Hess, 208.
20. Hess, 208; Kniffin, "Stone's River," 625; *Official Records*, Volume 20, Part 1, 927.
21. Fitch, 396; Hess, 208–09; Kniffin, "Stone's River," 625.
22. *Official Records*, Volume 20, Part 1, 846–47; Hess, 209.
23. Hess, 209; *Official Records*, Volume 20, Part 1, 735.
24. *Official Records*, Volume 20, Part 1, 432.
25. Hess, 210; *Official Records*, Volume 20, Part 1, 527; Catton, *Never Retreat*, 43.
26. Hess, 210–11; Catton, *Never Retreat*, 42–43; Kniffin, "Stone's River," 627.
27. Hess, 211.
28. *Official Records*, Volume 20, Part 1, 574, 597, 847–48.
29. Hess, 211; *Official Records*, Volume 20, Part 1, 848–49.
30. Catton, *Never Retreat*, 43; *Official Records*, Volume 20, Part 1, 783.
31. Kniffin, "Stone's River," 628; *Official Records*, Volume 20, Part 1, 493, 544.
32. Hess, 214; *Official Records*, Volume 20, Part 1, 493, 793–94.
33. Hess, 214–15; *Official Records*, Volume 20, Part 1, 783–84.
34. *Official Records*, Volume 20, Part 1, 194; Fitch, 400–01.
35. *Official Records*, Volume 20, Part 1, 662.

Chapter 11

1. Hess, 218; *Official Records*, Volume 20, Part 1, 194–95.
2. *Official Records*, Volume 20, Part 1, 450; Hess, 218; Kniffin, "Stone's River," 629.
3. *Official Records*, Volume 20, Part 1, 667; Hess, 218.
4. *Official Records*, Volume 20, Part 1, 667, 450; Catton, *Never Retreat*, 45.
5. *Official Records*, Volume 20, Part 1, 667–68; Kniffin, "Stone's River," 630.
6. Kniffin, "Stone's River," 630.
7. Hess, 219–20; *Official Records*, Volume 20, Part 1, 668.
8. *Official Records*, Volume 20, Part 1, 785.
9. *Ibid.*, 786; Hess, 220, 222.
10. Hess, 222–23; *Official Records*, Volume 20, Part 1, 591, 786.
11. *Official Records*, Volume 20, Part 1, 451.
12. Fitch, 404; *Official Records*, Volume 20, Part 1, 451, 786.
13. Kniffin, "Stone's River," 631; Hess, 224.
14. *Official Records*, Volume 20, Part 1, 195, 787.
15. *Ibid.*, 195–96.
16. *Ibid.*, 668–69.
17. Hess, 226; *Official Records*, Volume 20, Part 1, 669.
18. Hess, 227; *Official Records*, Volume 20, Part 1, 196.
19. *Official Records*, Volume 20, Part 1, 185–86.
20. *Ibid.*, 186.
21. J. B. Jones, *A Rebel War Clerk's Diary at the Confederate States Capital*, Volume 1 (Philadelphia: J. B. Lippincott, 1866), 228.
22. Fitch, 408; Roy P. Basler, ed., *The Collected Works of Abraham Lincoln*, Volume 6 (New Brunswick, NJ: Rutgers University Press, 1953), 424.
23. Hess, 227; *Official Records*, Volume 20, Part 1, 186.
24. *Official Records*, Volume 20, Part 1, 699.
25. *Ibid.*, 699, 682, 684, 683.
26. *Ibid.*, 698.

Chapter 12

1. Rosecrans, "Chattanooga," 129; Hess, 226.
2. Hess, 227–28; Woodworth, *Six Armies*, 9; *Official Records*, Volume 20, Part 1, 698–99.
3. Hess, 227–28; Woodworth, *Six Armies*, 10.
4. Woodworth, *Six Armies*, 10; Cozzens, *Terrible Sound*, 3.
5. Cozzens, *Terrible Sound*, 17; Woodworth, *Six Armies*, 14–15; James R. Sullivan, *Chickamauga and Chattanooga Battlefields* (Washington, DC: National Park Service, 1961), 5.
6. Woodworth, *Six Armies*, 15–16.
7. Gilbert C. Kniffin, "Maneuvering Bragg Out of Tennessee," *Battles and Leaders of the Civil War*, Volume 3, Robert Underwood Johnson and Clarence Clough Buel, eds. (New York: Thomas Yoseloff, 1956), 636; Woodworth, *Six Armies*, 16; *Official Records*, Volume 23, Part 1, 404.
8. Woodworth, *Six Armies*, 16–17; Kniffin, "Maneuvering," 636; *Official Records*, Volume 23, Part 1, 405.
9. Woodworth, *Six Armies*, 17.
10. Sullivan, 5
11. Woodworth, *Six Armies*, 20.
12. *Official Records*, Volume 23, Part 2, 119, 171.
13. *Ibid.*, 111.
14. Cozzens, *Terrible Sound*, 16.
15. *Official Records*, Volume 23, Part 2, 369.
16. *Ibid.*, Part 3, 376; Cozzens, *Terrible Sound*, 16.
17. *Official Records*, Volume 23, Part 1, 10.
18. Woodworth, *Six Armies*, 12–13.
19. *Official Records*, Volume 23, Part 1, 9–10.

Chapter 13

1. Woodworth, *Six Armies*, 19; *Official Records*, Volume 23, Part 1, 405.
2. *Official Records*, Volume 23, Part 1, 405; Cozzens, *Terrible*, 17.
3. Woodworth, *Six Armies*, 20–21; *Official Records*, Volume 23, Part 1, 405.
4. Mark K. Christ, ed., *Getting Used to Being Shot At: The Spence Family Civil War Letters* (Fayetteville, AR: University of Arkansas Press, 2002), 57.
5. Kniffin, "Maneuvering," 636; Cozzens, *Terrible*, 18.
6. Woodworth, *Six Armies*, 23.

7. Cozzens, *Terrible*, 18; *Official Records*, Volume 23, Part 1, 430; Kniffin, "Maneuvering," 636.
8. Woodworth, *Six Armies*, 24–25; *Official Records*, Volume 23, Part 1, 465–66.
9. Kniffin, "Maneuvering," 636–37.
10. *Official Records*, Volume 23, Part 1, 406; Aldrich, 50.
11. Woodworth, *Six Armies*, 28–29; Tower, 77.
12. Cozzens, *Terrible*, 18–19.
13. Woodworth, *Six Armies*, 30–31.
14. *Official Records*, Volume 23, Part 1, 618.
15. Woodworth, *Six Armies*, 32–33.
16. *Official Records*, Volume 23, Part 2, 884; Woodworth, *Six Armies*, 34–35.
17. *Official Records*, Volume 23, Part 1, 406–07.
18. *Ibid.*, 621–22.
19. Kniffin, "Maneuvering," 637; Woodworth, *Six Armies*, 40.
20. Woodworth, *Six Armies*, 40–41; Rosecrans, 130; *Official Records*, Volume 23, Part 1, 623–24.
21. Tower, 76; Aldrich, 51–52.
22. *Official Records*, Volume 23, Part 1, 408.
23. *Ibid.*; Tower, 77.
24. *Official Records*, Volume 23, Part 1, 425.
25. Cozzens, *Terrible*, 23; Basler, Volume 6, 373.
26. Rosecrans, 131.
27. *Official Records*, Volume 30, Part 1, 49–50; Woodworth, *Six Armies*, 52.
28. Woodworth, *Six Armies*, 52–53.
29. *Ibid.*, 53.
30. *Official Records*, Volume 23, Part 2, 948, 952–53.
31. Cozzens, *Terrible*, 21; Henry Cist, *The Army of the Cumberland* (New York: Charles Scribner's Sons, 1882), 170.
32. Sullivan, 8; Rosecrans, 131.
33. Woodworth, *Six Armies*, 60.
34. *Ibid.*; Rosecrans, 131; *Official Records*, Volume 30, Part 1, 53–53.
35. Sullivan, 8–9; *Official Records*, Volume 30, Part 1, 51; Woodworth, *Six Armies*, 56–57.
36. *Official Records*, Volume 30, Part 1, 51–52; Sullivan, 9.
37. Cozzens, *Terrible*, 30.
38. Rosecrans, 132; *Official Records*, Volume 30, Part 2, 27.
39. *Official Records*, Volume 30, Part 2, 27; Cozzens, *Terrible*, 56.
40. Rosecrans, 132; Woodworth, *Six Armies*, 62.
41. Rosecrans, 132; *Official Records*, Volume 30, Part 1, 53.

Chapter 14

1. *Official Records*, Volume 30, Part 1, 53; Woodworth, *Six Armies*, 62.
2. *Official Records*, Volume 30, Part 1, 53, 246–47, 486, 488, 493; Woodworth, *Six Armies*, 62–63; Sullivan, 9.
3. *Official Records*, Volume 30, Part 1, 479, 488; Cozzens, 63.
4. Sullivan, 10, 12; Woodworth, *Six Armies*, 67.
5. *Official Records*, Volume 30, Part 1, 247, Part 2, 27; Catton, *Never Retreat*, 243.
6. *Official Records*, Volume 30, Part 2, 27–28.
7. *Ibid.*, 28–29; Sullivan, 13.
8. Woodworth, *Six Armies*, 69; *Official Records*, Volume 30, Part 2, 29.
9. *Official Records*, Volume 30, Part 2, 301.
10. *Ibid.*, 301–02.
11. *Ibid.*, 29; Woodworth, *Six Armies*, 71.
12. *Official Records*, Volume 30, Part 2, 29.
13. *Ibid.*.
14. *Ibid.*, Part 4, 634.
15. *Ibid.*, 636.
16. *Ibid.*, Part 1, 54, Part 2, 30.
17. W. L. Martin, "Letter to the Southern Historical Society, February 3, 1883," *Southern Historical Society Papers*, 1883: 205–06. Tower, 93–94.
18. Woodworth, *Six Armies*, 73–74; *Official Records*, Volume 30, Part 1, 53, Part 3, 564–65.
19. *Official Records*, Volume 30, Part 1, 53–54; Rosecrans, 132.
20. *Official Records*, Volume 30, Part 1, 603–04; Cozzens, 81.
21. *Official Records*, Volume 30, Part 2, 30; Woodworth, *Six Armies*, 75.
22. *Official Records*, Volume 30, Part 2, 30.
23. *Ibid.*, 44.
24. *Ibid.*, 30–31.
25. Cozzens, *Terrible*, 86–87; *Official Records*, Volume 30, Part 4, 643.
26. Sullivan, 12–13; Catton, *Never Retreat*, 241.
27. Sullivan, 12.
28. Sullivan, 12; Catton, *Never Retreat*, 241.
29. D. H. Hill, "Chickamauga—The Great Battle of the West," *The Century*, April 1887: 946.
30. *Official Records*, Volume 30, Part 1, 54; Rosecrans, 132.
31. *Official Records*, Volume 30, Part 1, 54–55; Woodworth, *Six Armies*, 77.
32. *Official Records*, Volume 30, Part 4, 657; Cozzens, *Terrible*, 90.
33. Cozzens, *Terrible*, 90; Woodworth, *Six Armies*, 80.
34. Woodworth, *Six Armies*, 80–81; Hill, 946.
35. Woodworth, *Six Armies*, 81.
36. *Official Records*, Volume 30, Part 2, 451.
37. *Ibid.*, 451–52; Woodworth, *Six Armies*, 82.
38. *Official Records*, Volume 30, Part 1, 992, Part 2, 451–52; Sullivan, 15.
39. Sullivan, 15; *Official Records*, Volume 30, Part 1, 922–23, Part 2, 451–52.
40. *Official Records*, Volume 30, Part 1, 447, Part 2, 32, 239; Sullivan, 15; Woodworth, *Six Armies*, 83.
41. Cozzens, *Terrible*, 113–14; *Official Records*, Volume 30, Part 1, 55; Woodworth, *Six Armies*, 84.
42. *Official Records*, Volume 30, Part 1, 55–56, 248.
43. *Ibid.*, 55–56; Sullivan, 15.
44. Sullivan, 17–18.
45. *Ibid.*, 15.
46. Woodworth, *Six Armies*, 84; Cozzens, *Terrible*, 128.

Chapter 15

1. Catton, *Never Retreat*, 245.
2. *Official Records*, Volume 30, Part 1, 56, 249.
3. Woodworth, *Six Armies*, 86; *Official Records*, Volume 30, Part 1, 249, 400.
4. *Official Records*, Volume 30, Part 2, 32; Catton, *Never Retreat*, 246.

5. *Official Records*, Volume 30, Part 1, 249; Charles A. Partridge, *The Battle of Chickamauga: And the Part Played in it By A Portion of the Reserve Corps*. Paper read before George H. Thomas post of the Grand Army of the Republic, April 29, 1881.
6. *Official Records*, Volume 30, Part 1, 250, Part 2, 32.
7. Cozzens, *Terrible*, 141; Hill, "Chickamauga," 948.
8. Hill, "Chickamauga," 948; *Official Records*, Volume 30, Part 2, 78.
9. *Official Records*, Volume 30, Part 1, 250, Part 2, 131; Hill, "Chickamauga," 948.
10. *Official Records*, Volume 30, Part 2, 78.
11. Hill, "Chickamauga," 948.
12. *Official Records*, Volume 30, Part 1, 714, 730; Hill, "Chickamauga," 948.
13. *Official Records*, Volume 30, Part 2, 362, 370.
14. *Ibid.*.
15. *Ibid.*, 362.
16. *Ibid.*, Part 1, 56, 329, Part 2, 362.
17. Hill, "Chickamauga," 948; Cozzens, *Terrible*, 223–24.
18. *Official Records*, Volume 30, Part 1, 633, 654.
19. Hill, "Chickamauga," 948.
20. *Official Records*, Volume 30, Part 2, 79, Part 1, 250; Hill, "Chickamauga," 949.
2 . *Official Records*, Volume 30, Part 2, 154, Part 1, 539; Hill, "Chickamauga," 949.
22. *Official Records*, Volume 30, Part 2, 79, Part 1, 329.
23. Sullivan, 19; Thomas J. Doughman, "Civil War Recollections of Thomas J. Doughman," Center for Archival Collections, Bowling Green State University, Bowling Green, Ohio; *Official Records*, Volume 30, Part 1, 251.
24. Catton, *Never Retreat*, 247–48.
25. Sullivan, 19; *Official Records*, Volume 30, Part 2, 33; McPherson, 672.
26. *Official Records*, Volume 30, Part 1, 136.

Chapter 16

1. *Official Records*, Volume 30, Part 2, 33, 53.
2. *Ibid.*, 33; Tower, 123–24.
3. *Official Records*, Volume 30, Part 2, 33.
4. Hill, 951–52.
5. *Official Records*, Volume 30, Part 1, 58.
6. Tower, 97.
7. Sullivan, 19–20; Hill, 952; *Official Records*, Volume 30, Part 1, 278, 368.
8. *Official Records*, Volume 30, Part 2, 154–55.
9. Hill, 952; Catton, *Never Retreat*, 248.
10. *Official Records*, Volume 30, Part 1, 535, 252.
11. *Ibid.*, 635; Hill, 955–56; Gates P. Thruston, "The Crisis at Chickamauga," *Battles and Leaders of the Civil War*, Volume 3, Robert Underwood Johnson and Clarence Clough Buel, eds. (New York: Thomas Yoseloff, 1956), 663.
12. *Official Records*, Volume 30, Part 1, 635.
13. Sullivan, 21; *Official Records*, Volume 30, Part 1, 402, 656, 500.
14. Sullivan, 21; Thruston, 663–64; *Official Records*, Volume 30, Part 1, 580.
15. *Official Records*, Volume 30, Part 1, 59, 581; Rosecrans, "Chattanooga," 134; Catton, *Never Retreat*, 249.
16. *Official Records*, Volume 30, Part 1, 252–53; Sullivan, 22.
17. Thruston, 664; *Official Records*, Volume 30, Part 1, 60.
18. Sullivan, 22; Hill, 961.
19. *Official Records*, Volume 30, Part 1, 854; J.S. Fullerton, "The Reserve Corps at Chickamauga," *The Century*, April 1887: 962–63.
20. *Official Records*, Volume 30, Part 1, 854, 60.
21. *Ibid.*, 855.
22. Partridge, 10–11.
23. Fullerton, "Reserve Corps," 963–64; Sullivan, 23; *Official Records*, Volume 30, Part 1, 855, 860; Partridge, 11.
24. Sullivan, 23; *Official Records*, Volume 30, Part 1, 381.
25. *Official Records*, Volume 30, Part 1, 856, 860; Sullivan, 23.
26. *Official Records*, Volume 30, Part 1, 253.
27. *Ibid.*, 141.
28. Hill, 961; Sullivan, 23; *Official Records*, Volume 30, Part 1, 279.
29. *Official Records*, Volume 30, Part 1, 253–54; Sullivan, 24.
30. *Official Records*, Volume 30, Part 1, 142, 192.
31. *Ibid.*, 142–43.
32. *Ibid.*, 145.
33. *Ibid.*, 77; Sullivan, 24.
34. Tower, 124; Hill, 962.
35. *Official Records*, Volume 30, Part 2, 35.
36. *Ibid.*, Part 1, 146.
37. *Ibid.*, 148.
38. *Ibid.*, 149–50.
39. *Ibid.*, Part 2, 22.

Chapter 17

1. *Official Records*, Volume 30, Part 1, 168.
2. *Ibid.*, Part 3, 592, 594, 620.
3. *Ibid.*, 638, 655.
4. Grant, *Memoirs*, Volume 1, 581–82; Catton, *Grant Takes*, 29–30.
5. Grant, *Memoirs*, Volume 1, 582–83; Sherman, *Memoirs*, Volume 1, 375.
6. Sherman, *Memoirs*, Volume 1, 378.
7. James Longstreet, *From Manassas to Appomattox* (Old Saybrook, CT: Konecky & Konecky, n.d.), 466.
8. *Official Records*, Volume 30, Part 2, 36–37.
9. Catton, *Never Retreat*, 252; McPherson, 676; *Official Records*, Volume 30, Part 4, 706.
10. Woodworth, *Six Armies*, 144.
11. McPherson, 677; Catton, *Never Retreat*, 253; Woodworth, *Jefferson Davis*, 241–42.
12. McPherson, 677; Catton, *Never Retreat*, 253–54; Woodworth, *Jefferson Davis*, 241–42.
13. McPherson, 677; Catton, *Never Retreat*, 253–54; Woodworth, *Jefferson Davis*, 241–42.
14. *Official Records*, Volume 30, Part 1, 197–98.
15. Catton, *Never Retreat*, 255; *Official Records*, Volume 29, Part 1, 156.
16. Catton, *Never Retreat*, 255,56; Sullivan, 27.
17. *Official Records*, Volume 30, Part 1, 220–21.
18. Grant, *Memoirs*, Volume 2, 32–33.
19. *Ibid.*, 33–34.
20. James M. McCaffrey, *This Band of Heroes: Granbury's Texas Brigade, C. S. A.* (College Station, TX:

Texas A & M University Press, 1996), 84; Catton, *Never Retreat*, 256; W. F. G. Shanks, "Chattanooga, and How We Held It," *Harper's New Monthly Magazine*, January 1868: 145.
 21. McCaffrey, 84; Catton, *Never Retreat*, 256; *Official Records*, Volume 31, Part 2, 79.
 22. Briant, 253–54; L. G. Bennett and William M. Haigh, *History of the Thirty-sixth Regiment Illinois Volunteers, During the War of the Rebellion* (Aurora, IL: Knickerbocker & Hodder, Printers and Binders, 1876), 509; William R. Hartpence, *History of the Fifty-first Indiana Veteran Volunteer Infantry* (Cincinnati, Ohio: Robert Clarke Company, Printers and Binders, 1894), 189.
 23. Charles A. Dana, *Recollections of the Civil War* (New York: D. Appleton, 1902), 127–28.
 24. J. S. Fullerton, "The Army of the Cumberland at Chattanooga," *The Century*, May 1887: 137.
 25. Woodworth, *Six Armies*, 144.
 26. *Ibid.*, 147.
 27. *Ibid.*, 148; *Official Records*, Volume 30, Part 1, 218.
 28. Woodworth, *Six Armies*, 148–49.
 29. Grant, *Memoirs*, Volume 1, 583.
 30. *Official Records*, Volume 30, Part 4, 404; Grant, *Memoirs*, Volume 2, 17.
 31. Grant, *Memoirs*, Volume 2, 17–19; Van Horne, 394.
 32. Grant, *Memoirs*, Volume 2, 24–27; *Official Records*, Volume 30, Part 4, 455.
 33. *Official Records*, Volume 30, Part 4, 479.
 34. Grant, *Memoirs*, Volume 2, 26–27.
 35. Catton, *Grant Takes*, 35–36; Oliver O. Howard, "Chattanooga," *The Atlantic Monthly*, August 1876: 206.
 36. Howard, "Chattanooga," 206.
 37. Catton, *Grant Takes*, 36–37. Grant, *Memoirs*, Volume 2, 28.
 38. Grant, *Memoirs*, Volume 2, 28.
 39. Catton, *Grant Takes*, 40–41; Horace Porter, *Campaigning with Grant* (New York: Mallard Press, 1991), 4–5.

Chapter 18

 1. *Official Records*, Volume 31, Part 1, 70, 739; Grant, *Memoirs*, Volume 2, 28.
 2. Grant, *Memoirs*, Volume 2, 31.
 3. Woodworth, *Six Armies*, 154; Catton, *Grant Takes*, 44.
 4. *Official Records*, Volume 31, Part 1, 77; Woodworth, *Six Armies*, 154.
 5. *Official Records*, Volume 31, Part 1, 77; Catton, *Grant Takes*, 45.
 6. *Official Records*, Volume 31, Part 1, 77–78; Matt Spruill, *Storming the Heights: A Guide to the Battle of Chattanooga* (Knoxville, TN: University of Tennessee Press, 2003), 26–27; Woodworth, *Six Armies*, 154–55.
 7. *Official Records*, Volume 31, Part 1, 48–49, 53–54; Woodworth, *Six Armies*, 154–55.
 8. Grant, *Memoirs*, Volume 2, 28–29; Woodworth, *Six Armies*, 155.
 9. *Official Records*, Volume 31, Part 1, 712.
 10. *Official Records*, Volume 30, Part 3, 904–05, Volume 31, Part 1, 745.
 11. *Official Records*, Volume 31, Part 1, 713; Catton, *Grant Takes*, 48.

 12. *Official Records*, Volume 31, Part 1, 713.
 13. *Ibid.*, 739–40.
 14. *Ibid.*, 77–78.
 15. Catton, *Grant Takes*, 60; Fullerton, "Army Cumberland," 139.
 16. William B. Hazen, *A Narrative of Military Service* (Boston: Ticknor, 1885), 157; Kimberly, 60–62.
 17. Fullerton, "Army Cumberland," 139; *Official Records*, Volume 31, Part 1, 77.
 18. Catton, *Grant Takes*, 52; Kimberly, 61.
 19. Hazen, 157; Kimberly, 61–62.
 20. Kimberly, 62; Fullerton, "Army Cumberland," 139; *Official Records*, Volume 31, Part 1, 49, 78.
 21. Kimberly, 62; Fullerton, "Army Cumberland, 139; *Official Records*, Volume 31, Part 1, 54.
 22. Fullerton, "Army Cumberland," 130–40; John Bowers, *Chickamauga and Chattanooga: The Battles That Doomed the Confederacy* (New York: HarperCollins, 1994), 192–93; *Official Records*, Volume 31, Part 1, 54.
 23. Woodworth, *Six Armies*, 155–56; Bowers, 192–93.
 24. *Official Records*, Volume 31, Part 1, 217; Grant, *Memoirs*, Volume 2, 40–41; Fullerton, "Army Cumberland," 140; Longstreet, *Manassas*, 475–76.
 25. *Official Records*, Volume 31, Part 1, 114; Fullerton, "Army Cumberland," 140.
 26. Howard, "Chattanooga," 208; Woodworth, *Six Armies*, 166–67.
 27. Woodworth, *Six Armies*, 166–67; Howard, "Chattanooga," 208–09.
 28. *Official Records*, Volume 31, Part 1, 115; Woodworth, *Six Armies*, 166–67; James Longstreet, "Report of General Longstreet," *Southern Historical Society Papers*, July 1880: 268.
 29. Longstreet, "Report," 268.
 30. *Official Records*, Volume 31, Part 1, 56.
 31. Kimberly, 63.
 32. Grant, *Memoirs*, Volume 2, 38–39.
 33. Judith Lee Hallock, ed., *The Civil War Letters of Joshua K. Callaway* (Athens, GA: University of Georgia Press, 1997), 157, 166.
 34. Porter, 10–11.

Chapter 19

 1. *Official Records*, Volume 30, Part 2, 29.
 2. *Ibid.*, Volume 31, Part 3, 10.
 3. *Ibid.*, Part 1, 729, Part 3, 23.
 4. Grant, *Memoirs*, Volume 2, 46.
 5. *Ibid.*; Catton, *Grant Takes*, 57.
 6. *Official Records*, Volume 31, Part 3, 26.
 7. Grant, *Memoirs*, Volume 2, 47–48; Catton, *Grant Takes*, 57–58.
 8. Grant, *Memoirs*, Volume 2, 44.
 9. Woodworth, *Six Armies*, 173–74.
 10. Bowers, 196.
 11. *Official Records*, Volume 31, Part 3, 634; Longstreet, *Manassas*, 482; Grant, *Memoirs*, Volume 2, 49.
 12. Grant, *Memoirs*, Volume 2, 49.
 13. *Official Records*, Volume 31, Part 3, 73.
 14. *Ibid.*, 73–73, 76.
 15. Grant, *Memoirs*, Volume 2, 50; *Official Records*, Volume 31, Part 3, 84, 88.
 16. *Official Records*, Volume 31, Part 3, 216.

17. Woodworth, *Six Armies*, 173; Sherman, *Memoirs*, Volume 1, 388–89.
18. Sherman, *Memoirs*, Volume 1, 389; Howard, "Chattanooga," 210–11.
19. Sherman, *Memoirs*, Volume 1, 389; Van Horne, 410.
20. Grant, *Memoirs*, Volume 2, 54–56.
21. Ibid., 57–58.
22. Francis F. McKinney, *Education in Violence: The Life of George H. Thomas and the History of the Army of the Cumberland* (Detroit: Wayne State University Press, 1961), 281–82.
23. *Official Records*, Volume 31, Part 3, 145–46, 177; Grant, *Memoirs*, Volume 2, 51.
24. Grant, *Memoirs*, Volume 2, 52; Longstreet, *Manassas*, 483.
25. Catton, *Grant Takes*, 69.
26. Sherman, *Memoirs*, Volume 1, 391; Grant, *Memoirs*, Volume 2, 59.
27. Howard, "Chattanooga," 211; Catton, *Grant Takes*, 69.
28. Grant, *Memoirs*, Volume 2, 64–66; Catton, *Grant Takes*, 69–70; Van Horne, 412.
29. Grant, *Memoirs*, Volume 2, 61; Dana, *Recollections*, 142; Van Horne, 413.
30. Grant, *Memoirs*, Volume 2, 62; *Official Records*, Volume 31, Part 2, 32.
31. Woodworth, *Six Armies*, 180; Fullerton, "Army Cumberland," 141.
32. Howard, "Chattanooga," 211; Fullerton, "Army Cumberland," 141; McKinney, 286.
33. Van Horne, 414–15; McKinney, 288.
34. Montgomery C. Meigs, *The Three Days' Battle of Chattanooga, 23d, 24th, 25th November, 1864 [1863]: An Unofficial Dispatch From General Meigs* (Washington, DC: McGill & Witherow, Printers and Stereotypers, 1864), 3–4.
35. Spruill, 99; Fullerton, "Army Cumberland," 142.
36. Fullerton, "Army Cumberland," 142; McKinney, 289.
37. Fullerton, "Army Cumberland," 142.

Chapter 20

1. Catton, *Grant Takes*, 73.
2. *Official Records*, Volume 31, Part 2, 32; Woodworth, *Six Armies*, 185.
3. Van Horne, 418; *Official Records*, Volume 31, Part 2, 315.
4. Woodworth, *Grand Spectacle*, 57; *Official Records*, Volume 31, Part 2, 315.
5. Woodworth, *Grand Spectacle*, 57, 60; *Official Records*, Volume 31, Part 2, 315.
6. *Official Records*, Volume 31, Part 2, 315–16, 391.
7. Ibid., 143.
8. Howard, "Chattanooga," 213; Grant, *Memoirs*, Volume 2, 71–72.
9. Isaac C. Doan, *Reminiscences of the Chattanooga Campaign: A Paper Read at the Reunion of Company B, Fortieth Ohio Volunteer Infantry, at Xenia, O., August 22, 1894* (Richmond, IN: J. M. Coe's Printery, 1894), 13.
10. Fullerton, "Army Cumberland," 142–43; *Official Records*, Volume 31, Part 2, 144, 392.
11. Woodworth, *Grand Spectacle*, 61; *Official Records*, Volume 31, Part 2, 392–93; Grant, *Memoirs*, Volume 2, 71–72.
12. *Official Records*, Volume 31, Part 2, 393–94; Woodworth, *Grand Spectacle*, 62.
13. *Official Records*, Volume 31, Part 2, 394–95; Catton, *Grant Takes*, 73.
14. Fullerton, "Army Cumberland," 143; Howard, "Chattanooga," 214.
15. Paul M. Angle, ed., *Three Years in the Army of the Cumberland: The Letters and Diary of Major James A. Connolly* (Bloomington, IN: Indiana University Press, 1959), 153; Catton, *Grant Takes*, 74.
16. Woodworth, *Six Armies*, 187; Angle, 153.
17. *Official Records*, Volume 31, Part 2, 396; Woodworth, *Grand Spectacle*, 64.
18. *Official Records*, Volume 31, Part 2, 317, 398–99; Fullerton, "Army Cumberland," 143.
19. *Official Records*, Volume 31, Part 2, 664; Woodworth, *Six Armies*, 188.
20. Fullerton, "Army Cumberland," 143–44; *Official Records*, Volume 31, Part 2, 572.
21. Grant, *Memoirs*, Volume 2, 67; *Official Records*, Volume 31, Part 2, 573.
22. *Official Records*, Volume 31, Part 2, 573–74; Van Horne, 422.
23. Grant, *Memoirs*, Volume 2, 68–69; *Official Records*, Volume 31, Part 2, 573; S. H. M. Byers, "Sherman's Attack at the Tunnel," *Battles and Leaders of the Civil War*, Volume 3, Robert Underwood Johnson and Clarence Clough Buel, eds. (New York: Thomas Yoseloff, 1956), 712.
24. *Official Records*, Volume 31, Part 2, 573; Van Horne, 422–23.
25. *Official Records*, Volume 31, Part 2, 43.
26. Van Horne, 423; Fullerton, "Army Cumberland," 144; *Official Records*, Volume 31, Part 2, 573, 746.
27. Van Horne, 423; *Official Records*, Volume 31, Part 2, 574; Catton, *Grant Takes*, 77.
28. Woodworth, *Six Armies*, 190; Thomas Lawrence Connelly, *Autumn of Glory: The Army of Tennessee, 1862–1865* (Baton Rouge: Louisiana State University Press, 1971), 273.
29. *Official Records*, Volume 31, Part 2, 24–25.
30. Grant, *Memoirs*, Volume 2, 75; *Official Records*, Volume 31, Part 2, 43–44.

Chapter 21

1. Fullerton, "Army Cumberland': 143; Doan, 15.
2. Fullerton, "Army Cumberland," 144; *Official Records*, Volume 31, Part 2, 746.
3. Catton, *Grant Takes*, 77; *Official Records*, Volume 31, Part 2, 574.
4. Grant, *Memoirs*, Volume 2, 76; *Official Records*, Volume 31, Part 2, 574–75.
5. Byers, 713.
6. *Official Records*, Volume 31, Part 2, 636.
7. Ibid., 575, 749–50; Fullerton, "Army Cumberland," 144–45.
8. *Official Records*, Volume 31, Part 2, 575, 750; Woodworth, *Grand Spectacle*, 71.
9. Woodworth, *Grand Spectacle*, 71–72; Grant, *Memoirs*, Volume 2, 77.
10. *Official Records*, Volume 31, Part 2, 634, 750; Grant, *Memoirs*, Volume 2, 77.
11. *Official Records*, Volume 31, Part 2, 751; Woodworth, *Six Armies*, 192.

12. *Official Records*, Volume 31, Part 2, 575, 636–37.
13. Fullerton, "Army Cumberland," 145; Grant, *Memoirs*, Volume 2, 77; Catton, *Grant Takes*, 78.
14. *Official Records*, Volume 31, Part 2, 318; Grant, *Memoirs*, Volume 2, 78.
15. *Official Records*, Volume 31, Part 2, 318.
16. *Ibid.*, 319.
17. Grant, *Memoirs*, Volume 2, 77–78.
18. Fullerton, "Army Cumberland," 146; Van Horne, 429; Woodworth, *Six Armies*, 196–97.
19. Bowers, 221; *Official Records*, Volume 31, Part 2, 34.

Chapter 22

1. Grant, *Memoirs*, Volume 2, 79; *Official Records*, Volume 31, Part 2, 68.
2. Fullerton, "Army Cumberland," 146; Van Horne, 429.
3. Van Horne, 430; Angle, 157; Kimberly, 69.
4. Bowers, 221; Woodworth, *Six Armies*, 196–97.
5. Woodworth, *Six Armies*, 196–97; Bowers, 225–26.
6. Alfred G. Hunter, *History of the Eighty-second Indiana Volunteer Infantry, Its Organization, Campaigns and Battles* (Indianapolis: William B. Buford, Printer and Binder, 1893), 106.
7. Henry J. Aten, *History of the Eighty-fifth Regiment Illinois Volunteer Infantry* (Hiawatha, KS: Regimental Association, 1901), 135; *Official Records*, Volume 31, Part 2, 34; Woodworth, *Six Armies*, 197. Worsham, 100.
8. Kimberly, 69; William Wirt Calkins, *The History of the One Hundred and Fourth Regiment of Illinois Volunteer Infantry* (Chicago: Donohue & Henneberry, Printers, Engravers and Binders, 1895), 178; *Official Records*, Volume 31, Part 2, 190.
9. *Official Records*, Volume 31, Part 2, 34; L. G. Bennett, *Thirty-sixth*, 526.
10. *Official Records*, Volume 31, Part 2, 508, 459, 190–91.
11. *Ibid.*, 258, 264, 281.
12. *Ibid.*, 282, 69; Kimberly, 70.
13. *Official Records*, Volume 31, Part 2, 69; Fullerton, "Army Cumberland," 147.
14. Catton, *Grant Takes*, 83; W. H. Newlin, et. al., *A History of the Seventy-third Regiment of Illinois Infantry Volunteers* (Regimental Reunion Association, 1890), 266.
15. Bowers, 226; *Official Records*, Volume 31, Part 2, 264; Charles I. Switzer, ed., Ohio Volunteer: *The Childhood & Civil War Memoirs of Captain John Calvin Hartzell, OVI* (Athens, OH: Ohio University Press, 2005), 150; Ephraim A. Wilson, *Memoirs of the War* (Cleveland: W. M. Bayne Printing Co., 1893), 262.
16. Angle, 150; Worsham, 100.
17. Fullerton, "Army Cumberland," 148–49.
18. Woodworth, *Six Armies*, 200; Switzer, 149–50.
19. Switzer, 149–50.
20. Woodworth, *Six Armies*, 200–01.
21. Bowers, 231–32; Van Horne, 432.
22. Nixon B. Stewart, *Dan McCook's Regiment, 52nd O. V. I.* (Alliance, OH: Published by author, 1900) 75–76; Angle, 158; Switzer, 150.
23. Bowers, 232; Woodworth, *Six Armies*, 202.
24. *Official Records*, Volume 31, Part 2, 752; Catton, *Grant Takes*, 84.
25. *Official Records*, Volume 31, Part 2, 69.
26. *Official Records*, Volume 31, Part 2, 35, 191; Fullerton, "Army Cumberland," 149.
27. Catton, *Grant Takes*, 89–90; *Official Records*, Volume 31, Part 2, 192; Fullerton, "Army Cumberland," 149.
28. *Official Records*, Volume 31, Part 2, 36; William F. Fox, *Regimental Losses in the American Civil War, 1861–1865* (Albany, NY: Albany Publishing, 1889), 551.

Chapter 23

1. Woodworth, *Six Armies*, 203.
2. Grant, *Memoirs*, Volume 2, 84; Sherman, *Memoirs*, Volume 2, 393.
3. Woodworth, *Six Armies*, 204.
4. Grant, *Memoirs*, Volume 2, 91; Woodworth, *Six Armies*, 205.
5. *Official Records*, Volume 31, Part 2, 35.
6. Grant, *Memoirs*, Volume 2, 90–91.
7. Grant, *Memoirs*, Volume 2, 92; Sherman, *Memoirs*, Volume 2, 394.
8. Sherman, *Memoirs*, Volume 2, 394–95.
9. Orlando M. Poe, "The Defense of Knoxville," *Battles and Leaders of the Civil War*, Volume 3, Robert Underwood Johnson and Clarence Clough Buel, eds. (New York: Thomas Yoseloff, 1956), 90–91; Sherman, *Memoirs*, Volume 2, 395.
10. Grant, *Memoirs*, Volume 2, 98.
11. *Official Records*, Volume 31, Part 2, 665–66.
12. *Ibid.*, Volume 52, Part 2, 745.
13. *Ibid.*, Part 1, 618; Catton, *Grant Takes*, 97–98.
14. *Official Records*, Volume 31, Part 3, 430.
15. Catton, *Grant Takes*, 99–100.

BIBLIOGRAPHY

Books

Abernethy, Byron R., ed. *Private Elisha Stockwell, Jr. Sees the Civil War*. Norman: University of Oklahoma Press, 1958.

Aldrich, C. Knight. *Quest for a Star: The Civil War Letters and Diaries of Colonel Francis T. Sherman of the 88th Illinois*. Knoxville: University of Tennessee Press, 1999.

Ambrose, Stephen E. *Halleck: Lincoln's Chief of Staff*. Baton Rouge, Louisiana: Louisiana State University Press, 1962.

_____, ed. *A Wisconsin Boy in Dixie: The Selected Letters of James K. Newton*. Madison: University of Wisconsin Press, 1961.

Anderson, Mary Ann, ed., *The Civil War Diary of Allen Morgan Geer: Twentieth Regiment, Illinois Volunteers*. Denver: Robert C. Appleman, 1977.

Anderson, Nancy Scott and Dwight Anderson. *The Generals—Ulysses S. Grant and Robert E. Lee*. New York: Wings Books, 1994.

Angle, Paul M., ed. *Three Years in the Army of the Cumberland: The Letters and Diary of Major James A. Connolly*. Bloomington: Indiana University Press, 1959.

Aten, Henry J. *History of the Eighty-fifth Regiment Illinois Volunteer Infantry*. Hiawatha, KS: Regimental Association, 1901.

Athearn, Robert G., ed. *Soldier in the West: The Civil War Letters of Alfred Lacey Hough*. Philadelphia: University of Pennsylvania Press, 1957.

Badeau, Adam. *Military History of Ulysses S. Grant: From April, 1861, to April, 1865*, 3 Volumes. New York: D. Appleton and Company, 1885.

Bailey, Anne J. *The Chessboard of War: Sherman and Hood in the Autumn Campaigns of 1864*. Lincoln: University of Nebraska Press, 2000.

Barber, Lucius W. *Army Memoirs of Lucius W. Barber, Company "D," 15th Illinois Volunteer Infantry*. Chicago: J. M. Jones Stationery and Printing Co., 1894.

Barnes, James A., James R. Carnahan, and Thomas H. B. McCain. *The Eighty-sixth Regiment, Indiana Volunteer Infantry*. Crawfordsville, IN: Journal Company, Printers, 1895.

Basler, Roy P., ed. *The Collected Works of Abraham Lincoln*, 8 Vols. New Brunswick, NJ: Rutgers University Press, 1953.

Beach, John N. *History of the Fortieth Ohio Volunteer Infantry*. London, OH: Shepherd & Craig, Printers, 1884.

Beers, Fannie A. *Memories: A Record of Personal Experience and Adventure During Four Years of War*. New York:- Time-Life Books, 1985.

Bennett, L. G., and William M. Haigh. *History of the Thirty-sixth Regiment Illinois Volunteers, During the War of the Rebellion*. Aurora, IL: Knickerbocker & Hodder, Printers and Binders, 1876.

Bennett, Stewart, and Barbara Tillery, eds. *The Struggle for the Life of the Republic: A Civil War Narrative by Brevet Major Charles Dana Miller, 76th Ohio Volunteer Infantry*. Kent, OH: Kent State University Press, 2004.

Bering, John A., and Thomas Montgomery. *History of the Forty-eighth Ohio Vet. Vol. Inf.* Hillsboro, OH: Highland News Office, 1880.

Bickham, William D. *Roscrans' Campaign with the Fourteenth Army Corps, or The Army of the Cumberland: A Narrative of Personal Observations*. Cincinnati: Moore, Wilstach, Keys & Co., 1863.

Bircher, William. *A Drummer-boy's Diary: Comprising Four Years of Service with the Second Regiment Minnesota Veteran Volunteers*. St. Paul, MN: St. Paul Book and Stationery Co., 1889.

Bishop, Judson W. *The Story of a Regiment: Being a Narrative of the Service of the Second Regiment, Minnesota

Veteran Volunteer Infantry, in the Civil War of 1861–1865. St. Paul, MN: Regimental Association, 1890.
Blanchard, Ira. *I Marched with Sherman: Civil War Memoirs of the 20th Illinois Volunteer Infantry.* San Francisco: J. D. Huff, 1992.
Bowers, John. *Chickamauga and Chattanooga: The Battles That Doomed the Confederacy.* New York: HarperCollins, 1994.
Boyd, James P. *The Life of General William T. Sherman.* Philadelphia: Publishers Union, 1891.
Brewer, James D. *The Raiders of 1862.* Westport, CT: Praeger, 1997.
Briant, Charles C. *History of the Sixth Regiment Indiana Volunteer Infantry of Both the Three Months' and Three Years' Services.* Indianapolis: Wm. E. Burford, Printer and Binder, 1891.
Brinton, John H. *Personal Memoirs of John H. Brinton: Civil War Surgeon, 1861–1865.* Carbondale: Southern Illinois University Press, 1996.
Brown, Campbell H., ed. *The Reminiscences of Sergeant Newton Cannon.* Franklin, TN: Carter House Association, 1963.
Brown, Norman D., ed. *One of Cleburne's Command: The Civil War Reminiscences and Diary of Capt. Samuel T. Foster, Granbury's Texas Brigade, CSA.* Austin: University of Texas Press, 1980.
Calkins, William Wirt. *The History of the One Hundred and Fourth Regiment of Illinois Volunteer Infantry.* Chicago: Donohue & Henneberry, Printers, Engravers and Binders, 1895.
Canfield, Silas S. *History of the 21st Regiment Ohio Volunteer Infantry, in the War of the Rebellion.* Toledo, OH: Vrooman, Anderson & Bateman, Printers, 1893.
Carpenter, John A. *Sword and Olive Branch: Oliver Otis Howard.* New York: Fordham University Press, 1999.
_____. *Ulysses S. Grant.* NY: Twayne Publishers, 1970.
Carroll, John W. *Autobiography and Reminiscences.* Henderson, TN: (n. p.), 1898.
Catton, Bruce. *Grant Moves South.* Boston: Little, Brown, 1960.
_____. *Grant Takes Command.* Boston: Little, Brown, 1969.
_____. *Never Call Retreat.* Garden City, N.J.: Doubleday, 1965.
Christ, Mark K., ed. *Getting Used to Being Shot At: The Spence Family Civil War Letters.* Fayetteville: University of Arkansas Press, 2002.
Cist, Henry. *The Army of the Cumberland.* New York: Charles Scribner's Sons, 1882.
Clark, Olynthus B., ed. *Downing's Civil War Diary by Sergeant Alexander G. Downing, Company E, Eleventh Iowa Infantry.* Des Moines: Historical Department of Iowa, 1916.
Cluett, William W. *History of the 57th Regiment Illinois Volunteer Infantry.* Princeton, NJ: T. P. Streeter, 1886.
Coburn, Mark. *Terrible Innocence: General Sherman at War.* New York: Hippocrene Books, 1993.
Conger, A. L. *The Rise of U. S. Grant.* Freeport, NY: Books for Libraries Press, 1970.
Connelly, Thomas Lawrence. *Army of the Heartland: The Army of Tennessee, 1861–1862.* Baton Rouge: Louisiana State University Press, 1967.
_____. *Autumn of Glory: The Army of Tennessee, 1862–1865.* Baton Rouge: Louisiana State University Press, 1971.
Cooling, Benjamin Franklin. *Forts Henry and Donelson: The Key to the Confederate Heartland.* Knoxville: University of Tennessee Press, 1987.
_____. *Fort Donelson's Legacy: War and Society in Kentucky and Tennessee, 1862–1863.* Knoxville: University of Tennessee Press, 1997.
Coppee, Henry. *Life and Services of Gen. U. S. Grant.* Chicago: Western News Company, 1868.
Cozzens, Peter. *No Better Place to Die: The Battle of Stones River.* Urbana: University of Illinois Press, 1990.
_____. *This Terrible Sound: The Battle of Chickamauga.* Urbana: University of Illinois Press, 1992.
Cramer, Jesse Grant, ed. *Letter of Ulysses S. Grant to His Father and His Youngest Sister, 1857–78.* New York: G. P. Putnam's Sons, 1912.
Crist, Lynda Lasswell, ed. *The Papers of Jefferson Davis.* Baton Rouge: Louisiana State University Press, 1999.
Crummer, Wilbur F. *With Grant at Fort Donelson, Shiloh and Vicksburg.* Oak Park, IL: E. C. Crummer & Co., 1915.
Dana, Charles A. *The Life of Ulysses S. Grant.* Springfield, MA: Gurdon Bill & Company, 1868.
_____. *Recollections of the Civil War.* New York: D. Appleton and Company, 1902.
Daniel, Larry J. *Days of Glory: The Army of the Cumberland, 1861–1865.* Baton Rouge: Louisiana State University Press, 2004.
_____. *Shiloh: The Battle That Changed the Civil War.* New York: Simon & Schuster, 1997.
_____. *Soldiering in the Army of Tennessee.* Chapel Hill: University of North Carolina Press, 1991.
Davis, William C., ed. *Diary of a Confederate Soldier: John S. Jackman of the Orphan Brigade.* Columbia: University of South Carolina Press, 1990.
Day, Lewis W. *Story of the One Hundred and First Ohio Infantry.* Cleveland, OH: W. M. Bayne Printing Co., 1894.
Dodge, William S. *History of the Old Second Division, Army of the Cumberland, Commanders: M'Cook, Sill, and Johnson.* Chicago: Church & Goodman, 1864.
Downey, Fairfax. *Storming of the Gateway: Chattanooga, 1863.* New York: David McKay, 1960.

Doyle, Julie A., John David Smith, and Richard M. McMurry, eds. *This Wilderness of War: The Civil War Letters of George W. Squier, Hoosier Volunteer*. Knoxville: University of Tennessee Press, 1998.
Dyer, Frederick H. *A Compendium of the War of the Rebellion*. Des Moines, IA: Dyer Publishing Company, 1908.
Engle, Stephen D. *Don Carlos Buell: Most Promising of All*. Chapel Hill: University of North Carolina Press, 1999.
_____. *Struggle for the Heartland: The Campaigns From Fort Henry to Corinth*. Lincoln: University of Nebraska Press, 2001.
Evans, Clement A., ed. *Confederate Military History*, Vol. III. Atlanta: Confederate Publishing Company, 1899.
Ferrel, H. Robert, ed. *Holding the Line: The Third Tennessee Infantry 1861–1864*. Kent, OH: Kent State University Press, 1994.
Fiske, John. *The Mississippi Valley in the Civil War*. Boston: Houghton, Mifflin, 1900.
Fitch, John. *Annals of the Army of the Cumberland*. Philadelphia: J. B. Lippincott, 1864.
Fletcher, William A. *Rebel Private: Front and Rear, Memoirs of a Confederate Soldier*. New York: Dutton, 1995.
Folmar, John Kent. *From That Terrible Field: Civil War Letters of James M. Williams, Twenty-first Alabama Infantry*. Tuscaloosa: University of Alabama Press, 1981.
Fowler, John D. *Mountaineers in Gray: The Nineteenth Tennessee Volunteer Infantry Regiment, C.S.A.* Knoxville: University of Tennessee Press, 2004.
Fox, William F. *Regimental Losses in the American Civil War, 1861–1865*. Albany, NY: Albany Publishing Company, 1889.
Fuller, J. F. C. *The Generalship of Ulysses S. Grant*. New York: Da Capo Press, n. d.
Garland, Hamlin. *Ulysses S. Grant: His Life and Character*. New York: Doubleday & McClure Co., 1898.
Gosnell, H. Allen. *Guns on the Western Waters: The Story of River Gunboats in the Civil War*. Baton Rouge: Louisiana State University Press, 1949.
Grant, Ulysses S. *Personal Memoirs of U. S. Grant*. New York: Charles L. Webster & Company, 1885.
Grose, William. *The Story of the Marches, Battles and Incidents of the 36th Regiment Indiana Volunteer Infantry*. New Castle, IN: Courier Company Press, 1891.
Hale, Douglas. *The Third Texas Cavalry in the Civil War*. Norman: University of Oklahoma Press, 1993.
Hallock, Judith Lee, ed. *The Civil War Letters of Joshua K. Callaway*. Athens: University of Georgia Press, 1997.
Harden, H. O. *History of the 90th Ohio Volunteer Infantry in the War of the Great Rebellion in the United States, 1861 to 1865*. Stoutsville, OH: Press of Fairfield-Pickaway News, 1902.
Hartpence, William R. *History of the Fifty-first Indiana Veteran Volunteer Infantry*. Cincinnati, OH: Robert Clarke Company, Printers and Binders, 1894.
Haughton, Andrew. *Training, Tactics and Leadership in the Confederate Army of Tennessee: Seeds of Failure*. London: Frank Cass, 2000.
Hazen, William B. *A Narrative of Military Service*. Boston: Ticknor and Company, 1885.
Hess, Earl J. *Banners to the Breeze: The Kentucky Campaign, Corinth, and Stones River*. Lincoln: University of Nebraska Press, 2000.
Hicken, Victor. *Illinois in the Civil War*. Urbana: University of Illinois Press, 1991.
Hood, J. B. *Advance and Retreat*. Edison, NJ: Blue and Gray Press, 1985. Reprint.
Horn, Stanley F. *The Army of Tennessee*. Norman: University of Oklahoma Press, 1968.
_____. *Tennessee's War, 1861–1865: Described by Participants*. Nashville: Tennessee Civil War Centennial Commission, 1965.
Howard, Oliver Otis. *Autobiography of Oliver Otis Howard*. New York: Baker & Taylor, 1908.
Howe, M. A. DeWolfe, ed. *Marching With Sherman: Passages From the Letters and Campaign Diaries of Henry Hitchcock*. New Haven, CT: Yale University Press, 1927.
Hughes, Nathaniel Cheairs Jr. *The Pride of the Confederate Artillery: The Washington Artillery in the Army of Tennessee*. Baton Rouge: Louisiana State University Press, 1997.
Hunter, Alfred G. *History of the Eighty-second Indiana Volunteer Infantry, Its Organization, Campaigns and Battles*. Indianapolis: William B. Buford, Printer and Binder, 1893.
Johnson, R. W. *A Soldier's Reminiscences in Peace and War*. Philadelphia: J. B. Lippincott, 1886.
Johnston, William Preston. *The Life of Gen. Albert Sidney Johnston*. New York: Da Capo Press, 1997.
Jones, J. B. *A Rebel War Clerk's Diary at the Confederate States Capital*, 2 Vols. Philadelphia: J. B. Lippincott, 1866.
Jones, Thomas B. *Complete History of the 46th Regiment Illinois Volunteer Infantry*. Freeport, IL: W. H. Wagner & Sons, Printers, n. d.
Joslyn, Mauriel Phillips, ed. *A Meteor Shining Brightly: Essays on the Life and Career of Major General Patrick R. Cleburne*. Macon, Georgia: Mercer University Press, 2000.
Kimberly, Robert L., and Ephraim S. Holloway. *The Forty-first Ohio Veteran Volunteer Infantry in the War of the Rebellion, 1861–1865*. Huntington, WV: Blue Acorn Press, 1999.
Kinnear, John R. *History of the Eighty-sixth Regiment Illinois Volunteer Infantry*. Chicago: Tribune Company's Book and Job Printing Office, 1866.
Kiper, Richard L. *Major General John Alexander McClernand, Politician in Uniform*. Kent, OH: Kent State University Press, 1999.

Lewis, Lloyd. *Sherman: Fighting Prophet*. New York: Harcourt, Brace, 1932.
Longstreet, James. *From Manassas to Appomattox*. Old Saybrook, CT: Konecky & Konecky, n. d.
Losson, Christopher. *Tennessee's Forgotten Warriors: Frank Cheatham and His Confederate Division*. Knoxville: University of Tennessee Press, 1989.
Luvaas, Jay, Stephen Bowman, and Leonard Fullenkamp, eds. *Guide to the Battle of Shiloh*. Lawrence: University Press of Kansas, 1996.
McCaffrey, James M. *This Band of Heroes: Granbury's Texas Brigade, C.S.A*. College Stations: Texas A & M University Press, 1996.
McClure, A. K. *Abraham Lincoln and Men of War-Times*. Lincoln: University of Nebraska Press, 1996. Reprint.
McDonough, James Lee. *Chattanooga: A Death Grip on the Confederacy*. Knoxville: University of Tennessee, 1984.
McGee, Benjamin F. *History of the 72d Indiana Volunteer Infantry*. Huntington, WV: Blue Acorn Press, 1995. Reprint of 1882 edition.
McKinney, Francis F. *Education in Violence: The Life of George H. Thomas and the History of the Army of the Cumberland*. Detroit: Wayne State University Press, 1961.
McMorries, Edward Young. *History of the First Regiment Alabama Volunteer Infantry C.S.A*. Freeport, NY: Books for Libraries Press, 1970. Reprint of 1904 edition.
McMurray, W. J. *History of the Twentieth Tennessee Regiment Volunteer Infantry, C.S.A*. Nashville, TN: Publication Committee, 1904.
McPherson, James M. *Battle Cry of Freedom—The Civil War Era*. New York: Oxford University Press, 1988.
Morris, George W. *History of the Eighty-First Regiment of Indiana Volunteer Infantry in the Great War of the Rebellion, 1861 to 1865*. Louisville, KY: Franklin Printing Company, 1901.
Morris, W. S., L. D. Hartwell, and J. B. Kuykendall. *History of the 31st Regiment Illinois Volunteers*. Carbondale: Southern Illinois University Press, 1998.
Morrison, Marion. *A History of the Ninth Regiment Illinois Volunteer Infantry, With the Regimental Roster*. Carbondale: Southern Illinois University Press, 1997.
Newlin, W. H., D. F. Lawler, and J. W. Sherrick. *A History of the Seventy-third Regiment of Illinois Infantry Volunteers*. Regimental Reunion Association, 1890.
O'Connor, Richard. *Sheridan the Inevitable*. New York: Konecky & Konecky, 1993.
Patrick, Jeffrey L., ed. *Three Years with Wallace's Zouaves: The Civil War Memoirs of Thomas Wise Durham*. Macon, GA: Mercer University Press, 2003.
Payne, Edwin W. *History of the Thirty-fourth Regiment of Illinois Volunteer Infantry*. Clinton, IA: Allen Printing, 1902.
Perry, Henry Fales. *History of the Thirty-eighth Regiment Indiana Volunteer Infantry*. Palo Alto, CA: F. A. Stuart, the Printer, 1906.
Porter, Horace. *Campaigning with Grant*. New York: Mallard Press, 1991.
Pratt, Fletcher. *Civil War on Western Waters*. New York: Henry Holt, 1956
Prokopowicz, Gerald J. *All For the Regiment: The Army of the Ohio, 1861–1862*. Chapel Hill: University of North Carolina Press, 2001.
Reed, David W. *Campaigns and Battles of the Twelfth Regiment Iowa Veteran Volunteer Infantry*. Evanston, IL: n.p., 1923.
Rerick, John H. *The Forty-fourth Indiana Volunteer Infantry: History of Its Services in the War of the Rebellion*. LaGrange, IN: John H. Rerick, 1880.
Richardson, Albert D. *A Personal History of Ulysses S. Grant*. Hartford, CT: American Publishing, 1868.
Ridley, Bromfield L. *Battles and Sketches of the Army of Tennessee*. Dayton, OH: Press of Morningside Bookshop, 1978.
Roland, Charles P. *Jefferson Davis's Greatest General: Albert Sidney Johnston*. Abilene, TX: McWhiney Foundation Press, 2000.
Schofield, John M. *Forty-six Years in the Army*. New York: Century, 1897.
Shapiro, Larry ed. *Abraham Lincoln—Mystic Chords of Memory*. New York: Book-of-the-Month-Club, 1984.
Sheridan, Philip H. *Personal Memoirs of P. H. Sheridan*. New York: Charles L. Webster, 1888.
Sherman, William T. *Memoirs of Gen. W. T. Sherman, Written by Himself*. New York: Charles L. Webster, 1891.
Simon, John Y., ed. *The Papers of Ulysses S. Grant*, Volume 4. Carbondale: Southern Illinois University Press, 1972.
Simpson, Brooks D. *Ulysses S. Grant: Triumph Over Adversity, 1822–1865*. Boston: Houghton Mifflin, 2000.
_____, and Jean V. Berlin, eds. *Sherman's Civil War: Selected Correspondence of William T. Sherman, 1860–1865*. Chapel Hill: The University of North Carolina Press, 1999.
Smith, Barbara Bently, and Nina Bently Baker, eds. *"Burning Rails as We Pleased": The Civil War Letters of William Garrigues Bently, 104th Ohio Volunteer Infantry*. Jefferson, NC: McFarland, 2004.
Smith, Henry I. *History of the Seventh Iowa Veteran Volunteer Infantry During the Civil War*. Mason City, IA: E. Hitchcock, Printer, Binder, 1903.
Spruill, Matt. *Storming the Heights: A Guide to the Battle of Chattanooga*. Knoxville: University of Tennessee Press, 2003.

Stewart, Nixon B. *Dan McCook's Regiment, 52nd O. V. I.* Alliance, OH: Nixon B. Stewart, 1900.
Stillwell, Leander. *The Story of a Common Soldier of Army Life in the Civil War, 1861–1865.* New York: Time-Life Books, 1983.
Sullivan, James R. *Chickamauga and Chattanooga Battlefields.* Washington, DC: National Park Service, 1961.
Sutherland, Daniel E., ed. *Reminiscences of a Private: William E. Bevens of the First Arkansas Infantry, C.S.A.* Fayetteville: University of Arkansas Press, 1992.
Switzer, Charles I., ed. *Ohio Volunteer: The Childhood and Civil War Memoirs of Captain John Calvin Hartzell, OVI.* Athens: Ohio University Press, 2005.
Symonds, Craig L. *Stonewall of the West: Patrick Cleburne and the Civil War.* Lawrence: University Press of Kansas, 1997.
Thomas, Benjamin P., ed. *Three Years with Grant as Recalled by War Correspondent Sylvanus Cadwallader.* Lincoln: University of Nebraska Press, 1996.
Tower, R. Lockwood, ed. *A Carolinian Goes to War: The Civil War Narrative of Arthur Middleton Manigault, Brigadier General, C.S.A.* Columbia: University of South Carolina Press, 1983.
Tucker, Spencer C. *Unconditional Surrender: The Capture of Forts Henry and Donelson.* Abilene, TX: McWhiney Foundation Press, 2001.
United States War Department. *War of the Rebellion: A Compilation of the Official Records of the Union and Confederate Armies.* Washington, DC: Government Printing Office, 1880–1901.
Van Horne, Thomas B. *History of the Army of the Cumberland*, Vol. 1. Cincinnati, OH: Robert Clarke, 1875.
Wallace, Lew. *An Autobiography.* New York: Harper & Brothers, 1906.
Warner, Ezra J. *Generals in Blue.* Baton Rouge: Louisiana State University Press, 1964.
_____. *Generals in Gray.* Baton Rouge.: Louisiana State University Press, 1959.
Williams, Kenneth P. *Grant Rises in the West: The First Year, 1861–1862.* Lincoln: University of Nebraska Press, 1997.
Wilson, Ephraim A. *Memoirs of the War.* Cleveland: W. M. Bayne Printing Co., 1893.
Woodworth, Steven E. *Jefferson Davis and His Generals: The Failure of Confederate Command in the West.* Lawrence: University Press of Kansas, 1990.
_____. *Six Armies in Tennessee: The Chickamauga and Chattanooga Campaigns.* Lincoln: University of Nebraska Press, 1998.
_____. *No Band of Brothers: Problems in the Rebel High Command.* Columbia: University of Missouri Press, 1999.
_____. *This Grand Spectacle: The Battle of Chattanooga.* Abilene, TX: McWhiney Foundation Press, 1999.
Worsham, W. J. *The Old Nineteenth Tennessee Regiment, C.S.A.* Knoxville, TN: Press of Paragon Printing Company, 1902.
Worthington, Tom. *Brief History of the 46th Ohio Volunteers.* Washington, DC: n.p., 1878.
Wright, Henry H. *A History of the Sixth Iowa Infantry.* Iowa City, IA: State Historical Society of Iowa, 1923.
Young, Lot D. *Reminiscences of a Soldier of the Orphan Brigade.* Louisville, KY: Courier-Journal Job Printing Company, 1918.

Magazines, Diaries, Letters

Alexander, E. P. "Longstreet at Knoxville." *Battles and Leaders of the Civil War.* 4 Vols. Robert Underwood Johnson and Clarence Clough Buel, eds. New York: Thomas Yoseloff, 1956.
Badeau, Adam. "General Grant." *The Century.* May 1885.
Bankhead, Smith P. "Letter from Colonel Bankhead." *Southern Historical Society Papers.* January 1879.
Beauregard, P. G. T. "The Shiloh Campaign, Part I." *The North American Review.* January 1886.
_____. "The Shiloh Campaign, Part II." *The North American Review.* February 1886.
Buell, D. C. "Shiloh Revisited." *The Century.* March 1886.
Byers, S. H. M. "Sherman's Attack at the Tunnel." *Battles and Leaders of the Civil War.* 4 Vols. Robert Underwood Johnson and Clarence Clough Buel, eds. New York: Thomas Yoseloff, 1956.
Caldwell, Robert H. "Letter January 3, 1863." Robert H. Caldwell Papers. Center for Archival Collections. Bowling Green State University, Bowling Green, Ohio.
Canfield, George S. Paper read at the reunion of Company K, 21st Ohio, August 28, 1908. Center for Archival Collections. Bowling Green State University, Bowling Green, Ohio.
Carrington, Henry B. "Major General Lew Wallace at Shiloh." *The Bay State Monthly.* March 1885.
_____. "The Civil War in 1862: A Campaign of Contrasts." *The New England Magazine.* December 1886.
Crittenden, Thomas L. "The Union Left at Stone's River." *Battles and Leaders of the Civil War.* 4 Vols. Robert Underwood Johnson and Clarence Clough Buel, eds. New York: Thomas Yoseloff, 1956.
Cusac, Isaac. "Isaac Cusac Letter March 13, 1909." Center for Archival Collections. Bowling Green State University, Bowling Green, Ohio.

Doan, Isaac C. *Reminiscences of the Chattanooga Campaign: A Paper Read at the Reunion of Company B, Fortieth Ohio Volunteer Infantry, at Xenia, O., August 22, 1894*. Richmond, IN: J. M. Coe's Printery, 1894.
Doughman, Thomas J. "Civil War Recollections of Thomas J. Doughman." Center for Archival Collections. Bowling Green State University, Bowling Green, Ohio.
Fullerton, J. S. "The Reserve Corps at Chickamauga." *The Century*. April 1887.
_____. "The Army of the Cumberland at Chattanooga." *The Century*. May 1887.
Grant, F. D. "Halleck's Injustice to Grant." *The North American Review*. December 1885.
Grant, Ulysses S. "The Battle of Shiloh." *The Century*. February 1885.
Hannaford, Eban. "In the Ranks at Stone River." *Harper's New Monthly Magazine*. November 1863.
Heard, S. S. "Letter from Colonel S. S. Heard." *Southern Historical Society Papers*. January 1879.
Hill, D. H. "Chickamauga — The Great Battle of the West." *The Century*. April 1887.
Howard, Oliver O. "Chattanooga." *The Atlantic Monthly*. August 1876.
Johnston, William Preston. "Albert Sidney Johnston and the Shiloh Campaign." *The Century*. February 1885.
Jordan, Thomas. "Notes of a Confederate Staff-Officer at Shiloh." *The Century*. February 1885.
Kniffin, Gilbert C. "The Battle of Stone's River." *Battles and Leaders of the Civil War*. 4 Vols. Robert Underwood Johnson and Clarence Clough Buel, eds. New York: Thomas Yoseloff, 1956.
_____. "Maneuvering Bragg Out of Tennessee." *Battles and Leaders of the Civil War*. 4 Vols. Robert Underwood Johnson and Clarence Clough Buel, eds. New York: Thomas Yoseloff, 1956.
Lawrence, Eugene. "Grant on the Battle-Field." *Harper's New Monthly Magazine*. July 1869.
Lockett, S. H. "Controversies in Regard to Shiloh: A Staff Officer's Account of the Attack and Withdrawal." *The Century*, March 1886.
Longstreet, James. "Report of General Longstreet." *Southern Historical Society Papers*. July 1880.
Martin, W. L. Letter to Southern Historical Society, February 3, 1883. *Southern Historical Society Papers*. 1883.
McCook, Daniel. "The Second Division at Shiloh." *Harper's New Monthly Magazine*. May 1864.
Meigs, Montgomery C. *The Three Days' Battle of Chattanooga, 23d, 24th, 25th November, 1864 [1863]: An Unofficial Dispatch from General Meigs*. Washington, DC: McGill & Witherow, 1864.
Nicolay, John G. and John Hay. "Abraham Lincoln: A History, Tennessee and Kentucky." *The Century*. August 1888.
_____. "Abraham Lincoln: A History, the Mississippi and Shiloh." *The Century*. September 1888.
Olney, Warren. "The Battle of Shiloh, with Some Personal Reminiscences." *Overland Monthly and Out West Magazine*. June 1885.
Partridge, Charles A. *The Battle of Chickamauga: And the Part Played in It by a Portion of the Reserve Corps*. Paper read before George H. Thomas Post of the Grand Army of the Republic, April 29, 1881.
Perry, Leslie J. "The Rise of General Grant." *The Century*. November 1896.
Poe, Orlando M. "The Defense of Knoxville." *Battles and Leaders of the Civil War*. 4 Vols. Robert Underwood Johnson and Clarence Clough Buel, eds. New York: Thomas Yoseloff, 1956.
Rice, Allen Thorndike, ed. "Unpublished War Letters by Generals Grant and Halleck." *The North American Review*. March 1886.
Rosecrans, William S. "The Campaign for Chattanooga." *The Century*. May 1887.
_____. "Corinth." *The Century*. October 1886.
Ruggles, Daniel. "Letter from General Ruggles." *Southern Historical Society Papers*. January 1879.
Sandidge, L. D. "Letter from Captain Sandidge." *Southern Historical Society Papers*. January 1879.
Shanks, W. F. G. "Chattanooga, and How We Held It." *Harper's New Monthly Magazine*. January 1868.
_____. "Lookout Mountain and How We Won It." *Harper's New Monthly Magazine*. June 1868.
_____. "Recollections of Grant." *Harper's New Monthly Magazine*. June 1865.
_____. "Recollections of Sherman." *Harper's New Monthly Magazine*. April 1865.
_____. "Recollections of Thomas." *Harper's New Monthly Magazine*. May 1865.
Stevenson, C. L. "Original Rough Draft of Report of General C. L. Stevenson." *Southern Historical Society Papers*. July 1880st.
Taylor, Jesse. "The Defense of Fort Henry." *Battles and Leaders of the Civil War*. 4 Vols. Robert Underwood Johnson and Clarence Clough Buel, eds. New York: Thomas Yoseloff, 1956.
Thrall, James C. "Letter from Captain James C. Thrall." *Southern Historical Society Papers*. January 1879.
Thruston, Gates P. "The Crisis at Chickamauga." *Battles and Leaders of the Civil War*. 4 Vols. Robert Underwood Johnson and Clarence Clough Buel, eds. New York: Thomas Yoseloff, 1956.
Truman, Ben C. "A Spectacular Battle and its 'Ifs.'" *Overland Monthly and Out West Magazine*. August 1889.
Urquhart, David. "Bragg's Advance and Retreat." *Battles and Leaders of the Civil War*. 4 Vols. Robert Underwood Johnson and Clarence Clough Buel, eds. New York: Thomas Yoseloff, 1956.
Walke, Henry. "Operations of the Western Flotilla." *The Century*. January 1885.
Wallace, Lew. "The Capture of Fort Donelson." *The Century*. December 1884.

INDEX

Adams, Daniel W.: Stone's River 102–103; Chickamauga 144
Alexander's Bridge: location 133
Alpine, Georgia 125
Ammen, Jacob 71; Savannah 52; fugitives 64
Anderson, J. B. 171
Anderson, Nicholas: Shiloh 72
Anderson, Patton 90, 107; Stone's River 99, 101
Army of Tennessee 46, 104–105, 124; Murfreesboro 90; dissention 110; to Chattanooga 120; strength 131; crosses Chickamauga Creek, positions 134; enemy on right 135; Chickamauga losses, morale 154; dissention 155
Army of the Cumberland 88, 159; Stone's River 104; organization 112; occupies Chattanooga 125; strength, closes up 131; moves north, positions 134; Chattanooga 152; supplies 154; supply route 157; Thomas commands 159; sees victory 183; diversion 193; Missionary Ridge 195
Army of the Mississippi 79
Army of the Ohio 69, 79; Buell 43
Army of the Tennessee 69, 79
Aten, Henry: Missionary Ridge 196

Baird, Absalom 128, 129, 134, 192; Chickamauga 137, 143–144, 149; Missionary Ridge 193, 197
Baldwin, Philemon: Stone's River 97
Bane, Moses: Shiloh 62
Banks, Nathaniel P. 153
Barber, Flavell 23–24
Barber, Lucius: camp life 52
Bate, William B.: Hoover's Gap 117; Chickamauga 139, 146
Beatty, John: Stone's River 100; Chickamauga 144, 146
Beatty, Samuel 104, 106, 107; Stone's River 100–101
Beauregard, P.G.T. 11, 12, 19, 64, 67, 69, 70, 76, 81, 110; Corinth 45; organizes army 46; cancels attack 49; commands army 62; rests 65; to Cooper 68; retreats 74–75; at Corinth 82; evacuates Corinth 83; replaced 84
Bell Buckle Gap 111
Belmont, Missouri 10
Bennett, L. G.: Missionary Ridge 197
Berry, William: Stone's River 97
Bevens, William E.: Shiloh 60
Bishop, Judson: Shiloh dead 78

Blair, Frank P.: Missionary Ridge 185
Blanchard, Ira 61; Ft. Donelson cold 30; victory 31; Shiloh weather 53; Shiloh 56
Bowling Green, Kentucky 7, 8, 9, 11, 13, 35; abandoned 19
Bragg, Braxton 48, 50, 65, 68, 69, 90, 114, 115, 119, 122, 123, 167, 178, 186, 188; Corinth 45; Shiloh 60; army condition 76–77; replaces Beauregard 84; Kentucky 85; Perryville 86; Stone's River formation 92; Stone's River 102–105; retreats 107; conflict with generals 109–110; cavalry 118; abandons Tullahoma, morale 120–121; abandons Chattanooga 124; ends retreat 126; to Hindman 127–128; to Polk 129; Chickamauga Creek 130; battle plan 132–133; troop position 134; enemy on right 135; Chickamauga 138; divides command, attack on right 141–142; after victory 150; to Cooper 151; complaints 155; Knoxville 173; note to Grant 177; disappointed 184; strengthens center 196; Missionary Ridge 199; moves troops 200; rally troops 201; to Dalton, resigns 206
Brannon, John M. 129, 134, 136, 185; Chickamauga 137, 143, 145, 147
Bratton, John 168
Breckinridge, John C. 48, 50, 68, 69, 90, 92, 131, 134, 186; Shiloh 60; retreats 75–76; army condition 77; Stone's River 102–103; attacks 105–106; retreats 108; to Bragg 109; Chickamauga 144, 149; Missionary Ridge 196–197
Briant, Charles C.: Shiloh 69; low supplies 157
Bridgeport, Alabama 122, 160, 176; Union supply base 157
Brinton, John: Grant's treatment 42
Brown, John C.: Chickamauga 138–139
Brown's Ferry 162, 163, 170, 175, 179, 180
Buckland, Ralph: Shiloh 73
Buckner, Simon Bolivar 25, 29, 31, 90, 122, 123, 126, 133, 134; Ft. Donelson 22; command, surrender terms 30; to Knoxville 177–178
Buell, Don Carlos 6, 9, 35, 70, 82; history 5; to Lincoln 7; to Halleck 8; Nashville 36; fugitives 64; too slow 85; relieved 87
Buell, George: Chickamauga 139, 145
Burnside, Ambrose 114, 122, 176; in Knoxville 164; low supplies 172
Byers, S. H. M.: Missionary Ridge 185, 189

Cairo, Ill. 6, 10
Cairo: Union warship 33
Calkins, William: Missionary Ridge 197
Callaway, Joshua K.: 28th Alabama 170
Carlin, William: Stone's River 97; Chickamauga 139
Carondelet: Union warship 14, 16, 17, 20, 24, 79; damaged 22, 25
Carroll, John W.: Shiloh weather 53
Chalmers, James 69; Shiloh 62; Stone's River 101
Chattanooga, Tenn. 122, 131; importance 114; Union army to 150; location 156; casualties 202; open Deep South 206
Chattanooga Creek 181; bridge down 192
Chattanooga Valley 175
Cheatham, Benjamin 74, 90, 134, 181, 188; Shiloh 60; Stone's River 100; Chickamauga 137–138, 140, 144
Chickamauga Creek 130, 131, 141; fights to cross 133
Cincinnati: Union warship 14, 16
Cist, Henry 122
Clark, Charles: Shiloh 69
Clarksville, Tenn. 18, 39; deserted 33
Clayton, Henry: Chickamauga 138–139
Cleburne, Patrick 70, 90, 107, 126, 134; Shiloh attack 55; Stone's River position 92; Stone's River 96–102; to Bragg 109; Chickamauga 140, 144, 149; to Knoxville 177–178; Missionary Ridge 186, 189; launches attack 191; rear guard 201–202; Ringgold Gap 204
Cleveland, Tenn. 164
Cluett, William 67; camp life 52
Columbus, Kentucky: Confederate fortress 6, 8, 10, 11, 13
Conestoga: Union warship 14, 33
Connolly, James A.: Lookout Mtn. victory 183; Missionary Ridge 195; to wife 199; Missionary Ridge 201
Cook, John: Ft. Donelson 29
Cooper, Samuel: Confederate adjutant and inspector general 7, 68
Corinth, Miss. 36, 39, 49; Confederate army 44; railroad center 45; conditions, fortifications 82–83; evacuated 83
Corse, John 153; Missionary Ridge 189–190
Cowan House 103; Stone's River 101
Cram, George H.: Stone's River 106
Cravens, Robert: Lookout Mtn. farm 183
Crawfish Springs 134
Crittenden, Thomas L. 66, 88, 91, 92, 124, 129, 133, 134; Stone's River 106–107; 21st Corps 112; history 113; new campaign 116; Chattanooga 122; closes with Thomas 131; Chickamauga 138, 146
Croxton, John: Chickamauga 137
Cruft, Charles 26, 177; Ft. Donelson 28; Stone's River 101; Chickamauga 138; Lookout Mtn. 181–182; Missionary Ridge 192
Crummer, Wilber F.: Shiloh weather 53
Crump's Landing 43, 58; Union supply depot 51
Cullum, G. W. 35, 39; Halleck's chief of staff 20
Cumberland River 21
Cumming, Alfred: Missionary Ridge 191
Curtis, Samuel: Missouri 38

Dalton, Georgia 125; Confederate camp 206
Dana, Charles 177; Chickamauga 149; to Stanton 155, 156; on supplies, Rosecrans 158; retreats 159–160; Grant arrives 162; Missionary Ridge 198, 202
Davis, Jefferson 90; Confederate president 5; defends A. S. Johnston 37; Corinth 83; keeps Bragg 109; at Chattanooga 154–155
Davis, Jefferson C. 185; killed Nelson 86; Stone's River 96–98; Chickamauga 139, 143, 145
Department of the Missouri 4; description 5
Department of the Ohio: description 5
Department of the Pacific 5
Department of the Tennessee 86
District of West Tennessee: description 33
Doan, Isaac C.: Lookout Mtn. 182; flag 188
Dodge, Grenville: repair railroads 172
Donelson, Daniel: Stone's River 101
Donelson, J. L. 207
Doughman, Thomas J.: Chickamauga 141
Dover, Tenn. 13, 20, 21
Downing, Alexander: Shiloh battle 57
Dry Valley Road 134, 145; importance, route 132
Dug Gap 125, 128
Durham, Thomas: cold at Ft. Donelson 25, 28, 30
Dyer Road: location, importance 132, 134

Eads, James B.: ship builder 10
East Tennessee & Virginia Railroad 122
Eastport: Confederate warship 18
Eastport, Tenn. 43
Ector, M. D. 100–101; Stone's River 95–96
8th Illinois: Ft. Donelson 26
8th Kentucky: Lookout Mtn. Flag 188
8th Missouri: Ft. Donelson 28
18th Illinois: Shiloh 56
82nd Indiana: Missionary Ridge 196
85th Illinois: Missionary Ridge 196
88th Illinois 118; Stone's River 98
89th Illinois: Stone's River 95
89th Ohio: Chickamauga 141
11th Indiana: Ft. Donelson 25, 28
Essex: Union warship 14; damage 16
Ewing, Hugh 176; Missionary Ridge 185

Farmington, Miss. 83
Field Orders No. 1: Ft. Henry plan 15
Field Orders No. 5: troop condition 17
Field Orders No. 11: Ft. Donelson 20
1st Arkansas: Shiloh 60
5th Iowa: Missionary Ridge 185
5th Kentucky: Stone's River 97
15th Illinois 72; Shiloh 52
50th Illinois: Shiloh 62
53rd Ohio 73; Shiloh 55
54th Ohio: Shiloh 62
55th Illinois: Shiloh 62
57th Illinois 67; Shiloh 52
Florence, Alabama 18
Floyd, John G. 25, 28; commander Ft. Donelson 22
Foote, Andrew 11, 14, 16, 17, 24, 33, 79; Union flag officer 10; to Halleck 12; wounded 25
Forrest, Nathan Bedford 30, 90, 111, 118, 134, 136; Ft. Donelson 26
Fort Donelson 13, 14, 25; location 6; strengthened 19; prepared for attack 20; description 21; problems 32
Fort Heiman 10; description 15

Index

Fort Henry 10, 12, 13; location 6; description 14; evacuated 15; telegraph 37
Fort Pillow 38
Fort Wood 177
14th Iowa: Shiloh 63
14th Wisconsin: Shiloh 72
40th Ohio: Lookout Mtn. 182
41st Ohio 72, 169; Shiloh 64; Missionary Ridge 196–198
45th Illinois 56; Ft. Donelson 23; Shiloh 53
46th Ohio: Missionary Ridge 189
48th Illinois: Ft. Donelson 23
48th Ohio: Shiloh 55
49th Illinois: Ft. Donelson 23
49th Ohio: Shiloh 73; Stone's River 95
Foy, James C. 166
Franklin Pike 91, 92, 95
Frémont, John C. 4
Fullerton, J. S.: Chickamauga 147; Missionary Ridge 198
Fyffe, James P. 104, 105, 106; Stone's River 100–102

Garfield, James: Chickamauga 148–149
Geary, John 167, 177; Wauhatchie 168–169; Lookout Mtn. 181–184; flag 188; Missionary Ridge 192
General Orders No. 60: treatment of civilians 84
Gibson, William 105; Shiloh 72; Stone's River 95
Gladden, A. H. 49
Govan, Daniel: Chickamauga 137
Granbury, Hiram: Missionary Ridge 190
Granger, Gordon 85, 116, 177, 195, 202; Reserve Corps 112; Chickamauga 147–148; Missionary Ridge 198; to Knoxville 204
Grant, Julia: wife of Ulysses 15
Grant, Ulysses S. 37, 41, 51, 61, 63, 68, 75, 203; history 9; new campaign, meets Halleck 11; to Halleck 12; to Julia 15; to Halleck 17; Ft. Donelson 17; to Halleck 20; army position 21; to Walke 22; to Halleck 24; to Cullum 24; Ft. Donelson siege 25; attack, to Foote, philosophy 27–28; unconditional surrender 30; to Halleck 31; fame 32; new command, to Cullum 33; major general 35; Nashville 36; to Halleck 38; reports 39–40; cleared, to Halleck 42–44; defense, Sherman 50; no attack 52; Savannah, Pittsburg Landing, to Buell 58–59; fugitives 64–65; confident 66; no pursuit 76–77; to Halleck 78; criticism 80; on war 81; new command 82; move to Memphis, civilians 84–85; Vicksburg 114; injured 153; meets Stanton, new command 159; to Chattanooga 160–161; meets Thomas 161; bad roads 162; to Sherman, to Halleck 165; supply route open 169; salute 170; to Anderson, to Kilburn 171; Knoxville 173; unable to attack 174; new plans 175–176; to Burnside 176; begins assaults 177; to Sherman 186; to Halleck, continue attack 187; changes plan 191; Hooker attacks 192; different approach 193; wants results 194; impatient 195; questions attack 198; pursues Bragg 204; Burnside, Granger delay 205; general in chief 207
Greusel, Nicholas: Stone's River 98
Grose, William: Stone's River 105; Chickamauga 138, 144; Lookout Mtn. 181–182
Guy's Gap 111

Halleck, Henry W. 6, 76; history 4; to Lincoln 7; to Buell 8; to Lincoln 8–9; strategy 11; Ft. Henry, to McClellan 12; to Buell 13; clears Cumberland River 18; to Grant 19; reinforcements 19; to Foote 20; replaces Grant 34; to Cullum 37; Grant's complaints 38–39; warns Grant 40; western command 41; clears Grant 42; no advance 44; Pittsburg Landing 77, 79; no surprise 81; to Grant 82; Corinth 83; general in chief 84; to Buell 85, 86, 87; to Rosecrans 89, 113, 114, 121; to Grant, to Burnside 152
Hannaford, Eban: weather, destruction 91
Hanson, Roger 105; Stone's River 102
Hardee, William J. 7, 19, 48, 69, 76, 90, 92, 111, 119, 186; Shiloh 54; Stone's River 102; to Bragg 109; Missionary Ridge 202
Harker, Charles C. 92, 129; Stone's River 100–101; Chickamauga 146
Harris, Isham: Tennessee governor, Shiloh 74
Hartpence, William: low supplies 158
Hartzell, John: Missionary Ridge 199–201
Hascall, Miles S. 92
Haynie, Isham: Ft. Donelson 23
Hazen, William B. 123, 178 Shiloh 71; Stone's River 101–102; leads assault 165–166; Missionary Ridge 198, 200
Heg, Hans: Chickamauga 139
Helm, Benjamin: Chickamauga 144
Hickman Creek 21
Hill, Daniel 126, 134; Bragg critic 131; delays attack 142; Chickamauga 149; relieved 154
Hindman, Thomas C. 126, 134; Shiloh 60; history, to Bragg 127; delays attack, pulls back 128; Chickamauga 148
Hitchcock, Ethan A. 34
Hood, John Bell 133, 134, 173, 187, 188; Chickamauga 139, 145
Hooker, Joseph 163, 177; to Chattanooga 155; meets Grant 160; to Wauhatchie 167; new plan 175; Lookout Mtn. 180, 184; advance Missionary Ridge 192; pursuit 204
Hoover's Gap 111, 116
Hornet's Nest: Shiloh 60, 61, 63
Hotchkiss, Charles T.: Stone's River 95
Howard Oliver Otis 167, 175, 191; to Chattanooga 155; meets Grant 160; Wauhatchie 168
Hunter, Alfred G.: Missionary Ridge 196
Hunter, David 34
Hurlbut, Steven A. 55, 62, 63, 66, 73; Tenn. Expedition 43; Shiloh 58

Ireland, David: Lookout Mtn. 182
Island No. 10: Confederate fortress 6, 38; surrender 79

Jackman, John S.: diary 48–49; Shiloh 61
Jackson, John K.: Stone's River 102–103
Jackson, Stonewall 180
Jackson, William H.: Shiloh 62
Jenkins, Micah 167
Johnson, Bushrod R. 102, 133; Stone's River 99; Chickamauga 139, 147–148
Johnson, Richard W. 92, 95, 178; Stone's River 97–98; Liberty Gap 117; Chickamauga 137, 143–144, 149; Missionary Ridge 194, 197
Johnston, Albert Sidney 45, 50, 52, 61, 81; history 5; to Davis 7; saves Nashville 19; retreats 36; criticism, to Davis 37; Corinth 46; advances 48–49; confident 53; death 62

Johnston, Joseph E.: commands west 90; investigates Bragg 110
Johnston, William Preston: Shiloh 59
Jones, Charles: Shiloh 67
Jones, Samuel 173
Jordan, Thomas: Shiloh 74

Kershaw, J. B.: Chickamauga 147
Kilburn, C. L. 171
Kimberly, Robert: Missionary Ridge 198
Kirk, Edmund N.: Shiloh 72; Stone's River position 94–95
Knoxville, Tenn. 9, 123
Kyger, Tilmon D.: Missionary Ridge 199

La Fayette, Georgia 124, 125, 129; Bragg waiting 126
La Fayette Road 124, 129, 131, 139; importance, route 132; fight for 136
Lauman, Jacob: Ft. Donelson 29
La Vergne, Tenn. 91
Law, Evander 167; Wauhatchie 168–169
Lee, Robert E. 180
Lee and Gordon's Mill 126, 129, 131, 133, 136
Lexington, Kentucky 85
Lexington: Union warship 14, 63, 67
Liberty Gap 111, 117
Lick Creek 50; Pittsburg Landing 49
Liddell, St. John 100, 102; Stone's River 97–98; Chickamauga 137
Lincoln, Abraham 13, 41, 204; East Tennessee 3; to Halleck and Buell 7; to Buell 8; to Halleck 8; keeps Grant 81; to Rosecrans 108, 114; East Tennessee 121; to Rosecrans, to Halleck 150; East Tennessee 164; to Grant 187, 206
Lockett, S. H.: Shiloh 65
Logan, John A. 26
Longstreet, James 167, 176; to Chickamauga 130; Chickamauga 141; breakthrough 145–148; opportunity 154; Knoxville 155; Lookout Mountain 163; Wauhatchie 169; to Knoxville 173; pulls back 205
Lookout Creek 181
Lookout Mountain 122, 123, 126, 162; terrain 132; location 156; fortifications 157; importance 180; terrain, defenses 181
Lookout Valley 175
Loomis, John M.: Missionary Ridge 189, 191
Louisville, Kentucky 20
Louisville and Nashville Railroad 7, 88
Louisville: Union warship 24; damage 25

MacArthur, Arthur: Missionary Ridge 200
Maney, George: Stone's River 98, 101; Missionary Ridge 191
Manigault, Arthur: Stone's River 98–99, 101; cavalry 118; retreats, campaign 120; on Hindman 128–129; attack delay 142; waiting 144
Marmaduke, John S. 53
Marsh, C. Carroll 73–74; Shiloh 56
Martin, William L.: on Hindman 128
Mayfield, Kentucky 10
McArthur, John 26
McCallum, D. C. 207
McClellan, George B. 5, 34, 39, 41; history 4; general in chief 4; to Halleck 8; arrests Grant 38
McClernand, John A. 12, 15, 21, 25, 50, 60, 63, 66, 73–74, 75; Ft. Donelson 20; Shiloh attack 56–57

McClure, Alexander K.: meets Lincoln 81
McCook, Alexander 66, 88, 91, 119, 123, 125, 134; Shiloh 72; Stone's River position 93; holds position 94; 20th Corps 112; history 113; new campaign 116; Liberty Gap 117; joins Thomas 131; Chickamauga 143, 145–146
McCook, Daniel 67, 136, 147
McCown, John 90, 102, 107; Stone's River position 92; Stone's River 95–100
McFadden Ford: Stone's River 104
McFadden Lane 100, 101
McLaw, Lafayette: Chickamauga 148, 166, 173
McLemore's Cove 125, 128, 132, 134; Negley 126
McMinnville, Tenn. 111
McNair, Evander 97; Stone's River 95
McPherson, James B. 51, 66, 153, 171; history 20; enemy approach 58; sends trains 172
Meade, George: troops to Chattanooga 155
Meigs, Montgomery 113, 207; transportation 171; surprised 178
Memphis, Tenn.: importance 4
Memphis and Charleston Railroad 45, 85, 115, 156, 157, 160, 172; repair 153
Mendenhall, John 166; Union artillery 72; Stone's River 106
Military Division of Mississippi: Grant 159
Mill Springs, Kentucky 11; Union victory 7
Miller, Charles: Shiloh 74
Miller, John F. 106; Stone's River 101
Mills, Roger: Missionary Ridge 190
Minty, Robert 91; Guy's Gap 118; delays enemy 133
Missionary Ridge 132, 150, 178; fortifications 157; Sherman's advance 185; terrain 186; defenses 193–195; moving up 198; hand-to-hand 200; Confederate retreat 201; key to Chattanooga 203
Mitchell, John: Chickamauga 147
Mobile and Ohio Railroad 45
Moccasin Bend 162, 163, 165
Moccasin Point 162, 163, 166
Moore, David 53; Shiloh 54
Moore, John: Lookout Mtn. 183
Morgan, Daniel 90
Morgan, John 118
Morris, W. S.: under attack 26
Morrison, William: wounded Ft. Donelson 23
Morton, James St. Clair: Stone's River 100
Murfreesboro, Tenn. 36, 45, 90; Union occupies 108
Murfreesboro Pike 91

Nashville, Tenn. 9, 18; importance 4; Union occupies 35
Nashville and Charleston Railroad 92
Nashville and Chattanooga railroad 110, 114–115, 121, 160; 171; importance 112; repair 207
Nashville and Decatur Railroad 112; damage 172
Nashville Pike 92, 100, 101, 102
Negley, James S. 93, 100, 102, 134, 146; Stone's River 98; trap 126; 128; Chickamauga 139, 141; moves north 143
Nelson, William 63, 70, 71; to Nashville 35; Savannah 52; 63; Pittsburg Landing 64; killed 86
New Madrid, Missouri 38
Newton, James K.: Shiloh 74
9th Illinois: Shiloh 62
9th Kentucky: Stone's River 106
19th Ohio: Stone's River 106

19th Tennessee: Shiloh 60; Missionary Ridge 197
96th Illinois: Chickamauga 147
Nolensville Pike 91
North Chickamauga Creek 184

Oglesby, Richard 23; Ft. Donelson 26
Olney, Warren 62; 3rd Iowa 51; observes retreating men 57
104th Illinois: Missionary Ridge 197
105th Ohio: Missionary Ridge 199
111th Pennsylvania: Lookout Mtn. 182
137th New York: Wauhatchie 169
Orchard Knob 177, 193, 195; attack 178
Orphan Brigade: Kentucky Confederates 48; Shiloh 53
Osterhaus, Peter 153, 177, 180, 192; Lookout Mtn. 181–182
Owl Creek 50; Pittsburg Landing 49

Paducah, Kentucky 3, 12, 15
Palmer, John M. 91, 178; Chickamauga 137–138, 143–144, 149
Palmer, Joseph B. 115; Stone's River 102–103
Partridge, Charles: Chickamauga 147–148
Paulding, Leonard: commands *St. Louis* 14
Peabody, Everett 53
Perryville, Kentucky: battle 86
Phelps, S. L.: loyal citizens 18
Pigeon Mountain 125; Bragg waiting 126
Pillow, Gideon J.: Ft. Donelson, history 22; breaks out 25; pulls back 28–29; escapes 29; Stone's River 105
Pittsburg Landing 51, 69; campsite 43; terrain 50
Pittsburgh: Union warship 20, 24; damage 25
Polk, Leonidas 6, 48, 50, 69, 76, 90, 92, 110, 119, 129, 134; abandons Columbus 36; Corinth 45; history 47; Perryville 86; Stone's River 102; to Jefferson Davis 109; refuses to attack 130; attacks on right 141; Chickamauga 142; relieved 154
Polk, Lucius: Stone's River 99–100; Chickamauga 144
Pope, John 82, 83; Mississippi River 38; to Pittsburg Landing 78–79; Island No. 10 79
Porter, Horace 161
Porter, William: commands *Essex* 14
Post, Sidney: Stone's River 97
Prentiss, Benjamin M. 53, 54, 57, 60; Shiloh position 50; Shiloh attack 55; surrenders 63
Preston, William 62, 105; Stone's River 102–103
Price, Samuel: Stone's River 104
Price, Sterling: Kentucky 85; attacks Corinth 87

Quinn, Francis: Shiloh attack 55

Raccoon Mountain 157, 162, 163, 167
Rains, James E. 100; Stone's River 96
Rawlins, John A. 66; Grant chief of staff 14; to McPherson 171
Reed's Bridge: location, fight for 133
Reynolds, Joseph 117, 123, 129, 134; Chickamauga 137, 143–144
Rhoads, Frank L.: Ft. Donelson 26
Richmond, Kentucky 85
Ringgold, Georgia 125
Ringgold Gap 204
Roberts, George W.: Stone's River 98–99

Robinson, Milton S.: Chickamauga 149
Rosecrans, William S. 102, 103–104, 107, 118, 153; Corinth, replaces Buell 87; Army of the Cumberland, history 88; to Halleck 89; advances 90–91; Stone's River position 92–93; Stone's River 98; to Halleck, to Stanton 108; new campaign 111; to Meigs, to Halleck 113; new campaign 115–116; Tullahoma 120; to Halleck, supplies 121; Chattanooga 122; fools Bragg 123; pursues Bragg 124–125; to Halleck 126; concentrates army 129; moves north 134; Chickamauga 139–140; strengthens left, to Halleck 141; Chickamauga left 143; falls back 145–146; to Rossville 147; to Burnside, to Halleck 149; to Lincoln 150–151; to Lincoln 152; indecisive 156; politics 158–159; relieved 159–160; meets Grant 161
Rossville, Georgia 131, 146, 148
Rossville Gap 134, 150, 192
Round Forest: Stone's River 101, 102
Rousseau, Lovell H.: Shiloh 72–73; Stone's River 99–100
Rowley, W. R. 66
Ruggles, Daniel 63; Shiloh 60

St. Louis, Missouri 20
St. Louis: Union warship 14, 16, 24; damage 25
Sand Mountain, Tenn. 123
Savannah, Tenn. 18, 39
Schaefer, Frederick: Stone's River 98–99
Schofield, John M.: Knoxville 207
Schurtz, Carl 167; Wauhatchie 168–169
Scott, Thomas A.: U.S. assistant secretary of war 34
Scribner, Benjamin F.: Stone's River 100
2nd Iowa 72; Shiloh 63
2nd Minnesota: Shiloh 78; Missionary Ridge 201
Sequatchie Valley 157
7th Iowa: Shiloh 63
7th Texas: Missionary Ridge 190
17th Illinois: Ft. Donelson 23
17th Louisiana: Shiloh 67
71st Ohio: Shiloh 56
73rd Illinois: Missionary Ridge 199
76th Ohio: Shiloh 74
Shelbyville, Tenn.: Confederate camp 110, 119
Shepard, Oliver H.: Stone's River 100–101
Sheridan, Philip 92, 123, 178; enemy moves north 85; Perryville 86; Stone's River 98–100; Chickamauga 139, 143, 145; Missionary Ridge 194, 197–198; pursuit 202
Sherman, Francis T. 120; Stone's River 98; weather 118
Sherman, William T. 20, 50, 54, 60, 63, 66, 68, 75, 184; Pittsburg Landing 43; camps 51; confident 52; Shiloh attack 55–56; attacks 73; on Shiloh 79–80; moves east 153; hurries to Chattanooga 165; in Bridgeport 174; siege 175; rain delay 176; in position 179; crosses river, bridges 185; Missionary Ridge, troop position 186; Missionary Ridge attack 188–189; changes attack 190; Missionary Ridge, enemy attacks 191; tough defense 192; to Knoxville 205
Shiloh, Battle of: casualties 77
Shiloh Meetinghouse 50
Sill, Joshua: Stone's River 98
Sirwell, William: Chickamauga 139
6th Indiana: Shiloh 69

6th Mississippi: Shiloh losses 55
6th Ohio 91; Shiloh 72
61st Illinois: Shiloh 55
Slocum, Henry: to Chattanooga 155
Smith, Charles F. 10, 11, 12, 20, 21, 27, 31, 34, 42; Ft. Heiman 15; Ft. Donelson 29; surrender terms 30; replaces Grant 38–39
Smith, Edmund Kirby 90
Smith, Giles A. 153, 184
Smith, J. A.: Missionary Ridge 190
Smith, John E. 153; Missionary Ridge 185, 191
Smith, Morgan L.: Ft. Donelson 28; Missionary Ridge 185, 189–190
Smith, William F. 161; supply plan 163–164; supply route open 166
Smithland, Kentucky 12
Snake Creek 50
Snodgrass Hill: Chickamauga 146–148; casualties 148
South Chickamauga Creek 184
Squier, George W.: Shiloh 58; defends Grant 80
Stanley, David S. 88; cavalry command 112
Stanley, Timothy R.: Stone's River 99, 101; Chickamauga 146
Stanton, Edwin, U.S. secretary of war 34, 35, 39, 121; meets Grant 160
Starkweather, John: Stone's River 103–104
Steedman, James B.: Chickamauga 147–148
Steinwehr, Adolph von 167
Stemble, Roger N.: commands *Cincinnati* 14
Stevens Gap 123, 125
Stevenson, Alabama 115, 122, 157, 160
Stevenson, Carter L. 90, 188; Lookout Mtn. 184
Stewart, Alexander P. 101, 119; Stone's River 99; history 117; Chickamauga 138–139, 145–146; Missionary Ridge 192
Stewart, Nixon B.: Missionary Ridge 201
Stockwell, Elisha: Shiloh 72
Stone's River, Battle of: importance, casualties 108–109
Stoughton, William: Chickamauga 139, 148
Stovall, Marcellus: Chickamauga 144
Strahl, Otho: Chickamauga 137–138
Stuart, David 56, 62, 73; Shiloh position 50
Summerville, Georgia 125
Swett, Charles: Missionary Ridge 190

Taylor, Jesse 17; Ft. Henry damage 16
Taylor: Union warship 14
Telegraph Road 20
Tennessee River: route 3; Pittsburg Landing 50
10th Illinois: Missionary Ridge 199
Terrill, William: Union artillery 72
Thanksgiving Day: first 204
Thayer, John A. 26
Thedford's Ford 133
3rd Iowa 62; Shiloh 51
3rd Kentucky 91
3rd Tennessee: Ft. Donelson 23
31st Illinois: Ft. Donelson 26
32nd Indiana: Shiloh 72
34th Illinois: Stone's River 95
36th Illinois: Missionary Ridge 197
Thomas, George H. 11, 82, 88, 91, 93, 125, 188, 193; refuses command 86; Stone's River position 92; 14th Corps 112; new campaign 116; closes with Crittenden 131; moves to left 134; terrain 136–137; protects left 138; Chickamauga 141, 143–145; holds position 146–148; to Rossville 150; commands Army of the Cumberland 159–160; supplies 160; unable to attack 174; assists attack 175–176; Orchard Knob 177; reinforces Sherman 191; army ready 194; four divisions 195
Thomas, Lorenzo: Grant complaint 41
Tigress: Grant's ship 58
Tilghman, Lloyd: Ft. Henry, history 14; Ft. Henry design 15; surrenders 16
Triune, Tenn. 91, 115
Tullahoma, Miss. 119; Bragg headquarters 109–110; abandoned 120
Tunnel Hill 185, 186, 191
Tupelo, Miss. 83
Turchin, John B.: Chickamauga 138, 149; to Brown's Ferry 165–166; Missionary Ridge 201
12th Iowa: Shiloh 63
12th Michigan: Shiloh 55
20th Illinois 31, 56; Ft. Donelson 30; Shiloh 53
21st Alabama 48
21st Illinois: Grant's first command 10
21st Missouri: Shiloh 53
23rd Kentucky 166
24th Ohio: Shiloh 65
24th Wisconsin: Missionary Ridge 200
27th Missouri: Missionary Ridge 192
27th Tennessee: Shiloh 53
28th Alabama 170
29th Pennsylvania: Lookout Mtn. 182
Tyler: Union warship 14, 63, 67

Unaka Mountains 3

Van Cleve, Horatio P. 94, 104; Stone's River 100; Chickamauga 138, 143, 145
Van Derveer, Ferdinand: Chickamauga 144; Missionary Ridge 201
Van Dorn, Earl 83; to Corinth 82; Kentucky 85; killed 118
Vaughn, A. J.: Stone's River 102
Vaughn, John C. 100; Stone's River 98
Veatch, James C.: Shiloh 57
Vicksburg, Miss. 6, 114
Virginia and Tennessee Railroad 114, 155

Wagner, George D.: Stone's River 102–103
Walcutt, Charles C.: Missionary Ridge 189, 191
Walden's Ridge 157
Walke, Henry: commands *Carondelet* 14, 22; Ft. Henry 16
Walker, Moses: Stone's River 103–104
Walker, W. H. T. 127, 131, 134, 136, 178; reserve 133; Chickamauga 145, 149
Wallace, Lew 20, 21, 26, 59, 69, 75; to Ft. Donelson 24; about Grant 27; Shiloh position 51; Pittsburg Landing 66; attack 73
Wallace, W. H. L. 26, 55, 60; commands C. F. Smith's division 43; Shiloh position 51; Shiloh 58; death 63
Walthall, Edward: Chickamauga 137; Lookout Mtn. 181–183
Warfield, E.: Missionary Ridge 191
Wauhatchie, Tenn. 124, 163
Webster, J. D.: Grant's staff 63
Western and Atlantic Railroad 114, 123, 154, 204

Western Investigating Commission 41
Western Military Department: description 5
Wharton, Gabriel C. 92, 104; Stone's River 98
Wheeler, Joseph 90, 104, 111, 118, 134
Whitaker, Walter C. 166; Chickamauga 147; Lookout Mtn. 181–182
Widow Glenn's house 134, 141
Wilder, John T. 116, 123; Hoover's Gap 117; delays enemy 133–134; Chickamauga 145
Wilkinson Pike 92, 98, 99
Williams, James M.: letter 48; Missionary Ridge 192
Williamson, James: Missionary Ridge 192
Willich, August: Shiloh 72, 117, 178; Stone's River 94–95; Chickamauga 140, 144, 149; Missionary Ridge 197–200
Wilson, Ephraim: Missionary Ridge 199
Wilson, James 161
Withers, Jones M. 90; Shiloh 57; Stone's River 100–101
Wood, S. A. M. 129; Stone's River 99
Wood, Thomas J. 94, 129, 146, 178; to Murfreesboro 91–92; Stone's River 100; Chickamauga 139, 143; pulls out 145; Missionary Ridge 194–195, 197–198
Woodruff, William: Stone's River 97–98
Woods, Charles R.: Missionary Ridge 192
Worsham, W. J.: Shiloh 60; Missionary Ridge 197, 199

Young, Lot D.: Shiloh weather 53

www.ingramcontent.com/pod-product-compliance
Ingram Content Group UK Ltd.
Pitfield, Milton Keynes, MK11 3LW, UK
UKHW050531150426
5217IPUK00026B/1894